GRABBING BACK
Essays against
the Global Land Grab

Advanced praise for *Grabbing Back*:

"Part of the reason that knowledge about the current global land grab is so uncertain is the paucity of perspectives and analysis in defining the problem. This book fills the gap admirably. Think of it as a mix-tape, in which you're led from rural, urban, indigenous, Earth First!, Global North, Global South, policy wonk, insurgent, high theory, and high praxis. Listen for the new voices and the new ideas—you'll be humming them for years to come, and you'll have heard them here first." —**Raj Patel**, author of *Stuffed and Starved: The Hidden Battle for the World Food System*

"Grab back this sparkling mosaic of essays as a treasure of our new-old knowledge commons. Together these pieces replace dichotomies with dialectics, making explicit the inseparability of land and collective life." —**Maia Ramnath**, author of *Decolonizing Anarchism*

"As the forces of *thanatos* leave no stone unturned in their quest to dominate the entire planet, this anthology provides a much-needed antidote. Weaving together accounts from around the world, the authors advocate building grassroots movements aimed at subverting capital's incessant assault on our lives and land." —**George Katsiaficas**, author of *Asia's Unknown Uprisings*

"Never perhaps has the land question been so crucial for anti-capitalist movements, as we are witnessing a global process of enclosure that privatizes lands, waters, forests, displacing millions from their homes, and placing monetary gates to what we rightly considered our commonwealth. It is essential then that we understand what motivates this drive and its effects in all their social and spatial dimensions. *Grabbing Back* takes us through this process, identifying the 'reasons' and actors behind this global land grab and, most important, introducing us to the struggles that people are making across the world to resist being evicted from their lands and to reclaim the earth.

Bringing together an impressive group of authors, active in different social movements, it narrates a powerful story that, wherever we are, we will recognize as our own." —**George Caffentzis**, Committee for Academic Freedom in Africa

"The acquisition, control, and exploitation of land, as well as the simultaneous dispossession of land-based and peasant communities, is central to the processes of both colonialism and capitalism. As Fanon reminds us, egalitarian governance and stewardship of land is fundamental to the struggle for liberation and self-determination for all oppressed peoples. This makes *Grabbing Back* a necessary study for anticapitalist and anticolonial movements." —**Harsha Walia**, author of *Undoing Border Imperialism*

"Land grabs are a global phenomenon of our times, driven by the ever-increasing demands of both global corporations and the governments with which they are allied. But as this powerful and timely book demonstrates, small farmers and ordinary citizens around the world are standing up to defend their own with passion and ingenuity, and they are recording successes that are both extraordinary and inspiring." —**Oliver Tickell**, editor of *The Ecologist*.

GRABBING BACK
Essays against
the Global Land Grab

Edited by Alexander Reid Ross

PRESS

EDINBURGH · OAKLAND · BALTIMORE

AK Press
674-A 23rd Street
Oakland, CA 94612
USA
www.akpress.org
akpress@akpress.org

AK Press
PO Box 12766
Edinburgh EH8 9YE
Scotland
www.akuk.com
ak@akedin.demon.co.uk

The above addresses would be delighted to provide you with the latest AK Press
distribution catalog, which features the several thousand books, pamphlets, zines,
audio and video products, and stylish apparel published and/or distributed by AK
Press. Alternatively, visit our websites for the complete catalog, latest news, and
secure ordering.

Cover image by Margaret Killjoy | birdsbeforethestorm.net
Cover design by Kate Khatib | manifestor.org/design
Printed in the USA on acid-free paper.

When the peasant revolts, the student demonstrates, the slum dweller riots, the robber robs, he is reacting to a feeling of insecurity, an atavistic throwback to the territorial imperative, a reaction to the fact that he has lost control of the circumstances of life.

—George Jackson

Dedicated to political prisoners around the world.

CONTENTS

FOREWORD: TOWARD SOCIO-ECOLOGICAL SELF-MANAGEMENT

Javier Sethness Castro

"In schema borrowed from bourgeois sexual morality, technique
is said to have ravished nature, yet under transformed relations of
production it would just as easily be able to assist nature and on
this sad Earth help it attain what it perhaps wants."

—Theodor W. Adorno, *Aesthetic Theory*

As the numerous contributors to *Grabbing Back* dutifully show, we today confront a dialectical situation whereby the accumulated forces of
negation and absurdity—capital or, in German critical theorist Herbert
Marcuse's archetypal illustration, *thanatos* (the death drive)—carry the day
and largely determine the course of global affairs, *but not without challenge
from below*. Under conditions of capitalist hegemony, as Andrej Grubačić
notes, any attempt at exit from the system necessarily remains "partial,"
with movements toward autonomy being "relative" rather than absolute.
Nonetheless, conscious efforts to resist capitalist depredation—the examples of the EZLN and Black Panther Party, the Common Ground
Collective, radical workers, historical *jacqueries*, and so on—demonstrate,
again in Grubačić's words, that "place and territory are never completely
incorporated," that "they can be re-occupied and re-appropriated" towards
ends that contradict the exigencies of capital altogether. This realization,
at once empirical and theoretical, is the very basis for the *principle of hope*
that guides revolutionary thought and action—that is, taking from scott
crow, that our "emergency hearts" can perhaps through mass-rebellion take
down the death-system and so afford humanity the chance collectively
to manage its own affairs, bringing liberation that much closer. Plainly,
I will say that I share Grubačić's desire for a transition to an "anarchist
world-system," in place of the brutally authoritarian and ecocidal capitalist
system we today confront; with this end in mind, I am especially interested
in his concern for "strategies of escape," which he takes from James C.
Scott's luminous study of the vast highland stateless zone of Southeast
Asia, Zomia.[1]

---

1   James C. Scott, *The Art of Not Being Governed: An Anarchist History of Upland
    Southeast Asia* (New Haven, CT: Yale University Press, 2009).

One exit-strategy—or, at least, a precursor to such a strategy—would be, as Andrew Herod suggests in this volume, to map out geographies of resistance movements to capital—to study and share findings in "alternative area studies" (Grubačić), or *La Otra Geografía* ("The Other Geography"), as suggested by the neo-Zapatistas—and, more importantly, to help them develop rapidly and radically. While certainly there is a place for imagination, creativity, and fictional exploration within this project—consider Kim Stanley Robinson's *Mars* trilogy, written in the 1990s, wherein anarchist scientists abandon Earth for Mars, there to terraform it into a habitable planet on which they would build a new feminist and anti-capitalist society—it would seem that solidarity with unborn, nascent, and already-existing anti-systemic groupings in the world should carry greater weight. Consider the case of the Naxalites in central India who represent a radical counter-force to the imperialist devastation wrought on numerous *adivasi* (indigenous) communities inhabiting lands sought after by rapacious mining companies in the state of Chhattisgarh—the site of what has been termed the "largest land grab since Columbus." By directly confronting and subverting the mining companies and the police, military, and paramilitary forces conspiring there to promote "development"—that is to say, the wrecking-ball of society and nature—and by building a new, more emancipatory society in the regions liberated from governmental control (particularly in the Dandakaranya Forest, as Arundhati Roy explores in her *Walking with the Comrades*) the Naxalite insurgency provides a model whose spirit we should like to reproduce, wherever it is that we may find ourselves.

In terms of direct antagonism targeting the forces perpetuating environmental destruction, there are numerous examples provided in the illuminating piece "Environmental Group Events in Today's China," written by members of Yangtze River Delta Earth First! This EF! chapter documents the astronomical rise of environmentally related "group events"—better termed "mass disturbances," as they note—throughout China, in response to the super-exploitation of labor and nature, which has markedly worsened with the coming of economic liberalization and the concomitant transformation of China into the world's (slave) workshop, as facilitated by Deng Xiaoping's anti-Maoist reforms of 1979 and upheld by the Communist Party's ruthless military suppression of the worker-student revolts revolving around Tiananmen Square ten years later. Though the essay itself provides a veritable panoply of popular direct actions taken either to prevent or redress environmental decline, brief consideration of one such example will here suffice: in July 2012, some ten thousand residents of Qidong City (Jiangsu Province) stormed municipal offices to express their opposition to plans made by the Japanese-owned Oji Paper Company—among the largest paper manufacturing firms globally—to construct a pipeline that would release the plant's effluent directly into the Yellow Sea; protesters "stormed offices, smashing computers, toppling desks and throwing documents out of the windows" and apprehended Jianhua Sun, municipal committee secretary, as well as mayor Feng Xu, stripping the former naked and forcing the latter "to wear a T-shirt with protest messages." Plans for the construction of the discharge pipeline were thereafter expeditiously suspended. While the popular environmental resistance movements that have emerged in China have notable shortcomings, as the Yangtze River Delta EF! details, the model of militant, mass-direct action against capitalist depredation that is represented by these "disturbances" remains crucial to our present and any decent future we may hope for.

These examples from the global South notwithstanding, I do not wish to suggest that meaningful resistance to capitalism's genocidal and ecocidal operations are to be found only in the jungles and mountains of southeastern Mexico and eastern India, or in rural China: *Grabbing Back* importantly gives space to accounts of key struggles within the imperialist core (US) that aim at the dismantling of the catastrophic fossil-fuel complex, which is leading all of humanity and life into ruin. On the question of popular apathy and complicity, the most optimistic anti-authoritarian interpretations of this prevailing phenomenon claim ordinary peoples' non-engagement with political matters to be a *result* of capitalist dominance and hence contingent to the ongoing perpetuation of such; the suggestion here, then, is that people in general would involve themselves passionately in the management of society, if they felt they had access to an effective means to going about doing so. In this view are found the positive hopes of many of the Situationists as well as Takis Fotopoulos of the Inclusive Democracy project for workers' councils. In general terms, we can clearly say that the struggle against capitalist annihilation would be greatly helped along by the participation of far greater numbers of people within the sphere of radical political activism aimed at overturning capital; as George Katsiaficas writes, were People's Power to be "continually activated, we would have passed from the realm of prehistory to the realm in which human beings for the first time are able to determine for themselves the type of society in which they wish to live."[2]

It is here that I would like to suggest socio-ecological self-management as a concrete alternative to capital's omnicidal engine, both in terms of an end to be sought in itself, as well as a means to that end. As is well known, the concept of self-management bears much similarity to the idea of autonomy, which in its classical definition constitutes the exercise of one's own reason (or mind) freed from the direction of another (heteronomy). In essence, the call for socio-ecological self-management is really a call for the popular devolution of decision-making processes—for all power to be placed into the hands of the people, as the Black Panthers advocated, or, what is the same, for local communities to take control of social policy and the production and distribution of goods and resources, as suggested by Murray Bookchin's conception of libertarian municipalism and the participatory economics model (Parecon). Of course, no established social-scientific law promises that popular self-management would in the end produce more ecologically rational outcomes—a dramatic decrease in the various pressures asserted by humanity onto the non-human world through the abolition of economic growth, consumerism, and a great deal of industrialism, as well as the "rewilding" of significantly sized territories, the active removal of the enormity of human-created pollution and waste from the biosphere, and the effective protection of nature regions set aside for themselves, autonomous from human interference—yet the possibility remains.

On both empirical and theoretical grounds, ecological balance is essentially impossible within the current structuring of global society, as many of the contributors to *Grabbing Back* show. In practical terms, the Environmental Union Caucus of the Industrial Workers of the World recently demonstrated that a transition to decentralized renewable-energy resources, presumably coupled with a generalized decrease in material standards, could feasibly be achieved through the mass-recycling of the rare earth minerals contained within much of existing infrastructure and its waste-products; hence, such a transformation would not necessitate a vast expansion of the mining operations and resulting

---

2   George Katsifiacas, *Asia's Unknown Uprisings, Volume 2: People Power in the Philippines, Burma, Tibet, China, Taiwan, Bangladesh, Nepal, Thailand, and Indonesia, 1947–2009* (Oakland: PM Press, 2013), 377.

pollution that many critics worry about in terms of a conventional post-carbon transition.[3] Besides, a number of public-opinion polls conducted recently in the US show most people favor considerably more robust protections for the environment, just as they demonstrate public disapproval of militaristic excess ("intervention" in Syria, to consider the latest example) and support for greater measures of social support for the poor and vulnerable—in accordance with the people's decent impulses, which have not been suppressed entirely by the managers of society, their best efforts notwithstanding.

As the school of autonomous Marxism argues, then, it is largely on the subordinated to organize themselves and intervene in history in revolutionary fashion. As should be clear, the protracted history of State and elite rule over humanity is a long and sordid dialectic of hegemony and suppression of those developments that would have society become other than the way the powerful desire: the outrage that the French Revolution represented to reaction and feudalism explains the extent to which foreign powers sought to crush the radical institution in France of the principles of "liberty, equality, and solidarity," just as the estimated thirty thousand murdered by the French military upon its defeat of the popularly controlled Paris Commune of 1871 reflects the fears of the privileged of losing power and their concomitant desire to violently suppress the possibility of any future repetition of such autonomy within the minds of the subjugated. A similar dynamic is seen in the fate of recent uprisings in East and Southeast Asia—particularly Tibet, China, and Burma—as Katsiaficas shares in his newest work.[4] Noam Chomsky's concept of the Mafia Doctrine, which leads the imperial hegemon brutally to repress any significant socio-political alternative from developing on the world stage, is well-established, as the peoples of Cuba, Guatemala, Nicaragua, Vietnam, and several other societies can attest.[5] No one, then, can claim that an intensification of struggle from the oppressed against the capitalist system will necessarily proceed in an idyllic fashion, with few if any setbacks and a small number of casualties, both physical and psychological: indeed, the opposite seems a more likely outcome. And yet, to avoid the environmental apocalypse that

---

3   x356039, "Reinventing the Wheel—the Question of 'Rare' Earths," IWW-EUC, 26 June 2013. Available at http://ecology.iww.org/node/97.

4   Katsiaficas, *Asia's Unknown Uprisings, Volume 2*.

5   Noam Chomsky, *Hopes and Prospects* (Chicago: Haymarket Books, 2010), 55, 116.

capitalism promises—the descent of life on Earth into conditions that would justify Robinson's future-historical designation of this celestial body as "the planet of sadness"[6]—radical struggle and the construction of emancipatory alternatives become categorical imperatives. In the words of poet W.H. Auden, "We must love one another or die." Or, in Chris Hedges's more recent formulation: "Rise up or die."[7]

New York City, Bastille Day, 2013

---

6   Kim Stanley Robinson, *2312* (New York: Orbit, 2012).
7   Chris Hedges, "Rise Up or Die," *Truthdig*, May 19, 2013.

ACKNOWLEDGMENTS

This book originated in the tumultuous days of COP15 in 2009 during my days on the editorial collective of the *Earth First! Journal*. My position there, secured by Leah Rothschild, Jezzabell Dreamboat, and Donny Williams afforded me the time and circumstances necessary to follow the peoples' movement that crystalized on the streets of Copenhagen back to its sources in the Global South. I am therefore indebted to those brave, outstanding souls who let me loose on the archives and connections of the *Earth First! Journal*. I will always owe much to Grizzemily, Mike Ludwig, Kenton Cobb, Russ McSpadden, Ana Isabel Rodriguez, Panagioti Tsolkas, Luke Romano, and of course, Shay Emmons and Francis.

The theoretical and academic background for this work would not have been possible without the indefatigable interventions of my professors and mentors throughout my college years—particularly Vijay Prashad, whose course on corporations I took in 2003 at the tender age of nineteen years, and whose ongoing, benevolent correspondence since my graduation has helped me to no end. Katherine Lahti and Dario Euraque's advisory roles helped temper and forward my studies, and the enduring friendship of professors Maurice Wade and Luis Figueroa-Martinez have fortified my confidence in my professional and personal life.

Much of the research that brought this project into being was carried out through a spate of articles published in *CounterPunch* since 2011, and I am indebted to editors Joshua Frank, Jeffrey St. Clair, and the late, great Alexander Cockburn for holding me to stringent standards and valiantly defending that body of work that passed muster. While writing articles is often a solitary duty, I owe Lansana Coulibaly and David Da-Costa Shodeinde among others a great deal of gratitude for their intellectual as well as emotional guidance in mapping out present conditions, as well as Sam Moyo and Johannas Wilm, whose work was instrumental to the formulation of this book. More thanks are needed for Lim Lee Ching, Jeremy Fernando, and Yanyun Chang from the *Singapore Review of Books*, and Paul Bosheers, Jamie Allen, and the powerhouse that is Berit Soli-Holt at *continent*.

No words can express my gratitude towards AK Press for taking on this important work—especially Kate Khatib, who fought for *Grabbing Back* in its scrappy and disorganized formative stages, Charles Weigl for his guidance and advise, and Christa B. Daring for her enthusiastic encouragement. Deeper still are my eternal thanks to my family for the all-important dinnertime discussions on politics, culture, and world events that helped forge my understanding of life.

Last but not least, I must thank Ramsay Kanaan for encouraging me to follow up on this project, Kristian Williams and Will Munger for their support in this and other projects; Matt Landon for initiating the discussion in the Mountain Justice forum; Adam Weissman, Wendy Scher, Quinn Hethtkopf, Leah Mondragon, Christian Gutierrez, and Cindy for their courageous leaderships; Kazembe Balagun, Tibby Brooks, and Max Uhlenbeck for their principled mentorship; as well as my ramshackle community in Cascadia from the Free University project, Portland Rising Tide, Bark, and Portland IWW: Nicholas Ivan Caleb, Mike Losier, Stephen Quirk, Chau-Anh Nguyen, Akash Singh, Mike Lee, Tori Abernathy, Michael Hernandez, Jasmine Zimmer-Stucky, Tracy Mattner, Meredith Cocks, Alex P. Brown, Matthew Bristow, Christine Toth, Scottie Momo Skyles, Connor Chapman, Hollis Lichen, and many, many others.

EDITOR'S INTRODUCTION: THE GLOBAL LAND GRAB

Alexander Reid Ross

To paraphrase an old Palestinian parable, "the war doesn't come when they steal your land or your life, the war comes when they steal your stories." *Grabbing Back* is a book full of stories penned by people resisting the theft of their lives and land. These stories, though unique in their own lineages and features, are linked together in a global struggle against what is called the New Scramble for Africa, the New Great Game, the Global Land Rush, and the Global Land Grab. Large transnational corporations based in the North Atlantic countries, the Saudi states, and the BRICS (Brazil, Russia, India, China, South Africa) are grabbing millions of hectares of land from small farmers and indigenous peoples in Africa, South America, and Asia. Smaller countries with developing populations, like Singapore and South Korea, are also competing for the land. Experts compare the lawlessness and exploitation of the New Scramble for Africa to the Wild West, echoing the troubling fact that the quantity of land grabbed in just two years, between 2008 and 2009, amounts to an area the size of the state of California, plus much of Oregon. If military occupations and coups are included in the data set (and as Ben Dangl shows in his rousing article on Paraguay, they absolutely should be), the land grabs that have taken place around the world since 2009 would encompass the entire Western United States.[1] But as authors such as *Monthly Review*'s Fred Magdoff have shown, it is not gold that is leading the new expansion—it's agriculture.[2]

According to the World Bank, 464 land acquisition projects commenced between 2008 and 2009, and 22 million hectares were subject to acquisition between 2010 and 2011 alone. An important reason for these land grabs is that global power brokers want to bring food security to population-dense countries faced with erratic growing seasons (such as

---

1   This claim is based on the central position of natural resources, inter-imperialist rivalries, and agricultural lands in the political gambits of the Mali invasion, the Paraguay coup, and the overthrow of Bozize's regime in the Central African Republic. Counting the oil land leased in the Ecuadorian Amazon, these lands together equal nearly nine-hundred thousand square miles.

2   Fred Magdoff, "Twenty-First-Century Land Grabs: Accumulation by Agricultural Dispossession," *Monthly Review* 65, no. 6 (2013).

China, India, and South Korea). A vast majority of these massive global acquisitions took place in only seven African countries where land can cost less than $1 an acre. In Ethiopia, more than 25 percent of available, appropriate land was sold off between 2007 and 2008. By 2011, the Bank counted over fifty-six million hectares under acquisition in total, with the *Economist* citing a larger figure of eighty million hectares, and the International Land Coalition locating a whopping 203 million hectares of land grabs in a land matrix referencing the years 2000–2010.[3] But how and why did this all start?

There are five main reasons for the Global Land Grab: climate change, speculation, the Great Recession, resource scarcity and the ideology of "extractivism," and the history of colonialism. Each of these feeds off of the other, forming a feedback loop. The recession has generated the apparent need for further sources of revenue, thus bringing increased investment to extractive industries both domestically and in formerly colonized countries; however, due to over-extraction and growing urban populations, resources are becoming scarce, so there is a rush to open up new territory, cutting down more trees and pushing forward new production facilities that contribute to climate change. For instance, Brazil reported in 2013 that deforestation of the Amazon Rainforest had increased by 28 percent in just one year—chiefly due to encroaching infrastructure projects and farms. Climate change and industrial expansion put added strains on resources like water, which is a crucial factor in the refining and production processes of most resources and commodities. While hunger crises escalate, land grabs for resources such as water, food, fuel, and minerals will become increasingly brutal and violent. As climate-change-related disasters grow (such as Typhoon Haiyan, which left more than a million homeless and cost several thousands of lives), the triage will become more obvious: the powerful states will privilege industry and finance over people, while the effects of climate change will be borne by the poor and less fortunate.

Origins

1. Climate Change

One key reason for land grabs is food security. In 2008, the UN counted more than sixty countries hit by food crisis. In 2010, forty countries

---

3   Ward Anseeuw, Liz Alden Wily, Lorenzo Cotula, and Michael Taylor, *Land Rights and the Rush for Land* (International Land Coalition, 2012).

had entered into dialogue with the World Bank, due to skyrocketing food prices. That year, scorching drought and torrential floods belted Africa, from the Sahel valley to the Ethiopian plains, and the climate-driven famine had not relented, causing increasing crisis situations for the people. But the food crisis was not restricted to the South. Seeing dwindling grain stocks within its own borders, Russia placed an export ban on its wheat in 2010, further constricting the supply of food to the South, and causing prices to increase. In 2012, drought reduced crops in Russia by 25 percent, while obliterating a third of the harvest in Ukraine, leading to another export ban. The same year, the US experienced the heaviest dry spell in fifty years. Climate change is not only burning a hole in the breadbaskets of each continent; it is also causing increased flooding. In 2013, China imported more than 60 percent more wheat from Australia than it had done the year before, necessitated by heavy rainfalls. The list goes on, making more powerful countries increasingly concerned about their food security.

Food security brings national stability, so the race for land is often tied to keeping rebellion at home at bay. The impacts of the food crisis boiled over into the food riots of 2007, leading to brutal clashes between protesters and police in more than twenty countries. These mass movements were still simmering two years later as a hundred thousand protesters marched through the streets of Copenhagen in bright blue and green blocs to protest the COP15 climate change conference. Reasons for protests against COP15 were twofold: not only were protesters from the South, including *campesinos*, peasants, and indigenous peoples, frustrated with the lack of real solutions to carbon emissions, but they also expressed contempt for the financial industry of the North, which drove food prices up while trying to make money off of increasing food prices.

2. Financial Speculation

Beginning with the food crisis in 2007–8, global finance began to purchase growing plots of land while trading wheat futures in the short term to make money off of incremental rises in prices. This process is equivalent to buying grain in hopes that the investor can sell high at a later date. The commodities market, then, behaves like the stock market, with investor actions often causing volatile price changes, bubbles, and recessions. However, the commodities market is not like the stock exchange, because it deals with a finite resource, like wheat or corn—real things that people need to survive. A rapid increase in futures contracts often drives futures prices up, leading to concomitant trends in the cost of commodities, namely the price of food among starving populations. All of this even though the financial transactions usually do not entail any commodities physically changing hands. None of this would have been possible before the intervention of neoliberalism and financial deregulation, which several Third World leaders and organizations recognized as neo-colonialism long in advance.

Through the intervention of global financial institutions, developing countries were told to deregulate their protected markets. As the US deregulated its own financial system, beginning with the repealing of the Glass-Steagall Act, the US Treasury and the Big Five banks collaborated to add Financial Services Agreements (FSAs) to free trade agreements enforced by the World Trade Organization. Through the FSAs, banks could "open up markets" to derivatives trading—the same practice that created the housing bubble that led to the Great Recession. At the same time, the Commodity Futures Modernization Act was passed through US government, allowing traders to circumvent the Commodity Futures Trading Commission, which was essentially the only US institution that monitored and regulated commodity trades. The deregulation of financial institutions around the world drastically increased the US "over the counter" (deregulated) commodity trading from investment banks, hedge funds, pension funds, etc. Investment in commodities other than gold and metals rose from $5.85 trillion in 2006 to $7.05 trillion in 2007 to $12.39 trillion in 2009.[4] When the recession led investors to temporarily scale back their investments across the board, food and other commodity prices fell. However, after the bank bail outs, investment abroad increased again, and prices reflected the speculation, rising sharply again during the food crisis of 2010.[5]

3. The Great Recession

The connection between land grabs in the South, commodity prices, and the housing market in the North is not a new one. As early as 2003,

4   Bank for International Settlements, *BIS Quarterly Review*, September 2010, http://www.bis.org/publ/qtrpdf/r_qt1009.htm.

5   Jayati Ghosh, "Speculation and the food crisis," World Development Movement, October 2010, http://www.wdm.org.uk/sites/default/files/Commodity%20speculation%20and%20food%20crisis.pdf.

geographer David Harvey had already presciently identified the practice of "flipping houses" as part of the global structure of "accumulation by dispossession." A developer purchases a house, fixes it up, and sells it for a much higher amount, while the bank finds a buyer who is willing to take out a mortgage at as high an interest rate as possible. For at least a decade, politicians and banks worked together to encourage the working class (particularly people of color) to take out subprime mortgages with the highest interest rates. As this practice expanded, housing prices peaked, and when introductory interest rates kicked into ultra-high subprime interest rates, foreclosures proliferated. With foreclosures rising, the risk of this practice became apparent. Investors started to flee the market, leading to a wider crisis. Federal bailouts assuaged the repercussions felt throughout the financial industry—particularly with regards to credit default swaps—while leaving homeowners out to dry. After the housing market crashed and the banks were bailed out, investment flew to territorial expansion in the Global South, and homeowners were abandoned almost entirely.

Oakland Institute's Executive Director Anuradha Mittal explained the problem plainly in a 2010 interview with CNN: "The same financial firms that drove us into a global recession by inflating the real estate bubble through risky financial maneuvers are now doing the same with the world's food supply." The banks that cleared 9 million foreclosed properties and "erased" $7 trillion in home real estate values received federal bailouts, which provided hedge funds with investment capital to speculate on agribusiness projects around the world. As the British newspaper, *The Telegraph*, put it in September 2010, "Hedge funds that struck rich 'shorting' US sub-prime have rotated into the next great play of our era: 'long' soil."[6] This interplay between overaccumulation and territorial expansion that comprises the Global Land Grab provides an example of what Harvey calls a "spacio-temporal fix." Capital that is "overaccumulated" in one market must be reinvested, underwritten, or "switched" to territorial expansion and "primitive accumulation" in another. After house prices hit rock bottom, returns on land investments abroad padded bank deposit-to-loan ratios, but banks refused to lend to small home owners, using their deposits to purchase securities

---

6   Ambrose Pritchard-Evens, "The Backlash Begins Against the World Landgrab," *The Telegraph*, http://www.telegraph.co.uk/finance/comment/ambroseevans_pritchard/7997910/The-backlash-begins-against-the-world-landgrab.html.

(including bonds, stocks, and derivatives) that they could then leverage against new investments in stocks, companies, and commodity stores in the repo market. Thus, the pendulum swung back to the US and the Eurozone, so that today bank-led financial speculation sweeps through the cities of the North. Banks now own airports, ports, tollbooths, and major infrastructural points while transforming the demographic composition of entire continents through their renewed grip on the housing market.[7]

This is why a second wave of foreclosures has loomed over the current "housing market boom." The new boom is funded not by working families, but investment banks; in one year, Blackstone group raised $8 billion to buy homes, while JP Morgan Chase maneuvered to buy up five thousand houses. One housing strategist from Morgan Stanley left the bank to organize a billion dollar fund and purchase ten thousand houses. In hard-hit Florida, institutional investors make up seven out of ten home sales, or four out of ten in crisis-ridden cities like Atlanta. Homeownership for blacks and Latinos is the lowest on record and first-time ownership has fallen by 25 percent. In an article entitled, "It's Not a Housing Boom. It's a Land Grab," Imara Jones with Colorlines writes, "Wall Street is flipping homes into rental properties and then leasing them to the very people they pushed and priced out of the real estate market. Billionaire investor Warren Buffet sums it up this way, 'If I had a way of buying a couple-hundred thousand single-family homes, I would load up on them. I could buy them at distressed prices and find renters.'"[8]

Detroit is a frightening model for what is to come: not only massive foreclosures, but concentrated land grabs that push residents out of emptying neighborhoods, shut down city services, and propose a transition to, among other things, post-urban plantations. Sadly, the example of Detroit indicates that housing is just the beginning of the powers vested in the new bureaucratic figure of the Emergency Financial Manager (EFM). In one example, an EFM of Michigan barred the mayor of Benton Harbor, Michigan, from entering his office, and effectively fired the entire municipal government. The EFM then used his power to take over the valuable shoreline property of Jean Klock Park, a children's park donated to the municipality by wealthy benefactors long ago, and then

---

7   See Ellen Brown, "The Leveraged Buyout of America," *CounterPunch*, http://www.counterpunch.org/2013/08/27/the-leveraged-buyout-of-america/.

8   Imara Jones, "It's Not a Housing Boom. It's a Land Grab," *Colorlines*, May 30, 2013, http://colorlines.com/archives/2013/05/the_dangerous_new_housing_boom.html.

built a $500 million golf course-cum-residential development. The same EFM sold a $55 million sports arena, built with taxpayer money, to a developer for $583,000. Journalist David Bacon chronicles the misdeeds occurring throughout the state:

> Schools in Highland Park and Pontiac have now had three emergency managers, and one manager in Highland Park has been indicted for embezzling... In Hamtramck the financial manager stopped paying the mayor and City Council, and told the council members to stop meeting. In Ecorse and Highland Park financial managers made major layoffs to the firefighter and police departments, outsourcing many of the jobs to neighboring cities... More than half of Michigan's 1.4 million Black residents now live under rule by emergency managers, which effectively nullifies their right to vote. By contrast, only 1% of white residents live under managers.[9]

This trend foreshadows an extreme extension of "accumulation by dispossession" where public-private partnerships can dispense with public officials at will, along with public lands, services, and property such a museums, schools, and transportation, in order to displace local populations (most often poor people of color) for large development projects that service the rich. Incidentally, this situation is not unique— the role of the EFM is similar to the role of the neoliberal consultants who streamlined the public services of the Global South during the debt crisis, perhaps most famously in the case of Argentina, making the struggles of the oppressed in the Global South particularly instructive for our studies here. Under this stage of capitalism, the encroachment of corporations into every public sector, vis-à-vis public-private partnerships transforms the geographic, social, and economic composition of town and country, and in particular, how people relate to their city and each other and the land.[10]

---

9   David Bacon, "Detroit Residents on Bankruptcy—We Have No Democracy!" *Truthout*, August 15, 2013, http://www.truth-out.org/news/item /18196-detroit-residents-on-bankruptcy-we-have-no-democracy.

10 Prabhat Patnaik's term for this is "accumulation by encroachment," which he identifies with the inflation of food commodities resulting from supply-side shortages, speculation, and biofuel cultivation. See Patnaik, "The Accumulation Process in the Age of Dispossession," *Economic and Political Weekly* (June 28, 2008), 108–113. Found at http://www.indiaenvironmentportal.org.in/files/3_10.pdf.

4. Resource Scarcities and Extractivism

There is another agent responsible for the food crisis, price increase, and land grabs: resource scarcity. The price of oil, in particular, determines the price of food, since oil is a key factor in industrial agricultural production (transport, farm machines, etc.). The decline in supply of readily available sweet crude oil, met with the demand-side stimulus from urban development (for instance, petroleum products, such as plastics, and infrastructural development) creates a scramble for new points of extraction and refining of fuel and raw materials. Of course, financial speculation on the oil market has also increased since the deregulation of commodities markets, creating even more problems for food prices.

One attempted solution to peak oil is biofuels. As of 2011, only 25 percent of land acquisitions involved food crops, while an estimated 40 percent went to biofuels.[11] However, biofuels require vast tracts of land to produce, and large amounts of oil in the production process. The biofuel boom converts existing or potential farmland into palm oil, ethanol, or jatropha monocrops, so, while food crisis plagues the Global South, wealthy investors who sink their money into food speculation and biofuel production are taking food out of the mouths of starving populations, and becoming extremely wealthy in the process. Investors saw a 748 percent return on agricultural investment in 2010 according to the NCRIEF Investment Farmland Index—six times that of real estate (Schiller House Price Index) and quadruple that of gold.[12]

Land grabs are being enclosed not only for biofuels, but for new tar sands mines, oil shale operations, and natural gas drill-points. In one particularly egregious example, Ecuador sold off one-third of its Amazon Rainforest (three million hectares, an area larger than the state of Massachusetts) to the Chinese oil giant, China National Petroleum & Chemical, in order to service its outstanding debt (Ecuador even canceled previous forest protections to sweeten the deal).[13] Finance writer and position trader Leo Sun pointed out the historical significance of the land grab taking place in spite of seven non-consenting indigenous

---

11 Ward Anseeuw, Liz Alden Wily, Lorenzo Cotula, and Michael Taylor, "Land Rights and the Rush for Land," *International Land Coalition* (January 2012), 24.

12 Black Sea Agriculture, "Investing in farmland funds trumps 'The Big Three' investments of our time," http://blackseaagriculture.com/charts_data.html.

13 Tim Fernholz, "Ecuador abandons rainforest protection to pay its China debts," *QZ.com*, August 19, 2013, http://qz.com/116321/ecuador-terminates-a-3-6-billion-plan-to-protect-the-amazon-from-oil-drilling/.

groups who inhabit the land: "The deal marks a return to the status quo similar to the one the Ecuadorian government shared with Texaco between 1964 and 1992. Texaco left the country in 1992 after drilling in the rainforest for 28 years, and was subsequently sued by residents of the Ecuadorian Amazon, who claimed that its drilling operations had caused severe health problems for over 30,000 residents in the region."[14] Tar sands projects are also projected for Venezuela, Mexico, and in three different bioregions of the US. The practice of fracking for natural gas as a "clean" alternative fuel has also skyrocketed worldwide, while the increase of coal extraction, along with other raw materials like copper and rare earths, continues apace with the rapid development of BRICS countries.

The notion that the global economy will be propelled by a colossal uptick in resource extraction is contributing to more domestic land grabs in the North as well. The Department of Agriculture's Forest Service mandated a 20 percent increase in logging throughout the US's national forests for the years 2012–2014, further encroaching into protected areas.[15] The deforestation has little economic merit, considering that the timber companies employ seasonal, low-wage loggers, often paying less than 5 percent in taxes, while exporting upwards of 70 percent of their yield in raw log form in order to forgo sawmills—the last refuge of the timber unions. The Forest Service openly identifies public lands as "plantation land" on a thirty-year cycle, and senators from the logging states of Oregon, Montana, and Idaho, have urged Obama to increase logging while "modernizing" and "streamlining" the National Environmental Protection Act (NEPA).

Streamlining NEPA would have broader impacts than on forestland, as oil production recovered with the sharpest spike in recent memory between 2011 and 2012. The future of oil is foreshadowed by the Bureau of Land Management's leasing of 810,000 acres (more than 1,265 square miles, or twice the size of the Alberta Tar Sands) including parts of Utah, Colorado, and Wyoming for oil shale and tar sands mining operations—other tar sands operations are slated for Kentucky and Alabama.

---

14 Leo Sun, "China Commits to Ecuador: Out With the Old, in With the New," *The Montley Fool*, July 3, 2013, http://beta.fool.com/leokornsun/2013/07/03/china-commits-to-ecuador-out-with-the-old-in-with/39224/.

15 Rob Chaney, "US Forest Service plans to boost timber production, forest health work," *The Missoulian*, February 3, 2012, http://missoulian.com/news/local/us-forest-service-plans-to-boost-timber-production-forest/article_710829e8-4e16-11e1-aff9-001871e3ce6c.html.

The "clean energy alternative," natural gas production is only projected to increase, though it has already risen from 19 million cubic feet to 25.3 million cubit feet since 2005, hitting an all-time record in 2012 as towns from Texas to California run dry due to the tremendous strain that fracking places on water supplies. In only the most recent example of this coast-to-coast gas grab, the federal government leased four thousand acres of public land for natural gas fracking in Ohio without even warning state officials or the public. Meanwhile, coal production steadily increases in the Powder River Basin, as new infrastructure routes for fossil fuels trace—to use Galeano's famous phrase—the opening veins of North America.

Farmland in the US is also being increasingly bought up by foreign investment as industrial extraction encroaches into rural towns and places. According to the Department of Agriculture, foreign investment in US forests and farmland increased by 6.7 percent in 2010, growing to an area the size of Indiana.[16] Outside ownership of farmland in Illinois increased by 66 percent to 73 percent of all sales.[17] In the span of one year, the land rush drove farmland prices up by 23 percent in the Midwest.[18] Over the next twenty years, as farm holdings cross from one generation to the next, four-hundred thousand acres, half of the US's farmland, is set to change hands. Small farmers who lack sufficient access to capital are already struggling to compete with large-scale farms. "There is a buyout on the horizon," according to the Oakland Institute, where institutional investors from Wall Street and beyond could "expand their presence in this untapped, and, until recently, largely overlooked market."[19]

The Global Land Grab can be circumscribed in three interlocking economic spheres: the *foreclosure crisis* "freed up" capital to expand *holdings in the Global South* while producing the apparent necessity to buoy up the economy through increased *resource extraction* in the North and South. With borders "opened up" by neoliberalism, there is no "great

---

16   Chuck Raasch, "Foreign Investment in US Land on the Rise," *USA Today*, July 25, 2012, http://usatoday30.usatoday.com/news/nation/story/2012-07-18/foreign-investing-US-farm-timber-land/56466674/1.

17   National Family Farm Coalition, "US Farmland: The Next Big Land Grab," *National Family Farm Coalition*, May 2012, http://www.nffc.net/Learn/Fact%20Sheets/US%20Land%20Grab%20backgrounder_5.24.12.pdf.

18   Mariwyn Evans, "Farm Land Rush," *Realtor Mag*, September 2011, http://realtormag.realtor.org/commercial/feature/article/2011/09/farm-land-rush.

19   Lukas Ross, *Down on the Farm: Wall Street: America's New Farmer* (Oakland: Oakland Institute: 2014), 9.

frontier" to be crossed by pioneers and explorers settling the new "Wild West." As Andrej Grubačić says, today's borders can be found through the defense of peasant and indigenous lands, radical ecologists defending public lands and common spaces, neighborhoods resisting evictions and creating autonomous infrastructure, women and LGBQTTI people fighting for safe and livable places to live free from abuse, radical workers blocking the extraction and transportation of commodities garnered through greed and avarice, and "unoccupied" lands that are "informal properties" of their ancestral inheritors who continue to fight against encroaching extractive industrial areas and speculators from the global centers of capital.

5. Imperialist History

"It is only a step from the market to the colony," explains historian Fernand Braudel. "The exploited have only to cheat or to protest, and conquest immediately follows."[20] In the midst of rising neo-colonialism, it is important to recognize how colonialism and market economics have historically intertwined, and how that history affects the current world-system. The territorial expansion of capital into the South, particularly Africa, has historical roots in colonialism. European countries maintained colonial outposts in coastal Africa after the sixteenth century, but much of the interior remained resistant to colonial expansion for centuries. Portugal's early attempts to make inroads into the Kingdom of Kongo were thwarted by King Alfonso, for example, who accepted Catholicism, but rejected Europe's right to purchase property and practice the slave trade. After Alfonso's death, Portugal opened more land and ports to the slave trade, but was forestalled by violent Dutch competition. The warrior queen, Nzinga, used Dutch intervention as leverage to reclaim land from the Portuguese, defeating the Portuguese army on at least one occasion. For two hundred years, violence plagued the region, and Europe was not able to penetrate deeply into the mainland, much less rule the continent.

Leaving much of Africa unexplored, Europe drew raw materials from the "New World" to glut the coffers of a rising merchant elite. By the nineteenth century, however, the colonies of the New World had begun to cast off their colonial chains, and with the industrial revolution

---

20   Fernand Braudel, *Civilization and Capitalism, 15ᵗʰ–18ᵗʰ Century, Vol. I* (Berkeley: University of California Press, 1992), 102.

in full swing, the developing bourgeoisie craved more raw materials to manufacture into goods for Europe's increasingly insatiable metropolitan centers. Along with the newly developed productivity in manufactured goods and trade capacity, the Empires of Europe could expand their military powers into *terra incognita*, and expropriate more raw materials and labor power from colonial territories in the hinterland of Africa. Hence, the European powers would step over each other in a frantic race to grab hold of parts of the world that had previously held out against colonial expansion.

Hannah Arendt explains the territorial expansion of imperialism at the time of the Scramble for Africa in *The Origins of Totalitarianism*. Arendt calls the Imperialists "owners of superfluous capital... the first section of the [bourgeoisie] class to want profits without fulfilling some real social function." Quoting from JA Hobson's portrayal of the era, Arendt notes that imperialists' habit of being "content with investing 'large portions of their property in foreign lands,' even if this tendency ran 'counter to all past traditions of nationalism,' (...) merely confirmed their alienation from the national body on which they were parasites anyway."[21] The Imperialists summoned all of Europe's military powers to ensure that their vast landholdings would be secure, both in the colonies and Europe, itself. Military campaigns in the colonies as a result of indigenous unrest and inter-imperialist rivalries became a way of dispensing with the restless working class of Europe while keeping the bourgeoisie rich enough to suppress workers' agitation at home. Indeed, such an outlet was needed, since the people of Europe revolted against the rootless bourgeoisie every couple of decades, with massive popular uprisings breaking out in 1830, 1848, and 1871.

After the discovery of diamonds and gold in South Africa, the British went to war with the Boer population and the natives in order to keep the territory out of French hands. Later on, England would lay claim to Nigeria and spread its administrative influence thickly over the Ottoman-controlled countries of the Nile (excepting Ethiopia, which was never colonized). The British also built railroads to the coast of Mozambique, enabling their large private companies to operate in an area violently contested by Arabs and the Portuguese. For its part, France took over much of the north and center of Africa, killing a third of the population

---

21 Hannah Arendt, *The Origins of Totalitarianism* (Meridian Books: New York, 1958), 149.

of Algeria in the process (the invasion of Mali was warmly contextualized as part of the colonial mandate across the Algerian press).[22] Smaller players included Belgium, with the notoriously genocidal reign of Leopold II, who murdered half of the population of the Congo over the span of but a few decades;[23] Spain, which held part of Morocco and the Western Sahara; and Portugal, with holdings in Angola and Mozambique. The German establishment, having agreed upon national unification as late as 1866, longed for greater colonial holdings in Africa, forming an alliance with Austria-Hungary and subsequently a triple alliance with Italy to create a counter-power to the feuding English and French Empires.

As Germany pushed into an arms race with England, using colonies as bargaining chips in the rush to create a "balance of power" arrangement, Russia expanded into Central Asia, challenging Britain's colonial hold on India. The ensuing struggle between the militaries of England, Russia, China, and Afghanistan, would become known as The Great Game, a paroxysm of inter-imperialist rivalry that prefigured the First World War. The Great Game spilled over to the twentieth century with a tenuous pact between Russia and England, which was underscored by intrigue and sabotage. It was thus in the context of African and Asian colonialization, marked by intense military agitations, alliances, and arms build-ups, that the whole of Europe would drag much of the world into a devastating World War.

The consequences of WWI were myriad. Russia invaded West Asia, joining with the Arab Revolt of 1916 to cause the disintegration of the Ottoman Empire. The following year, Russia, itself, would succumb to revolutionary fervor. Former Ottoman countries, Turkey, Syria, Lebanon, Israel, Jordan, and Iraq, were split up between France and Europe, with France taking Lebanon and Syria. After the Second World War, the colonial powers of the North lost nearly all of their strongholds in Africa and Asia, and the Soviet Union gained substantial influence in Syria as well as the Central Asian states of Afghanistan and Pakistan. Thus, during the Cold War, Syria and Libya became crucial allies against the hegemony of NATO in the region—particularly US allies Egypt, Israel, and Saudi Arabia. When Russia threatened to attack Saudi Arabia in response to the threat of a US and French aerial

---

22   Algeria Embassy, http://www.algeriaembassy.com/country/index.html.
23   Adam Hochschild, *King Leopold's Ghost: A Story of Greed, Terror, and Heroism in Colonial Africa* (Boston: Houghton Mifflin Company, 1998).

bombardment campaign against Syria, the historical arrangements that amount to a modern balance of powers suddenly came into clarity. Soon after, Ukraine would erupt into a 19th Century Imperialist re-run of the Crimean War—this time between NATO powers and Russia over strategic positions, land, and resource flows from and to Central Asia and the Levant.

Inter-Imperialist Rivalries

Now that we know at least five key causes for the Global Land Grab, we can look towards one primary geopolitical problem that it has created: namely, a disruption in the dynamic balance of power, or global hegemony. As former National Security Advisor to Jimmy Carter, Zbigniew Brzezinsky, declared before the UK and France abandoned support of the US's warmongering, "I am struck how eager Great Britain and France appear to be in favor of military action. And I am also mindful of the fact that both of these two powers are former imperialist, colonialist powers in that region... I do not see the context for [military action]. I am concerned that its participants are too narrowly based, that is, it is America and former colonial powers. That seems to me to create a political problem immediately."[24] The clearest interpretation of Brzezinsky's apprehensive comments is that there did not appear to be a context for invasion outside of colonial dominance.

As Nafeez Ahmed pointed out, Syria had thumbed its nose at a Western-backed pipeline spearheaded by Qatar and Saudi Arabia while working with Iran to contract a pipeline carrying Iranian oil and gas through Iraq to the Mediterranean.[25] As the US encourages Israel's policy of encroachment into Palestinian lands, defying international law in brazen attempts to expedite the ethnic cleansing of Arabs (in one most recent example, fifty to seventy thousand Palestinian Bedouins are slated to be "relocated" from historic desert lands into state-planned urban tenements to make them more governable), Syria joined with Iran in a hegemonic bloc. Syria's move appeared to counter the alliance between the US, Israel,

---

24 "Brzezinsky: Syria strategy is a 'well-kept secret,'" *Deutsche Welle*, August 27, 2013, http://www.dw.de/brzezinski-syria-strategy-is-a-well-kept-secret/a-17045802.

25 Nafeez Ahmed, "Syria intervention plan fueled by oil interests, not by chemical weapon concern," *The Guardian*, August 30, 2013, http://www.theguardian.com/environment/earth-insight/2013/aug/30/syria-chemical-attack-war-intervention-oil-gas-energy-pipelines.

and Saudi Arabia, and it would prove a crucial step towards civil unrest. The US funded and supported Al Qaeda organizations to undermine the Assad Regime in Syria, with a critical climax coming on November 19, 2013, when a double car bomb went off at the Iranian embassy in Beirut. Although Iran blamed "Zionist" agents, journalist Pepe Escobar correctly observed, "What happened in Beirut was a terror attack, cheered by Israel, and fully enabled by Saudis."[26]

Without question, Washington, DC's relationship with Iran and its neighbors has been terrible since the 1979 revolution against the US-backed Shah (among other CIA and military operations). The US has funded numerous terrorist organizations throughout West and Central Asia to undermine domestic rule. The spread of terrorist cells is staggering, running from Syria to the Islamic Movement in Uzbekistan, and the network becomes stronger with every US intervention—most recently, the US backing of Al Qaeda in Syria. As a result of the US draw-down in Afghanistan, much of Central Asia (namely, Tajikistan and Uzbekistan) becomes more vulnerable to Islamist attack and destabilization, which places the US's covert and overt interventions in a different kind of arena.[27] Consequently, Russia has pulled its Central Asian allies closer with security agreements, while Kyrgyzstan has called for a closure of the critical US airbase in Manas. As Central Asia moves away from the US, China is developing "the New Silk Roads," redeveloping Manas into an airport, creating an Agricultural Free Trade Zone in Tajikistan, and pumping large amounts of natural gas from Turkmenistan through an inter-regional pipeline network. With Uzbekistan standing out against the other Central Asian states as an outpost of US hegemony in the region, the mixture of US-Russia relations, Islamist rebels, and the increasing influence of China in the global rush for land and resources (particularly oil, gas, and food) leaves the region open for internal conflict in the coming years. Such geopolitical factors have surely been involved during recent upheavals in Africa that have completely transformed power relations in the region, beginning with the invasion of Libya in 2011.

---

26 Pepe Escobar, "The Wahhabi-Likudnik war of Terror," November 20, 2013, *Asia Times*, http://www.atimes.com/atimes/Middle_East/MID-03-201113.html.

27 Clara Weiss, "NATO's Afghan draw-down stokes Kremlin's fear of clash with US," *World Socialist Web Site*, September 2013, http://www.wsws.org/en/articles/2013/09/03/ruaf-s03.html.

Libya

In 2013, Russia and China found themselves defending Syria with Iran not simply because the four have historic political and economic ties, but also because of the failure of NATO's invasion in Libya. After the NATO invasion, which Vladimir Putin derided as a "crusade," Russia faced a loss of $10 billion in investment. $20 billion of Chinese investment was threatened in the post-revolutionary Libya. In the years leading up to the invasion, the BRICS invested in Qadaffi's Libya, and Qaddafi invested in Africa. When Qaddafi was deposed, Africa's balance sheet registered the change. Beginning in 2008, Libya announced plans to invest $10 million in Egypt over the following year while increasing its $5 billion investment in Morocco. Libya's money helped power the African Development Bank along with the African Union, and numerous corporations throughout the continent. The year before his ouster, Qaddafi promised to invest an additional $60 billion in Africa. Under the auspices of ousting an oppressive dictator (as US-backed regimes in Bahrain and Saudi Arabia persecuted pro-democracy movements with terrible wrath), US-French forces toppled Qaddafi with the help of Islamist militants who had been persecuted under the regime. When Qaddafi was executed without trial by a band of rebels, the Russian government expressed outrage. Subsequently, the attack against the US Embassy in Benghazi by Islamic militants on September 11, 2012, provoked mordant reactions from Russian officials, such as this Twitter response from Russia's Foreign Affairs Committee head, Aleksei K. Pushkov: "Under Qaddafi they [Libyans] didn't kill diplomats. Obama and Clinton are in shock? What did they expect—'Democracy?' Even bigger surprises await them in Syria."[28]

Mali

While Libya flew into chaos, Islamic militants swept south into the former French colony of Mali, where the moderate, though corrupt and unpopular, reign of Amadou Toumani Touré (ATT) would prove an easy target. ATT's presidency was infamous for inaction as drug trafficking proliferated and hunger took hold of the Sahel region. With

---

28   Ellen Barry, "Russians Say Anti-US Attack in Libya Vindicates their Position," *The New York Times*, September 12, 2012, http://www.nytimes.com/2012/09/13/world/europe/russians-say-anti-american-attack-in-libya-vindicates-their-position.html?_r=0.

an extensive drought encroaching on the daily lives of the small farmers, villages, and cities of Mali, ATT reportedly sold off large swaths of land and industries to foreign investors. In 2008, ATT dedicated upwards of a hundred thousand acres of land in the region known as Office du Niger to Qaddafi's Libya for a joint China-Libya venture to cultivate rice for Libyan food security. China would contribute 30 percent to the project, consisting of seeds and expertise, while Libya would provide the 70 percent of administration funding needed to get the project off the ground.[29] The joint corporation created around the project, Malibya, also brought in Chinese contractors to dig a thirty-mile canal for irrigation, diverting much-needed water from the Niger River. It appeared to business elites in the North that the African states were collaborating on a new chain of power relations with Libya as a semi-periphery and China as a core. By 2009, France's main body of transnational corporate interests, Medef International, had already clearly suggested a solution to the problem of "Chinese competition." In a public speech given in Senegal, Patrik Lukas, the head of Medef's Africa Division, declared, "There is a real issue that goes beyond the issue of the private sector. The French government should definitely help the private sector working in Africa."[30] Medef's insistence on French intervention against China in Mali might be taken as a gesture towards "diplomacy by other means," to invert the famous saying in the tradition of Michel Foucault.

The canal was a dangerous gamble for the Malian state, not only due to French displeasure, but also its strain on local populations. First, the government had to forcefully remove the villages that populated the hundred thousand-acre land grab. Then, the diversion of water into the canal had to be achieved. As author of *Land Grabbers*, Fred Pearce, observed in 2011, "[the canal] will enhance Libyan food security at the expense of Malian food security by sucking dry the river that feeds

---

29   See Deborah Brautigam, "Whatever Happened to Those Chinese Agricultural Investments?," *China in Africa: The Real Story*, November 20, 2012, http://www. chinaafricarealstory.com/2012_11_01_archive.html.

30   Translated from French: "il y a un vrai sujet qui dépasse la problématique du secteur privé." "Le gouvernement français doit absolument aider le secteur privé qui travaille en Afrique, en particulier les secteurs du BTP et du bois qui ont été les premiers touches." Found in "France/Chine en Afrique: 'nous ne sommes pas à armes égales,'" *AFP*, February 13, 2009, http://www.google.com/hostednews/ afp/article/ALeqM5j0JPaS6PVx9I1nFk-GX8nK2BW79Q?hl=fr.

the inland delta, diminishing the seasonal floods that support rich biodiversity—and thriving agriculture and fisheries vital to a million of Mali's poorest citizens—on the edge of the Sahara desert." Pearce presaged a situation where, "with Al Qaeda busy recruiting disaffected people such as the Tuareg nomads around Mali's borders, any disruption to the traditional way of life could feed its violent agenda."[31] The rebel advance in fact did occur when mostly secular Tuareg fighters waging a long-term war of independence against the Malian state seized the opportunity to engage in conflict as the Islamist rebels advanced from Libya.

Within months, the combined (though not aligned) rebel forces had spread up the Niger River like wildfire. The military's frustration with ATT's inaction in the face of rebellion brought on a coup, led by US-trained Captain Sanogo, against ATT, which provided an important window of opportunity for French and US interests to become involved. When the US and France invaded, ostensibly for the quite valid reason of combating the human rights abuses being carried out, they also had in mind the protection of Libya's economic investments, as well as keeping access to Mali's plentiful unexploited natural resources, such as vast reserves of natural gas, in their control. By the time the French declared victory, half a million Tuareg and Arab refugees were scattered throughout five neighboring countries, while food scarcity reached a historic high. But France only intervened to "protect its interests," according to President Hollande—a statement whose meaning came into focus a month after rebel-conquered territory in Mali had been retaken, when the capitol city of neighboring Central African Republic (CAR) was suddenly and brutally overrun by rebels.[32]

Central African Republic

Once known as the Cinderella of the French Colonies, CAR's economy relies heavily on mineral wealth, including a thriving diamond industry in which European interests remain deeply involved. However, according to former CAR head of security Guy-Jean Le Foll

---

31   Fred Pearce, "Africa's Flourishing Niger Delta Threatened by Libya Water Plan," *Environment360*, February 3, 2011, http://e360.yale.edu/feature/africas_flourishing_niger_delta_threatened_by_libya_water_plan/2366/.

32   Inti Landauro, "Hollande: France Doesn't Protect Regime in Central African Republic," *Wall Street Journal*, December 27, 2012, http://online.wsj.com/article/SB10001424127887324669104578204813106938602.html.

Yamande, the French would intervene in the country's political situation if it ever tried to live up to its potential as the "Switzerland of Africa." Although it had prior knowledge about a 2010 attack by a group called Convention of Patriots for Justice and Peace (CPJP), Yamande insisted shortly before his assassination, France refused to inform President François Bozizé in order to become "a stone in the shoe" of the sovereign development of Africa.[33] The CPJP are linked today with the rebel Séléka coalition that took the country by surprise in late-2012, but more damningly, the Séléka rebels invading CAR from Chad are also clearly linked to Al Qaeda and human rights abuses. The French had every reason to intervene in defense of human rights and CAR's uranium deposits. However, the CAR was already selling their uranium to South Africa—a move that would bring development to a region that the imperial powers wanted to keep strategically underdeveloped, according to Bozizé.

In a speech delivered shortly after his flight from the CAR capitol city of Bangui, the ousted president protested: "Why did they start raping, killing and hurting the Central African population? (…) We gave them everything. Before giving oil to the Chinese, I met Total in Paris and told them to take the oil, nothing happened, I gave oil to the Chinese and it became a problem. I sent counselor Maidou in Paris for the Uranium dossier, they refused. I finally gave it to the South Africans."[34] In a later interview with the BBC, Bozizé claimed that it was Chadian Special Forces aided by the French who struck the final blow against CAR by attacking the barracks of South African forces.[35] There is a long history of this sort of underdevelopment in Africa; in fact, historian Walter Rodney mentions the Central African Republic, specifically, when discussing the unnecessary colonization of lands for the sake of keeping other Imperialist

---

33 See Mads Brügger, *The Ambassador* (Documentary Film), 2011.

34 From a December 27, 2012 speech, quoted by Julie Owono, "Who Wants to Overthrow Central African Republic President François Bozizé," *Global Voices Online*, December 30, 2012, http://globalvoicesonline.org/2012/12/30/who-wants-to-overthrow-central-african-republics-president-francois-bozize/. Bozizé later told the BBC French Service that the final blow against CAR came not from Seleka, but from Chadian Special Forces working with France.

35 See Antoine Roger Lokongo, "Central African Republic: the hidden hands behind 'yet another good coup,'" *Pambazuka News*, April 17, 2013, http://www.pambazuka.org/en/category/features/87025. Also, "Car's ousted leader Bozizé says Chad aided rebels," *BBC*, April 3, 2013, http://www.bbc.co.uk/news/world-africa-22012772.

countries away from resources that might, at some later point, be either discovered or plundered or both.[36]

The victory of the rebels coincided with an important summit of the major BRICS parties in Durban, South Africa. After the BRICS held their crucial talks to launch a development bank of the South, Séléka rebel commander and self-appointed leader of CAR, Michel Djotodia, issued the final word on investment in the war-ravaged country: "We will rely on the European Union to help us develop this country. When we have been sick, the European Union was at our bedside. It will not abandon us now." Djotodia's loving terms for the EU have fed suspicion that EU countries were more involved than they appeared to be. According to Yun Sun, a Visiting Fellow at the Brookings Institute, "China… sees a double standard in France's decision to dispatch troops [to Mali] since it disregarded a similar request for military assistance from Central African Republic," and is most worried about the precedent for "neo-interventionism."[37] Indeed, between 2011–2013, US-France intervention (or conspicuous lack thereof) in its former African colonies (as well as Libya) cost the BRICS countries billions of dollars in lost contracts and investments, while deepening the crises of hunger, dependency, and dispossession.

In terms of North Atlantic relations to the Global South, if there is a driver of historical continuity from the Colonial period to the contemporary era, it is that rabid class of capitalists rampaging throughout the world and snatching up as much of its land and resources as possible, while subjecting the indigenous populations to the worst brutality imaginable. As Arendt explains, "Expansion then was an escape not only for superfluous capital. More important, it protected its owners against the menacing prospect of remaining entirely superfluous and parasitical. It saved the bourgeoisie from the consequences of maldistribution and revitalized its concept of ownership at a time when wealth could no longer be used as a factor in production within the national framework and had come into conflict with the production ideal of the community as a whole."[38]

---

36 Walter Rodney, "The Imperialist Partition of Africa," *Monthly Review* 21, no. 11 (1970): 103–114. Found at http://www.marxists.org/subject/africa/rodney-walter/works/partition.htm.

37 Yun Sun, "How China Views France's Intervention in Mali: An Analysis," *Brookings*, January 23, 2013, http://www.brookings.edu/research/opinions/2013/01/23-china-france-intervention-mali-sun.

38 Arendt, *The Origins of Totalitarianism*, 150.

Each essay in *Grabbing Back* speaks to the extremities of capitalist accumulation in the Global South from the position of horizontal resistance movements against the Global Land Grab. Whether resistance to land grabs going on in the US, the BRICS countries, or what Vijay Prashad calls, "the poorer nations," we will find the macro and micro analysis of land-based struggles in constant tension with the principles and values of capital.

Timeless Struggle

The uprisings of 2011–2013 manifest the early popular reactions to economic and geographic conditions surrounding the Global Land Grab. These struggles, which include and are often led by the peasants, the landless, the indigenous, and urban slum dwellers, Partha Chatterjee describes as "extraordinary, apocalyptic, timeless moment of a world turned upside down." The event where everyday resistance surges into rebellions of indigenous, rural, and peasant peoples "gives us a glimpse of that undominated region in peasant consciousness and enables us to see the everyday and the extraordinary as parts of a single unity in historical time."[39] It is a historic struggle for survival, and in another sense, the struggle for history. Who will tell the history of the Global Land Grab? Who will be there to remember how it took place, and what was done?

In 2011, 180,000 "group events" were registered in China, having grown apace at 26 percent every year since 1996—a majority of these took place in rural areas resisting land grabs.[40] Throughout the Arab world, mass protest movements sparked by political oppression and skyrocketing food prices toppled three major governments. Africa, too, has seen its share of riots, revolts, and even revolutions—for example, the movement against land grabs in Madagascar recently led to the ouster of the government. At the same time, the devastating impact of the foreclosure crisis, the recession, and the collapse of the US financial sector brought multitudes to the streets in protest against the lack of economic security and political representation, while ecological resistance in Canada generated a new wave of solidarity movements, with First Nations

---

39 Partha Chatterjee, "For an Indian History of Peasant Struggle," *Social Scientist* 16, no. 11 (1988): 15.

40 Elizabeth C. Economy, "A Land Grab Epidemic: China's Wonderful World of Wukans," *Council on Foreign Relations*, February 7, 2012, http://blogs.cfr.org/asia/2012/02/07/a-land-grab-epidemic-chinas-wonderful-world-of-wukans/.

at the fore. From Bolivia to Indonesia, Mozambique to Coast Salish Territory, the people are grabbing the land back.

The full-scale revolt against the government of Turkey began after a much-publicized heavy-handed police response to peaceful protests against the bulldozing of the smallest park in Istanbul to make way for a shopping mall in the style of an Ottoman-era barracks. What has emerged out of the contradictions is something much larger—the movement in Turkey is not only about a small park, or even about public participation in urban planning; the revolt is poised against the autocratic governance of multinational Empire. As George Jackson wrote years ago from his Solidad prison cell, the rebelling subject manifests "an atavistic throwback to the territorial imperative, a reaction to the fact that he has lost control of the circumstances of life."

In Europe, an extended protest movement against corruption in Bulgaria has ousted one government so far this year, with the next one hanging on by its fingernails. Fittingly, the pro-democracy protests were separated by a popular movement against natural gas drilling, which resulted in a complete moratorium against fracking. Following the moratorium, scores of activists crossed the border to Romania to join a mass mobilization against natural gas drilling on World Environment Day—throughout the summer of 2013, anti-fracking protests continued to rock Romania, leading to Exxon's withdrawal, and a growing social movement that deploys rural direct action. From Hungary to the Philippines to the State of Oregon, fields of genetically modified crops are being destroyed, banned, and abandoned. The fight for clean water, air, and land, and sovereignty moves beyond the borders of nation states as it bridges alliances and forms the bulwark of popular organizing.

In 2013, Egypt was again seized by paroxysms of revolution, with reports of millions of people taking to the streets—the reasons for protest being oppressive rule, a shrinking economy, and, again, rising food prices. At the same time, ten thousand Ethiopian citizens took to the streets against corruption and improper use of political powers. In Libya, oil workers refuse to go to work for the new neoliberal regime. Around the world, the throngs of the oppressed grow into forces of political counterpower, and are met with the heavy hand of military brutality. The statist interventions in Syria that threaten to bring about international civil war expose a feuding elite teetering on the precipice of global class war.

As large parts of Asia, Africa, and Europe emerge into this new era with revolt, the struggle for economic and social justice in Latin America continues on many fronts. In June 2013, Brazilian Indians joined the poor and middle classes in the streets railing against lavish displays of wealth showered upon sporting and luxury events in the midst of dire poverty. The political movement, MPL, declared before a meeting with President Rousseff on June 24, "We hope that this meeting marks a change in the federal government's position and that this will extend to other social battles: to the indigenous peoples, for example the Kaiowá-Guaraní and the Munduruku, who have been attacked by landowners and public bodies; to the communities affected by evictions; to the homeless; to the landless; and to the mothers whose children were murdered by the police in the peripheral neighborhoods."[41] Davi Kopenawa, a spokesperson for both the MPL and the Yanomami tribe declared, "In my world, nature is with me and she is listening. She is seeing the errors of the authorities of this country. They should respect our country, respect the peoples of the city, the communities and respect Brazilian indigenous peoples' rights."[42]

As the people rise up, plutonomy tightens its grip on as much land as possible, trying to squeeze as much resources and profits as possible from the earth and its billions of working poor until the intensity of class struggle makes either position no longer tenable. As the rich buy up more land through forceful acquisition, their bureaucrats lose legitimacy, and can only maintain power through a deepened status quo of surveillance and "security." Today, these fault lines quake under the strain of whistle blowers, leakers, and hackers, and the organization of the people against the grasp of the Global Land Grab.

This book is by no means an exhaustive study of every land grab and every popular rebellion. Admirably, organizations such as GRAIN, the

---

41 "Brazil: Protesters call on President to Uphold Indigenous Rights," *Survival International*, July 1, 2013, http://www.survivalinternational.org/news/9349.

42 Ibid. As a result of the unity in the streets of Brazil, the government made some real concessions, promising to invest all oil revenues into healthcare and education while ramping up prosecution of corruption. This maneuver is a stopgap that leaves the landed elite relatively unscathed by the fires of social unrest. In Brazil, less than 10 percent of farms take up nearly 80 percent of total cultivated area (according to the Instituto Brasileiro de Geografia e Estatística, "Censo agropecuário 2006," http://www.ibge.gov.br/home/estatistica/economia/agropecuaria/censoagro/default.shtm.). However, Brazil has done more than many countries to stop US investors, fleeing high farm prices, from buying up soya land in the Amazon.

International Land Coalition, and the Oakland Institute have produced extensive online resources, articles, and journals dedicated to scholarship on these matters. Instead, this book represents an illustrative field-guide to the ways that people power responds to the Global Land Grab. It is a book about front-line attempts to organize and struggle against neo-colonialism in the South as much as solidarity and resistance in the North.

Grabbing Back

I have split *Grabbing Back* into two main geographic and thematic parts: the first part dealing largely with the Global South, and the second pertaining to activist responses to land grabs in the US and Canada. The first part of the book looks at movements in the BRICS countries, the poorer nations, and native groups in North America who are grabbing back. The second part of the book will focus on the backlash to the Global Land Grab in the North Atlantic. Whether the struggle comes in the form of land-based movements for community education, housing justice, ecological defense, or food security, *Grabbing Back* makes connections between popular movements of the North and South, opening up new possibilities for liberation, emancipation, and decolonization.

Struggle in the South

Grabbing Back begins with a chapter about decolonization struggles, but every article might as well be placed under this imperative. Decolonization begins with a broader look at the geopolitics of the Global Land Grab by analyzing the causes and effects. We begin with an investigation into the hubs of the Global South, because these important nations exist as not only exploiters, but also as a part of the Global South as it is exploited by the North Atlantic's financial institutions. The "Locomotives of the South," which are meant to pull the North out of the quagmire of debt, forge bonds of South-South Cooperation, because they remain, in many ways, on the side of the "developing members of the WTO."[43] Although they represent "neoliberals with Southern Characteristics," the hegemons of the South continue to

---

43 According to Wu, found in Vijay Prashad, *Poorer Nations* (New York: Verso, 2012), 210.

be shut out of what Prashad calls "the saturated consumer-driven debt economies of the North (mainly the United States)."[44] Thus, South-South Cooperation amongst the BRICS and their client states is both developmentalist *and* neoliberal, which leads to problematic methods of both capital and resource accumulation. As Prashad notes, "Overall growth [in Brazil, India, China, and South Africa] came not only from dynamic sectors such as information technology (a very small percentage of GDP), but significantly from cannibalistic economic activity (privatization, land grabs for real estate speculation)."[45]

Opening the discourse of internal neocolonialism, Vandana Shiva begins the chapter with an impressive article that shows how landless peasants, small farmers, and the dispossessed become important allies and participants in the struggle against fossil fuel infrastructure and the patriarchal power structure. Exposing "globalization as neocolonization," Shiva explains how land grabs are "facilitated by the creation of a police state and the use of colonial sedition laws." Ward Anseeuw and Mike Taylor of South Africa's University of Pretoria and International Land Coalition come next with a provocative look at the political and economic dynamics of the Global Land Grab, followed by a close-up of the horrific situation in Ethiopia by Graham Peebles. My own article investigating the colonial roots of the palm oil industry, as well as the hidden transcripts and exilic spaces that have defined the global resistance, comes after.

The EF! contingent from the Yangtze River Delta follows with a birds-eye view of modern land and environmental activism against development in China. Silvia Federici's revelations of women's movements against land grabs around the Global South surges forward. Shifting the focus to the Americas, Guillermo Delgado-P deconstructs the colonial mind and its approach to land in his fabulous essay exposing the problems of colonialism that we have inherited today. Ben Dangl shows how the recent coup in Paraguay indicates a frightening return to the North-Atlantic-based politics of colonial conquest over land. Last but not least, is Keisha-Khan Perry's close-up look at the micropolitics of a black women's neighborhood assembly resisting urban development in Brazil.

---

44   Ibid.
45   Ibid., 175.

Closing Remarks

If the present situation comes into focus as nothing less than a global phenomenon of the accumulation of capital in its most recent form, the challenge of our new century, then, is to mount a struggle on the symbolic and territorial of land. This is no simple task, however, as the authors of *Grabbing Back* point out, it is a struggle that has existed throughout the Global South for numerous decades. Brilliant Latin American thinkers like Gloria Anzaldúa, Walter Mingolo, Anibal Quijano, and Raúl Zibechi have worked to explore the aspects of representation, territory, autonomy, and self-determination within social movements of, for example, Argentina, that have had to reckon with the hostile takeovers of neoliberalism. We have from them a gift of thinking about Indigeneity, territoriality, and coloniality, which brings crucial content to current revolutionary practice (as opposed to the volatile cocktail of drug cartels, gangs, paramilitaries, and economic displacement that is deployed by corrupt politicians profiting from the drug war to upset social solidarity in Central America).[46]

It makes sense to attend to Maia Ramnath's placement of solidarity in decolonization as something that can take place in the North today: "Grassroots mobilizations that focus on manifestations of transnational corporate capitalism, engaged in the unmasked act of accumulation by dispossession, also function as implicit indictments of the neoliberalized state. So land acquisition struggles can easily be seen as continuing resistance to colonization, or at any rate to the economic processes included historically within the colonial package. This is what enclosure of the commons looks like."[47] As we reassert ourselves on this apparently new (but really almost atavistic) terrain of struggle, part of the project of *Grabbing Back* becomes finding a common language to express our needs, desires, actions, and to claim what, in reality, is already ours to obtain. As in Latin America during the 1990s and 2000s, the fight against austerity brings people together to reterritorialize their places of struggle.[48]

46 See Robert Muggah and Steven Dudley, "The Most Dangerous City in the World is Not Where You Think It Is," *The Atlantic*, August 28, 2013, http://www.theatlantic.com/international/archive/2013/08/the-most-dangerous-city-in-the-world-is-not-where-you-think-it-is/278963/.
47 Maia Ramnath, *Decolonizing Anarchism: An Antiauthoritarian History of India's Liberation Struggle* (Oakland: AK Press, 2011), 234.
48 See Raúl Zibechi, *Autonomías y emancipaciones, Programa Democracia y Transformación Global* (Lima: Universidad Nacional Mayor de San Marcos, 2007).

With *Grabbing Back*, the authors hope to recover and reclaim the language, thought, and collective memories of marginalized people, moving beyond Occupy to produce decentralized and localized power in solidarity throughout the world. Women struggling for place, workers fighting for land and stability amidst neoliberalism, indigenous peoples generating self-determination, farmers and concerned citizens blocking forced displacement and environmental devastation—all of these we see as united in the popular movement against the Global Land Grab.

PART ONE

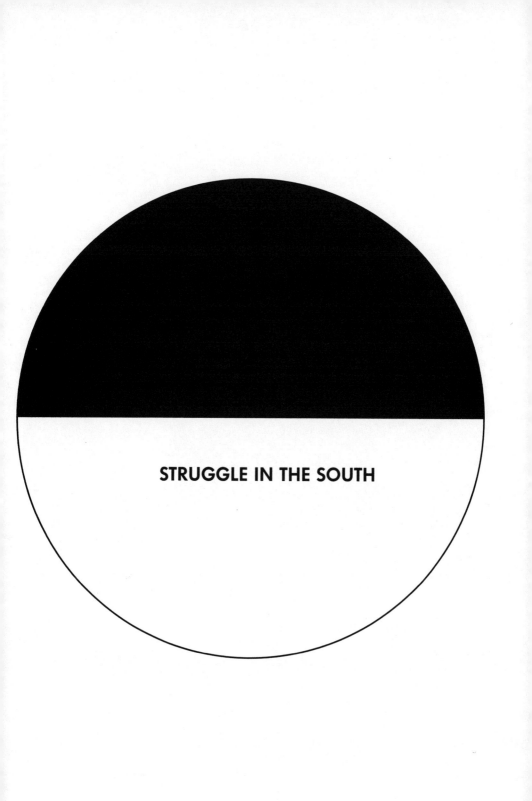

STRUGGLE IN THE SOUTH

LAND WARS AND THE GREAT LAND GRAB

Dr. Vandana Shiva

> "The Earth upon which the sea, and the rivers and waters, upon which food and the tribes of man have arisen, upon which this breathing, many life exits."

> — Prithvi Sukta, *Atharva Veda*

Land is life. It is the basis of livelihoods for peasants and indigenous people across the Third World, and is also becoming the most vital asset in the global economy. As the resource demands of globalization increase, land has emerged as a key site of conflict. In India, 65 percent of the people are dependent on land. At the same time, a global economy, driven by speculative finance and limitless consumerism, needs the land for mining and industry, for towns, highways, and biofuel plantations. The speculative economy of global finance is hundreds of times larger than the value of real goods and services produced in the world. Financial capital is hungry for investments and returns on investments. It must commodify everything on the planet—land and water, plants and genes, microbes and mammals. The commodification of land is fueling the corporate land grab in India, both through the creation of Special Economic Zones (SEZs) and through foreign direct investment in real estate.

Further, the global economy based on limitless consumerism has a rapacious appetite for natural resources. With trade liberalization, it has been increasingly turning to countries of the South and, within the South, to indigenous and peasant land. As globalization generates more luxury consumption by the rich, the demand for cars grows. More cars means more automobile factories, more iron and bauxite mining, and more steel and aluminum manufacturing. The land grab for mining and industry has triggered major conflicts, including those in Orissa's bauxite and iron-ore mining, in steel plants, at Ford's car manufacturing plants in Tamil Nadu, and the Tata's Nano factory in West Bengal, which had to be abandoned due to protests. Land grab has become the most significant economic activity and the most significant source of profits for corporations like Vedanta, Mittal, Tata, Essar, and Reliance. Corporate profits grow by stealing land through brute force from the poorest farmers and tribals. Mining profits have jumped from 50 Rupees per ton to 50,000 Rupees per ton.

Land, for most people in the world, is Terra Madre, Mother Earth, Bhoomi, Dharti Ma. The land is people's identity; it is the ground of culture and economy. The bond with the land is a bond with Bhoomi, our Earth. In the Third World, 75 percent of the people live on the land, and are supported by the land. The Earth is the biggest employer on the planet. For people of the South, 75 percent of the wealth is in land.

Land grabs are being justified by two false arguments. First, that agriculture has become unviable and farmers should abandon the land. For farmers, soil is not a prison from which they need to escape to an industrial job. It is their support, their means of livelihood, their security, their identity. The peril state farmers find themselves in is a result of the corporatization of agriculture. The high costs of inputs like seeds and agrochemicals push up production costs. At the same time, trade liberalization is pushing down crop prices. The result is a negative economy, with costs higher than returns, leaving farmers facing debt and suicide. However, there are alternatives to this negative economy: lowering costs of production through seed sovereignty and ecological farming, and increasing returns to the farmers through fair and just trade. We have achieved this in Navdanya, and there is no reason farmers should be denied prosperity and dignity through being *annadatas*, our food providers.

The second argument to justify land grab is that India must "industrialize" to have economic growth. *The Economist* concluded that Indian farmers could escape suicides if they "could escape the soil." However, today's economic growth is jobless growth. It is not labor-intensive and employment-generating. India will not be a "super power" with millions rendered destitute through land grabs. Furthermore, SEZs, a favored tool of industrialization, are for real estate companies, developers, and for the IT sector, which are already growing industries and do not provide basic needs. No society can become a post-food society. If India destroys her fertile farmlands for concrete jungles, and uproots her small farmers for a speculative economy, there would not be enough land in other countries to provide the food for India's one billion people. Land is inelastic. Fertile land is a very precious and very scarce resource. It needs to be protected and conserved as an asset of the farmers and as a national heritage to be passed on to future generations. It cannot be destroyed for the passing wave of short-term greed and speculation driving the corporate land grab. Climate change and peak oil should wake us up to the consequences of destroying our local food economies.

Colonization was based on the violent take over of land. Now, globalization as recolonization is leading to a massive land grab in India, Africa, Latin America. Land is being grabbed for speculative investment, urban sprawl, mines and factories, highways and expressways. Land is being grabbed from farmers after trapping them in debt and pushing them to suicide.

In India, land grab is facilitated by the toxic mixture of a colonial Land Acquisition Act of 1894, the deregulation of investments, and commerce through neo-liberal policies, and with it the emergence of the rule of uncontrolled greed and exploitation. It is facilitated by the creation of a police state and the use of colonial sedition laws, which define defense of the public interest and national interest as anti-national.

The World Bank has worked for many years to commodify land. The 1991 World Bank structural adjustment reversed land reform, deregulated mining, roads, ports. While the laws of independent India to keep land in the hands of the tiller were reversed, the 1894 Land Acquisition Act was untouched. Thus, the state could forcibly acquire the land from the peasants and tribals and hand it over to private speculators, real estate corporations, mining companies, and industry.

Across the length and breadth of India, from Bhatta in Uttar Pradesh (UP) to Jagatsinghpur in Orissa to Jaitapur in Maharashtra, the government has declared war on our farmers, our *annadatas* in order to grab their fertile farmland.

Their instrument is the colonial Land Acquisition Act of 1894 used by foreign rulers against Indian citizens. The government is behaving as the foreign rulers did, appropriating land through violence for the profits of corporations: Jaiprakesh Associates in UP for the Yamuna expressway, POSCO for Orissa, and AREVA French company in Jaitapur—land grab for private profits, and not for public purpose by any stretch of imagination, is rampant in the country today.

These land wars have serious consequences for one's democracy, our peace and our ecology, our food security and rural livelihoods. The land wars must stop if India is to survive ecologically and democratically.

While the Orissa government prepares to take over land in Jagatsinghpur, from people who have been involved in a democratic struggle against land acquisition since 2005, Rahul Gandhi makes it known that in a similar case in Bhatta, UP, he stands against forceful land acquisition. The Minister of Environment Mr. Jairam Ramesh admitted that he gave the green signal to pass the POSCO project under great pressure. One may ask, pressure from whom? This visible double standard when it comes to the land question must stop.

In Bhatta Parsual Greater Noida (UP) about six thousand acres of land is being acquired by infrastructure company Jaiprakash Associates to build luxury townships and sports cities, including a Formula 1 race track in the garb of building the Yamuna Expressway. In total, the land of 1,225 villages is to be acquired for the expressway. The farmers have been protesting this unjust land acquisition. Four people died, and many were injured during a clash between the protesters and the police on May 7, 2011. If the government continues its land wars in the heart of India's breadbasket, there will be no chance for peace.

In any case, money cannot compensate for the alienation of land. As eighty-year-old Parshuram, who lost his land for the Yamuna Expressway, said, "you will never understand how it feels to become landless."[1]

While land has been taken from farmers at 300 Rupees per square meter by government using the Land Acquisition Act, it is sold by developers at 600,000 Rupees per square meter—a 200,000 percent increase in price and, hence, profits. This land grab, and the profits, contribute to poverty, dispossession, and conflicts.

Similarly, in Jaitapur Maharashtra, police opened fire on peaceful protesters demonstrating against the proposed Nuclear Power Park at Jaitapur, Ratnagiri, Maharashtra. One person died and about eight were seriously injured on April 18, 2011 when this incident took place. The Jaitapur nuclear plant will be the biggest in the world, and is being built by the French company AREVA. After the Fukushima disaster, the protest has intensified, as has the government's stubbornness.

Today a similar situation is brewing in Jagatsighpur Orissa where twenty battalions have been deployed to assist in the anti-constitutional land acquisition to protect the stake of India's largest Foreign Direct Investor—the POSCO Steel project. The government has set the target of destroying forty betel farms a day to facilitate the land grab. The betel farms bring the farmers an earning of 400,000 Rupees an acre. The Anti POSCO movement, in its five years of peaceful protest, has faced state violence numerous times, and now is gearing up for another perhaps

---

1   Quoted in Jyotika Sood, "Road to Disaster," *Down to Earth*, June 15, 2011, 39.

final non-violent and democratic resistance against a state that uses violence for its undemocratic land grab for corporate profits, overlooking due-process and constitutional rights of the people.

The largest democracy of the world is destroying its democratic fabric through the land wars. While the constitution recognizes the rights of the people and the *panchayats* (traditional assemblies) to democratically decide the issues of land and development, the government is giving a go-by to these democratic decisions (as is evident from the POSCO project where three *panchayats* have refused to give up their land). The use of violence and the destruction of livelihoods that the current trend is reflecting is not only dangerous for the future of Indian democracy, but the survival of the Indian nation-state, itself. That today India may claim to be a growing or booming economy, yet is unable feed more that 40 percent of its children, is matter of national shame. Land is not about building concrete jungles as proof of your growth and development, but is the progenitor of food and water, a basic for human survival. It is thus clear what India needs today is not a land grab policy through an amended colonial land acquisition act, but a land conservation policy that conserves our vital eco-systems, such as the fertile Gangetic plain and coastal regions, for their ecological functions and contribution to food security.

Handing over fertile land to private corporations who are becoming the new *zamindars* cannot be defined as public purpose. Creating multiple, privatized superhighways and expressways does not qualify as necessary infrastructure. The real infrastructure India needs is the ecological infrastructure for food security and water security. Burying our fertile food producing soils under concrete and factories is burying the country's future.

FACTORS SHAPING THE GLOBAL LAND RUSH

Ward Anseeuw and Mike Taylor

Struggles over land were one of the defining features of movements to overcome poverty, hunger, discrimination, and political repression in the last century. The first decade of the twenty-first century suggests that competition for land and natural resources is likely to continue and even intensify. Growing demand for food, feed, fuels, and other commodities, combined with a shrinking resource base and the liberalization of trade and investment regimes, are driving a new global rush for land. Lands that, only a short time ago, seemed marginal to the global economy are now being sought by international investors and speculators to an unprecedented degree, in direct competition with local communities.

This "land rush" is being driven by diverse and growing global market demands—not least for food, biofuels, other non-food agricultural commodities, timber, minerals, and carbon-offsetting opportunities.[1] There is little in present findings to suggest that the term "land grabbing" is not widely deserved.[2] Poor, resource-dependent communities disproportionately bear the costs. Women, who typically do not have secure land rights and may be excluded from decision-making processes, yet are often primarily responsible for household food security, face grave risks of further exclusion. Likewise, pastoralists and forest-dependent people, whose land-use and management practices are not recognized, are particularly vulnerable. Meanwhile, the trend towards greater land concentration creates a poor environment for social justice, peace, and stability.[3]

This land rush has grabbed global attention and prompted debate within the media, national parliaments, civil society, and global bodies such as the Committee for World Food Security. Efforts are under way to develop benchmarks or standards of good practice for large-scale land

---

1   Annelies Zoomers, "Globalisation and the foreignisation of space: seven processes driving the current global land grab," *Journal of Peasant Studies* 37, no. 2 (2010): 429–47.
2   Ward Anseeuw, Liz Alden Wily, Lorenzo Cotula, and Michael Taylor, "Land Rights and the Rush for Land: Findings of the Global Commercial Pressures on Land Research Project" (Rome: International Land Coalition, 2010).
3   Ibid.

acquisition and investment in agriculture, such as the "Voluntary Guidelines on the Responsible Governance of Tenure of Land, Fisheries and Forests," and "The Principles for Responsible Agricultural Investment." The problem is the impact of global market forces in the context of governance failures at global, national, and local levels. Only by addressing these failures can growing global demands for food and other commodities be met in a way that is sustainable, equitable, and respectful of the rights of the world's rural poor.

The rush for land must be seen as a broad, historically and politically embedded phenomenon. Specifically, it is shaped by several failures of governance. These are most notably:

• The failure to recognize and protect customary land rights, including particularly the rights of women and common property rights;

• The failure to support smallholder agriculture, and the commensurate enthusiasm for a modernist vision of agriculture driven by foreign direct investment;

• The failure to give due weight to human rights and sustainability considerations;

• The failure to take decisions affecting the future of land-use as well as agricultural systems of rural societies—not to mention global food security and ecosystems—in a way that is transparent, fair, and inclusive.

In the rush to sign large-scale deals by governments and prospective land acquirers, decision making is ignoring the wider social and ecological functions of land. Secure access to land provides a foundation for dignified employment, a safety net for the poorest, and a foundation for cultural identity. As such, we observe the rush for land taking place in a manner that firmly subordinates the economic, social, and cultural rights of millions of the rural poor.

Weak Democratic Governance

Land acquisition for commercial ventures implies policy decisions about the type of agricultural development that is envisaged and promoted. It concerns the sustainable management of the nation's natural resources, the entry of the state into commitments with external parties, and the discretionary use of powers typically held by the state over the allocation of land. Democratic governance is thus a cross-cutting issue.

Today, "neo-patrimonialism" is pronounced in many, and perhaps most, of the countries where lands are being acquired at scale by investors, from Cambodia to Mali, DRC to Indonesia. Such regimes combine the architecture of seemingly modern democratic states with the informal reality of persisting "personalized, unaccountable power and patron-client ties." These often reach down to the local level through chiefs and connected fixers, but leave the majority poor without a say.[4] The partial integration of judiciaries in such networks can make recourse to justice difficult. More specific problems include lack of transparency and corruption; decision making and negotiations for land deals usually happen behind closed doors. Only rarely do local landholders have a say in such negotiations, and few contracts are made available to the public. This reduces scope for public scrutiny and creates a breeding ground for corruption.

Transparency International defines corruption as "the abuse of entrusted power for private gain."[5] Defined in these broad terms, corruption is endemic in many key countries leasing lands at scale, including much of Africa and parts of Asia. In Transparency International's "Corruption Perceptions Index," Sudan, Laos, and Cambodia are close to the bottom of the ranking (172nd, 154th, and 154th out of 178, respectively), while other key investment recipient states like the Philippines (134th), Madagascar (123rd), Ethiopia, Mali, Mozambique, and Tanzania (all four at 116th) score only marginally better. It is not just high-level corruption on a large scale that is at stake. Case studies from the Philippines[6] and from Nepal illustrate the role of corruption at all levels of government.[7]

A vital aspect of governance is the following of due process in decisions that affect rural land users. The principle of obtaining free, prior, and informed consent, in particular, is central to understandings of the right to freedom from eviction and respect for other rights such as the rights of indigenous peoples. Breaches of such due process are widely exhibited.

---

4   Larry Diamond, *The Spirit of Democracy: The Struggle to Build Free Societies Throughout the World* (London: Times Books, 2008).

5   Transparency International, CPI 2010, http://www.transparency.org/policy_research/surveys_indices/cpi/2010/in_detail.

6   RJG de la Cruz and ILC/AR Now!, *The new conquistadores and one very willing colony: A discussion on global land grabbing and the Philippines experience*, AR Now! contribution to ILC Collaborative Research Project on Commercial Pressures on Land (Rome: International Land Coalition, 2011).

7   Bharat Shrestha, *The Land Development Boom in Kathmandu Valley*, CDS contribution to ILC Collaborative Research Project on Commercial Pressures on Land (Rome: International Land Coalition, 2011).

For example, local communities are not often informed and may be evicted in the context of logging concessions.[8] Thousands of communities in Indonesia affected by the oil palm boom have no means of complaint or recourse to justice.[9] A case study from the Philippines shows how local officials routinely turn a blind eye to irregular development on foreshore lands, dispossessing local fishing communities.[10] In the context of the Polepally SEZ in India,[11] studies describe a process of (mis)information and extraction of consent that makes a mockery of required due process.

A further problem concerns the limited development of genuinely decentralized local government, which can legally represent the interests of rural communities. Following political reforms in the 1990s a wave of "government devolution" occurred in Africa and Asia. In some cases, as in Francophone West Africa, this included decentralization of land administration. In practice, such developments have (with exceptions) been either cosmetic or have decentralized only certain powers, leaving land-related decision making vested in the central government or remote provincial or regional state entities.[12]

Land Governance That Fails the Rural Poor

As shown in the previous chapters, large-scale land acquisitions are resulting in the widespread dispossession of existing land users. Dispossession

8   Augusta Molnar, Keith Barney, Michael De Vito, Alain Karsenty, Dominic Elson, Margarita Benavides, Pedro Tipula, Carlos Soria, Phil Sherman, and Marina France, *Large acquisition of rights on forest lands for tropical timber concessions and commercial wood plantations*, Rights and Resources Initiative (RRI) contribution to ILC Collaborative Research Project on Commercial Pressures on Land (Rome: International Land Coalition, 2011).

9   Marcus Colchester, *Palm oil and indigenous peoples in South East Asia*, FPP contribution to ILC Collaborative Research Project on Commercial Pressures on Land (Rome: International Land Coalition, 2011).

10 Dennis Calvan and Jay Martin S. Ablola, *Highly extractive fishing activities and privatization of foreshore lands: Impact on the everyday lives of municipal fisherfolks*, NFR ccontribution to ILC Collaborative Research Project on Commercial Pressures on Land (Rome: International Land Coalition, 2011).

11 Vidya Bhushan Rawat, Mamidi Bharath Bhushan, and Sujatha Surepally, *The impact of special economic zones in India: A case study of Polepally*, SEZ contribution to ILC Collaborative Research Project on Commercial Pressures on Land (Rome: International Land Coalition, 2011).

12 Elizabeth Daley, *Gendered impacts of commercial pressures on land*, contribution to ILC Collaborative Research Project on Commercial Pressures on Land (Rome: International Land Coalition, 2011).

may take place through an *illegal* transfer, but it is far more common in the context of the current land rush for landholders to be legally dispossessed. Legal dispossession may occur through compulsory acquisition, or, far more commonly, through the expropriation of land and other resources that are possessed by local communities under traditional forms of tenure.

The failure of laws to thoroughly define procedures enables officials to stretch the boundaries of their powers to dispose of public lands. In Kenya, for example, this is such a problem that these practices have for some time been referred to as "irregular" allocations of public land in order to distinguish them from illegal allocations.[13] Often, policies and laws may provide broad consideration of what is a lawful, public purpose for governmental expropriation of titled, occupied, or customarily held land. Public-interest grounds have been repeatedly used to facilitate expropriation for the establishment of Special Economic Zones (SEZs) in India, for example.[14]

There are several features common among contemporary land governance systems that facilitate such dispossession.

- All untitled lands are frequently vested in the state. Several versions of this are common: Government Lands, State Lands, and Public Lands. Laws tend to describe the first two as the private property of the state, or government. Public Land tends to refer to lands that the state owns in trust for the nation, or for populations living in those areas (such as where native areas or tribal lands still exist). In practice, all three turn the government of the day into the effective landowner or landlord of all untitled lands. This is common in both Asia and Africa. Certain resources are also frequently vested directly in the state. While this includes subsoil resources like oil and minerals in most of the world, in many African and Asian countries, state ownership extends to land and surface resources like the foreshore, water resources, and sometimes forests.
- Governments often regard only lands that have been made formally subject to statutory entitlement as private property deserving protection by the law. This often occurs in circumstances where very

---

13   Erin O'Brien and Kenya Land Alliance, *Irregular and illegal land acquisition by Kenya's elites: Trends, processes, and impacts of Kenya's land grabbing phenomenon*, KLA contribution to ILC Collaborative Research Project on Commercial Pressures on Land (Rome: International Land Coalition, 2011).

14   Rawat, et. al., *The Impact of special economic zones.*

little of the national area is under such title. For example, no more than 10 percent of all rural lands in Sub-Saharan Africa are subject to statutory entitlements, and most of this acknowledged "private property" relates to former white-owned farms in South Africa, Namibia, and Zimbabwe.

• In many agrarian countries, there is a legal failure to recognize that lands held through customary/indigenous tenure systems amount to real property, therefore deeming these lands to be merely occupied, or possessed, but not *owned*. This normally affects most of the rural population in these countries, and an estimated half a billion people in Sub-Saharan Africa.

• In some cases, there is even a failure to acknowledge that large parts of traditionally-held lands are even *occupied or used*. This places the greater portion of the customarily held estate in Africa and Asia in the category of not just being unowned, but "vacant and idle" and "available to investors." This occurs even though these lands are actively used and may constitute an even greater source of livelihood than farm production.

There are exceptions to these trends. Several states have always given customary land rights due legal respect as property interests—Ghana being the main example in the African continent, and Botswana being another in certain respects.[15] Recent tenure reforms in Tanzania, Uganda, and Mozambique have given rural lands a similar status, presuming them already privately owned under customary law. This makes the state sale or lease of these lands more difficult in these countries, requiring local communities to first either surrender their lands voluntarily to the state, or to reach agreement themselves with the investor. However, in practice, governments in these countries have found ways to coerce or manipulate access to large areas of community-held lands.[16]

There are also a number of other countries in Africa that have improved, if not entirely reformed, the legal status of properties held under customary tenure. Benin, Burkina Faso, Madagascar, and Africa's newest state, Southern Sudan, are among these. However, such improvements are

---

15   Elizabeth Alden Wily, *The tragedy of public lands: The fate of the commons under global commercial pressure*, contribution to ILC Collaborative Research Project on Commercial Pressures on Land (Rome: International Land Coalition, 2011).

16   Elizabeth Alden Wily, "'The Law is to Blame': Taking a Hard Look at the Vulnerable Status of Customary Land Rights in Africa," *Development and Change* 42, no. 3 (2011).

seriously impeded by one or another condition, such as requiring customary land owners to formally survey and register their holdings, or limiting formal recognition to house plots and farms, leaving the much more expansive collective land assets of communities exposed. Even where the rights of communities to regulate customary landholding is given legal recognition, there may be several shortfalls in the *de facto* protection of rural land-holders. An exception is Tanzania, where local governments, designated as the lawful land authority, are elected at the village level.

A last key avenue of dispossession occurs where local elites coerce or manipulate access to community lands for investors. In Kenya, the trustee owners of customary lands are partially elected county councils whose land administration powers are, by law, shared with the centrally located Commissioner of Lands. While both are bound to act in the presumed interest of communities, state law neither defines that interest, nor requires popular consultation. Accordingly, in one case, the Siaya and Bondo County Councils were legally able to lease 6,900 hectares of community wetlands to a US investor for rice production, even though these lands are crucial to local rice production, grazing, reed cutting, and fishing.[17] In a similar example, over one million hectares of Ghana's community lands have been leased by chiefs to seventeen biofuel developments.[18]

As another case study in Nicaragua describes, such developments can pit local elites against poorer community members who are likely to be most dependent upon communal resources.[19] Institutionally weaker sections of communities are particularly vulnerable to dispossession. This is usually acute for women who are likely to be disproportionately more negatively affected by decisions made outside their realm of control.[20] A case study for Ethiopia[21] illustrates how pastoralists are also very

17   FIAN, *Land grabbing in Kenya and Mozambique. A report on two research missions—and a human rights analysis of land grabbing* (Heidelberg: FIAN International Secretariat, 2010).

18   George C. Schoneveld, *Potential land use competition from first-generation biofuel expansion in developing countries*, Occasional paper 58 (Bogor, Indonesia: CIFOR, 2010).

19   David Monachon and Noémi Gonda, *Liberalization of ownership versus indigenous territories in the North of Nicaragua: The case of the Chorotegas*, AVSF/CISEPA contribution to ILC Collaborative Research Project on Commercial Pressures on Land (Rome: International Land Coalition, 2011).

20   Elizabeth Daley, *Gendered impacts of commercial pressures on land.*

21   Messele Fisseha, *A case study of the Bechera agricultural development project, Ethiopia*, contribution to ILC Collaborative Research Project on Commercial

vulnerable, especially given the large number of land deals that affect pastoral areas such as in Mali, Ethiopia, and Sudan.

Economic Governance That Fails the Rural Poor

Economic governance includes both domestic economic policy, and the international rules and institutions that make up global, regional, and bilateral trade and investment regimes, as well as international human rights law.

Within host countries, large-scale land acquisitions are greatly facilitated by an economic policy paradigm that sees the private sector as the main, if not the only, engine of economic growth. Host countries are going to great lengths to attract and legally protect foreign direct investment, including in agriculture and extractive industries. Measures include the creation of tax relief and other incentives for investors to purchase or lease lands.[22] Other measures include the creation of investment promotion agencies to identify lands for investors and speedily facilitate their lease. These bodies usually also provide technical assistance and advisory services to large-scale investors. Investment projects may also be given insurance, for example, through the World Bank's Multilateral Investment Guarantee Agency or the African Trade Insurance Agency accords.[23] Another particularly important measure is the maintenance of very low prices for land purchase or

Pressures on Land (Rome: International Land Coalition, 2011).

22   See Michael Ochieng Odhiambo, *Commercial pressures on land in Africa: A regional overview of opportunities, challenges, and impacts*, RECONCILE contribution to ILC Collaborative Research Project on Commercial Pressures on Land (Rome: International Land Coalition, 2011); Roel Ravanera and Vanessa Gorra, *Commercial pressures on land in Asia: An overview*, IFAD contribution to ILC Collaborative Research Project on Commercial Pressures on Land (Rome: International Land Coalition, 2011); and Elisa Wiener Bravo, *The concentration of land ownership in Latin America: An approach to current problems*, CISEPA contribution to ILC Collaborative Research Project on Commercial Pressures on Land (Rome: International Land Coalition, 2011).

23   Elisabeth Bürgi Bonanomi, "Trade law and responsible investment," in Simone Heri, Albert ten Kate, Sanne van der Wal, Elisabeth Bürgi Bonanomi, and Katja Gehne, *International instruments influencing the rights of people facing investments in agricultural land*. WTI/SOMO/ON contribution to ILC Collaborative Research Project on Commercial Pressures on Land (Rome: International Land Coalition, 2011).

lease, particularly in Benin,[24] Zambia,[25] Kenya,[26] and Ethiopia.[27]

Large-scale land acquisition is also enabled by the rapid development of international law over the past few decades. This has strengthened the legal protection of investment and investors in acquiring large areas of lands. The signing of the WTO agreement and related treaties, including the Agreement on Agriculture, signaled a new wave of trade liberalization that has reduced barriers to trade in agricultural commodities.[28] Trade liberalization has also been pursued through a growing number of bilateral or regional free trade agreements, while the EU and African, Caribbean, and Pacific states are negotiating comprehensive Economic Partnership Agreements.

In addition to trade liberalization, a booming number of investment treaties (over 2,600 by 2010, and growing) have considerably strengthened international safeguards for foreign investment by bringing investment disputes to international arbitration rather than domestic courts. Investment treaties usually require host governments not to discriminate against investors from the other state party, to treat investors in a fair and equitable way, and to pay compensation in case of expropriation. Investment treaties may also strengthen the legal value of investor-state contracts by requiring states to respect their contractual commitments vis-à-vis investors from the other state parties.[29]

Depending on how investment treaties are interpreted and applied, their implications may be far-reaching. For example, regulatory measures that undermine the viability of a land-based investment—such as revising a contract's water allocation to meet the water needs of other users—may be considered as an expropriation of that investment. In these cases, the host would be required to compensate the investor

---

24 Paulin Jésutin, *Evolution and impacts of coastal land use in Benin: The case of the Sèmè-Podji Commune*, VADID contribution to ILC Collaborative Research Project on Commercial Pressures on Land (Rome: International Land Coalition, 2011).

25 John T. Milimo, Joy H. Kalyalya, Henry Machina, and Twamane Hamweene, *Social impacts of land commercialization in Zambia: A case study of Macha mission land in Choma district*, ZLA contribution to ILC Collaborative Research Project on Commercial Pressures on Land (Rome: International Land Coalition, 2011).

26 O'Brien, *Irregular and illegal land acquisition.*

27 Fisseha, *A case study of the Bechera agricultural development project.*

28 Bürgi Bonanomi, "Trade law and responsible investment."

29 Lorenzo Cotula, *Land deals in Africa: What is in the contracts?*, Research Report (London: IIED, 2011).

for the losses suffered. This raises concerns over where host state action genuinely pursues a public purpose. Where public finances are strained, an obligation to pay compensation may make it more difficult for host governments to act in the public interest.

If an investor feels that the host government has breached its obligations under a land deal or an applicable investment treaty, it may refer the dispute to international arbitration. Where breaches were found, international arbitrators have awarded investors large amounts of public money in compensation. And where governments are unwilling to pay up, investors may choose to seize host state assets held abroad, encouraging enforcement. In addition, governments are often under pressure to comply with contracts in order to keep attracting investment.

The legal playing field is therefore arguably uneven for host states, let alone for local communities who are affected by large-scale land acquisitions. Bürgi Bonanomi shows that investment treaties seldom define investor obligations with regard to social and environmental matters, although they normally provide an international standard of protection for investors.[30]

On the other hand, international conventions supporting the land rights of indigenous peoples and communities (most notably ILO 169 and the 2007 UN Declaration on the Rights of Indigenous Peoples) lack legal teeth. A detailed legal analysis of international investment and human rights law carried out by Lorenzo Cotula shows that human rights law provides much weaker protection than investment law—in terms of both substantive standards of treatment and legal remedies.[31] For example, while investment treaties typically enable investors to access international arbitration directly, human rights law requires domestic remedies to be exhausted before petitions can be filed with human rights courts. Considering that domestic remedies may themselves involve several stages, including appeals, this requirement can make international processes significantly less accessible. Also, under the American Convention on Human Rights and the African Charter on Human and Peoples' Rights, petitioners must first bring the dispute to a commission, which may then refer it to the relevant regional court. The African

---

30   Bürgi Bonanomi, "Trade law and responsible investment."
31   Lorenzo Cotula, *Human Rights, Natural Resource and Investment Law in a Globalised World: Shades of Grey in the Shadow of the Law* (New York: Routledge, 2011).

Commission's non-binding decisions contrast with the final and binding nature of awards issued by investment arbitrators. Even for the binding judgments of the African Court (for those states that have ratified the African Court Protocol), enforcement mechanisms are less effective than those established to enforce arbitral awards.[32]

In addition, advances in international human rights and environmental law have not been widely ratified and adopted into domestic legislation.[33] In Africa, for example, only one country has ratified the above-mentioned ILO Convention No. 169 of 1989 on indigenous and tribal peoples. Only about half of African states have ratified the African Court Protocol, meaning that the other countries can only be held accountable before the African Commission on Human and Peoples' Rights.

Only one recent decision of the Commission (*CEMIRIDE and Minority Rights Group International v. Kenya*) has dealt directly with the protection of local land rights against arbitrary dispossession. The content of that decision was greatly influenced by the fact that the group affected was indigenous, and holds a special status under international law. Therefore, it is not clear whether the reasoning and safeguards developed in the *CEMIRIDE* decision would be found to be applicable to the land rights of non-minority groups. In any event, the decision of the Commission was not legally binding, but served only as a strong recommendation to the government of Kenya (which at the time of writing it has yet to apply).

Many other developments towards the rights of communities affected by large-scale land acquisitions are even weaker, having the status of voluntary guidelines that investors and host governments may adopt at their will.

The Side-Lining of Smallholder Agriculture

The rush for land comes against a background of an under-performing smallholder sector. Against this background, interest by global investors in large-scale, industrialized agriculture has been seen by many host countries as a new way forward, even as a solution to the problem of

---

32 Cotula, *Land deals in Africa.*
33 Simone Heri, "Human rights mechanisms to safeguard the food/land rights of people facing land use shifts," in *International instruments influencing the rights of people facing investments in agricultural land.*

rural development. Large land acquisitions are thus enabled by a policy
bias, and indeed an ideological bias, towards such industrialized agriculture. On one hand, the underinvestment in family farms make farm
lands vulnerable to commercial interests,[34] mining,[35] tourism, and urban
development investments.[36] On the other hand, with reduced public
spending and official development assistance, the renewed interest of
investors (private, public, or parastatal) is seen as an opportunity to
overcome gaps and attract investment funds into agriculture and land-
based activities. Why has smallholder agriculture come to be seen as
such a lost cause?

Two factors explain this neglect. The first has to do with scarcity of
public resources. This in turn stemmed, especially in Africa, from a shift
in donor-sector support to demands of urbanization and infrastructure.[37]
In many countries, agriculture has suffered from neglect in public policies and investment programs for several decades.[38] Structural adjustment in the 1980s and 1990s exacerbated this problem, and forced many
states to further limit support to agriculture. The second set of factors
relates to prioritization in the allocation of available resources. For many
governments, agriculture has not been a priority due to perceptions that

34   Adrián Tambler and Gabriel Giudice, *The competition for family dairy farmers'
     land in Uruguay and their strategies for confronting it*, CCU/CISEPA contribu-
     tion to ILC Collaborative Research Project on Commercial Pressures on Land
     (Rome: International Land Coalition, 2011).
35   A. Durand, *No Man's lands? Extractive activity, territory, and social unrest in
     the Peruvian Amazon: the Cenepa River*, SER/CISEPA contribution to ILC
     Collaborative Research Project on Commercial Pressures on Land (Rome:
     International Land Coalition, 2011); Zulema Burneo and G. Chaparro, *The
     process of land concentration in Peru*, CEPES contribution to ILC Collabora-
     tive Research Project on Commercial Pressures on Land (Rome: International
     Land Coalition, 2011).
36   Paulin Jésutin, *Evolution and impacts of coastal land use in Benin: The case of the
     Sèmè-Podji Commune*, VADID contribution to ILC Collaborative Research
     Project on Commercial Pressures on Land (Rome: International Land Coali-
     tion, 2011).
37   Ward Anseeuw and Augustin Wambo, "Le volet agricole du Nouveau parte-
     nariat pour le développement de l'Afrique (NEPAD) peut-il répondre a la crise
     alimentaire du continent?," *Herodote—Revue de géographie et de géopolitique* 131
     (2008): 40–58.
38   Rivo Andrianirina-Ratsialonana, Landry Ramarojohn, P. Burnod, and A. Teys-
     sier, *After Daewoo? Current status and perspectives of large scale land acquisitions in
     Madagascar*, OF/CIRAD contribution to ILC Collaborative Research Project
     on Commercial Pressures on Land (Rome: International Land Coalition, 2011).

agriculture is a backward sector, that smallholder farming cannot be competitive in global markets, or that other economic sectors are more promising in terms of job creation and revenue generation.

The sentiment against smallholder farming was prevalent in the colonial era as well as much of the post-colonial era development discourse—its legacy is reflected in governments' commitments towards agriculture, and to smallholder farming in particular. For example, by signing the Maputo Declaration in 2004, African governments pledged to spend 10 percent of their national budget on agriculture. In practice, only four of the fifty-three country signatories had in fact done so by 2009.[39] In Asia, although several countries developed major agrarian reforms from the 1960s, most remained unimplemented, including developments that required significant injections of support to small farmers. This was true, for example, in India, Indonesia, the Philippines with its controversial Comprehensive Agrarian Reform Program,[40] Nepal, and Pakistan.[41] In a similar vein, the Green Revolution of the 1960s and 1970s managed to effectively increase food production overall, but it did so in a manner that primarily benefited upper-middle-class farmers.

The long-standing neglect of agriculture in many developing countries has resulted in dwindling agricultural production and productivity. Although most of the population remains dependent upon self-produced food, Africa has become a net importer of basic food commodities since the 1970s. Angola, for example, was exporting food in 1980, but now imports half its food needs. In 2007, the continent as a whole, imported 15 percent of its basic consumption at a cost of US$119 billion.[42]

In Ethiopia, foreign investment rose from $135 million in 2000 to $3.5 billion in 2008 according to UNCTAD.[43] Much of this is for production for export, including flowers, vegetables, cereals and rice,

---

39 Augustin Wambo, *La gouvernance des politiques publiques en Afrique subsaharienne en période postajustement structurel. Une critique de la valeur ajoutée du NEPAD face au défi agricole*, Thèse de Doctorat en Économie (Paris: Université Paris-Sud, 11, 2009).

40 Roel Ravanera and Vanessa Gorra, *Commercial pressures on land in Asia: An overview*, IFAD contribution to ILC Collaborative Research Project on Commercial Pressures on Land (Rome: International Land Coalition, 2011).

41 Alden Wily, *The tragedy of public lands*.

42 Anseeuw and Wambo, "Le volet agricole du Nouveau partenariat."

43 UNCTAD, "Rapport sur l'investissement dans le monde: sociétés transnationales, production agricole et développement en 2009," *Rapport—Vue d'ensemble* (New York: UNCTAD, 2009).

livestock, and biofuels. This production stands in stark contrast to the risk of periodic famines, including the current food crisis in the Horn of Africa. Over one million hectares have already been leased for these purposes with planned expansion up to 2.7 million hectares (10,424 square miles), 986,000 ha of which is one regional state, Benshanguel Gumuz.[44] Tremendous institutional support has been given to foreign investment, including the establishment of the Agricultural Investment Support Directorate to find lands for investors and facilitate development. Incentives to produce for export include five-year tax holidays, low land-use fees, and availability of concessional lending for up to 70 percent of the investment from the Development Bank of Ethiopia. Companies from India, Germany, Israel, and Saudi Arabia have actively responded. Saudi Star Agricultural Development PLC already exports rice from 10,000 ha in Gambella Regional State with plans to expand to 500,000 ha.[45]

But none of this means that family farming is intrinsically less productive than large-scale farming. There are long-standing arguments that, all else being equal and while acknowledging much diversity in contexts and crops, efficiency considerations tend to favor family-sized units in agriculture, partly because of issues linked to labor costs and supervision. It is often pointed out that in now-developed countries, family farming has been the traditional norm. Large-scale agriculture, particularly plantations, have proved profitable, but it is not possible to conclude from this that they are more productive. Economies of scale favoring large-scale agriculture tend to exist not in production, but upstream (e.g. access to credit, fertilizers, etc.) and downstream (processing), and these factors may contribute towards greater concentration in primary production.

Conclusions—Are We Reaching a Tipping Point?

Two billion people, or one third of humanity, are dependent on five-hundred million smallholder farms and pastoral production. Yet their land and production rights are increasingly jeopardized. Their future capacity to feed themselves may depend on decisions being taken now in the context of the global land rush. But there is also more than food security

---

44 Odhiambo, *Commercial pressures on land in Africa*.
45 Oakland Institute, *Understanding Land Investment Deals in Africa: Ethiopia* (Oakland: The Oakland Institute, 2011).

at stake. Decisions over land use and ownership carry great potential for promoting empowerment, sustainable livelihoods, and dignity, but as much potential for expanding and entrenching poverty, inequality, and disempowerment.

The land rush is opening up ever-greater land areas to commercial exploitation, including land held under customary regimes that previously has not been available for such exploitation.[46] This also implies the expanding and deepening commercialization of rural communities and farming systems with local production systems and societies increasingly having to adapt to the demands of global commodity markets. This is illustrated in several case studies, perhaps most clearly in those relating to land market liberalization in Nicaragua,[47] land concentration and social unrest in Peru,[48] land conversions in the Kathmandu Valley of Nepal,[49] and in studies conducted in the Philippines.[50]

But these trends, in themselves, are nothing new. They are a continuation of processes that began with colonization, and the legacy of colonialism is apparent in many of the factors that are shaping and enabling the current wave of large-scale land acquisitions. What is new is the rate of change since 2005, and the prospect that today's enhanced investor interest in land resources is unlikely to go away for the foreseeable future. Rural communities throughout the South have had to live for decades with insecure and threatened claims to land, but now increasingly face the prospect of finally losing access to these resources to a new wave of expropriation. We may be said to be facing something of a crisis or tipping point, beyond which we will see large-scale and irreversible changes in ownership and control over land and water, in agricultural systems, and in rural societies.

Indeed, the current wave of investment itself can be seen as further aggravating some of the governance failures that are shaping it. Global capital flows and government efforts to attract capital can have a

---

46 Chris Huggins, *A historical perspective on the "'Global Land Rush,"* contribution to ILC Collaborative Research Project on Commercial Pressures on Land (Rome: International Land Coalition, 2011).

47 Monachon and Gonda, *Liberalization of ownership.*

48 Burneo, *The process of land concentration*; Durand, *No Man's lands?*

49 Bharat Shrestha, *The Land Development Boom in Kathmandu Valley*, CDS contribution to ILC Collaborative Research Project on Commercial Pressures on Land (Rome: International Land Coalition, 2011).

50 de la Cruz, *The new conquistadores*; Calvan and Ablola, *Highly extractive fishing activities.*

profound influence on key areas of national policy, including land governance, labor law, environmental regulation, and agricultural policies, while also driving corruption. Weak land-administration systems may be overwhelmed, while the mere prospect of a large-scale land acquisition creates uncertainty for potentially affected land users, undermining their *de facto* security of tenure and acting as a deterrent to investment. Finally, large-scale land acquisitions and the priority given by governments to attracting and supporting large-scale schemes are putting small-scale production systems under further pressure.

But it would be wrong to imagine that rural communities are merely passive bystanders of these processes. Social movements and popular resistance are increasingly a major factor in determining the effects global commodity prices and investment flows have within target countries. In many of the case studies, popular discontent has taken the form of peaceful advocacy and protest movements.[51] In Indonesia, NGOs have recorded 630 land disputes between local communities and palm oil companies. But where injustice is seen as unresolved, the risk that such disputes and movements will lead to violent confrontations is real.[52] Such "political risks" for investors and governments, whether peaceful or not, are likely to have an increasing impact on the number and type of investments that are agreed and successfully implemented.

---

51   Rawat et al., *The impact of special economic zones*; de la Cruz, *The new conquistadores*; Calvan and Ablola, *Highly extractive fishing activities*.
52   Colchester, *Palm oil and indigenous peoples*.

DESTRUCTIVE DEVELOPMENT AND LAND SALES IN ETHIOPIA

Graham Peebles

Land to many is much more than a resource or corporate commodity to be profitably exploited. Identity, cultural history, and livelihood are all connected to "place." Indeed for many whose families have lived in the same area for centuries the sense of self is intimately tied up with their homeland. The Anuak People who constitute the majority tribal group in the southwest Ethiopian region of Gambella are such a group, so too the Kwegu, Bodi, Mutsi, Suri, and Nyangatom tribes of the Lower Omo Valley. To these ancient, noble people, the land is who they are. It's where the material to build their homes is found and the source of traditional medicines and food. This land is where their ancestors are buried, and where their history rests. By driving such people off their land and into large settlements in order to make way for industrial-sized farms, mostly owned and run by foreign corporations, the government is denying them their livelihood and stealing their identity.

The erosion of traditional values and morality (including the observation of human rights and environmental responsibility) are just some of the negative effects of the global neoliberal economic model, with its focus on short-term gain and material rewards. The commercialization of everything and everybody has become the goal of multinationals and corporate governments driven by a narrow understanding of development, which is largely reduced to the economic sphere with its emphasis on increasing Gross National Product figures month on month, year on year, and turning over glowing returns to the insatiable global monetary bodies—the World Bank and International Monetary Fund—no matter the human impact or environmental cost. In many parts of the world, such development has become an invisible cloak under which all manner of state-sponsored atrocities and human rights violations are committed.

The United Nations Human Development Index widens the assessment of development, and the UN has a detailed and thorough definition of "Sustainable Development," which "meets the needs of the present without compromising the ability of future generations to meet their own needs." The concept of "need," primarily of the world's poorest people, is the "overriding priority."[1] Commonly understood, "need" is nothing more than meeting the fundamental physical requirements for living: adequate food and water, shelter, together with access to education and health care, all of which are seen as basic human rights and enshrined as such in the United Nations Declaration of Human Rights Article 25. An aspirational set of statements, Article 25 is made in the recognition of humankind's innate equality and the fundamental rights of all people to share in the bounty of the Earth, rights that will only be met when the resources of the world are shared equitably amongst the people of the world. Such a commonsense idea would be a good place from which to build a new, fair, and just economic system to address the needs of all.

Overflowing with contradictions (and despite the UN guidelines), "development" is often employed to dignify government and corporate activities, which commonly amount to no more than exploitation and profiteering. This is certainly so in the case of the worldwide appropriation of land to irresponsible, profit-driven foreign corporations, private hedge funds, and equity fund managers—speculators who boast of returns between 20 and 40 percent on "investments" in agricultural land in developing countries. These rates of return provide delicious promises, which Anuradha Mittal of the Oakland Institute (OI) says are luring in "endowments including university endowments such as Harvard University, Vanderbilt University" and others.[2] This cocktail of irresponsible investors, Friends of the Earth state, "are stimulating land grabbing, which is destroying thousands of communities worldwide."[3] The financial sector, they rightly insist, "must take responsibility for their activities and ensure their investments respect human rights and abide by local environmental regulations," and in line with the image of sustainable development that meets the "needs" of native people.

An expanded definition of development would include: the fulfillment of an individual's innate potential; the continuation and expansion

1   World Commission on Environment and Development, *Our Common Future* (Oxford: Oxford University Press, 1987), http://www.un-documents.net/ocf-02.htm.
2   "Oakland Institute's Ethiopia Land Grab Report, Executive Director Anuradha Mittal on CNN," July 14, 2011, http://www.youtube.com/watch?v=g7YD1X7wDpg.
3   David Kureeba and Kirtana Chandrasekaran, "European Banks and Pension Funds Fuel Land Grabs in Uganda," Friends of the Earth International, May 21, 2013 http://www.foei.org/en/media/archive/2013/european-banks-and-pensions-funds-fuel-land-grabs-in-uganda.

of traditional lifestyles and cultures; and the integrated development of individuals. Such ideas grow out of the UN definition of development, which recognizes the importance of meeting people's needs beyond limited GNP or GDP measurements, globalization statistics, and Power Point clichés, which see everything as a commodity and everyone as a consumer. The homogenization of life—a further consequence of globalization and the market economy (with its inherent inequality and lack of social justice), cultivates conformity and denies individuality, squashes or appropriates culture to the market, and imposes competition in all areas of life. It is a destructive recipe creating injustice and division, fueling anger and frustration that, long suppressed, seems now to have surfaced in the popular uprisings recently witnessed throughout the world.

With growing unity and confidence, people are expressing their collective will and crying out for freedom, justice, and equality, and to be listened to by governments and international institutions. The scale and breadth of recent protests is unprecedented: people, in many cases suppressed for years, are awakening. The young lead the charge, seeing clearly the need for a new way of living, one that observes human rights and allows, indeed encourages, freedom of expression and new inclusive political systems free from the ideological constraints of the past. It is a new time, a new millennium, indeed a new cosmic age or cycle, with its unique qualities and creative opportunities. It is a time of transition, and lasting change takes time. The impulse of the new is strong, but the form is embryonic still. Perennial values of old—freedom and justice, sharing, equality, and brotherhood—are the goals of those pressing for change, heartfelt values denied by the present systems. New imaginative forms (political/economic and social) are required, ones that look beyond the current competitive model that separates and divides, to a peaceful world at ease with itself, where the basic requirements and human rights of everybody are met.

Movements calling for change have found their way into almost every corner of the world, including Ethiopia, where the people have been suppressed and controlled for generations. Under the leadership of Ethiopian Peoples Revolutionary Democratic Front (EPRDF), freedom of expression has been curtailed, and an atmosphere of fear and intimidation fostered. Contrary to the constitution, peaceful assembly has not been allowed and political dissent is stamped out. Against this repressive background, on Sunday, June 2, 2013, the Smayawi (Blue)

Party, organized demonstrations at various sites across Addis Ababa.
Throngs of mainly young people marched through the city, demanding
that the "government releases political leaders and journalists, and tack-
les corruption and economic problems," *The Guardian* report.[4] Protesters
carried banners reading "Justice! Justice! Justice! We call for respect of
the constitution." In addition to these extraordinary scenes, local people
are rising up against unjust government land-development projects in
the Lower Omo Valley and Gambella. With over 65 percent of the population of Ethiopia under twenty-five years of age, and a median age of
just seventeen, the young are an army; peaceful, unified, and motivated,
the youth is the great hope of the country. They know well that sharing
and justice are the keys to peace and freedom—common sense truths
that the ruling party, acting from narrow ideological positions that dis-
tort and corrupt, does not understand. The political elites cling to power
and privilege, fearful of the changes that the people demand. Unity is a
worldwide need and the way forward for humanity; in Ethiopia, where
over seventy different tribal groups, speaking dozens of dialects, contribute to the rich cultural tapestry of the country it is essential if there is to
be fundamental, lasting change.

Three quarters of all worldwide land acquisitions have taken place in
Sub-Saharan Africa, where poverty-ridden and economically vulnerable
countries (many with poor human rights records) are encouraged to attract foreign investment by donor partners and their international guides:
The World Bank, International Monetary Fund, powerful institutions
that by "supporting the creation of investment-friendly climates and land
markets in developing countries" have been a driving force behind the
global rush for agricultural land, the OI report in *Unheard Voices*.[5]

Poor countries make easy pickings for multinationals negotiating
deals for prime land at giveaway prices with all manner of government

4   Reuters in Addis Ababa, "Ethiopian human rights protesters take to streets
     in Addis Ababa," *The Guardian*, February 6, 2013, http://www.guardian.co.uk/
     world/2013/jun/02/ethiopian-rights-protestors-addis-ababa.
5   Wendy Liu, G. Alex Sinha, and Rikki Stern, *Unheard Voices: The Human Rights
     Impact of Land Investments on Indigenous Communities in Gambella* (Oakland:
     Oakland Institute, 2013), http://www.oaklandinstitute.org/unheard-voices
     -human-rights-impact-land-investments-indigenous-communities-gambella.

sweeteners. Sealed without consultation with local people, contracts lacking transparency and accountability offer little benefit for the host country (certainly none for indigenous groups), and as Oxfam makes clear, "have resulted in dispossession, deception, violation of human rights and destruction of livelihoods."[6] Ethiopia is a prime target for investors looking to acquire agricultural land. Since 2008, the government has leased around 3.6 million hectares for commercial farm ventures. Land is cheap, and along with long-term leases, the government offers a neat bundle of carrots, including tax incentives and unrestricted export clauses, incentives that the OI state "deny African countries economic benefits" from land deals that the EPRDF regime wraps up neatly with its complete disregard for the human rights of indigenous people. In their desperation to attract foreign investment, and "to make way for agricultural land investments," the Ethiopian government has "committed egregious human rights abuses, in direct violation of international law."

Together with the Lower Omo Valley in the South East of the country, the fertile Gambella region (where 42 percent of land is available), borders South Sudan with its lush vegetation and flowing rivers. A large percentage of land sales in the country have taken place here. Indian corporations have acquired the largest chunk, leasing around six-hundred thousand hectares (2,317 square miles) concentrated in Gambella and afar, split between ten investing companies. Karuturi Global, the world's largest grower of roses, leads the charge as they diversify into food production, leasing 311,700 ha in Gambella, for $1.10 per ha, snapping up land without even seeing it. For the Indian giant, it is, as John Vidal in *Land Grab Ethiopia* says, "the sale of the century."[7] "Green Gold" is how Mr. Karuturi, describes his 300,000 ha of Ethiopian soil, "for which he pays $46 per ha per year including water and labour and expects at least $660 [per ha] in profit per year."[8] Another major Indian company leasing land in Gambella is BHO Bioproducts. Chief Operating Officer Sunny Maker told Bloomberg in 2010 that they have "plans to invest more

---

6   Bertram Zagema, *Land and Power: The Growing Scandal Surrounding the New Wave of Investments* (Oxfam, 2011), http://policy-practice.oxfam.org.uk/publications/land-and-power-the-growing-scandal-surrounding-the-new-wave-of-investments-in-l-142858.

7   John Vidal, *Land Grab—Ethiopia*, Guardian Films, Journeyman Pictures, http://www.youtube.com/watch?v=DeQFCBFYlwY.

8   *Slideshow: Who's behind the land grabs?*, GRAIN (2012), http://www.grain.org/article/entries/4576-slideshow-who-s-behind-the-land-grabs.

than $120 million in rice and cotton production," which, by 2017, should "generate about $135 million a year from sales divided equally between domestic [Indian] and international markets."[9] He added that the "incredibly rich fertile land," will all be "cleared within the next three years." Cleared yes, violently, indiscriminately, and totally. Villages, people, forests, woodland, all destroyed, burnt, displaced, relocated, desecrated.

Land deals in the Gambella region are made possible by the EPRDF's "villagization program," which is forcibly clearing indigenous people off ancestral land and herding them into State-created villages. The widely criticized villagization scheme proposes to resettle 1.5 million people nationwide; 225,000 over three years from Gambella alone. The same process is taking place in the beautiful Lower Omo Valley, home to a group of eight ancient tribes—indigenous people who have lived upon the land for thousands of years, leading self-sufficient, simple lives in harmony with the environment. They live east and west along the 760 km (472 miles) long Omo River, the heartbeat of their lives, which flows from Ethiopia into Kenya, where it comes to rest in Lake Turkana.

Murder, rape, false imprisonment, and torture are being committed by the Ethiopian military as they implement the federal governments policy of land clearance and resettlement. One Anuak man told the NGO Inclusive Development International, "My village was forced by the government to move to the new location against our will. I refused and was beaten and lost my two upper teeth." His brother "was beaten to death by the soldiers for refusing to go to the new village," he says. "My second brother was detained, and I don't know where he was taken by the soldiers."[10] The government guarantees investors that any land leased will be cleared of everything and everyone, and in addition, they agree to "provide free security against any riot, disturbance or any turbulent time," OI reports. Bulldozers operating in Gambella are destroying the "farms, and grazing lands that have sustained Anuak, Mezenger, Nuer, Opo, and Komo peoples for centuries," *Cultural Survival* records.[11] The

9   William Davison, "BHO Bioproducts of India to Spend $120 Million on Ethiopia Farms," *Bloomberg*, September 25, 2012, http://www.oaklandinstitute.org/bho-bioproducts-india-spend-120-million-ethiopia-farms.

10   "Ethiopians Demand Accountability from World Bank for Contributing to Grave Human Rights Abuses," Inclusive Development International (2012), http://www.inclusivedevelopment.net/ethiopia-gambella-villagization-program/.

11   "Ethiopia: Stop Land Grabbing and Restore Indigenous Peoples' Lands,"

government's attitude is summed up by a village elder in Batpul, Gambella: "since you do not accept what [the] government says, we jail you."[12] True to their word, the military jailed him without charge in Abobo where he was held for more than two weeks, during which time, he says, "they turned me upside down, tied my legs to a pole, and beat me every day for seventeen days until I was released." Many indigenous people tell of such violent intimidation, beatings, arbitrary arrests and detention, torture in military custody, rape and extra-judicial killings. Genocide Watch considers the state criminality "to have already reached Stage 7 (of 8), genocide massacres" against the Anuak (in Gambella), as well as the people of Oromia, Omo and the Ogaden region.[13]

Hundreds of thousands of villagers in both Gambella and the Lower Omo Valley are being relocated, Human Rights Watch (HRW) state, "through violence and intimidation, and often without essential services," such as education, water, and health care facilities—public services promised to the people and donors in the EPRDF's program rhetoric.[14] "The government promises us paradise, but we know that we are going to hell," says a member of the aggrieved Bodis tribe from the Omo Valley. "Between tribes we have always found a solution when a land conflict has arisen, but with the government it's impossible."[15] Contrary to their policy of Ethnic Federalism, which outlines a federal state united and diverse, the governments approach has been to divide and rule, setting tribes and ethnic groups against one another, encouraging division and competition for resources including all forms of humanitarian aid, which is being illegally distributed by government officials on a partisan basis.

⁂

By driving people off their land and into large settlements, the government is not only destroying their homes, in which they have lived for

---

Cultural Survival (February, 2012), http://www.culturalsurvival.org/take-action/ethiopia-stop-land-grabbing-and-restore-indigenous-peoples-lands/ethiopia-stop-land.

12   Human Rights Watch (2013), http://www.hrw.org/node/109149.

13   "Ethiopia," *Genocide Watch*, http://www.genocidewatch.org/ethiopia.html

14   "Human Rights in Ethiopia," Human Rights Watch (2013), http://www.hrw.org/africa/ethiopia.

15   *Omo: Local Tribes Under Threat* (Oakland: Oakland Institute: 2013), www.oaklandinstitute.org/sites/...org/files/OI_Report_Omo_Ethiopia.pdf.

generations, it is stealing their identity. Land rights are complex, and while the Ethiopian constitution—a broadly liberal document (written by the ruling regime but used at its convenience)—states that all land ultimately belongs to the state, but the only land appropriate to be leased is land described as "marginal," "unused," or "wasteland," the land leased to foreign corporations and appropriated by the state is prime land, well irrigated with bountiful water supplies. "Because the land is traditionally owned, under international law the traditional owners have the right to it as property. Changes to its use or seizure are illegal without the consultation and compensation of the lands' traditional owners," HRW make clear in their report, *What Will happen If Hunger Comes*.[16] As well as protecting indigenous people, the constitution also safeguards agro-pastoralists, who are the majority of affected tribal groups: Section 40(5) explains, "Ethiopian pastoralists have the right to free land for grazing and cultivation as well as the right not to be displaced from their own lands."[17] Driving local people off their ancestral land, which supplies their food and medicine, also breaches the International Covenant on Civil and Political Rights, which states, "in no case may a people be deprived of its own means of subsistence." Add to this the violation of the Right to Culture and Religion and the Right to Health and a substantive legal shield forms around the tribal people in Gambella and the Lower Omo Valley from government development plans. These are rights that the people need to be made aware of, and which donor partners acting with all due ethical responsibility should demand the Ethiopian regime observe.

The government is also legally required to involve indigenous people in any decisions relating to development projects that impact on their lives, and must obtain the "Free, Prior and Informed Consent" of any groups it plans to move, in accordance with the International Labor Organization Convention 169 and the /UN Declaration on the Rights of Indigenous Peoples.[18] However, far from consulting and obtaining

---

16   "'What Will Happen if Hunger Comes?': Abuses against the Indigenous Peoples of Ethiopia's Lower Omo Valley," Human Rights Watch (2013), www.hrw.org/sites/default/files/reports/ethiopia0612webwcover.pdf.

17   Ethiopian Constitution, unofficial English-language draft (University of Pennsylvania: 1994), http://www.africa.upenn.edu/Hornet/Ethiopian_Constitution.html.

18   FPIC is the principle that a community has the right to give its consent to proposed projects that may affect their lands, resources, livelihoods, and communities. This principle is protected by international human rights law as "all peoples have the right to self-determination" and "all peoples have the right to

consent, Niykaw Ochalla of the Anywaa Survival Organization explains, "when [the government] comes to take their [tribal groups] land, it is without their knowledge, and in fact [the government] says that they no longer belonged to this land, [even though] the Anuak [in Gambella] have owned it for generations." Indeed, according to Nyikaw Ochalla, "there is no consultation at all, sometimes people are warned they have to move." OI discovered that the military "instruct people to get up and move the same day." And "for their loss of livelihood and land," people receive no compensation whatsoever. Throughout sweeping research in Gambella, OI "did not find any instances of government compensation being paid to indigenous populations evicted from their lands."[19]

Indeed, far from consulting with native people, encouraging them to participate, and allowing them the right to speak out freely, military units regularly visit villages in Gambella and in the Lower Omo Valley, where HRW record that they "suppress dissent related to the sugar plantation development [and associated resettlement plans]. According to local people anything less than fully expressed support for [government] sugar development was met with beatings, harassment, or arrest."[20] *The Guardian* reports that killings and repression are now common, recounting the story of a villager who says he "was shot with a bullet in my knee. That day eleven people were killed and the soldiers threw four bodies off Dima Village Bridge. They were eaten by hyenas."[21] Rape is another military weapon being employed in the Lower Omo Valley, Gambella, and elsewhere in the country to frighten and intimidate. OI relay the particularly distressing account of "the gang rape of a young herd boy. They took a small boy that was herding cattle. They had sex with him for a long time in the forest. He was screaming. The boy couldn't walk afterward. He had to be picked up and carried."[22] With such levels of

freely pursue their economic, social and cultural development." It is enshrined in the International Labour Organization Convention 169 and the UN Declaration on the Rights of Indigenous Peoples, http://www.culturalsurvival.org/node/10635.

19 "Ethiopia: Lives for Land in Gambella," Oakland Institute, August 1, 2013, http://www.oaklandinstitute.org/ethiopia-lives-land-gambella.

20 HRW, "What Will Happen if Hunger Comes?," 2.

21 John Vidal, "Ethiopia dam project is devastating the lives of remote indigenous groups," *The Guardian*, 6 February 2013, http://www.theguardian.com/global-development/2013/feb/07/ethiopian-dam-project-devastating-remote-tribes

22 Will Hurd, "Understanding Land Investment Deals in Africa: Ignoring Abuse

cruelty and inhumanity, the people feel desperate, as one displaced individual told HRW in *Waiting Here for Death*, the government "brought the Anuak people here to die. They brought us no food, they gave away our land to the foreigners so we can't even move back."[23]

🃏

Remote and culturally diverse, with prized United Nations Educational Scientific and Cultural Organization World Heritage status, the Lower Omo valley is home to over two-hundred thousand indigenous tribal people, including the Kwegu, Bodi, Mutsi, Suri, and Nyangatom tribes. Their ancient way of life and the delicate ecosystem is being threatened "by the construction of a massive hydroelectric dam, known as Gibe III, on the Omo River and associated plans for large-scale irrigated agriculture," HRW report.[24] The Gilgel Gibe III dam was started in 2006, and is now 62 percent complete. Funding for the $2 billion project has come from a range of sources, including the Industrial and Commercial Bank of China (ICBC). The European countries looked at the project, and, concerned by the lack of impact assessment studies, culturally appropriate project consultations (required under the constitution), and under heated pressure from a range of NGOs, wisely decided not to get involved, as did the World Bank. Gibe III is part of the Gibe family and follows on from the Gibe I Dam and the Gibe II power station (which draws its water from the Gibe I reservoir) and the yet-to-be-built dam duo of Gibe IV and V. With these major projects the government is driving a developmental sledgehammer into the heart of the previously tranquil Omo Valley with plans to transform the area into an agro-industrial powerhouse. This is all part of the EPRDF's ambitions to turn Ethiopia's agrarian economy (85 percent of the population work in agriculture) into an urbanized, industrial one.

A number of deeply concerned international and regional aid organizations, Survival International (SI) among them, believe that "the Gibe III Dam will have catastrophic consequences for the tribes of the

---

in Ethiopia DFID and USAID in the Lower Omo Valley" (Oakland: Oakland Institute, 2013), 6.

23   HRW, "Waiting Here for Death: Displacement and 'Villagization' in Ethiopia's Gambella Region," Human Rights Watch (2012), 24.

24   HRW, "What Will Happen if Hunger Comes?"

Omo River, who already live close to the margins of life in this dry and challenging area."[25] Gibe III, no doubt much to the delight and misplaced pride of the government, will be the largest dam of its kind in Africa (243 meters, nearly eight hundred feet tall, about the size of the tower known as The Shard in London, UK). It would double Ethiopia's energy capacity, while causing some of the worst environmental and human carnage in the region by seriously impacting the lives of tribal groups of the Lower Omo area, as well as the three-hundred thousand people who live around Lake Turkana in Kenya. According to the NGO International Rivers, the Gibe III dam "will dramatically alter the Omo River's flood cycle, affecting ecosystems and livelihoods all the way down to the world's largest desert lake [and one of the planet's oldest], Kenya's Lake Turkana," which receives 90 percent of its water from the Omo River. The lake's ecosystems go through a dramatic annual cycle driven by the Omo flows, the microscopic plants and algae that underpin the lakes food chains are fed by the river, and "the rising water level floods the Omo delta… and the bays and shallows around the lake [create] an ideal habitat for foraging and breeding fish species among the dense architecture of bank-side vegetation in the shallows and riverine floodplain. These seasonal breeding cycles also create opportunities for fishermen, birds and crocodiles to catch fish in near-shore areas during and after their reproduction."[26]

Water from the dam will be stored in a giant reservoir, which will feed the plantations in the valley (445,000 ha has so far been earmarked by the government for development) via hundreds of kilometers of pipelines. "Up to 200 kilometers [125 miles]" of such primary irrigation canals have already been built, along with an "earthen dam" to water the plantations which, OI tell us, "has stopped the annual flood that all people along the river depend on for agriculture, and in the process inundated cultivation sites of the Bodi and Kwegu people upstream." In addition, SI makes clear, the combined effects of the projects "will result in the drying out of much of the riverine zone and will eliminate the Riparian Forest. Indigenous people such as the Kwegu who rely almost exclusively on fishing and hunting will be destitute." One could be

---

25   "The Omo Valley Tribes," *Survival International*, http://www.survivalinternational
      .org/tribes/omovalley.
26   *The Downstream Impacts of Gibe III: East Africa's "Aral Sea" in the Making?*,
      International Rivers, January 2013, http://www.internationalrivers.org/files/
      attached-files/impact_of_gibe_3_final.pdf.

forgiven for thinking that the EPRDF government is working to intentionally decimate native peoples' lives, cause ethnic and national conflict,
and shatter the delicate ecology of the region.

𝕊

The construction of the Gibe III dam in the Lower Omo Valley and the
interconnected development project of leasing ancestral land for agricultural use (including biofuels), are being pursued by the government
in a manner that is violating a range of human rights, as well as internationally binding legal agreements. Ideologically conditioned and driven
solely by the quest for economic development and growth, the EPRDF
is pursuing a development strategy including the land sale policy, which
is causing enormous suffering to the lives of hundreds of thousands of
indigenous people throughout the country. With the Lower Omo Valley
projects there is a real risk that, according to HRW, "the livelihoods of
five-hundred thousand people may be endangered, tens of thousands will
be forcibly displaced, and…the region will witness increased inter-ethnic
conflict as communities compete for scarce resources."

According to OI, over 375,000 ha of fertile land in the Lower Omo
valley—is being turned into "industrial scale plantations for sugar and
other monocrops." Such methods damage the soil ecology, create dependency on pesticides and fertilizers (all good for the agro-chemical
giants), and require the use of lots of water. HRW estimate around
100,000 ha is being made available to private "investors," corporations
from Malaysia, India, Italy, and South Korea who are planting biofuels
and cash crops (e.g. cotton and maize).[27] State-owned sugarcane and
cotton plantations run by the Ethiopian Sugar Corporation, an umbrella organization of the central government, has taken 150,000 ha of
"rich and fertile" tribal land for itself, and "will [negatively] impact the
people of the Lower Omo most, especially the 170,000 along the river,"
according to OI.[28]

Mass displacements are accompanying these development projects
in the Lower Omo Valley. OI report "260,000 local people from 17 ethnic groups in the Lower Omo and around Lake Turkana [in Kenya]—
whose waters will be taken for plantation irrigation—are being evicted

---

27   HRW, "What Will Happen if Hunger Comes?"
28   Hurd, "Understanding Land Investment Deals," 4.

from their farmland and restricted from using the natural resources they have been relying on for their livelihoods."[29] HRW reports that "on the east bank of the Omo River, where farms are being cleared, grazing lands have been lost, and livelihoods are being destroyed."[30] More than two thousand soldiers have been drafted into the area downstream of the dam. *The Guardian* reports, "most of the Omo valley is now off limits to foreigners," including international media and NGOs.[31] "Virtually no NGOs work in the area, and members of indigenous communities have been warned not to speak to outsiders, especially to foreigners." The picture of state intimidation is a familiar one. Refugees in Dadaab, Kenya, from the Ogaden region of Ethiopia, recall stories of the same type of abuse as those from Gambella. A former commander of the Liyuu police told me that "the first mission for all the military and the Liyuu is to make the people of the Ogaden region afraid of us," a policy objective achieved by the use of violent means, such as murder, rape, torture, and destruction of property. From a wealth of information collated by HRW and the OI, it is clear that the Ethiopian military operating in Gambella and the Lower Omo Valley is following the same criminal script. "We were at home on our farm," a seventeen-year-old girl from Abobo in Gambella told HRW, "when soldiers came up to us: 'Do you accept to be relocated or not?' 'No.' So they grabbed some of us. 'Do you want to go now?' 'No.' Then they shot my father and killed him."[32] A villager from Gooshini (in Gambella), now in exile in South Sudan, described how those in his settlement "that resisted... were forced by soldiers to roll around in the mud in a stagnant water pool then beaten."

The new settlements that make up the villagization program in Gambella and in the Omo Valley are built on land that is "typically dry and arid," completely unsuitable for farming, and miles from water supplies, which are reserved for the industrial farms. The result is increased food insecurity amongst local dispossessed people, leading in some cases to starvation. HRW documented cases in Gambella of people being forced off their land during the "harvest season, preventing them from

29 Oakland Institute, "Ignoring Abuse in Ethiopia."
30 HRW, "What Will Happen if Hunger Comes?," 2.
31 Vidal, "Ethiopia dam project devastating the lives of remote tribes."
32 HRW, "Ethiopia: Army Commits Torture, Rape," Human Rights Watch, August 28, 2012, http://www.hrw.org/news/2012/08/28/ethiopia-army-commits-torture-rape.

harvesting their crops."[33] OI explains that people are barred from "cultivating their own fields and [with the military] destroying crops and grain stores to cause hunger. People are then lured to the [resettlement] sites with food aid from international agencies."[34] In 2011, former Prime Minister Meles Zenawi, asserted that the construction of industrial farms in the Awash Valley in the North East would "benefit the people of this area and hundreds of thousands of other Ethiopians, by creating employment." Hollow political rhetoric; the only jobs created were low-paid plantation work, and Zenawi crucially failed to mention that tribal groups in the region lost their homes and their way of life. They are now dependent on food aid to feed their families. In addition, with the arrival of foreign workers, plus two thousand soldiers in this previously quiet, hidden corner of Ethiopia, the people of the Lower Omo Valley have become exposed to a spate of health concerns. Prostitution is flourishing, and the refusal to use condoms is contributing to the rapid spread of HIV/Aids. OI states that "numerous cases of Hepatitis B, a disease transferred through blood and sex" have also been reported in the area.[35] Food insecurity, violent evictions (including killings and rape), cultural carnage, environmental destruction, prostitution, and HIV/Aids: all brought to the beautiful Lower Omo Valley by the government, and all in the name of development.

In the face of such government atrocities the people feel powerless, but change is afoot and like many suffering injustice throughout the world, the people of Gambella and the Omo Valley are beginning to act. "We don't have any means of retrieving our land," Mr. O from the village of Pinykew in Gambella, told *The Guardian*.[36] "Villagers have been butchered, falsely arrested, and tortured, the women subjected to mass rape." Enraged by such atrocities and donor countries' involvement, he is bringing what could be a landmark legal case against Britain's Department for International Development (DFID). Leigh Day & Co, solicitors

---

33   HRW, "Waiting Here for Death," 48.
34   Oakland Institute, "Understanding Land Investment Deals in Africa," 6.
35   Oakland Institute, "Omo," 10.
36   Clar Ni Chonghaile, "Ethiopia's resettlement scheme leaves lives shattered and UK facing questions," *The Guardian*, January 22, 2013, http://www.guardian.co.uk/global-development/2013/jan/22/ethiopia-resettlement-scheme-lives-shattered.

based in London, have taken the case, "arguing that money from DFID is funding the villagization program… breaches the department's own human rights policies." DFID administer the £324 million given to Ethiopia, making it the biggest recipient of aid from Britain. They deny supporting forced relocation, but their own documents reveal that their funds pay the salaries of local government officials responsible for the implementation of the scheme and infrastructure of the state-created villages. In an account that rings with familiarity, Mr. O, now in Dadaab refugee camp, says he was forced from his village at gunpoint by the military. At first he refused to leave, so "soldiers from the Ethiopian National Defense Force beat me with guns." He was arrested, imprisoned in military barracks, and tortured for three days, after which time he was taken to the new village, which "did not have water, food, or productive fields," and where he was forced to build a new house.

In the Lower Omo Valley, frustrated, angry, and seeing no alternative, members of the Suri tribe on the west bank of the Omo river have taken up arms against the military. The government has decimated their land, clearing trees and grass to "allow Malaysian investors to establish plantations, water has also been diverted from the mainstay Koka River to these plantations leaving the largely pastoral Suri without water for their cattle," according to OI. Government forces are maintaining a brutal campaign aimed at the Suri people. Friends of Lake Turkana, a Kenyan NGO reported in May 2012 that, "government forces killed 54 unarmed Suri in the marketplace at Maji in retaliation [to Suri actions against the military]. It is estimated that between 57 and 65 people died in the massacre and from injuries sustained on that day. Five more Suri have been killed since then… [and] Suri people are being arrested randomly and sentenced to 18, 20, and 25 years in prison for obscure crimes."[37]

The government unsurprisingly denies all allegations of widespread human rights abuses connected with land deals and the villagization program specifically. They continue to espouse the "promised public service and infrastructure benefits" of the scheme that "by and large," OI assert, "have failed to materialize." The regime is content to ignore documentation provided by human rights groups and NGOs, and until recently had refused to cooperate with an investigation by the World Bank into allegations of abuse raised by indigenous Anuak people

---

37   *Friends of Lake Turkana* (2013), http://www.friendsoflaketurkana.org/.

(incidentally, the World Bank gives Ethiopia more financial aid than any other developing country—$920 million last year alone). Former regional president Omod Obang Olum oversaw the plan in Gambella and assures us resettlement is "voluntary" and "the program successful." Predictable, duplicitous comments that Inclusive Development International (IDI) says "are laughable." An independent, non-profit group working to advance human rights in development, IDI has helped the Anuak people from Gambella "submit a complaint to the World Bank Inspection Panel implicating the Bank in grave human rights abuses perpetrated by the Ethiopian Government." The complaint alleges "that the Anuak people have been severely harmed by the World Bank-financed and administered Providing Basic Services Project (PBS)." OI describes PBS as "expanding access and improving the quality of basic services in education, health, agriculture, water supply and sanitation."[38] However, IDI make clear that "villagisation is the principle vehicle through which PBS is being implemented in Gambella," and they claim that there is "credible evidence" of "gross human rights violations" being committed in the region by the Ethiopian military. HRW found that donors are "paying for the construction of schools, health clinics, roads, and water facilities in the new [resettlement] villages. They are also funding agricultural programs directed towards resettled populations and the salaries of the local government officials who are implementing the policy."

IDI's serious allegations further support those made by many people from the region and Mr. O in his legal action against DFID. The World Bank's inspection panel have said the "two programs (PBS and villagization) depend on each other, and may mutually influence the results of the other." The panel found that "there is a plausible link between the two programs but needs to engage in further fact-finding." All groups involved in land sales have a moral duty, a civil responsibility, and a legal obligation to the people whose land is being leased. That includes the Ethiopian government, the foreign corporations leasing the land, and the donors—the World Bank and DFID, who, through PBS, are funding the villagization program.

The Ethiopian government is in violation of a long list of international treaties that, in keeping with their democratic pretensions, they

---

38   Development Assistance Group Ethiopia, PBS, http://www.dagethiopia.org/
     index.php?option=com_content&view=section&layout=blog&id=14&Item
     id=16 (accessed May 2013).

are happy to sign up to, but less enthusiastic to observe—from the International Convention on Civil and Political Rights to the Convention on the Rights of the Child (CRC) and all points legal in between. If not legally obliged, investors are certainly morally bound by the United Nations' "Protect, Respect and Remedy" Framework, which makes clear their duty to respect and work within human rights law.[39] To turn a blind eye to widespread government abuse and to support schemes, that whether directly or indirectly, violate human rights and cause suffering to the people is to be complicit in state criminality that is shattering the lives of hundreds of thousands of indigenous people in Gambella, the Lower Omo Valley, and indeed elsewhere in the country. Donors' responsibility, first and last, is to the people of Ethiopia.

Whilst economic development in Ethiopia is essential, it must be rooted in human rights and international law and should take place in a measured, just manner that respects the wishes of the community and shares any rewards equitably. Indigenous groups, villagers, and pastoralists must be encouraged to participate in all decisions that affect them, and a community spirit of inclusion and unity fostered.

---

39 *Guiding Principles on Business and Human Rights*, United Nations Human Rights Office of the High Commissioner, www.ohchr.org/Documents/.../ GuidingPrinciplesBusinessHR_EN.pdf.

BIOFUELS, LAND GRABS, REVOLUTION

Alexander Reid Ross

Hand in Glove: Global Trade and Colonialism

Palm oil went from being a traditionally used, small-scale product local-ized almost entirely in some parts of Africa to being found in close to 50 percent of consumer goods, including food-stuffs and soaps (and, increas-ingly, biofuels). In recent years, roughly 40 percent of total land acquisi-tions have been for biofuels—a land grab that leads to food shortages and worsens the climate crisis. By looking into the past, present, and projected future of palm oil, we can gain some insight into the hypocritical colonial and neo-colonial roots of the industry that is deepening some of the most serious human rights and environmental violations in the world.

After the US Revolution, Britain shifted its focus from the slave trade in North America to the commodity trade in Africa. "In Britain," writes scholar Walter Rodney, "the notorious slave trading port of Liv-erpool was the first to switch to palm oil early in the nineteenth century when the trade in slaves became difficult or impossible. This meant that Liverpool firms were no longer exploiting Africa by removing its labor physically to another part of the world. Instead, they were exploiting the labor and raw materials of Africa *inside* Africa."[1] Colonial resource ex-traction in Africa brought the continent into the capitalist world system, requiring an attendant shift in labor markets.

It was only through a direct and corollary movement of colonialism that the slave trade was abolished and Africa set up as a peripheral zone for the North Atlantic countries.[2] In what became known as the Scram-ble for Africa, between 1841 and the outbreak of the first world war,

1   Walter Rodney, *How Europe Underdeveloped Africa* (Washington, DC: Howard University Press, 1987), 156.
2   Wallerstein explains: "one of the very factors explaining the rapidity of the growth of palm oil production—given of course the indispensible (and new) European demand for fats and oil for industrial lubrication, personal hygiene, and candlepower—was the previous massive growth of the slave trade which had stimulated African demand for foreign goods, expanded the network of trading communities, and (which is frequently overlooked) expanded 'the eco-nomic infrastructure of markets, roads, and currencies.'" Immanuel Wallerstein, *The Modern World-System III: The Second Era of Great Expansion of the Capitalist World-Economy, 1730s–1840s* (New York: Harcourt Brace: 1989), 107.

Western European powers descended on Africa to enclose new colonies, break the spirits of the traditional societies, and render the vast territory a peripheral zone within the capitalist world system. In 1917, at a time when nearly all of Africa and Southeast Asia languished under colonialism, WEB Du Bois described the setting:

> Colonies we call them... they are those out-lands where like a swarm of hungry locusts; white masters may settle to be served as kings; may wield the lash of slave drivers; may rape girls and wives, grow rich as Croesus and send homeward a golden stream. They belt the earth, these places, but they cluster in the tropics with its darkened peoples: in Hong Kong and Anam, in Borneo and Rhodesia, in Sierra Leone and Nigeria, in Panama and Havana—these are the El Dorados toward which the world powers stretch itching palms.[3]

Immanuel Wallerstein explains, "of all countries, Britain had the most to gain from the proper functioning of the capitalist world economy, so it took the lead in abolishing the slave-trade and substituting 'legitimate trade,'—that is, encouraging the production by Africans of cash crops (for example, palm oil) for the world market."[4] But other colonial interests sought to gain access to these markets as well, accounting for the apparently arbitrary partition of Africa into European protectorates and territories. "The flagpoles seem to have been stuck in the ground without rhyme or reason," writes Rodney, but the very deliberate wedge of French Dahomey and German Togo formed between Britain's Gold Coast and Nigeria, because the former countries sought to protect their palm oil interests. Meanwhile, German firms lapped up more than half of palm kernel exports and one third of palm oil from British Lagos, because it used palm-kernal cake for livestock feed, its proletariat utilized palm oil as a cheap cooking oil, its railway expansion required lubrication, and Hamburg held the only machines in Europe dedicated to crushing palm kernels.[5] Thus, palm oil among other cash crops, and

3   W. E. B. Du Bois, "Of the Culture of White Folk," *The Journal of Race Development* 7, no. 4 (1917): 444.

4   Immanuel Wallerstein, "Africa in a Capitalist World," *A Journal of Opinion* 10, no. ½, Tenth Anniversary Issue (1980): 29.

5   Walter Rodney, "The Imperialist Partition of Africa," *Monthly Review* 21, no. 11 (1970): 103–114, http://www.marxists.org/subject/africa/rodney-walter/works/partition.htm.

of course diamonds, gold, and minerals, played a defining role in the political economy of the Scramble and what was to come.

One of the principle beneficiaries of the "Scramble for Africa" was and has been the Anglo-Dutch corporation Unilever. A brief history of Unilever helps shed light on the palm oil trade. After the British entrepreneur, William H. Lever, developed his "Sunshine" soap, his small factory outside of Liverpool expanded into a large township, and soon multiplied into a multinational enterprise with factories around the world under the auspices of a new corporation called Lever Brothers. To supply his soap with the key ingredient of palm oil, Lever sought out concessions in Africa. After being turned away in the Gold Coast and Liberia, Lever went to the Congo Free State under the rule of King Leopold II, purchasing vast concessions for palm oil cultivation and bringing machines to convert palm seeds into oil. The Lever Brothers swept into the Congo in the aftermath of the vicious drive for rubber that led to the slaughter of 50 percent of the Congolese populous—upwards of ten million Congolese people. In this grotesque environment, Lever (soon to be known as First Viscount Leverhulme) became a sponsor of the brutality of "forced labor" that occurred on his lands.

According to Jules Marchal, who spent forty years in the Belgian diplomatic service, Leverhulme "did not want to devote money to ensuring fair remuneration of Africans, who, given such circumstances, would have worked quite willingly. Instead, he adopted the method generally used during this period to make Africans work, namely, coercion." Leverhulme would send his emissaries throughout several "circles" of property granted to him by the "Free State." Palm fruit was plentiful, so rather than deforesting large areas, the Lever Brothers simply planted more trees, and forced villagers to produce a certain amount of fruit or risk fines and penalties such as lashings with the notorious *chicotte*—a deadly, razor-sharp whip made from rhino hide. In many cases, Leverhulme's officials relocated Africans to squalid work camps, taking villagers away from their own fields and food sources to work for nothing. Although Leverhulme considered himself a philanthropist in the tradition of "free trade," Marchal calls the Lever Brothers' enterprise nothing more than "a sordid affair of large-scale profiteering, not heeding the harm done to Africans."[6] According to a medical report, released in 1928 by Dr. René Mouchet, forced labor on Lever Brothers lands included children as young as eight years old and caused such a crisis that "the companies exploiting the region do not seem to have grasped that development is itself threatened by the drop in population."[7] The report goes on to plead, "What are a few thousand lives saved by our serums and vaccines when compared to the millions of deaths for which we are responsible?"[8]

As the Lever Brothers expanded into Nigeria, villages closed themselves off to the presence of the colonists, and company representatives grew accustomed to greetings of arrow volleys and bullets when they tried to enter. The year after Mouchet's report, the Women's Market Rebellion swept through neighboring Nigeria, where British colonial forces attempted to impose a head tax on women in the palm oil producing province of Owerri. When the tax collector, Okugo, sent a messenger to count the women in one village, a woman named Nwanyerua asked him, "Did you count your mother, too?" A scuffle ensued, and a meeting of women was held—called by the sending of palm leaves to distant communities. The women occupied the grounds of Okugo's house, dancing around it and singing songs until he came out. They then mobbed him, damaged his house, and brought him to court. Tens of thousands of women made sure that Okugo was convicted in a sweeping movement that included the act of camping outside of the state house, the assault of tax collectors in other regions, the destruction of sixteen court houses, and the burning of numerous "European stores."

The next year, the revolt of the Pende struck Leverhulme's concessions in Congo, breaking economic involvement with the Lever Brothers, and effectively decolonizing Pende regions of the Congo. Though cast as a religious specter (Europeans referred to the African movement as *satana*, and the freedom fighters were labeled "fetish-worshippers"), the Pende revolted largely against high head taxes, which, at the time of low palm oil prices, consumed most of the laborers' income (they also revolted against other accumulated outrages, such as the failure of the company to pay African laborers their due wages, insulting of African chiefs, the intrusion of missionaries who sought to suppress African social organization, and the proliferation of unchecked thefts and abuses).

---

6   Jules Marchal, *Lord Leverhulme's Ghost* (New York City: Verso, 2008), 4.
7   Ibid., 117.
8   Ibid., 127.

As violent repression escalated, pitched battles ensued. At the height of the revolt, the corpse of a murdered colonial agent was dismembered, and his parts sent to different regions of the Congo, which became "shatter zones" against forced labor (as illustrated by the difficulty the British and Dutch forces had reclaiming the body parts of the late agent). Eventually the bloody revolt was put down by the *chicotte* and the barrel of the machine gun, and the Lever Brothers cemented their brutal hold on the Africans' land for the time being. The repression of the Pende would become so shocking that it was the first-ever documented British act in Africa condemned by other European governments.

By the time of the Pende revolt, the Lever Brothers had become so powerful that they could not only wage war against the Africans, but they could wage economic war against the shipping monopoly, the West African Lines Conference, through Lever's subsidiary shipping corporation, the United Africa Company (UAC), which Rodney refers to as the "African capitalist octopus."[9] Unilever's economic warfare relied on former employees who held key positions in the Oil and Fats Division of the British Ministry of Food while still receiving wages from the company. The Oil and Fats Division set the buying quotas for the Association of West African Merchants, which was dominated by the UAC anyway, so Unilever could determine prices and quantities of palm oil available from West Africa.

"It is no wonder," declares Rodney, "that the companies had government aid in keeping prices down in Africa and in securing forced labor when necessary. It is no wonder that Unilever then sold soap, margarine, and such commodities at profitable prices within a market assured by the British government."[10] Palm oil became the ingredient of the century, finding itself in "soaps, detergents, margarine, lard, ghee, cooking oil, canned foods, candles, glycerin, oil cake, and toilet preparations such as toothpaste."[11] It was used in explosives during the world wars, and then used during the post-war period of national liberation as a weapon of imperialist global trade.

---

9 Rodney, "The Imperialist Partition of Africa."
10 Rodney, *How Europe Underdeveloped Africa*, 170.
11 Ibid., 182.

Following World War II, African peoples rose up in mighty struggles across the continent to decolonize their homelands. Congo revolted against Imperial forces, which included the 9.5 million acres of mining and agricultural lands that had been given by Leopold II to largely US-backed firm La Société internationale forestière et minière (Forminière) with such powerful backers as Rockefeller, Guggenheim, and others. The elected government of Patrice Lumumba was forcibly shut down by these interests when Forminière led the region of Kasaï to secede from the Congo, withdrawing, along with Katanga, a majority of tax revenue from Congo's coffers. US and Belgian forces would soon assassinate Lumumba, and put their favorite, Mobutu Sésé Seko, into power.

This era of national liberation was plagued by such intrigues of foreign governments and corporations—particularly those as large as Forminière and Unilever. In 1965, one year before the CIA-backed coup that would end his term prematurely, the democratically elected President of Ghana, Kwame Nkrumah, would complain that "over 90 percent of world ocean shipping is controlled by the imperialist countries. They control shipping rates and, between 1951 and 1961, they increased them some five times in a total rise of about 600 percent, the upward trend continuing."[12] During the three decades of Pan-African national liberation, the UAC octopus was deemed "the Alternative Government" in Ghana and Nigeria, where it became the biggest private sector employer. But as time passed, Unilever expanded into "high modernist" monocrop production, and found more failures than successes—in one notorious example from Tanzania, their attempts to harvest millions of hectares of peanuts produced only 10 percent of it potential, and was abandoned within three years (a lesson, perhaps, to today's land grabbers).

Unilever continued to operate in Nigeria and Ghana as the national liberation impetus ebbed under the back-breaking onus of debt. Due to political volatility, the tendency of African nations to nationalize private corporations in a process known as Africanization, and the economic dependency of consumers on global commodity prices (particularly oil), by 1988, Unilever incorporated UAC into its structure, signaling a decrease of African operations.[13] Yet, as palm oil production shrunk in

---

12 Kwame Nkrumah, *Neocolonialism, The Last Stage of Imperialism* (New York: International Publishers, 1966), http://www.marxists.org/subject/africa/nkrumah/neo-colonialism/ch01.htm.

13 Benefiting from this "commodity boom" of liberal markets and developmentalist production of national liberation, which included a decade of rising consumer

West Africa, it advanced in South East Asia where colonial powers had been busy for centuries, and where companies like Unilever now obtain the majority of their palm oil.

Colonialism and the Seeds of Strife

Indonesia and Malaysia are the biggest producers of palm oil in the world today. The two countries currently produce 89 percent of all global palm oil exports, so much that they are out-producing their capacity. But this conversion was not achieved in a smooth, swift motion of history. Considering the *longue durée*, we can see how a Tamil Muslim merchant's capital was colonized, then liberated, and then turned towards ruthless plantation expansion via neo-colonialism.

In the third-century BC, Malacca, a small city-state on the western coast of the Malayan Peninsula, arose as a particularly important link between the Indian Ocean, the Java Sea, and the South China Sea. Though power changed hands many times, Malacca remained a hub of the commodity trade for well over a millennium, until the early-fifteenth century when the Portuguese explorer Afonso de Albuquerque colonized the small city-state and mercilessly slaughtered its Tamil Muslim population. Power changed hands again two centuries later—this time to Holland in a ruthless play that Marx captures in *The Critique of Political Economy*: "To secure Malacca, the Dutch corrupted the Portuguese governor. He let them into the town in 1641. They hurried at once to his house and assassinated him to 'abstain' from the payment of £21,875, the price of his treason." After the Portuguese governor paid Malacca's ransom in his own blood, the Dutch abandoned the island as the center of commerce in Southeast Asia, shifting operations to Java. "Wherever [the Dutch] set foot, devastation and depopulation followed," continues

status among Africans, Unilever's African profits rose to £1.1 billion, compared to £873 billion in North America. Approximately one decade later, their profit from the Third World would comprise 10.3 percent of sales, as opposed to profit from North America, which amounted to just 8.5 percent. In the 1980s, the World Bank induced structural adjustment policies in Nigeria led to such increases as a quadrupling of operating profits and an increase in service and technical sales profits of over a hundred times for UAC within just five years, yet the debt that underwrote the SAPs caused a crashing economic failure, bringing substantial political blow back. See Patrick Smith, "Corporate Profile: (UAC) United Africa Company 'The Alternative Government,'" *Multinational Monitor*, June 1989, http://www.mcspotlight.org/beyond/unilever/uac.html.

Marx, "Banjuwangi, a province of Java, in 1750 numbered over eighty thousand inhabitants, in 1811 only eighteen thousand. Sweet commerce!"[14] Two hundred years later, the Napoleonic Wars created the subtext for the British Empire to occupy the spaces of fading Dutch hegemony.

During the 1950s, communist insurgencies tore through the colonial powers of Malaysia, which responded by forcibly removing some half million rural, indigenous Malayans to "New Villages"—concentration camps surrounded by barbed wire and watch towers. The forced removal of Malayans presented a way of separating indigenous populations from the Chinese Malaysians, thus flaring up ethnic tensions and enhancing fears of "Red China." The disastrous act also "freed up" vast tracts of rural land for further plantation expansion. After liberation, Malaysia designed fledgling policies to integrate indigenous peoples into the world economy by privileging industrial and agricultural growth. In the coming decades, further displacement came along with the increase of palm oil production. By 1980, Malaysia was the world's largest exporter of palm oil and hardwoods.

In *Seeing Like a State*, James C. Scott asks, "Why did the Malaysian state elect to establish large, costly, bureaucratically monitored settlements in the 1960s and 1970s when the frontier was already being actively pioneered by large-scale voluntary migration?... As an economic proposition, the huge rubber and palm oil concerns established by the government made little sense. They were enormously costly to set up, the capital expenditure per settler being far beyond what a rational businessman would have invested." The answer, for Scott, is that the frontier was being laid out by the state in order to ensure a population "more amenable to control from above and outside."[15] Today, in the palm-oil-producing state of Sabah, Indonesia's second most populous state, one-third of the 3.2 million residents are migratory—the palm oil plantations provide a means of control. Children are no longer afforded state-sponsored education, so thousands of child workers bear the brunt of the palm oil industry in the plantation.[16] To wit, the plantations did not attain an ordered

14 Karl Marx and Friedrich Engels, *Capital Vol. 1*, Marx/Engels Internet Archive (marxists.org) 1999, 477.

15 James C. Scott, *Seeing Like a State* (New Haven: Yale University Press, 1999), 190–191.

16 Jason Motlagh, "Palm Oil for the West, Exploitation for Young Workers in Malaysia," *The Atlantic*, April 8, 2013, http://www.theatlantic .com/international/archive/2013/04/palm-oil-for-the-west-exploitation

and "well-administered" population, but they did create the conditions by which the population could be monitored and subjected to capitalist exploitation. As historian Fernand Braudel remarked at the time, "if one form of slavery is abolished, another springs up. Yesterday's colonies have all gained their independence, or so we are told in every political speech; but the rattling of chains in the third world is deafening."[17]

🔀

As Anseeuw and Taylor explain in their article, more than 630 protests against biofuels have been recorded in recent years in Malaysia's archipelagic neighbor, Indonesia, but where did this mass movement begin?

As the US actively subverted nominally leftist national liberation struggles in Africa, it pursued the same course in Asia. Under the more radical leadership of Sukarno during the early 1960s, Indonesia's policies of "Guided Democracy" staved off foreign investment and nationalized the Dutch plantations on which the colonists had cultivated palm oil. By nationalizing colonial industries, Sukarno sought, with other post-colonial nations, to create a new world system centered in an economic life liberated from the misery of Dutch colonial influence. But moves to pull formerly colonial operations under the purview of the state brought increased tension between Indonesia and the US.

In 1955, Sukarno held a summit of leaders from the Global South in the small town of Bandung, where a new Third World movement was generated. The US frowned upon such a world system, and by the early 1960s decided to cut off higher diplomatic relations with Indonesia. In one particularly revealing internal dispatch, US Ambassador Marshall Green insists, "A presidential meeting (between Lyndon Johnson and Sukarno) would be an open invitation for others to emulate Sukarno. It would show that the bad boys are the ones that get the attention. It would have decisively serious impacts on countries like Korea, Vietnam and perhaps even Thailand and the Philippines as far as the Far East is concerned. God knows how the Africans would react."[18] By 1965, the

---

-for-young-workers-in-malaysia/274769/.

17 Fernand Braudel, *Civilization and Capitalism: 15ᵗʰ–18ᵗʰ Century, Volume 2: Wheels of Commerce* (Berkeley: University of California Press: 1992), 514.

18 *Foreign Relations 1964–1968, Volume XXVI, Indonesia; Malaysia-Singapore; Philippines*, "Sukarno's Confrontation With the United States December 1964–September 1965," 89. Intelligence Memorandum, OCI No. 2057/64

same year Nkruma was removed from office in Ghana, covert CIA operations had subverted the relatively democratic government of Sukarno, and it was soon overthrown by a CIA-backed coup.

Within three years, Sukarno's successor, General Suharto, butchered over half a million people and launched a full-scale national investment program to expand the palm oil industry exponentially. Between 1968 and 1985, the palm oil industry expanded five times over. From 1985 and 2003, the acreage covered by palm oil increased another seven fold. As Indonesian industry churned out palm oil for global consumption, the neo-liberal discourse lauded the "Asian Tigers"—financial centers of Singapore, South Korea, Taiwan, and Hong Kong that have played important roles in palm oil expansion—while lamenting the "tragedy of Africa."[19] However, the top palm oil suppliers are Indonesian and Malaysian companies that are, today, increasing land holdings in Africa. While these companies are not based in the North Atlantic, they join companies in the North in the cannibalistic march to consume as much land and labor as possible.

After the fall of Suharto in 1998, indigenous peoples joined with rural and urban workers in decentralized efforts to resist government coercion—including the encroachment of palm oil plantations. The chief methods that the Dayak and others employed included active sabotage, court cases, and persisting to occupy and survive in zones of refuge. For example, the indigenous Dayak Temuan and Meratus peoples have engaged in ongoing struggle, sometimes through legal means and other times by setting fire to the offices and equipment of illegal palm oil operations. The Dayak who find refuge from the state in the majestic Meratus Mountains live as migratory hunter-gatherers practicing swidden farming, living in fluid, dispersed kinship units, and are, to the mind of many Indonesian citizens, "pagans."[20] Perforce, the government is trying to hound the Dayak into roadside settlements from their place of refuge in the jungle, due to their practice of "disorderly agriculture"

Washington, December 2, 1964, http://2001-2009.state.gov/r/pa/ho/frus/johnsonlb/xxvi/4443.htm.

19 See Vijay Prashad, *Everybody was Kung Fu Fighting* (Boston: Beacon, 2001), 42.
20 Scott, *Seeing Like a State*, 188.

No.	Date	Company (PT)	Location (District)	Problem	Action by the People
1	May '98	Malindo Jaya (ML)	Beng-kayang	The company tricked the village head with an inaccurate map and began operating without a permit	Unanimously rejected: grow pepper, rubber
2	Sept. '98	Rana Wastu Kencana (RWK)	Sambas	Took over land including cemeteries and tembawang through trickery: obtained a false signature on blank paper	Held company machines, sought compensation and went to court: lost
3	May '99	Aimer Agromas (AA)	Landak	The company cut the peoples' adat forest	The company had to pay an adat fine
4	Dec. '98	Multi Prima Entakai (MPE)	Sekadau	Did not convert plasma lands. People demanding at least 3–4ha/family	Demo at district legislature
5	Feb. '00	MPE	Sekadau	The company promised to build a road, but built a factory instead	People were hungry and destroyed the company's office
6	Jan. '99	Multi Jaya Perkasa (MJP)	Sekadau	Did not convert plasma lands for local people, only transmigrants	Demo both at district legislature and at company's office in Pontianak
7	June '99	MJP	Sekadau	The plasma lands still not converted. People feel deceived and apprehensive for their future.	The people burned the company camp and all their heavy machinery
8	Aug. '01	MJP	Sekadau	The company did not fullfil its promises to the people, which made life difficult for them	People threaten to take over the company
9	July '99	Harapan Sawit Lestari (HSL)	Ketapang	The company violated village land rights	Two-thousand ha re-occupied and 400 oil palms cut down
10	Jan. '00	HSL	Ketapang	The company cleared land under crop, sacred forest and land about to be opened for swidden	People demanded justice from the Ketapang District Legislature
11	May '00	HSL	Ketapang	The company manipulated data to receive an inflow of foreign investment and sold *kapling* to officials	Demo at the district legislature
12	Dec.' 99	MAS	Sanggau	The company deceived the people about their activities, arbitrarily clearing their crops	They seized the company's tools despite police intervention

(*pertanian yang tidak teratur*), and in order to open up their lands to palm oil. According to Ana Lowenhaupt Tsing, the Dayak caught on to the government's attempts at intervention, and developed a farcical political relationship by building villages with clustered housing in order "to look good if the government comes to visit."[21] The "public transcript," to use Scott's phraseology, of deference disguises the "hidden transcript" of indigenous life in defiance to the order of the state.

The Dayak's ongoing mobility, depicted as the source of their "pre-organized," atavistic culture by the state, allows them thorough access to much of the region, and in February 2013 two surveyors were caught mapping indigenous forest by the Dayak Meratus. After the plans for a palm oil plantation were uncovered, the Dayak Meratus immediately rejected the destruction of the local ecosystem, and the company offered them three choices: compensation for the land, plasma farming (a process by which the indigenous people will be assigned plots, or "ponds," of land to farm for the plantation corporation), or removal. The Dayak Meratus are perhaps lucky to have found out about the project at all—in one instance, the governor of East Kalimantan unlawfully granted permission to a palm oil company to log over 1 million hectares of the Dayak's land (he was eventually arrested for his involvement in such illegal activities, but the environmental damage and dispossession had already been done).

There is relatively little daylight between the prospect of "removal" and the promise of plasma farming. In one chilling account of the behavior of Wilmar subsidiary, PT BDU, Pak Subuk of the indigenous Batin Sembilan (Malay) people explains,

> PT BDU was being nice to us. They promised us cocoa, oil palm and plasma. We signed the KKPA. Was this their tactic to expand their land? We don't know. At the time, we already had planted fruit trees and cocoa plants on our customary lands. We trusted PT BDU. But after we had signed, PT BDU came and burned down our forests to plant their oil palm. They burned our graves at the same time. When we resisted, the company pointed guns in our faces. As for the KKPA that they promised to us before planting. 1,500 ha of land had been promised us, from Pinang Tinggi to Bulit Balut, marked by signposts 650B and 649A. When PT BDU began to harvest the oil palm fruit, they took down the signposts. We had been tricked into giving up our lands.[22]

---

21   Anna Lowenhaupt Tsing, *In the Realm of the Diamond Queen* (Berkeley: Princeton University Press, 1993), 93.

22   Marcus Colchester, Patrick Anderson, Asep Yunan Firdaus, Fatilda Hasibuan, and Sophie Chao, *Human rights abuses and land conflicts in the PT Asiatic Persada concession in Jambi*, Forest Peoples Programme (HuMa, Sawit Watch, November

According to one report, the Wilmar subsidiary bulldozed into surrounding creeks the long-standing settlements of protesting Batin Sembalin people—concrete foundations and all—while private security guards opened fire. This form of oppression is quite pervasive; in 2008, for example, Sawit Watch documented 518 instances of conflict involving military or police violence against local communities, including women who bear much of the brunt of labor in the palm plantations.

In the words of staff members of the Wilmar International subsidiary PT AP, the indigenous people are "nomads, so their rights to land are fully questionable," and "they are thieves, and their leaders are coordinators of thieves."[23] PT AP thinks that the land belongs to the company, because nomads have no legal claim to any land whatsoever. If palm trees are planted, the company has the rights, according to their logic. However, for the Batin Sembilan and the Dayak, the land is clearly theirs by dint of their memory, demarcated by burial grounds. Like any nation, the people lay claim to the land based on their history with it. One Barin Sembalin person named Adi from a bulldozed settlement explains, "Our grandmothers are still alive, they can still tell our history, so we continue to claim this land."[24] As Vandana Shiva asserts, "land is life," the living memory of the land tells the story of how the indigenous peoples came to survive and maintain their traditions as links in the fabric of the world that they come to know and recreate. It is no surprise, then, that the encroachment of palm oil deprives native communities of their access to food and water. In the words of Pak Butar, a Batin Sembalin person:

> We are surrounded by the oil palms. We are oppressed. We don't have enough to make a livelihood; we are just surviving now. Before, no one went hungry. Now, with all this oil palm, there are no livelihoods at all....The company is planting oil palm everywhere; less

---

2011), http://www.forestpeoples.org/sites/fpp/files/publication/2011/11/final-report-pt-ap-nov-2011-low-res-1.pdf.

23 Ibid., 23. The comment about being thieves is probably in regards to the work of collecting berondol (the lone fruits that are left to rot after falling from a bunch) often carried out by women and children farm workers. See Julia and Ben White, *The gendered politics of dispossession: oil palm expansion in a Dayak Hibun community in West Kalimantan, Indonesia* (paper presented at the International Conference on Global Land Grabbing, 2011).

24 Colchester, et. al., *Human rights abuses and land conflicts*, 47.

than a meter from the river, which is illegal, and sometimes even right in the middle of the rivers. We cannot catch fish like we used to. PT AP lets us pick the loose fruit but we are only paid 300 Rp./kilo, which is below the minimum wage. A kilo of rice alone costs 8,500 rupiah. Is this not oppression? People need to eat. We are economically weak; we are left behind and our livelihoods have been ripped away from us.[25]

The indefensible practices of industrial palm cultivation are spreading, as palm oil plantations expand anew in Africa. Even after pledging to convert to sustainable practices, in 2012 the multinational corporation Sinar Mas violated the land rights of the Bagyeli people by failing to consult them before commencing their logging operations on 33,000 hectares of Bagyeli land. According to a press release by the Forest Peoples Program, "As the affected Bagyeli communities have told us, the forest is their memory. If they lose it, they lose their past, their present and their future. They will no longer be Bagyeli. To destroy the forest is to reduce them to nothingness."[26] Sinar Mas's attempts to appear kinder and gentler seem laughable to environmentalists who recall the infamous Greenpeace demonstration of 2009, during which police joined Sinar Mas guards in punching and kicking activists staging a peaceful lockdown at corporate headquarters in Singapore. As well as Sinar Mas, other organizations from China, South Korea, Singapore, India, the US, and other countries are moving to take up 5.6 percent of the total landmass of Liberia with African palm production, 10 percent of Sierra Leone, and over 3 million hectares (about the size of Belgium) in Benin, Nigeria, Gabon, the Republic of Congo, and the Democratic Republic of Congo.

※

Although new demand for "sustainable palm" is growing, according to Friends of the Earth, "[it] is simply leading to the expansion of other palm oil plantations onto forested land." According to Wetlands International, by 2022, palm oil could destroy 98 percent of Indonesia's rainforest.[27] In

---

25 Ibid., 36.

26 http://www.forestpeoples.org/topics/palm-oil-rspo/news/2012/11/press
    -release-new-oil-palm-land-grabs-exposed-asian-palm-oil-compa.

27 Vandana Shiva, "The Agricultural Industrial Complex," in *Global Industrial Complex: Systems of Domination*, ed. Steven Best, Richard Kahn, Anthony J. Nocella

Malaysia alone, the past seven years has seen 350,000 hectares of peat swamp forests cleared—that's one third of the total—and 520,000 hectares drained. Draining peat swamps in Malaysia has caused the release of twenty million tons of carbon dioxide, while clearing peat swamp forest contributes to about 10 percent of total greenhouse gases released into the environment every year worldwide.[28] Given the disastrous implications of deforestation related to palm oil, the European Commission has estimated that palm oil biofuels involve 105 grams of carbon dioxide per megajoule energy in total—only two grams behind oil extracted from the tar sands and almost forty grams ahead of regular crude oil.[29]

The conversion of land to palm oil plantation, specifically, has led to an average deforestation rate of 2 percent per year in Malaysia—three times the rate of the rest of Asia.[30] Malaysian Borneo has the longest list of endangered species on the planet, and palm oil has claimed the lives of fifty thousand orangutans in the last two decades—90 percent of the species' habitat has been destroyed by deforestation.[31] The Asian Rhinoceros, the Pygmy Elephant, and Clouded Leopard are also threatened along with three-hundred thousand other animal species and three thousand tree species, while thousands of species are discovered every year.

Thus, the main aspects separating palm oil cultivation today from its colonial heritage are not human rights and environmental sustainability, but mass clear-cutting of indigenous forest and the spreading of chemical fertilizers—a task largely entrusted to women. According to a Rainforest Action Network fact sheet, "Women are often assigned tasks that seem less onerous, but which are actually more dangerous and physically demanding than that of their male counterparts. In Indonesia, women are often designated to spray pesticides because it is less physically taxing than other plantation work. Unfortunately, they are rarely given proper protective gear like gloves and masks. When they return home, they have

II, and Peter McLaren (Plymouth, UK: Lexington Books, 2011), 180.

28 Tom Young, "Malaysian palm oil destroying forests, report warns," *The Guardian*, February 2, 2011, http://www.theguardian.com/environment/2011/feb/02/malaysian-palm-oil-forests.

29 Damian Carrington, "Leaked data: Palm biodiesel as dirty as fuel from tar sands," *The Guardian*, January 27, 2012, http://www.guardian.com/environment/damian-carrington-blog/2012/jan/27/biofuels-biodiesel-ethanol-palm-oil.

30 Arthur Max, "Malaysia Deforestation is Three Times Faster Than Rest of Asia Combined," *Huff Post Green*, September 7, 2012, http://www.huffingtonpost.com/2011/02/05/malaysia-deforestation-is_n_816779.html.

31 Thomas King, *Say No to Palm Oil*, http://www.saynotopalmoil.com/.

to prepare food for their families, often with pesticide residue still on their skin and clothes."[32]

The plantations often resort to slave labor to conscript workers into these toxic and unethical conditions. According to one account given to Rainforest Action Network reporter, Ashley Schaeffer, "After work, Ferdi and Volario were forced inside the camp where they'd stay overnight under lock and key, guarded by security. If they had to use the bathroom, they'd do their best to hold it until morning or relieve themselves in plastic bags or shoes." Another account from a forty-two-year-old Java resident: "Suroso was approached by another oil palm company with the prospect of a well-paid career, along with promises of schooling, access to a local hospital, and all the protective gear necessary to take on the job of 'opening the land,' or clearing natural forests to make way for rapidly expanding palm plantations... After two months of backbreaking work and barely livable conditions, Suroso was paid 200,000 rupiah ($22) for clearing 60 hectares of land."[33]

🔖

Today, the populations of the Third World are subjected to sweat shops and extractive industries, made sacrosanct by International Financial Institutions and global trade partnerships. Even as the Pacific island of Kiribati disappears into the ocean, typhoons obliterate large parts of Southeast Asia—as Ban Ki-moon insists "climate change...is lapping at our feet—quite literally in Kiribati and elsewhere"—new free trade agreements are seeking to stimulate increased production and trade of biofuels and African palm.[34] Although Malaysia refused an IMF package in 1997, avoiding some of the more debilitating effects of the debt crisis, it is now the locus of a new US-driven free trade agreement called the Trans-Pacific Partnership. Underwriting the Trans-Pacific Partnership is the expectation that, as manufacturing in China decreases due to intensified (and successful) struggles against pollution, land grabs, and

---

32 Rainforest Action Network, "Hostile Harvest," factsheet.
33 Ashley Schaeffer, "Slave Labor For Palm Oil Production," *The Understory*, December 7, 2010, http://understory.ran.org/2010/12/07/slave-labor-for-palm-oil-production/.
34 Audrey Young, "Climate Change laps at our feet—UN Head," *New Zealand Herald*, September 6, 2011, http://www.nzherald.co.nz/nz/news/article.cfm?c_id=1&objectid=10749749.

corruption, industry will be ushered into the more "competitive" labor markets of Vietnam and Malaysia. These industries will provide convenient import markets for energy, so Canada has projected the Keystone XL and Gateway pipelines to traverse North America, bringing tar sands oil to terminals where it will be shipped to Southeast Asia. Furthermore, Australian coal giant, Ambre Energy is working hard to bring coal mined in the Powder River Basin of the US (the so-called "Saudi Arabia of coal") to the new export terminals on the Pacific in order to provide increased coal for Southeast Asia. In exchange, Malaysia will be able to provide cheaper raw materials and cheaply made manufactured goods to US corporations for biofuels and other household commodities.

The attempted greening of the energy industry through biofuel production has created carbon markets that fit free trade agreements. At the UN's 2011 Conference of the Parties meeting (COP17) in Cancun, agreements were made to pursue the path of REDD+ (Reducing Emissions from Deforestation and Degradation) agreements, which in some cases favors a high margin of profit for cultivation of palm oil.[35] REDD+ agreements also place blame for ecological destruction on small farmers like the Dayak, whose traditional practice of swidden farming is migratory and relies on a fallow period for forest growth. REDD+ agreements threaten to intensify farming in non-forested areas, while forcibly removing indigenous peoples from newly minted ecological reserves to prevent native farming practices and self-sufficiency. Rather than climate resilience, REDD+ leads to simple monocrop farming, which destroys topsoil, deploys hazardous and toxic pesticides and fertilizers, and pollutes water resources.[36]

With the TPP in place, REDD+ agreements may cause dispossession of indigenous peoples who inhabit forests, while creating even more intensive agricultural complexes and sticking countries with the bill if corporations happen to lose profits. This process can be seen as forcing a migratory and "ungovernable" population like the Dayak into sedentary existence, ensuring that their land and social structures become legible

35 U. Martin Persson, "Conserve or convert? Pan-tropical modeling of REDD–bioenergy competition," *Biological Conservation* 146, no. 1 (2012): 81–88, http://earthemphasis.com/key-research-articles/conserve-or-convert -pan-tropical-modeling-of-redd-bioenergy-competition/.

36 Christian Erni, *Shifting the Blame? Southeast Asia's Indigenous Peoples and Shifting Cultivation in the Age of Climate Change* (paper presented at Adivasi/ST Communities in India Conference, Delhi, 2009).

to state and economic planners (forests for wildlife and plantations for humans, and ne'er the two shall meet). Meanwhile, the carbon credits garnered from biofuel plantations will allow environmentally unaccountable states to wash their hands of the coal and oil underwriting the manufacturing boom that will bring sweatshop labor to the hundreds of thousands dispossessed by the enclosures caused by growth in the plantation economy. It's greenwashing, plain and simple.

Pushed to the brink of existence by the forces of global extraction and commerce, desperate people return to old ways of resisting Empire, forming pockets of piracy off the coast of Somalia and the Gulf of Guinea. The Somali pirates, for instance, are notorious for holding tanker-ships hostage, collecting several million dollars in ransom, and releasing their captives. In one such occasion in early May 2011, an Indonesian vessel carrying twenty-eight thousand tons of palm oil was seized by Somali pirates. The crew and vessel were released for a high ransom, but the pirates kept four South Korean sailors hostage as bargaining chips for the release of five Somali pirates in South Korea. After fourteen harrowing months, the pirates released the sailors for additional ransom. According to TradeMark Southern Africa, "The total cost to the global economy of the piracy off Somalia was over $6.5 billion last year [2011] and the $160 million shipping companies paid in ransoms was outstripped by the far bigger sums they spent on preventing attacks."

As palm oil holdings increase in West Africa, along with other extractive enterprises, more piracy has occurred in the Gulf of Guinea, leading to the deaths of five hostages (as opposed to no fatalities at the hands of Somali pirates). The pirates of the Gulf of Guinea also differ from their Somalian counterparts in that they typically expropriate the hijacked commodities, rather than asking for ransom. According to Aegis Advisory, "The Gulf of Guinea pirates may not look like much, but their activities have far-reaching financial consequences"—namely increased export costs for commodities produced in West Africa, such as palm oil from Togo and oil from Nigeria.

Against the Biofuel Wasteland

Piracy is on the rise in West Africa partly because of increased security off the coast of Somalia, and partly because export-oriented extraction in

Africa is expanding, and with it dispossession, corruption, and strife—but the pirates are not alone in resisting the new expansions of global trade. For example, when the people of Madagascar learned that more than three million hectares of land, approximately half of the available arable land in the country, had been given to foreign investors (half to Europeans, the other half to South Korean giant, Daewoo; Indian corporation, Varun; and other interests from South Africa and Australia) in largely rent-free concessions for jatropha, maize, and palm oil plantation land they overthrew the government. By alerting different land-based indigenous communities throughout Madagascar to the fact that their land was being sold literally from under their feet, the Collective for Defense of Malagasy amassed a sweeping movement that rallied in cities and towns across the island. According to Mamy Rakotondrainibe an organizer with the Collective, "the land deal with Daewoo corporation was one of the major points of the 2009 protests against the Madagascar government of Marc Ravalomanana, now exiled in South Africa."[37]

Little has been shared about the revolutionary tumult that toppled the presidency of Marc Ravalomanana, but it is absolutely critical to note the relationship involved between forestry, politics, rural self-management, and dual power. Anthropologist David Graeber notes the isolation of the rural populous from the central government as an example of dual power. Graeber explains, "the government had ceased to exist and the people had come up with ingenious expedients of how to deal with the fact that there was still technically a government, it was just really far away."[38] According to the United Nations Food and Agriculture Organization's report, *Accommodating Multiple Interests in Forestry*, the "environmental mediator" who goes between rural areas and political or economic agencies is "selected by the rural community (*fokon'olona*)."[39] However, according to an important report by the International Land Coalition, the intermediaries are "consultants who position themselves as 'jack of all trades,' typically retired or

---

37   Stefan Christoff, "Madagascar: Community resistance to corporate land theft," *farmlandgrab.org*, April 6, 2011, http://farmlandgrab.org/post/view/18406.

38   Ellen Evans and Jon Moses, "Interview with David Graeber," *The White Review*, 2013, http://www.thewhitereview.org/interviews/interview-with -david-graeber/.

39   Food and Agrigcultural Organization of the United Nations editorial, "Unasylva - No. 194 - Concilier des intérêts multiples en foresterie," 62, http://www. fao.org/docrep/w8827f/w8827f02.htm.

public officials," who have networks among civil society and significant agronomic knowledge.[40] Their relationships with the government and corporations are spotty at best.

Graeber insists that the Malagasy government's attempts "to make [*fokon'olona*] the grassroots cells for local democracy...never really works...largely because these [*fokon'olona*] aren't formal bodies at all, but assemblies brought together around a particular problem."[41] To wit, Graeber describes the *fokon'olona* as "a way of invoking the power of the ancestors,"[42] distinct from legal principles, which pose "only one, relatively minor, consideration."[43] The traditional notion of governance in the *tanindrazana*, or the "land of the ancestors," draws not simply on the brutal history of Imperial oppression for Madagascans, but on a territorialization of the memories of ancestors, themselves—the "matter of placing the living in an historical landscape created by the dead."[44] Rather than conceive of their history as one of resistance to oppression, Malagasy traditions incorporate their inherited knowledge through stories of magic and myths always intertwined with the land. Like the Malay who prize burial grounds and the living memory of their grandmothers, and the Bagyeli who identify memory with land, the "infra-politics" of the indigenous Malagasy are tied to ancestral memories and the land, rendering communication between rural communities and the formal nation-state a "charade," in Graeber's words.

An evaluation by the German nonprofit Bertelsmann Stiftung from just before the political crisis exposes the corruption involved in the cultural appropriation of indigenous organization for political purposes: "corruption is notorious in the environmental sector [of Madagascar]. If the government were to prove prepared to allow international consortia access to large areas of land for agro-industrial production (corn, palm oil, biodiesel material or other crops), thereby neglecting environmental and social aspects, the ecological sustainability record of

---

40 Rivo Andrianirina Ratsialonana, Landry Ramarojohn, Perrine Burnod, and André Teyssier, *After Daewoo? Current status and perspectives of large-scale land acquisitions in Madagascar* (Rome: International Land Coalition, 2011), 30.

41 David Graeber, *The Democracy Project* (New York: Spiegel & Grau, 2013), 230.

42 Graeber, "Catastrophe—Magic and History in Rural Madagascar," *Campos* 5, no. 1 (2004), 14.

43 Ibid., 19.

44 Graeber, "Painful Memories," *Journal of Religion in Africa* XXVII, no. 4 (1994): 374.

the Ravalomanana government would need to be re-examined."[45] In lieu of such a formal re-examination of the Ravalomanana government, it seems like the 2008–2009 crisis that toppled the president manifested a powerful rebellion against the state before being contained by a charismatic leader (the mayor of capital city Antananarivo, Andry Rajoelina). Like other rebellions, the political crisis of 2009 created more distance between the state and the people, allowing spaces of refuge to persist against land grabs and industrial domination without hegemony.

In Latin America, coups and paramilitary forces have been directed against small campesinos and indigenous peoples.[46] Above all else, this means that land is being taken away from rural populations, and placed in the hands of multinational corporations that siphon profits back to hegemonic centers and semi-centers of the world economy.

The biofuel boom is truly an extension of a prolonged colonial affair designed to displace subsistence, food-based autonomy for global commodity production. In Honduras, for example, the US-orchestrated coup against President Zelaya in 2009 was heavily aided by the country's wealthiest man, biofuel magnate Miguel Facussé, who has been suspected of cocaine trafficking by the US government since 2004.[47] Facussé's biofuel enterprises are protected by a paramilitary security force, which has killed more than fifty campesinos since the coup. According to reports, Honduran paramilitaries are being trained by Colombians who are emerging from their own paramilitary war in the name of biofuels.[48]

In Colombia, the department of El Choco-Darien, one of the world's top ten most critical ecological hot spots, has been taken over by the government with plans, initiated by the Uribe regime, to turn the

45 BTI 2010, "Madagascar Country Report," http://www.bti-project.org/countryreports/esa/mdg/2010/.

46 Joan Baxter, "Africa: Palm Oil Fuels Land Grabs in Africa," September 15, 2011, http://allafrica.com/stories/201109160960.html.

47 US Embassy, Honduras, "Drug Plane Burned On Prominent Honduran's Property," March 19, 2004, found at cablegatesearch.net, http://www.cablegatesearch.net/cable.php?id=04TEGUCIGALPA672&q=facusse%20miguel.

48 Annie Bird, "Honduras: Aguán Massacres Continue to Support Production of Biodiesel," *Upside Down World*, August 28, 2011, http://upsidedownworld.org/main/news-briefs-archives-68/3198-honduras-aguan-massacres-continue-to-support-production-of-biodiesel.

western-most part of Colombia into a massive African palm plantation. Not, however, before military and paramilitary forces worked in tandem to displace virtually the entire population of the region, inhabited by indigenous peoples like the Embera as well as Afro-Colombians who now comprise one of the largest internally displaced populations on the planet.[49] In this case, the legacy of Empire wraps around the world economy like an Ouroboros: Afro-Colombians, descendants of Africans brought to Colombia as slaves, are forced off of their land, which is then replaced with African palm plantations—a prime symbol of the colonization of Africa. Biofuel production is also expanding to vast proportions of the land base in Brazil, where it is fought by the Landless Worker's Movement (MST), Mexico, where villagers of Chiapas resist its spread, and Peru, where the Singaporean private equity firm, Asian Agri, is planning to concentrate a $100 million expansion.

Implications for global markets remain critical. Although oil production is increasing in the US, global oil production has plateaued over the last several years, and is expected to begin to decline by 2020. Meanwhile, Malaysia and Indonesia are running out of land for oil palm plantations. What we have to look forward to, then, is a twenty-first century full of oil palm land grabs. As biofuels like palm oil and ethanol arrogate the land of the world's food producers—small farmers—the cost of food increases, leading to enhanced speculation in commodity markets, such as grain, and an even sharper rise in international food prices.[50] As droughts and unpredictable weather patterns make harvests increasingly unreliable, the cultivation of biofuel crops decreases the amount of food production on the horizon. It is precisely this precariousness of global food markets that played a large role in the lead up to the 2011 uprisings, and will continue to provoke mass action until the memory and lives of the people of the world are respected, and those who displace, desecrate, and arrogate are brought to account for their misdeeds.

---

49   David Bacon, "Blood on the Palms: Afro-Colombians Fight New Plantations," *Upside Down World*, July 18, 2007, http://upsidedownworld.org/main/colombia-archives-61/816-blood-on-the-palms-afro-colombians-fight-new-plantations.

50   Scott Baier, Mark Clements, Charles Griffiths, and Jane Ihrig, "Biofuels Impact on Crop and Food Prices: Using an Interactive Spreadsheet," Board of Governors of the Federal Reserve, System International Finance Discussion Papers, Number 967, March 2009, http://www.federalreserve.gov/pubs/ifdp/2009/967/ifdp967.pdf.

ENVIRONMENTAL GROUP EVENTS IN TODAY'S CHINA

Yangtze River Delta Earth First!

From Individuals to Mass

Individual or elitist acts of "ecoterrorism" (such as the sporadic and isolated presence of the Earth Liberation Front and Animal Liberation Front) have not enjoyed a "harmonious" environment in China. Although several uninfluential, naïve, and nonviolent actions have been carried out, they typically represent little more than empty threats. On the other hand, environmental "group events" (a vogue buzzword nowadays for "mass disturbances" in China) are increasingly emerging as unceasing and uncontrollable forms of public protest. Forms of group events include road blockades, sabotage, mass demonstrations, and arson.

Numerous group events originate from land seizures. For that reason, it is necessary to describe the Chinese land system briefly. The Constitution stipulates that land in the cities is owned by the State; that land in the rural and suburban areas is owned by collectives; and that house sites and privately farmed plots of cropland and hilly land are also owned by collectives. In the meantime, the Land Administration Law claims that all units and individuals that need land for construction purposes shall apply for the use of State-owned land. In fact, almost all land is controlled by the government (to be more exact, the local governments instead of the central government). And the right to the use of land may be transferred (i.e., sold) to various companies or real estate developers when the latter want to erect factories or buildings. The system used to strike the landlords or speculators and protect the peasants, but nowadays it is utilized for providing the capitalist class with the price differential and a huge margin of reselling their usufruct.

Forced demolitions and evictions were totally lawful before the new Requisition and Compensation Ordinance of Housing on State-owned Land was signed on January 20, 2011. The area of land requisitioned annually for development is a secret to local governments, though the total requisitioned area of the whole country is public information in *Communiqué on Land and Resources of China* published by the Ministry of Land and Resources. The area of requisitioned land is secret, because it could be used to estimate the financial strength-and-debt ratio of each local government, which would probably become an obstacle to calling for various subsidies from the central government. In addition, land owned by collectives will be able to enter the free market directly if the Land Administration Law is passed, which means that there will be more land grabs in the future.

Largely peasant-driven group events have acted not only by resisting direct land seizure, but also indirect dispossession by way of heavy pollution. Compared to the environment itself, the scanty harvests and extra medical costs that come with pollution are more painful to most peasants. Particularly in the earlier decade of environmental group events (1996–2005), mass disturbances occurred as much, if not more, on the terrain of economic survival than ecological circumstances.

Vice-minister of the State Environmental Protection Administration Yue Pan stated that group events evoked by pollution increased at an average rate of 29 percent per year between 1996 and 2005. In 2005, there were fifty thousand relevant disputes throughout China, characterized by markedly higher degrees of confrontation than group events in other fields. The growth trend is continuing. *The Blue Book of Society 2010*, released on December 21, 2009 by Institute of Sociology of Chinese Academy of Social Sciences, points out that "environmental issues have become one of the significant factors which lead to social conflicts." Chaofei Yang, the chief of Department of Policies, Laws and Regulations of the Ministry of Environmental Protection (MEP), claimed that the number of major environmental group events increased by 120 percent from 2011 to 2012, and pollution presently stands as ninth among the top ten causes of group events nationwide.

The growth in resistance is surprising, since the number of environmental emergencies (including water, air, ocean, solid wastes, noise, and vibration) have decreased in recent years, according to the *China Statistical Yearbook* compiled by the National Bureau of Statistics of China. This contradiction might be understood in light of the implementation of China's Environmental Emergency Response Plan on January 24, 2006, which combines with timely reactions and interference of the mass ahead of prospective industrial constructions to preempt environmental emergencies. Also, the ongoing adjustment of China's economic structure transfers industries to poorer countries, mitigating domestic pollution.

Characteristics of Group Events

In terms of chronological order and movement building, analogous group events divide into two types: prophylaxis beforehand and response *post hoc*. According to other scholars, five types of group events can be identified concerning their purposes, features, and targets: demands for safeguards, events out of indignation, riots, disputes, and organized crimes.

Generally, the characteristics of these events could be sketchily concluded as follows: (1) general: happening across a variety of social sectors and frequent in every place; (2) non-political: swift to mobilize interested stakeholders while stirring the sympathy of outsiders; (3) escalating: taking a long time for brewage, fermentation, and preparation before bursting out, erupting again and again while escalating and upgrading continuously; (4) cooperative: channeling strong antagonism in multiple ways, unleashing negative sentiment and resentment on environmental issues, imitated and copied by other regions.

And their weaknesses are conspicuous: (1) Environment issues are only the breaking point of some "environmental" events. Thus the mass are satisfied with the supply and distribution of compensation, or the settlement of other economic issues including broader land seizures and labor employment, etc. (2) Most people only want to clear up their own backyard, ending at the edges of neighboring communities, and are indifferent to whether the same projects are relocated to others' backyards. Nationwide movements or organizations haven't appeared. (3) Leaders failed to hide themselves in the multitude, and many of them get arrested. (4) The success of resistance depends to a great extent on the internal factions and strife amongst other backstage enterprises and dominant capitalists, while the majority of participants seek help from external powers like the "neutral" government or media. Spontaneous sabotage by the mass hasn't developed into conscious struggles or revolutions, or mounted onto the stage of history as a potent force. (5) Officials of local governments maintain social stability by canceling controversial projects, mainly for the sake of quelling riots, calming down mass rallies, and thereby saving their bureaucratic position. Governments of other places scramble for projects canceled by mass protests, and industry remains welcome in nearby provinces by bureaucrats and capitalists. Large-scale outcry and actions yield apparent and short-term fruit instead of long-term effects; they alleviate symptoms rather than cure the disease—this is also one of crucial causes of similar events arising and subsiding over and over.

The Anger of Lexington

We can trace the trend of environmental disturbances back to 1990s. Sewage from a chemical fertilizer plant severely polluted the tillage and water source of Dachuan Village, Gansu Province. In 1996, the mayor of the village led over two hundred villagers to breach the gate of the plant. Meanwhile, local youths drove ten tractors fully loaded with polluted water up to the site, threw the rubber hoses over the bounding wall, and poured water into the factory district. This demonstration lasted ten days.

Fast forward to the year 2000. Dongxing Village, Jiangsu Province, earned the title of "cancer village" in *China Business Journal*, after opening Yancheng Julong Chemical Co., Ltd. in March 2000. Rice harvested in autumn was polluted right away. Sheep and pigs became sick, and the vegetables started to reek. Villagers at the leeward side could not endure the exhaust gas anymore, so they went to the chemical works in the spring of 2001 to remove the flues, smash the windows, and block up the water inlet. Julong was eventually closed in 2007.

Another extended campaign in Baisha Town, Fuchuan Yao Autonomous County, saw villagers engage in a seesaw battle with an arsenic factory for ten years, climaxing when several hundred people clashed with the police for two days in September 2003.

These events took place during the nascent stage of ecotages and environmental struggles. An integrated survey of national society in China's urban areas in 2003 showed that 77 percent (3,878 people) of those asked (5,069 people in all) reported that they, themselves, or their families once suffered from environmental damages; but only 38 percent among the 3,878 had carried out resistance, which meant that 61 percent comprised the silent majority who failed to do anything.

During five months in the summer and autumn of 2005, everything changed. Three group events with at least one thousand participators touched off in Zhejiang Province. From then on, eco-sabotages in China literally stepped into the era of large-scale movements.

Huashui Town built up Zhuxi Industrial Park in 2001, hosting thirteen heavy, pollution-producing companies specializing in plastics, chemical engineering (such as toxic fertilizers), printing, and dyeing. Vegetables died; villagers' well water became polluted, nasty, and colored; rice declined in yield; fruit trees bloomed without bearing fruits; metasequoias and seedlings blighted; fish and shrimps disappeared; water quality of the river became worse than Grade V in 2002; and five deformities or stillbirths occurred in 2004. On March 3, 2005, peasants began to set up bamboo sheds and roadblocks along the roads outside of the industrial park in order to obstruct chemical raw materials transportation. In the wee hours of the morning on April 10, 3,500 law enforcement officers set off to dismantle the sheds forcibly, encountering little resistance at first. When police were ready to evacuate the scene, elderly villagers acting as guards lit firecrackers, attracting twenty- to thirty thousand people. The police were encircled and pounded around, and sixty-nine automobiles (a dozen police cars and over fifty police buses) were damaged in the hail of rocks costing 3.8 million RMB ($620,700). As a result, eight villagers were convicted, and leading officials of Dongyang City were given administrative sanctions. Preposterously, after that, basic-level governments in neighboring provinces of Jiangsu, Anhui, and Jiangxi held investment invitation activities in Huashui Town to attract these small polluting companies.

The second major event took place after the Qingshan Industrial Park in Xinchang County, Shaoxing City, which brought the water quality of the Xinchang River down from Grade II in 1996 to Grade IV in 1997 to Grade V in 1998, and worse than Grade V in 1999. After years of destruction of farmland, degradation of villagers' health, and government inaction, on July 15, 2005, nearly ten thousand peasants converged from neighboring villages and besieged the factory from all sides.

The third group event took place at an accumulator factory of Changxing Tianneng Power Co., Ltd. in Meishan Town, Changxing County, which brought about a mass lead and cadmium pollution episode. Thousands of the masses confronted more than a hundred cadres and 150 riot policemen. Both sides threw rocks and tear gas at each other, many people fell injured and two police cars were damaged. At eight o'clock that night, a small number of people sneaked into the factory by starlight to attack the building and to burn the finished-product warehouses, processing workshops, and offices. The number of accumulator companies in Changxing County was decreased by the government from 175 to fifty over the next two years.

A Series of Events Concerning PX Projects

PX is a petroleum product used in plastic bottles and fiber, and its manufacture creates highly toxic pollution. By virtue of grassroots collective
resistance or ecotages, and the divergence of interests among capitalists
in different industries, a dozen similar projects precipitated violent clashes between the police and the mass, followed by the swift suspension of
the projects by the government.

Xiamen Event in 2007 was the starting point of numerous PX
events and a watershed of Chinese environmental movements. A petrochemical enterprise called Dragon Aromatics of Xiang Lu Dragon
Group proposed to initiate "the largest industrial project throughout
Xiamen's history" in a Taiwanese merchant investment zone in Xiamen
City, Fujian Province. After the rejection of a proposal from National Committee members of the Chinese People's Political Consultative
Conference to change the site, citizens started to mobilize by means of
websites, short messages, BBS and QQ (an instant messaging tool). The
citizens agreed to meet on May 17 and march through Xianmen (called
"collective walking"). Although NGOs renounced public objections and
the government suppressed reports of the protests, over ten thousand
citizens occupied the main streets. One month later, the provincial and
municipal governments resolved to move the production lines to Gulei
Peninsula in Zhangzhou City, Fujian Province. Unfortunately, Gulei PX
project burst during a trial commissioning.

Another group event involving PX came after the conglomerate
Hebang Chemical Co., Ltd initiated preparations to build a project
of 250,000 tons of aromatics per annum. As the Hebang factory developed, it started using sulfur-rich heavy oil without the approval of
the Bureau of Environmental Protection, magnifying its processing
capacity to four-hundred thousand tons per annum, and violating the
24th Article of Law of the People's Republic of China on Evaluation
of Environmental Effects. Hydrogen sulphide in the exhaust emission
made villagers feel dizzy, nauseated, and even foam at the mouth. After a leak in March 2008, symptoms worsened and swept through the
village. A week later, nine villagers of Beihai Village spontaneously
blocked the entry of Hebang for two days and one night. The raw materials inlet pipe leaked again, and conditions became more severe than
in the previous incident. This time, a phalanx of at least four hundred

villagers in seven rows sealed the pathway, poured oil on all access roads to make vehicles skid, and attacked the security room with rocks and even tractors. On the third night, over six hundred policemen in twenty-eight cars bulldozed the area, and villagers dispersed. Beihai villagers did not relent, uniting instead with thousands of people in Maao town and nearby Xiaosha town. Fighting together, the villagers forced Zhoushan's government to get involved in the negotiation. The chemical firm wheedled the villagers into going home, dismissed them with 200 RMB a month per person and one gas canister a month per household. It also promised to relocate the exhaust emission source by October (the source has not been moved as of writing). On October 18, the villagers organized and, in groups, tactically entered onto the square in front of the government waving banners, yelling slogans, and kneeling down collectively in order to attract attention from the mass media. Such local road-blocking actions took place at least fifty times from 2008 to 2012, persisting even today.

Citizens continue to resist other PX projects. In 2010, tens of thousands of people gathered at the central plaza of Dalian City, Liaoning Province, to demand the relocation of a PX project co-invested in by Fujia Group and Dahua Group Co., Ltd., which had begun operations before official approval. On October 22, 2012, more than one thousand citizens overturned a private car and a police car, threw rocks and bricks, marched in protest, and blocked traffic against an integrated project of fifteen million tons of oil refining and 1.2 million tons of ethylene per annum in Ningbo City, Zhejiang Province. The scene was getting out of hand, and finally the government called for a lull in the PX project.

The official suppression of group events has bordered on absurd. Responding to a march ("collective walking") of two hundred citizens against an oil refinery financed in part by China National Petroleum Corporation (CNPC), the local government altered the weekend to weekdays in order to silence the discontent ahead of the Fortune Global Forum. CNPC's refinery comprises one of the auxiliary infrastructures of Sino-Burma crude oil pipelines, which just entered the Industrial Park of Anning City, Yunnan Province in 2013. The pipeline stands at the windward of the "City of Eternal Spring" and upstream side of the "City of Water Shortage," Kunming. After three thousand citizens protested on the square of the civic center around May 4 and 16, authorities severely restricted purchase of respirators as well as photocopying and typing services and the sale of white T-shirts.

Urban Struggles in Other Fields After 2007

PX is not the sole burning fuse. Environmental group events often occur in three fields: (1) infrastructure constructions in large and medium-sized cities, transportation (such as road widening, subway building, and airport extension), electric power (power lines, transmission and transformer equipment), and garbage crematories; (2) waste drainage in small towns and rural areas; (3) mega-projects of industrial enterprise behemoths.

In 2006, the government of Haidian District, Beijing declared intention to build a garbage incineration power plant atop the waste landfill site in Liulitun Village. Local residents collectively marched to the State Environmental Protection Administration to petition on the World Environment Day in 2007. Exactly a week later, SEPA recommended the government postpone it before the further technical argument. The incineration plant was relocated to a disused mine in Dagong Village in November 2010. It has not been completed at the time of writing.

On May 31, 2010, nearly two hundred home-owners of Sakura Garden Residential Quarter in Nanbanbidian Village, Beijing, staged a sit-in against the ongoing construction and upcoming sound pollution of Terminal 3 and the third runway of Beijing Capital International Airport. They may still have to move their houses in the next several years.

Guizhentang Pharmaceutical Company's plans to build a factory were canceled in 2012 after facing the kneeling down of a performance artist Pianshankong on February 22, a protest by Shenzhen citizens on February 26, and a popular documentary *Moon Bear*, which revealed the backstage interest groups—State Forestry Administration and Ministry of Public Security.

Art has also been used to stimulate and inspire group events. On April 3, 2012, the opening ceremony of a polycarbonate project of 260,000 tons per annum marked the beginning of ten days' collective walking in Dagang District, Tianjin. The project's owner is Sinopec Sabic Petrochemical Co., Ltd., with the support of Saudi Basic Industry Corporation. A climax of several thousand walkers came on April 13 and snarled traffic, forcing the government to compromise. In another aesthetic action, protesters from Wuhan City, Hubei Province, came to the construction site of the

Wuhan-Huangshi Inner-city Railway for symbolic "collective military exercises." Together, their performance consisted of using red-tasseled spears, carrying the red flag; wearing military caps and uniforms of the Long March; standing sentry; and performing patrolling drills among other maneuvers. Their creativity deserved success.

In contrast to these peaceful actions, there are two important examples of more volatile group events. Shifang City, Sichuan Province, suffered heavy loss of life and major damage to infrastructure during the 2008 earthquake. By 2012, Sichuan Hongda Group had laid the foundation for a new plant, which would refine forty thousand tons of molybdenum and four-hundred thousand tons of copper annually. The magnificent commencement ceremony brought news of the plant to most local people for the first time. On July 1, the raging waves of a crowd gathered in the center of the city and forced through the cordon, pushing over the gate and breaking the government's equipment, destroying the public facilities, jamming the crucial roads, and demanding the suspension of the project. The police used stun grenades and tear gas to cope with the flying flowerpots, water bottles, and miscellaneous junk of tens of thousands of protesters. Two days later, the local government announced the suspension of construction. Protests continued, because the twenty-seven detained protesters had not been released. Late in the evening, authorities released twenty-one protesters; the other six remained in custody facing criminal and administrative charges. On May 5, the head of Shifang served as a contented scapegoat, and was replaced rather than demoted in administrative rank.

It is a universal truth that profits go upstream in the international capital market, and pollution downstream. Oji Paper Company, Ltd., the sixth-largest paper manufacturing company in the world in terms of revenue, belongs to Mitsui Zaibatsu, one of the four largest corporate conglomerates in Japan. Its paper production base in Qidong City, Jiangsu Province wanted to construct a large pipeline to discharge its sewage into the Yellow Sea, which would likely adversely affect the fishing industry and drinking water. On July 28, 2012, at least ten thousand people swarmed into the municipal government and overturned five vehicles. An estimated thousand protesters stormed offices, smashing computers, toppling desks, and throwing documents out of the windows while rummaging about and searching out many things irrelevant to administrative management and public service, such as luxury wine and tobacco, cash gifts, and pictures of scenic spots. The municipal committee secretary, Jianhua Sun, was stripped naked, and Mayor Feng Xu was forced to wear a T-shirt with a protest messages. But these leading officials remained quite moderate and controlled, generally speaking. On this morning, the government promised to permanently suspend the pipeline project, which would also have affected the business of real estate developers. Here, the environmental issue acted as the concentrative flash point and best vent of various interests or claims (land expropriation, fishery loss, and so on), owing to its legitimacy, rationality and non-political nature, although anti-Japanese sentiment became an unfortunate facade over the actual economic demands.

Rolling Waves in Rural Areas after 2007

In addition to such metropolises or cities, there are also big fish splashing in small ponds, where much courage is exhibited. The targets of urban and rural residents differ in types, and the poor and helpless peasants behave more violently and radically when wreaking havoc on their enemies, free from the impact of the peaceful and mild collective walking. A few examples are worth recounting before a final analysis is taken.

The paper pulp workshop of Zhongtaifu Paper Co., Ltd. in Botang Town, Guangxi Zhuang Autonomous Region, drained polluted sewage into neighboring water sources. Over a hundred villagers made use of wood and rocks as obstacles outside the gate of the manufacturer and shattered police cars on January 10, 2007. In the same region, only a little over three years later, several thousand people in various villages of Xinjia Township attacked the bulldozers of Xinfa Aluminum Smelter and the boss's private car with homemade bombs, napalm, and rocks, but were suppressed by armed police.

In March and April 2011, hundreds of people protested at the government of Xinshi Town, Zhejiang Province, because of the lead pollution of Haijiu Battery Co., Ltd. As a result, Deqing lost the title of Ecological Demonstration Area, and Haijiu suspended operations.

On May 11, 2011, an ethnic Mongol herdsman, opposed to the grasslands development, was killed by an ethnic Han coal-truck driver in West Ujimqin Banner, Inner Mongolia Autonomous Region. On May 14, another Han coal miner drove a forklift and hit a Manchu in Abag Banner. Then, the first large-scale ethnic Mongol protest in some twenty years occurred in the capital of Inner Mongolia, Hohhot, which actually reflected the previous long-term contradictions between the coal-mine capital and the ordinary peasants and herders beneath the cover of ethnic conflicts.

On August 26, 2011, a river full of dead fish astonished the villagers in Hongxiao Village, Zhejiang Province. On September 15, more than five hundred people stormed JinkoSolar Holding Co., Ltd. and overturned eight cars inside the factory. JinkoSolar was already one of the world's largest crystalline solar manufacturers, with its IPO in New York City.

On December 20, 2011, several hundred people occupied the government of Haimen Town, Guangdong Province, destroying the windows and office equipment there while opposing the plan of the power plants of China HuaNeng Group and China Huadian Corporation. On December 23, two thousand demonstrators got together at the toll station of the Shenzhen-Shantou Expressway to block the entrance while coming under fire from the tear gas of two hundred military policemen.

Final Analysis

The shortcomings of such small-scale producers of scattered and fragmented economic holdings are compendiously described in an article by Mao Zedong, entitled "On Correcting Mistaken Ideas in the Party" (written in December 1929). Quotations here might be helpful:

> [On the Purely Military Viewpoint] They become conceited when a battle is won and dispirited when a battle is lost.
>
> [On Individualism] "Small group" mentality. Some comrades consider only the interests of their own small group and ignore the general interest. Although on the surface this does not seem to be the pursuit of personal interests, in reality it exemplifies the narrowest individualism and has a strong corrosive and centrifugal effect. ...
>
> [On the Ideology of Roving Rebel Bands] Some people want to increase our political influence only by means of roving guerrilla actions, but are unwilling to increase it by undertaking the arduous task of building up base areas and establishing the people's political power.

Furthermore, three deadly defects of Chinese peasants in social revolutions can be found in William Howard Hinton's book, *Fanshen: A*

Documentary of Revolution in a Chinese Village, which is not out of date in analyzing these environmental group events:

> The ruthless way in which the slightest defiance on the part of ten-ants and laborers was suppressed over the years created in the peas-ants a deep, almost instinctive, reluctance to mount an attack against the power of the gentry. ... It is no wonder, then, that only the most severe provocation could overcome the peasants' great reluctance to act, and set them in motion. But once in motion they tended to extremes of cruelty and violence. If they struck, they struck to kill, for common sense and millenniums of painful experience told them that if they did not, their enemies would inevitably return another day to kill them....
>
> The first of these weaknesses was an all-pervading individual-ism engendered by the endless, personal struggle to acquire a little land and to beat out the other fellow in the market place. Peasants individually driven to bankruptcy viewed economic disaster not as a social but as a personal matter, to be solved in isolation by whatever means came to hand....
>
> A second crucial weakness was the lack of vision that arose di-rectly out of small-scale production with its rudimentary division of labor and indirectly out of the cultural isolation which this type of economy, with its limited market, imposed on the community. ...
>
> The despair of men standing up to their necks in water coupled with the ignorance engendered by a "well-bottom" view of social rela-tions led inevitably to impetuosity in action—a third great weakness of the peasants. ... Therefore, when they did act, they were not pre-pared for two or three years, not mention decades, of bitter struggle and were easily discouraged when revolt did not quickly bring any improvement in their situation."[1]

Environmental group events can be very complex. As shown above, they are often spearheaded by peasants, but can include sectors of society such as home-owners, fishing interests, the real estate industry, small-scale industrial interests, and even nationalists. While the combined force of social unity has a powerful effect on local issues, the coalitions dwindle

---

1   William Hinton, *Fanshen: A Documentary of Revolution in a Chinese Village* (Berkeley: University of California Press, 1997), 54–56.

when immediate victory is declared. Solidarity and cooperation across regions and classes would bring the growing struggle against land grabs to a level of revolutionary power capable of transforming the social, political, and economic relations of contemporary state capitalism in China.

WOMEN, LAND-STRUGGLES, AND GLOBALIZATION:

An International Perspective[1]

Silvia Federici

Women Keep the World Alive

Until not long ago, issues relating to land and land struggles would have failed to generate much interest among most North Americans, unless they were farmers or descendants of the American Indians for whom the importance of land as the foundation of life is still paramount, culturally at least.

For the rest of the population, land issues seemed to have receded into a vanishing past, as in the aftermath of massive urbanization drives, land no longer appeared the fundamental means of reproduction, and new technologies claimed to provide the power, self-reliance, and creativity that people once associated with agriculture.

This has been a great loss, if only because this amnesia has led to the creation of a world where the most basic questions about our existence—where our food comes from, whether it nourishes us or, instead, it poisons our bodies—remain unanswered and often unasked. This indifference to land among urban dwellers is coming to an end, however. Concern for the genetic engineering of agricultural crops and the ecological impact of the destruction of the tropical forests, together with the example offered by the struggles of indigenous people, like the Zapatistas who have risen up in arms to oppose land privatization, have created a new awareness in Europe and North America about the importance of the "land question," not long ago still identified as a "Third World" issue.

There has also been a conceptual shift, in the last twenty years, concerning our understanding of the relation between land and capitalism. This shift has been promoted by Maria Mies and the circle of activist-scholars who have worked with her.[2] They have shown us that land is

---

1   This piece is excerpted from a larger essay first published in *Journal of Asian and African Studies* 39, issue 1/2 (January/March 2004): 47–62.

2   Maria Mies, *Patriarchy and Accumulation on a World Scale: Women in the*

not a largely irrelevant "factor of production" in modern capitalism. Land is the material basis for women's subsistence work, which has been the main source of "food security" for millions of people across the planet. Mies sees in this subsistence work also the paradigm of a new social perspective, providing a realistic alternative to capitalist globalization.

It is against this political and conceptual background that I look at the struggles that women are making worldwide not only to re-appropriate land, but also to boost subsistence farming and a non-commercial use of natural resources. I argue that these efforts are extremely important not only because, thanks to them, billions of people are able to survive, but also because they point in the direction of the changes that we have to make if we are to regain control over the means of production and construct a society, where reproducing ourselves neither comes at the expense of other people, nor presents a threat to the continuation of life on the planet.

Struggles for Subsistence and Against "Globalization" in Africa, Asia, and the Americas

Faced with a renewed drive toward land privatization, the extension of cash crops, and the rise in food prices in the age of globalization, women have resorted to many strategies pitting them against the most powerful institutions on the planet.

The primary strategy women have adopted to defend their communities from the impact of economic adjustment and dependence on the global market has been (again) the expansion of subsistence farming also in the urban centers.

Exemplary is the case of Guinea Bissau studied by Galli and Funk, which shows that, since the early 1980s, women have planted small gardens with vegetables, cassava, and fruit trees around most houses in the capital city of Bissau and other towns; and in times of scarcity they have preferred to forfeit the earnings they might have made selling their

---

International Division of Labour (London: Zed Books, 1986); Maria Mies and Vandana Shiva, Ecofeminism (London: Zed, 1993); Veronika Bennholdt-Thomsen and Maria Mies, The Subsistence Perspective: Beyond the Globalised Economy (London: Zed, 1999); Veronika Bennholdt-Thomsen, Nicholas Faraclas, and Claudia von Werlhof, eds., There is an Alternative: Subsistence and Worldwide Resistance to Corporate Globalization (London: Zed, 2001).

produce to ensure their families would not go without food.[3] Still with reference to Africa, this picture is confirmed by Christa Wichterich who speaks of women subsistence farming and urban gardening as "cooking pot economics." She notes too that, in the 1990s, it was revived in many of Africa's cities—the urban farmers being mostly women from the lower class:

> There were onions and papaya trees, instead of flower-borders, in front of the housing estates of underpaid civil servants in Dar-es-Salaam; chickens and banana plants in the backyards of Lusaka; vegetables on the wide central reservations of the arterial roads of Kampala, and especially of Kinshasa, where the food supply system had largely collapsed... In [Kenyan] towns [too]...green roadside strips, front gardens and wasteland sites were immediately occupied with maize, plants, *sukum wiki*, the most popular type of cabbage.[4]

To expand food production, however, women have had to battle to expand their access to land, which international agencies' drives to privatize land and commercialize agriculture have further jeopardized.

This may be the reason why, in the case of Guinea Bissau, many women have chosen to remain in the rural area, while most of the men have migrated. As a result, there has been a "feminization of the rural areas, with many villages now consisting of women farming alone or in women's coops."[5]

Regaining or expanding land for subsistence farming has been one of the main battles also for rural women in Bangladesh, leading to the formation of the Landless Women's Association that has been carrying on land occupations since 1992. During this period, the Association has managed to settle fifty thousand families, often confronting landowners in pitched confrontations. According to Shamsun Nahar Khan Doli, a

---

3   In Bissau, women planted rice during the rainy season in plots on the peripheries of town. During the dry season more enterprising women try to get access to nearby plots in order to plant irrigated vegetables not only for domestic consumption but for sale. (Rosemary Galli and Ursula Frank, "Structural Adjustment and Gender in Guinea Bissau," in *Women Pay the Price: Structural Adjustment in Africa and the Caribbean*, ed. Gloria T. Emeagwali (NJ: Africa World Press, 1995), 20.)

4   Christa Wichterich, *The Globalized Woman: Reports from a Future of Inequality* (London: Zed, 2000), 73.

5   Galli and Funk, "Structural Adjustment and Gender," 23.

leader of the Association to whom I owe this report, many occupations are on "chars," low-lying islands formed by soil deposits in the middle of a river.[6] Such new lands should be allocated to landless farmers, according to Bangladeshi law, but because of the growing commercial value of land, big landowners have increasingly seized them. But women are now organizing to stop them, defending themselves with brooms, spears of bamboo, and even knives. Women have also set up alarm systems, to alert other women to gather when boats with the landowners or their goons approach, and to stop the attackers from landing.

Similar land struggles are being fought in South America. In Paraguay, for example, the Peasant Women's Commission (CMC) was formed in 1985 in alliance with the Paraguayan Peasant's Movement (MCP) to demand land distribution.[7] As Jo Fischer points out, the CMC was the first peasant women's movement that went into the streets in support of its demands. It incorporated in its program women's concerns, also condemning "their double oppression, both as peasants and as women."[8]

The turning point for the CMC came when the government granted large tracts of land to the peasant movement in the forests close to the Brazilian border. The women took these grants as an opportunity to organize a model community, joining together to collectively farm their strips of land. As Geraldina, an early founder of CMC pointed out,

> We work all the time, more now than ever before, but we've also changed the way we work. We're experimenting with communal work to see if it gives us more time for other things. It also gives us a chance to share our experiences and worries. This is a very different way of living for us. Before, we didn't even know our neighbors.[9]

Women's land struggles have included the defense of communities threatened by commercial housing projects constructed in the name of "urban development." "Housing" has often involved the loss of "land" for food production, historically. An example is the struggle of women in the Kawaala neighborhood of Kampala (Uganda), where the World Bank, in conjunction with the Kampala City Council, in 1992–1993,

---

6   This report is based on oral testimony at the Prague "Countersummit" of 2000.
7   Jo Fisher, *Out of the Shadows: Women, Resistance and Politics in South America* (London: Latin American Bureau, 1993), 86.
8   Ibid., 87.
9   Ibid., 98.

sponsored a large housing project that would destroy much subsistence farmland around or near people's homes. Not surprisingly, it was women who most strenuously organized against it, through the formation of an Abataka (Residents) Committee, eventually forcing the World Bank to withdraw from the project. According to one of the women leaders:

> While men were shying away, women were able to say anything in public meetings in front of government officials. Women were more vocal because they were directly affected. It is very hard for women to stand without any means of income.... most of these women are people who basically support their children and without any income and food they cannot do it...You come and take their peace and income and they are going to fight, not because they want to, but because they have been oppressed and suppressed.[10]

Aili Mari Tripp points out that the situation in the Kawaala neighborhood is far from unique.[11] Similar struggles have been reported from different parts of Africa and Asia, where peasant women's organizations have opposed the development of industrial zones threatening to displace them and their families and contaminate the environment.

Industrial or commercial housing development often clashes, today, with women's subsistence farming, in a context in which more and more women even in urban centers, are gardening (in Kampala women grow 45 percent of the food for their families). It is important to add that, in defending land from assault by commercial interests and affirming the principle that "land and life are not for sale," women again, as in the past against colonial invasion, are defending their peoples' history and their culture. In the case of Kawaala, the majority of residents on the disputed land had been living there for generations and had buried their kin there—for many in Uganda the ultimate evidence of land ownership. Tripp's reflections on this land struggle are pertinent to my thesis:

> Stepping back from the events of the conflict, it becomes evident that the residents, especially the women involved, were trying to

---

10   Aili Mari Tripp, *Women and Politics in Uganda* (Oxford: James Currey, 2000), 183.

11   Tripp concludes that "the Kawaala struggle is in many ways a microcosm of some of the changes that are occurring in Uganda" (Mari Tripp, *Women and Politics in Uganda*, 194).

institutionalize some new norms for community mobilization, not just in Kawaala but more widely in providing a model for other community projects. They had a vision of a more collaborative effort that took the needs of women, widows, children, and the elderly as a starting point and recognized their dependence on the land for survival.[12]

Two more developments need to be mentioned in conjunction with women's defense of subsistence production. First, there has been the formation of regional systems of self-sufficiency aiming to guarantee "food security" and maintain an economy based on solidarity and the refusal of competition. The most impressive example in this respect comes from India where women formed the National Alliance for Women's Food Rights, a national movement made of thirty-five women's groups. One of the main efforts of the Alliance has been the campaign in defense of the mustard seed economy that is crucial for many rural and urban women in India. A subsistence crop, the seed has been threatened by the attempts of multinational corporations based in the United States to impose genetically engineered soybeans as a source of cooking oil.[13] In response, the Alliance has built "direct producer-consumer alliances" to "defend the livelihood of farmers and the diverse cultural choices of consumers," as stated by Vandana Shiva, one of the leaders of the movement. In her words: "We protest soybean imports and call for a ban on the import of genetically-engineered soybean products. As the women from the slums of Delhi sing, 'Sarson Bachao, Soya Bhagaa,' or, 'Save the Mustard, Dump the Soya.'"[14]

Second, across the world, women have been leading the struggle to prevent commercial logging and save or rebuild forests, which are the foundation of people's subsistence economies, providing nourishment as well as fuel, medicine, and communal relations. Forests, Shiva writes,

---

12 Ibid., 94.

13 This attempt was given a boost in 1998 when the mustard-seed cooking oil locally produced and distributed was mysteriously found to be adulterated to such a point that forty-one people died after consuming it. The government then banned its production and sale. The National Alliance responded by taking the case to court and calling on producers and consumers not to cooperate with the government's ban (Vandana Shiva, *Stolen Harvest: Hijacking of the Global Food Supply* (Boston: South End Press, 2000), 54).

14 Vandana Shiva, *Stolen Harvest*.

echoing testimonies coming from every part of the planet, are "the highest expression of earth's fertility and productivity."[15] Thus, when forests come under assault, it is a death sentence for the tribal people who live in them, especially the woman. Therefore, women do everything to stop the loggers. Shiva often cites, in this context, the Chikpo movement—a movement of women, in Garhwal, in the foothills of the Himalaya who, beginning in the early 1970s, embrace the trees destined to fall, and put their bodies between them and the saws when the loggers come.[16]

While women in Garhwal have mobilized to prevent forests from being cut down, in villages of Northern Thailand they have protested the Eucalyptus plantations forcibly planted on their expropriated farms by a Japanese paper-making company with the support of the Thai military government.[17] In Africa, an important initiative has been the "Green Belt Movement," which under the leadership of Wangari Maathai is committed to planting a green belt around the major cities and, since 1977, has planted tens of millions of trees to prevent deforestation, soil loss, desertification, and fuel-wood scarcity.[18]

But the most striking struggle for the survival of the forests is taking place in the Niger Delta, where the mangrove tree swamps are being threatened by oil production. Opposition to it has mounted for twenty years, beginning in Ogharefe, in 1984, when several thousand women from the area laid siege to Pan Ocean's Production Station demanding compensation for the destruction of the water, trees, and land. To show their determination, the women also threatened to disrobe should their demands be frustrated—a threat they put in action when the company's director arrived, so that he found himself surrounded by thousands of women naked, a serious curse in the eyes of the Niger Delta communities, which convinced him at the time to accept the reparation claims.[19]

---

15 Vandana Shiva, *Staying Alive: Women, Ecology and Development* (London: Zed Books, 1989), 56.

16 Shiva, *Staying Alive*.

17 Yayori Matsui, *Women in the New Asia: From Pain to Power* (London: Zed Books, 1996), 88–90.

18 Wangari Maathai, "Kenya's Green Belt Movement," in *Africa*, ed. F. Jeffress Ramsay (Guilford, CT: The Dushkin Publishing Group, 1993).

19 Terisa E. Turner and M.O. Oshare, "Women's Uprisings Against the Nigerian Oil Industry," in *Arise! Ye Mighty People!: Gender, Class and Race in Popular Struggles*, ed. Terisa Turner (Trenton: Africa World Press, 1994), 140–141.

The struggle over land has also grown since the 1970s in the most unlikely place—New York City—in the form of an urban gardening movement. It began with the initiative of a women-led group called the "Green Guerrillas," who began cleaning up vacant lots in the Lower East Side. By the 1990s, 850 urban gardens had developed in the city, and dozens of community coalitions had formed, such as the Greening of Harlem Coalition that was begun by a group of women who wanted "to reconnect with the earth and give children an alternative to the streets." Now it counts more than twenty-one organizations and thirty garden projects.[20]

It is important to note here that the gardens have been not only a source of vegetables and flowers, but have served community-building and have been a stepping stone for other community struggles (like squatting and homesteading). Because of this work, the women came under attack during Mayor Giuliani's regime, and for some years now one of the main challenges this movement has faced has been stopping the bulldozers. Over the last decade, a hundred gardens have been lost to "development," more than forty have been slated for bulldozing, and the prospects for the future seem gloomy.[21] Since his appointment, in fact, the mayor of New York City, Michael Bloomberg, like his predecessor, declared war on these gardens.

The Importance of the Struggle

As we have seen, in cities across the world at least a quarter of the people depend on food produced by women's subsistence labor. In Africa, for example, a quarter of the people living in towns say they could not survive without subsistence food production. This is confirmed by the UN Population Fund, which claims that "some two hundred million city dwellers are growing food, providing about one billion people with at least part of their food supply."[22] When we consider that the bulk of the food subsistence producers are women, we can see why the men of Kedjom, Cameroon, would say, "Yes, women subsistence farmers do good for humanity." Thanks to them, the billions of people, rural and urban, who earn one or two dollars a day do not go under, even in times of economic crisis.

---

20   Peter Lamborn Wilson and Bill Weinberg, *Avantgardening: Ecological Struggles in the City and the World* (New York: Autonomedia, 1999), 36.

21   Wilson and Weinberg, *Avantgardening*, 61.

22   United Nations, *The World's Women 1995: Trends and Statistics* (New York: UN, 1995).

Equally important, women's subsistence production counters the trend by agribusiness to reduce cropland—one of the causes of high food prices and starvation—while ensuring control over the quality of food and protecting consumers against manipulation of crops and poisoning by pesticides. Further, women subsistence production represents a safe way of farming, a crucial consideration at a time when the effects of pesticides on agricultural crops is causing high rates of mortality and disease among peasants across the world, starting with women.[23] Thus, subsistence farming gives women an essential means of control over their health and the health and lives of their families.[24]

Most important, we can also see that subsistence production is contributing to a non-competitive, solidarity-centered mode of life that is crucial for the building of a new society. It is the seed of what Veronika Bennholdt-Thomsen and Maria Mies call the "other" economy, which "puts life and everything necessary to produce and maintain life on this planet at the center of economic and social activity and not the never-ending accumulation of dead money."[25]

---

23 See, for example, L. Settimi et al., "Cancer Risk Among Female Agricultural Workers: A Multi-Center Case-Control Study," *American Journal of Industrial Medicine* 36 (1999):135–141.

24 Bennholdt-Thomsen and Mies, *The Subsistence Perspective.*

25 Ibid., 5.

LAND, TERRITORY, ENTROPY

Guillermo Delgado-P.

"Compare the tree to a factory, or a cow to a reactor. Like the people it is not amenable to efficiency and control in a factory sense. You can't boss over the science of photosynthesis."

—Nicholas Xenos[1]

In the face of the entropy of the ongoing environmental crisis, it is time to both retrieve and advance indigenous concepts of land and territory. Indigenous peoples commonly inhabit climate-sensitive ecosystems and, as place-based communities, they persist in considering themselves as well as the other-than-human world, infused with life. Indigeneity privileges a common understanding of territory as a living entity. As Gary White Deer suggests:

> To Native America, the world is composed of both spirit and matter. This, of course, is not a new concept, as the world is full of variations on this common theme. What is important for our consideration is that to Native America, burials are sacrosanct, certain geographies are counted as holy places, and the earth itself is a living entity.[2]

This commonality is particular to indigenous thought. After the 1960s, the emergence of ethnic-peasant movements contributed to the dissemination of this ancient conviction regarding the notion of belonging to the land throughout the world. In Latin America by the 1990s, an indigenous-peasant social movement had repositioned the struggle for land and identity simultaneously with the emerging movement of landless peasants who actively joined contemporary struggles.

Globalization entails concrete challenges to the ways Indigenous peoples conceive permanence on earth. For instance, biotechnology can be considered a strategy to obtain definitive control over biodiversity and traditional ecological knowledges found and protected, not coincidentally,

---

1   Nicholas Xenos, *Scarcity and Modernity* (New York: Routledge, 1989).
2   Gary White Deer, "Return of the Sacred. Spirituality and the Scientific Imperative," in *Native Americans and Archaeologists: Stepping Stones to a Common Ground*, ed. N. Swidler, K. Dongoske, R. Anyon, and A. S. Downer (Walnut Creek: Altamira, 1997), 41.

in areas inhabited by Indigenous peoples today. The struggle for land became more radicalized as it emphasized a conservationist agenda while critiquing the emergence of genetically modified organisms and the food industry's "globalitarianism." Soon, land-based struggles directed their collective fury against full neoliberal deruralization and dispossession (as has been seen in global summits from Seattle 1999 to Cancun 2003 to Copenhagen 2009).

Indigenous peoples acknowledge a sort of multidimensionality and polyculturality in which terms such as "progress" (as excess) give way to alter-Native thinking inspired in pluriversities and environmental preservation. Hayes and Timms explain, "The idea of humans being part of (rather than in control of) an environmental system has gained increased importance as we recognize the impact of overexploitation of environmental goods and the problems associated with the distribution of those goods to a growing world population."[3] Yet not only is *land* the issue today, but water and biomass as well. Land struggles, along with water struggles, reach large cohorts of people who offer combative, localized, and vivid examples of how humans belong to the earth, rather than the earth to humans.

Cosmic Time and Industrial Time

As humans, we are impacted by imperiling events—global warming, ocean acidification, ozone layer depletion, atmospheric testing of nuclear weapons, nuclear disasters, and cosmic entropy.[4] Here, we are clearly confronting two or more concepts of time and nature. Not in sync with "cosmic time," "industrial and atomic time" is global society's present context, representing that synchronized time of a society increasingly, and almost consciously, self-destructing itself. So far, the entropic consequences can be called "environmental colonialism" expressed as "climate change."[5]

Fifteen years ago, it was affirmed that "on a global scale, scientists estimate that twenty-seven thousand species are being lost each year

---

3   James Hayes and Benjamin Timms, "Physical Geography: The Human Environment Connection," in *Placing Latin America*, ed. Edward L. Jackiewicz and Fernando J. Bosco (Lanham, MD: Rowman and Littlefield, 2012), 13.

4   I am using the term "entropy" to suggest destruction and bound or unavailable energy in the system.

5   William Nordhaus, *The Climate Casino: Risk, Uncertainty, and Economics for a Warming World* (New Haven: Yale University Press, 2013), 32–34.

in the rainforests alone... the loss of species through extinction is only one aspect of the biological impairment that has resulted from human destruction of wildlife habitat."[6] We must remember that humanity needed only two hundred years to trash the habitat we call Earth. These years coincide with the emergence of the Industrial Revolution, and although urbanization seems to be a *fait accompli*, large portions of the world remain rural, where peasants following nature's "cosmic time" till the land to survive and feed the cities for cheap. Because peasants seldom receive social security assistance from the state, this is a very good deal for urban dwellers.

As we noticed previously, Native notions of territory come with a sense of ecological integrity and complexity. For Native peoples, territory has to be preserved and defended as a co-entity in which humans are just other players along with insects, seeds, and water—that is, a pluriverse. Descola notes the importance of context in ecological knowledge: "In spite of their internal differences, all [Native Peoples] have as a common characteristic that they do not operate clear-cut ontological distinctions between human, on the one hand, and a good many species of animals and plants, on the other."[7]

The Native concept of "territory" runs parallel to the term "land," yet it has almost disappeared from our epistemology. We must remember that Columbus's enterprise in 1492 proclaims this word as soon as it glances upon the first signs of what are now called the Caribbean Islands: "Tierra! Tierra!" With these looters also came the term "empty land," or "wild lands." At first, they were not so interested in "land," itself, but rather gold and silver. But as the metals are exhausted, meager, and scattered, "land" becomes the thing to claim and possess.

To conquer and colonize means to appropriate and administer land, and to parcel and fracture territory, above all, to de-ontologize it. As inheritors of colonial history today, we talk about "wild lands," "empty land," "virgin forest," "free land," "idle land," "law of the land," "landscape," "public land," "private land." The word takes on a more abstract meaning—an intangible entity. These terms, relevant to "land" and the commodification of land, imply a constant subdivision, dangerously

---

6   Edward J. Heisel, "Biodiversity and Federal Land Ownership: Mapping a Strategy for the Future," *Ecology Law Quarterly* 25 (1998): 235.

7   Philip Descola, "Ecology as cosmological Analysis," in *The Land Within: Indigenous Territory and the Perception of Environment*, ed. Alexandre Surrallés and Pedro García Hierro (Copenhagen: IWGIA, 2005), 24.

disrupting the ecological and self-sustaining complexity of territory. Land fracturing has been the rule since colonial agriculture:

> If the lands were not currently suited to intensive agriculture, cultivation would force the land to submit to the discipline of production. Any reluctance on the part of Indigenous peoples to participate in intensive agriculture or resource extraction was simply more justification for moving them off the land and bringing in European settlers who were ready to use the land productively.[8]

In a twist of irony, the demand "to use the land productively" actually backfired, and rates of depletion and fragility dwindle into determinate scarcity, thus colonization meant the expropriation of riches, land, territory, and human labor, shaping the accumulation of capital in a process Marx called "primitive accumulation." Under "primitive accumulation," conquest and dispossession create the conditions for the systematic transfer of wealth from one region to another, including labor (the classic example constituting slavery as a mode of production). Primitive accumulation triggered ecological collapse by introducing technologies of systematic depletion often based on monocultures, mining of ores, and transferring of biota (seeds and animals through the manipulation of rivers and construction of dams, etc.). It is this process that is called the ontological transformation of nature. Once the territory has been destroyed, land is good only for "development."

Physiocrats in the eighteenth century were interested in the value of productive land as agricultural products reached higher demand. But for peasants, land was necessary only to consume nature's bounty for survival. If surplus was available, then it was shared, stored, or bartered. With the invention of advanced storage systems and food preservation, the emergence of bureaucrats who controlled food surplus, land, and water gave rise to the origin of the modern state, itself. Bureaucracies, priests, and armies were fed, while they accumulated information on land's productive capacity that, in turn, reproduced control and coercion, suppressing the new "free peasantry." The "free peasantry," itself, signified the contestation of two perceptions of time: cosmic time and industrial

---

8   Anne Ross, K.P. Sherman, J.G. Snodgrass, H.D. Delcore, and R. Sherman, *Indigenous Peoples and the Collaborative Stewardship of Nature: Knowledge Binds and Institutional Conflicts* (Walnut Creek: Left Coast Press, 2010).

(computerized or synchronized) time, which is really the control over productivity and the limiting of free time. Because industrial time signifies the domestication of time and the worker, we could probably say that, through it, time became a technology of numbers. On the other hand, "cosmic time" is slow, antiessential, and an obstacle to the purposes of synchronized speed, accumulation, and management.

Native Land Systems

The possession of land in the "New World" meant depopulation of First or Originary Peoples. That is, to facilitate arbitrary appropriation by systemic dispossession, subversion, and destruction of previous pre-industrial agricultures. Colonialism's aim was precisely "to dominate nature," meaning that "there is no nature outside of history, [and] there is nothing natural about nature."[9] In Latin America these new possessions of *Terra Nullius* were called *"Encomienda," "Mission," "Mercedes Reales," "Presidio," "Colony."* All were institutions of dispossession and criminalization based on the acquisition of lands and administration of fractioned, de-ontologized territories. These colonial terms required previous pluriversal indigenous systems of land tenure, such as the Inka's *Ayllu*, the Nahuatl's (Aztec) *Kalpulli*, the Taino's *Conuco*, the Guaraní's *Chaco*, to be ignored and substituted by the homogenizing colonial process based on the *Hacienda* and the Plantation.

Let's consider the case of the Inkas. The Quechua term *"Jallpa"* (land) has been historically administered through the *Chakra*, a polyculture plot, by the state-minded Inkas in three ways: one, to satisfy the needs of the *Panakas*, the ruling clans; two, to assure surplus was redistributed evenly throughout the state; and three, to offer the God Sun its share by sending surplus to the temple (heliolatry), where bureaucrats silently stored it and eventually redistributed it as the "gift of the gods." The idea was to avoid the presence of hunger. In the process, bureaucrats ensured the preservation of territory through the isolation of a portion of land, called the *Sapsi* (commons), ready to be activated if a family or community hit disgrace and could not feed itself. So the *Sapsi* is a traditional polyculture plot protected as the commons, a territorial reserve that rests until it is worked collectively every seven years. The *Jallpa* of the *Sapsi* are treated as

---

9   Arturo Escobar, "After Nature: Steps to an Antiessentialist Political Ecology," *Current Anthropology* 40, no. 1 (February 1999), 2.

a human being—the *Sapsi* "rests" in order to produce and save the lives of those whose plots failed. Thus, a plot is never exhausted. These examples form the bases of what we think of today as "sustainability."

However, as one important article notes, "sustainability is only important if one is concerned about the quality of life on earth in the future, and individuals, corporations, and governments may ignore potential future problems of resource availability while focused on short-term goals and economic growth."[10] With colonialism, a shift in ekistics (perception of settlement space) came about. The land-to-human ratio was turned on its head.[11] Crops and livestock from opposite hemispheres affected water kinetics and provoked erosion (think of the feeding habits of a llama, bison, turkey versus a goat, pig, sheep, chicken, or horse).[12] On the other hand, the same changes in land and water use lowered productivity in territories that were previously considered highly productive.

In numerous cases, such upsetting changes involved transferring Originary Peoples as things from the land they inhabited. Thus, several "free peasantries" became the agricultural workers of their own states. The new owner, an *Encomendero*, distorted the land-to-human ratio, because "land grants" farming were based on early forms of monoculture and corvée labor involving sugar, cotton, rice, wheat, potato. The land-to-human ratio was also distorted, because migrating populations from one place to another brought people to unknown territories. Ecological niches and paleo-technologies were different, unfamiliar, so displaced migrants often contributed to deteriorating ecological sustainability by introducing different crops requiring different agricultural technologies (e.g. of irrigation, terracing, fallow lands, raised beds), and finally provoking environmental depletion due to the (mis)use of different agricultural instruments and techniques—for example, the use of digging hoes such as the Andean *Chakit'aqlla*, a well adapted digging stick for terrace agriculture where plow and ox were impractical and damaging.

In most areas where the Native Peoples of the Americas have been demographically resilient, "colonial legacies" continue to work against

---

10   Hayes and Timms, "Physical Geography," 13.
11   Sofía Monsalve Suárez, "Gender and Land," in *Promised Land: Competing Visions of Agrarian Reform*, ed. Peter Rosset, Raj Patel, and Michael Courville (Oakland: Food First Books, 2006), 192–207.
12   Richard P. Schaedel, "Late Incaic and Early Spanish Changes in Land Use: Their Effect on Dry Land, The Peruvian Coast," Ibero-Amerikanisches Archive (N.F.) Jg 7 (H. 3) (1981): 309–319.

them today. Very rarely do Native Peoples rest on rich lands, for they have been pushed out and "removed" to arid lands. They have been dismembered. This is very contrary to the survival of small bands of hunters and gatherers into the twenty-first century who are aware of the fact that rainforests are not to be cultivated but maintained. Hunters and gatherers plant polyculture gardens sporadically rather than systematically, since their nomadism allows circulation rather than sedentarism. When they plant, they avoid disturbing their environments as much as possible. They know that their environment, as territory, depends on the complexity of the canopy. The phrase, "All our relations," offered by Native Peoples as a greeting or farewell, relates this symbiosis. Without localized knowledge, monocultures automatically turn the soil infertile, and it erodes very fast, turning into sand.

Among the Maya, swidden farming does not just imply clearing the *land*. A producing plot is considered already an infraction against nature, but the true owners—*Yumilo'ob K'axo'ob*, wilderness lords—grant a sort of temporary permit for a plot, a *Milpa*, to be worked. Eventually, the *Milpa* is returned to them, but it is never abandoned.[13] Here, there is an obvious need to conserve the "wilderness" (*Yum k'ax*) as a reservoir, or as sp(l)aces[14] of regenerative fertility connoting dimensions other than monocultural nations of "arable land." Suddenly, the discarded terrain (*el monte*) is the cradle of biodiversity. The Maya scholar Victor Montejo[15] reminds us of the Mesoamerican Yukatek Maya, who believe in the *Kusansum*, an umbilical cord that connects the earth and the sky. The *Kusansum* reflects the connection not only between all things on earth, but of a greater cosmology, a pluriverse.

Amidst the Maori of New Zealand, according to Maori scholar Fiona Cram, "The interconnectedness of life on this planet stems from all species being descended from Papatuanuku (Earth Mother) and

---

13 Alejandra García-Quintanilla, "El Dilema de Ah Kimsah K'ax, 'El que mata al Monte': Significados del Monte entre los Mayas Milperos de Yucatán," *Mesoamerica* 39 (2000): 267, 283, 285.

14 Guillermo Delgado-P., "Bordering Indigeneities. Two Notes on Decolonization and Sp/l/ace," *Indigenous Research Center of the Americas* (Davis: University of California Press, 2009), http://irca.ucdavis.edu/2009/12/bordering-indigeneities-two-notes-on-decolonization-and-splace/.

15 Victor Montejo, "The Road to Heaven: Jakaltek Maya Beliefs, Religion, and Ecology," in Indigenous Traditions and Ecology: The Interbeing of Cosmology and Community, ed. John A. Grim (Cambridge, MA: University of Harvard Press, 2001), 181.

Ranginui (Sky Father). Everything possesses a *Mauri* (life force), in-cluding animals, fish, birds, land, forests, and seas. *Mauri* is the source of the link between things."[16] But, at the outset of the twenty-first century, the norm is the persistent resistance of indigenous people against neo-colonial land grabs.

Agriculturalist Resistance to Land Grabbing

As a current study shows, between 1985 and 2007, the expansion of agri-cultural lands in Latin America was the highest in the world. "Specifically in Bolivia," the study states, "it went from 13,891 square kilometers to 25,365 square kilometers."[17] But land grabbing is not isolated to Bolivia. One recent case of land grabbing is found in Alto Paraguay, where ancient Amerindians—largely Guaraní—are graphically being dispossessed from the lands where they lived throughout these last centuries. While today, the African land grab has outpaced Latin America, the outcome remains the same—territories are decimated in a neo-colonial rush for land. In the twenty-first century, forms of neo-slavery have been found on lands that are, presumably, part of modern, monocrop capitalism. *The New York Times* reports about thirty-five enslaved workers in the state of Pará, Brazil:

> Inspectors found the employees on Senator João Ribeiro's ranch working 78 hours a week with no medical assistance, no days off and living in sub-human conditions. The inspectors found that the workers racked up debts to the ranch for food and equipment, which were deducted from their wages and left them permanently indebted and unable to leave.[18]

It can be inferred that modern capitalism needs forms of enslaved labor through an old system called "debt-peonage"—the never-ending cycle

---

16   Fiona Cram, "Backgrounding Maori Views on Genetic Engineering," in *Sovereignty Matters: Locations of Contestation and Possibility in Indigenous Struggles for Self-Determination*, ed. Joanne Barker (Lincoln: University of Nebraska Press: 2005), 54.

17   Karl S. Zimmerer, "'Conservation Booms' with Agricultural Growth?: Sustain-ability and Shifting Environmental Governance in Latin America, 1985–2008 (Mexico, Costa Rica, Brazil, Peru, Bolivia)," *Latin American Research Review* 46, Special Issue (2011): 102.

18   "Brazil: Senator is Accused of Keeping 35 Workers in Slavelike Conditions," *New York Times*, February, 25, 2012, A5.

of debt that a plantation or ranch worker enters, very often passing it along to their children. Frequently, in these circumstances, the term "landlessness" crops up at the moment that a tax is imposed on the free agriculturalist, who are usually autonomous peasants.

In the twenty-first century we must be aware that globalization denotes the last capitalistic movement to commodify everything. As Max Broswimmer explains, "The exploitation of nature was universalized and commodified. In the end, the imperatives of late modernity produced the global framework in which ecocidal tendencies greatly accelerated."[19] Here, the processes to commodify land are equal to the destruction of territory. The terms "free land," "empty land," "wild lands," "landscape," "land development," acquire new meanings after entering a process of full commoditization including water and air. Just think about the term "urban sprawl," which Edward Heisel explains, "has even spread into more remote and scenic regions of the country as Americans have become more mobile and recreational outposts have sprouted into full-fledged cities."[20]

But civil societies and their social movements have not remained passive. Indeed, according to Zimmerer, Latin American countries "now account for nearly 15 percent of global coverage of protected areas."[21] Agriculturalists value the notion of community, and reject the full individualist socialization brought in by neoliberalism to areas where reciprocity and recognition of others are privileged as an endeavor between or within human and nature. Knowledge and paleotechnologies available to unrelenting agriculturalists around the world allow old forms of production that proved reliable or sustainable to be reconsidered. As observed recently in Peru by anthropologist Frédérique Apffel-Marglin, this is the case of biochar, a clean charcoal made from agricultural biomass.

One European example of *longue durée* land use in Burgundy, France, may show that depletion and exhaustion of the land is not always correlated with European practices like those introduced in the Americas. It is exquisite, as it relates to wine making, which takes us back to the first millennium AD and the term "clos." "*Clos* designates a

---

19   Franz J. Broswimmer, *Ecocide: A Short History of the Mass Extinction of Species* (Virginia: Pluto Press, 2002), 10.
20   Heisel, "Biodiversity and Federal Land Ownership," 231.
21   Zimmerer, "'Conservation Booms' with Agricultural Growth?," 83.

walled enclosure that has been distinguished from other plots. The term often suggests that the plot has been valued for its grapes—enough at least to build a wall."[22]

Another positive and more contemporary example of sustainability could be environmentally friendly and socially-responsible use of privatized lands, small and organic producers of coffee in Costa Rica, Oaxaca, or Bolivia where, aided by fair trade practices, growers are able to sustain their way of life, aware of the fact that their lands are nurtured and their incomes are not inspired by blind maximization of profits but by producer/consumer responsibility and nurturing. In this case, it is the consumer that is also indirectly involved in environmental sustainability and regeneration.

Zimmerer helps here to distinguish the opposite: "Still, the bulk of expanded export agriculture and new national production has tended, on the whole, to contribute to environmental destruction under neoliberal policies that predominated in [Mexico, Costa Rica, Brazil, Peru, and Bolivia] between 1987 and 2008."[23] Zimmerer's observation correlates with a long-term state practice:

> Under the label of "government projects for collective well-being," indiscriminate intervention into specific ecosystems occupied by indigenous communities from time immemorial, in Mexico and other Latin American countries, has produced severe alterations of those systems and traumatic changes in traditional ways of life.[24]

---

22 Roderick Coover, "Working with Images, Images of Work," in *Working Images: Visual Research and Representation in Ethnography*, ed. Ana Isabel Alfonso, Laszlo Kurti, and Sarah Pink (New York: Routledge, 2004), 187.

23 Zimmerer, "'Conservation Booms' with Agricultural Growth?," 81.

24 Ángel Julián García-Zambrano, "Calabash Trees and Cacti in the Indigenous Ritual Selection of Environments for Settlement in Colonial Mesoamerica," in *Indigenous Traditions and Ecology: The Interbeing of Cosmology and Community*, ed. John A. Grim (Cambridge, MA: Harvard University Press, 2001), 351.
    Other Recommended Works: Hans Baer and Merrill Singer, eds., *Global Warming and the Political Ecology of Health: Emerging Crises and Systemic Solutions* (Walnut Creek: Left Coast Press, 2008). Joseph Bastian, *Mountain of the Condor: Metaphor and Ritual in an Andean Ayllu* (St. Paul, MN: AES, 1978). Vivienne Bennett, Sonia Dávila, and María Nieves Rico, eds., *Opposing Currents. The Politics of Water and Gender in Latin America* (Pittsburgh: University of Pittsburgh Press, 2005). Mario Blaser, *Storytelling Globalization from the Chaco and Beyond* (Durham: Duke University Press, 2010). Icíar Bollaín, Director, *Even the Rain* (Film) (2010). Marijosé Amerlink de Bontempo,

Agriculturalists are interested in recomposing the subdivided lands, undoing the feuds that created a culture of allotment, giving time for land to be idle, to regenerate, to "rest." Several ancient anthropogenic plots (*Milpa, Chaqra, Conuco, Chinampa, Kusansum, Chaco*) continue productively in Latin America to this day. The survival of such agriculturalists and their anthropogenic practices depends on their ability to remain caretakers of their seeds. Once they lose the preservation and regeneration of seeds, they fall into commercial seed dependency. Thus, the reconstitution of lands includes the *remembering* of territory through such agro-ecologies

"'Praedium,' 'Fundum,' 'Villa,' y Hacienda: La perspectiva de los agrónomos latinos," in *La Heterodoxia Recuperada. En Torno a Angel Palerm*, ed. Susana Glantz (Mexico: Fondo de Cultura Económica, 1987), 375–395. Gregory Button, *Disaster Culture: Knowledge and Uncertainty in the Wake of Human and Environmental Catastrophe* (Walnut Creek: Left Coast Press, 2010). Alf Hornborg and Carole L. Crumley, *The World System and the Earth System: Global Socioenvironmental Change and Sustainability since the Neolithic* (Walnut Creek: Left Coast Press, 2006. Barbara Rose Johnston, ed., *Life and Death Matters: Human Rights, Environment and Social Justice* (Walnut Creek: Left Coast Press, 2010). Richard P. Schaedel, "The Archaeology of the Spanish Colonial Experience in South America," *Antiquity* 66 (1992): 217–242. Shiv Visvanathan, "Between Cosmology and System: The Heuristics of a Dissenting Imagination," in *Another Knowledge is Possible. Beyond Northern Epistemologies*, ed. Boãventura de Sousa Santos (London: Verso, 2007), 182–218. Frédérique Apffel-Marglin, *Subversive Spiritualiaties: How Rituals Enact the World* (New York: Oxford University Press, 2011).

A COUP OVER LAND:

The Resource War Behind Paraguay's Crisis[1]

Benjamin Dangl

Each bullet hole on the downtown Asunción, Paraguay, light posts tells a story. Some of them are from civil wars decades ago, some from successful and unsuccessful coups, others from police crackdowns. The size of the hole, the angle of the ricochet, all tell of an escape, a death, another dictator in the palace by the river.

On June 22, 2012, a new tyrant entered the government palace. The right-wing Federico Franco became president in what has been deemed a parliamentary coup against democratically-elected, left-leaning President Fernando Lugo.

What lies behind today's headlines, political fights and struggles for justice in Paraguay is a conflict over access to land; land is power and money for the elites, survival and dignity for the poor, and has been at the center of major political and social battles in Paraguay for decades. In order to understand the crisis in post-coup Paraguay, it's necessary to grasp the political weight of the nation's soil. Here, a look at the history of Paraguay's resource war for land, the events leading up to the coup, and the story of one farming community's resistance places land at the heart of nation's current crisis.

The Coup and the Land

Hope surrounded the electoral victory of Fernando Lugo in 2008, a victory that ended the right wing Colorado Party's sixty-one-year dominance of Paraguayan politics. It was a victory against the injustice and nightmare of the Alfredo Stroessner dictatorship (1954–1989), and a new addition to the region's left-leaning governments. The election of Lugo, a former bishop and adherent to liberation theology, was due in large part to grassroots support from the *campesino* (small farmer) sector, and Lugo's promise of long-overdue land reform.

Yet Lugo was isolated politically from the very beginning. He needed to ally with the right to win the election. His vice president, Federico

---

1   Excerpts from this article are taken from Benjamin Dangl, *Dancing With Dynamite* (Oakland: AK Press, 2011).

Franco, is a leader in the right wing Liberal Party, and was a vocal opponent of Lugo since shortly after Lugo came to power. Throughout Lugo's time in office, the Colorado Party maintained a majority in Congress, and there were various right wing attempts to impeach the "Red Bishop." Such challenges impeded Lugo's progress, and created a political and media environment dominated by near-constant attacks.

At the same time, Lugo was no friend of the campesino sector that helped bring him into power. His administration regularly called for the severe repression and criminalization of the country's campesino movements. He was isolated from above at the political level, and lacked a strong political base below, due to his stance toward social movements and the slow pace of land reform. None the less, many leftist and campesino sectors still saw Lugo as a relative ally and source of hope in the face of the right wing alternative.

The issue that finally tipped the scales toward the June 22 Parliamentary coup against Lugo was a conflict over land. In April 2012, sixty landless campesinos occupied land in Curuguaty, in northeastern Paraguay. This land is owned by former Colorado Senator Blas N. Riquelme, one of the richest people and largest landowners in the country. In 1969, the Stroessner administration illegally gave Riquelme fifty thousand hectares of land that was supposed to be destined to poor farmers as a part of land reform. Since the return to democracy in 1989, campesinos have been struggling to gain access to this land. The April occupation of land was one such attempt. On June 15, security forces arrived in Curuguaty to evict the landless settlement. The subsequent confrontation during the eviction (the specific details of which are still shrouded in confusion) led to the death of seventeen people, including eleven campesinos and six police officers. Eighty people were wounded.

While certainly the bloodiest confrontation of this kind since the dictatorship, it was one of dozens of such conflicts that had taken place in recent years in a nation with enormous inequality of land distribution. The right's response to such conflicts typically involved siding with the land owners and business leaders, and criminalizing campesino activists. With the tragedy of Curuguaty, the right saw yet another opportunity to move against Lugo.

The right blamed Lugo for the bloody events at Curuguaty, an accusation that was unfounded, but served as fodder for the ongoing political attacks against the president. In response to critics, Lugo replaced his

Interior Minister with Colorado Party member Candia Amarilla, a former State Prosecutor known for his criminalization of leftist social and campesino groups, and who was trained in Colombia to export Plan Colombia-style policies to Paraguay. Lugo also made the police commissioner, Moran Arnaldo Sanabria (who was in charge of the Curuguaty operation), the National Director of Police.

In this way, Lugo handed over the state's main security and repressive powers to the Colorado Party. The move was an effort to avoid impeachment from the right, but it backfired; the Liberal Party opposed Lugo's replacements, and, empowered by the criticisms leveled against Lugo's handling of Curuguaty, collaborated with the Colorado Party and other right wing parties in Congress to move forward with the impeachment.

The process began on June 21, and within twenty-four hours the Senate gathered and officially initiated the trial, granting Lugo only two hours to defend himself. The next day, Lugo was removed from office in a thirty-nine to four vote. He was accused of encouraging landless farmers' occupations, poor performance as president, and failing to bring about social harmony in the country. Lugo stepped down, and Vice President and Liberal Party leader Federico Franco took his place.

This Parliamentary coup was condemned as undemocratic and illegal by many Latin American leaders, who refused to recognize Franco as the legitimate president. In response to the coup, Latin American trade and political blocs, such as Unasur and Mercosur, have suspended Paraguay's participation in their organizations until next year's elections. Unsurprisingly, the Organization of American States decided to not suspend Paraguay's membership in the group because, according to OAS secretary general Jose Miguel Insulza, doing so would create further problems in the country and isolate it regionally. This is the second such coup in the region in recent years. In June 2009, Honduran president, Manuel Zelaya, was ousted under similar circumstances.

The backdrop to this political fight is a struggle over how to control, use and distribute Paraguay's vast land. Approximately 2 percent of landowners control 80 percent of Paraguay's land, and some eight-seven thousand farming families are landless. While Lugo failed to meet many of his campaign promises to the campesino sector, he did in fact work to block many of the right's policies that would worsen the crisis in the countryside. For example, Lugo and his cabinet resisted the use of Monsanto's transgenic cotton seeds in Paraguay, a move that likely

contributed to his ouster. Yet even before Lugo was elected, political alliances and victories were shaped by the question of land. Multinational
agro-industrial corporations are fully entrenched in Paraguayan politics,
and their fundamental enemies in this resource war have always been the
Paraguayan campesino.

A Sea of Soy

For decades, small farmers in Paraguay have been tormented by a tidal
wave of GMO soy crops and pesticides expanding across the countryside.
Paraguay is the fourth largest producer of soy in the world. Soy makes up
40 percent of Paraguayan exports and 10 percent of the country's GDP.
An estimated twenty million liters of agrochemicals are sprayed across
Paraguay each year, poisoning the people, water, farmland, and livestock
that come in its path.

Managing the gargantuan agro-industry are transnational seed,
agricultural, and agro-chemical companies including Monsanto, Pi-
oneer, Syngenta, Dupont, Cargill, Archer Daniels Midland (ADM),
and Bunge. International financial institutions and development banks
have promoted and bankrolled the agro-export business of monoculture
crops—much of Paraguayan soy goes to feed animals in Europe. The
profits have united political and corporate entities from Brazil, the US,
and Paraguay, and increased the importance of Paraguay's cooperation
with international businesses.

Since the 1980s, national military and paramilitary groups connected to large agribusinesses and landowners have evicted almost a hundred thousand small farmers from their homes and fields and forced the
relocation of countless indigenous communities in favor of soy fields.
While more than a hundred campesino leaders have been assassinated
in this time, only one of the cases was investigated, with results leading to the conviction of the killer. In the same period, more than two
thousand other campesinos have faced trumped-up charges for their
resistance to the soy industry. The vast majority of Paraguayan farmers
have been poisoned off their land either intentionally or as a side effect
of the hazardous pesticides dumped by soy cultivation in Paraguay every
year. Beginning in the 1990s, as farmers saw their animals dying, crops
withering, families sickening, and wells contaminated, most packed up
and moved to the city.

The havoc wreaked by agro-industries has created some of the most grave human rights violations since Stroessner's reign. A report produced by the Committee of Economic, Social, and Cultural Rights of the United Nations stated that "the expansion of the cultivation of soy has brought with it the indiscriminate use of toxic pesticides, provoking death and sickness in children and adults, contamination of water, disappearance of ecosystems, and damage to the traditional nutritional resources of the communities."

The expansion of the soy industry has occurred in tandem with the violent oppression of small farmers and indigenous communities who occupy the vast land holdings of the wealthy. Most rural Paraguayans cultivate diverse subsistence crops on small plots of ten to twenty hectares, but do not have titles to their land, nor do they typically receive assistance from the state. The Paraguayan government has historically represented the soy growers in this conflict by using the police and judicial system to punish campesino leaders.

The small farming community of Tekojoja has been on the front line of this struggle for years. Its history and struggle is representative of countless other farming communities in the Paraguayan countryside.

Tekojoja's Resistance

The first of several buses we would take from Asunción toward Tekojoja in April of 2009 heated up like a sauna as polka played on the radio. Hawkers came on the bus selling sunglasses, radios, and pirated DVDs. Particularly dedicated salesmen gave impassioned speeches about the superior characteristics of their product, pushing samples onto the unwilling and bored passengers. One sales pitch promised that garlic pills could cure insomnia and cancer.

We passed countless fields of soy and Cargill silos, but also vegetable stands from small farmers and simple roadside restaurants where people could escape into the shade with a cold beer. The dirt road from Caaguazú toward Tekojoja was a rutted expanse of churning red sand; it took us three hours to travel fifty kilometers. The bus fought its way over the deep potholes, the engine reaching a fevered pitch, and every one of its metal bones rattling along with those of its passengers.

That same night, we arrived in Tekojoja and went to Gilda Roa's house, a government-made structure without running water (though the government built the buildings, it never completed the plumbing). A land and farmer rights activist, Roa's shirt portrayed plants breaking through a bar code. Inside her house, the walls were covered with anti-soy and anti-GMO posters. She pulled up plastic chairs for us in front of the garden with bright stars as a backdrop, and began talking. Roa spent 2000–2002 in Asunción studying to be a nurse, and had worked as one in a nearby town. At the time of our visit, in April of 2009, she was dedicated exclusively to activism in her community. As Paraguayan folk music played on the radio, and moths bounced around the lights, Roa told us the story of her community and its fight against GMO soy.

The community of Tekojoja is home of the Popular Agrarian Movement (MAP) of Paraguay. It is a place that has faced enormous repression from the soy farmers and their thugs, and led a legendary resistance against them, producing many campesino leaders.

Tekojoja stands on land given to campesinos as part of a Public Land Reform Program. In the 1990s, Brazilian soy farmers—with armed thugs, lawyers, and political connections to protect them—gradually expanded onto the community's land, forcing a series of violent evictions of the farming families. In 2003, the MAP began to recover the lands taken from them by Brazilians, but corrupt judges and the mercenaries hired by soy producers kept pushing the farmers off their land.

On December 2, 2004, Brazilian land owners accompanied by police burned down numerous houses and farmland in Tekojoja as part of an eviction process. A statement from the MAP described this brutal act:

> After the tractors destroyed our crops, they came with their big machines and started immediately to sow soy while smoke was still rising from the ashes of our houses. The next day we came back with oxen and replanted all the fields over the prepared land. When the police came, we faced them with our tools and machetes. There were around seventy of us and we were ready to confront them. In the end they left.

The campesinos' houses and crops were destroyed, and they had no assurances that the Brazilians would not orchestrate another eviction. Still, as most had no place to go, the community members decided to persevere, staying on the land and fighting for legal recognition as the owners. Roa explained, "We planted seeds with fear as we didn't know if our crops would be destroyed. And we began to reconstruct the houses." But again at 4 AM on June 24, 2005, the Brazilians and police attacked the community. "They arrested children, blind people, old men, and pregnant women, everyone, throwing them all in a truck." Roa said. "They threw gas and oil on the houses, burning them all down as the arrests went on."

In this standoff between the thugs, police, and unarmed campesinos, two farmers, who the Brazilians mistakenly identified as MAP leaders and brothers Jorge and Antonio Galeano, were killed by gunfire. One of the victims was Angel Cristaldo Rotela, a twenty-three-year-old who was about to be married, and had just finished building his own home the day before the police burned it to the ground. The wife of Leoncio Torres, the other victim, was left a widow with eight children. A memorial stands in the center of the community in memory of the fallen campesinos.

After the murders, campesinos and activists from around the country rallied in support of Tekojoja, supplying the besieged community members with tarps and food. Finally, the Supreme Court ruled that the land should go to the local farmers, and as part of the reparations for the violence the community suffered, President Nicanor Frutos commissioned the building of forty-eight homes. The plight of Tekojoja sheds light on the situation many farming communities are finding themselves in across Paraguay. While the residents of Tekojoja remain on their land, many others are forced to flee to slums in the city as soy producers push them off their land.

Roa explained this cycle of displacement:

> When the small farmers are desperate, and the pesticides are hurting them, there is no money, and so they sell their land for a little money, which is more than they've ever had, thinking that life in the city will be better, easy—but it's not so easy. A lot of people who end up gathering garbage in the city are from the countryside. They don't know how to manage their money, so for example, they'll spend all their money on a used, broken-down car first, and then end up in the city broke, without any jobs or place to stay.

The victory of Tekojoja was due to the tenacity of the farmers who refused to leave their land for the false promise of rich city life. But their fight is far from over. Though they tore the soy plants out of their land, residents live sandwiched between seemingly limitless expanses of soy, and they, their animals, and their crops continue to suffer from exposure to toxic pesticides.

By dawn the next day, most of Roa's neighbors were already up, getting to work before the sun made labor unbearable. Chickens milled about houses, the red dirt yards were still damp from the night's dew, and radios tuned in to a community radio station mixing music with political commentary in Guaraní. A neighboring community activist invited us to his house to start the day with Paraguayans' essential beverage, yerba maté served hot in the morning and specially prepared with coconut and rosemary. We sat in his kitchen as the sun streamed through the cracks between the boards in the wall, illuminating ribbons of smoke from the fire, while his children and pigs played on the dirt floor.

An ominous presence loomed over this bucolic scene. The neighboring Brazilian soy farmers had already shown up with their tractors, spraying pesticides on nearby crops. I could smell the chemicals in the air already. We walked toward the fields until the sweet, toxic odor grew stronger. We passed one tractor very closely as clouds of the pesticides drifted toward us. I began to feel a disorienting sensation of dizziness and nausea. My eyes, throat, and lungs burned, and my head ached—something the locals go through on a daily basis. The physical illness caused by the pesticides contributes to breaking down the campesino resistance.

I am reminded that this is a besieged community, not just because of the soy crops that circle these islands of humanity, or the pesticides that seep into every water source, crop, and conversation, but also because the Brazilian soy farmers live next to, and drive through, these impoverished communities with total impunity, and with the windows of their shiny new trucks rolled up tightly. Mounted somewhat precariously on the back of a few mopeds, we bounced along the dirt roads, which petered out into paths to another cluster of homes. On our way there, we passed one Brazilian who glared at us until we were out of sight. Roa knew him: he had participated in the razing and burning of their homes. The fact that he was still free added insult to injury. And if the locals were to accuse him, said Roa, or even yell at the murderers, police would show up and haul them off to jail. "This is the hardest part," she explained. "That we see them, and can't do anything."

The Moped rolled to a stop in front of Virginia Barrientos's home, a few miles from Roa's, directly bordering a soy field. The land Barrientos lived on for the past four years is a peninsula jutting into the sea of soy. She occupied her land, which used to be covered with soy, in February of 2005, and won legal ownership to it. But life since gaining the land has been far from easy. Pesticides have terrorized her family since they moved there.

"Just before we harvest our food the Brazilians will spray very powerful pesticides," Barrientos explained. "This spraying causes the headaches, nausea, diarrhea we all suffer." Her thin children were gathered with her on the porch of the home. "There are a lot of problems with the water," she continued. "When it rains, the pesticides affect our only water source."

Barrientos said the pesticides affected her plants and animals as well, making some of the crops that do actually grow taste too bitter to eat. Her pigs' newborn babies died, and the chickens were ill. Part of the problem, she pointed out, is that the Brazilian soy farmers intentionally choose to fumigate during strong winds, which blow the poison onto her land. We passed dead corn stalks on the way to her well. It was located at the end of a long field of soy, so that the runoff from the field dripped into the well, concentrating the pesticides in her only water source. The family lives in a poisoned misery, while the soy producer responsible for it lives in comparative luxury away from his fields.

Isabel Rivas, a neighbor of Barrientos' with a big smile and loud laugh in spite of her grim living situation, told us, "When we drink the water we can smell the chemicals. It turns out they were washing the chemical sprayers in our source of water, in a little stream nearby." Barrientos stood in front of her house while breastfeeding her baby as chickens pecked at peanuts in the yard. Her children stared at us with wide eyes. "We can't go anywhere else."

While Lugo's inability and unwillingness to sufficiently address such hardships was a betrayal of this grassroots sector, the recent coup against Lugo was also a coup against hope, a coup against Barrientos and her children, Roa and her neighbors, and the hundreds of thousands of farmers struggling the countryside. Behind this coup lies the vast land, some of it poisoned, some still fertile, and much of it tear and blood-soaked. Until the demand of land justice is realized, there will be no peace in Paraguay, regardless of who sleeps in the presidential palace.

BLACK WOMEN ON THE EDGE:

A Conversation on the Gendered Racial Struggle for Urban Land in Salvador, Brazil[1]

Keisha-Khan Y. Perry and Ana Cristina da Silva Caminha

A Context of Grassroots Struggle

On August 4, 2007, at an official ceremony in the open space of the historic São Paulo Fort in the Gamboa de Baixo neighborhood, community leaders of Salvador, Brazil, signed the landmark agreement to take possession of land for local families. This political act was the result of decades of struggle over land tenure, and promised to benefit the majority group of black residents who had been living on and using the land since the colonial period.

The legal possibility of land tenure sparked much discussion among Gamboa de Baixo residents in attendance who questioned the meaning of signing a contract "allowing the use of navy land." Dona Vilma, having lived in the neighborhood for over fifty years, asked government representatives present at the ceremony: "Is my house considered to be on navy land? Will I be able to receive my title?" Dona Vilma's question reflected the concern of other residents who were distressed for the same reason, and began asking a series of other questions, such as, "What is the length of navy land?" Also, they inquired into whether or not the land agreement was partial, authorizing use but not ownership, and that some regions of the neighborhood would be kept out of the agreement. The agreement only normalized local use and control of land owned by the State, leaving out significant portions of land belonging to other legal entities, such as the Catholic Church (and now Odebrecht construction firm). In addition to the navy, there were several competing "owners" of the land who were missing from this legal agreement. Doubts about the meaning of the collective right to land in the city of Salvador have

---

1   We would like to give a special thanks to Sasha, the organizer of this edited volume, who completed the initial translation of segments of the article we co-authored in Portuguese, "Daqui não saio, daqui ninguém me tira: Poder e política das mulheres negras da Gamboa de Baixo, Salvador" (*Gênero* 9, no. 1 (2008): 127–158) and the conversation we recorded in 2007 that is excerpted in this essay.

caused many residents to view the tenure and titling process with suspicion and call into question the potential for partial land ownership in the areas of Gamboa de Baixo.

Black women neighborhood association leaders are at the forefront of these debates on land rights, and this was not the official document for which they had waited so long. Signifying more than just the physical space where families live, work, and build social and political networks, urban land represents the ability of poor blacks to pass resources from one generation to the next. As blacks migrate to Brazilian cities in increasing numbers and form neighborhoods, they rearticulate their sense of belonging to and owning these urban spaces. But institutional roadblocks to winning full state recognition of land ownership mean that poor blacks throughout Salvador suffer the threat of eviction and violent displacement. The neighborhood association of Gamboa really wanted a document that made it legal for them to stay in their homes permanently and acknowledged collective ownership. One activist, Rita, educator and adviser of the Center for Studies of Social Action (CEAS), which has played a key role in mobilizing the community for more than ten years, led chants among the residents of the names of black national heroes: "Zumbí, Dandara, and Luiza Mahim," and "Long live the black people!" She wanted to remind residents of the tradition of resistance of blacks and black women for the right to live with dignity and material resources such as land. Dona Lenilda, a former community leader, began to sing the Gamboa de Baixo political anthem and was also promptly accompanied by the residents present:

"From here, I will not leave
No one can take me away,
From here, I will not leave
No one can take me away,
Where am I going live?
Oh Lord, have the patience to wait,
especially for me with so many children,
Where am I going to live?"

At that moment, in the singing of the song, residents expressed that the many-decades-long struggle of those with no civil rights for land in downtown Salvador could not end with a partial government contract.

The black women-led struggle for land rights in Gamboa de Baixo brings up a problem that troubles popular movements in the predominantly black communities of Salvador: how to claim rights in a context wherein government actions generally ignore gendered racism as a structural element of social inequalities, and disregard the participation of this group in the articulation and implementation of public policy? This question implies also reflecting on how representatives of the government have contributed to stereotypical views of urban black communities, generally, and black women, specifically, who are seen as unable to negotiate their own demands.

To expose the gendered, racial nature of land struggle in Salvador and to show how black women have come to lead the intense debates about public policies that distribute land access rather than displace entire neighborhoods, a brief history of Gamboa de Baixo's neighborhood movement is in order. The following historical context will frame a conversation that took place between the two authors, both black women activists and scholars, in January 2007, less than a year before the government's attempt to reach a tenure agreement. The struggle began long before we sat down to speak.

A Brief Political History

The history of political development in Gamboa de Baixo is essentially a history of leadership of black women. Gamboa de Baixo is a small, secular, black community of fishermen and fisherwomen situated on the coast of the Baía de Todos os Santos (All Saint's Bay), below the street named Contorno Avenue between the Museu de Arte Moderna (MAM) and the elite residential district of Vítoria. The political formation of this community began in the 1960s when the government of Bahia started construction on the Contorno Avenue, which separated Gamboa de Baixo from its surrounding communities (Politeama, Campo Grande, and Aflitos).

Some of the residents of this region resisted the demolition of their homes, but lost the fight against forced relocation. In fact, after the construction of the Contorno Avenue, the community of Gamboa de Baixo suffered the consequences of geographic isolation through the actual physical lack of a formal access to other areas of the city as well as basic infrastructural services (sanitation, potable water, and electricity) that were becoming regularized throughout the city-center. The construction of the Contorno Avenue created a real "apartheid" city which solidified socio-spatial inequalities and subsequent territorial disputes. Local activists now understand this early, government-supported geographic isolation and social abandonment as an initial strategy to force local displacement from the coveted coastal lands to the periphery of the city during the urban modernization of the 1970s, '80s, and '90s.

Local residents fought against imposed physical and social isolation, and black women residents took the helm of this struggle. They mobilized as a Women's Association (Associação de Mulheres) to demand government resources from the food and milk programs initiated by city officials in the 1980s, and they were a key force in building the first wooden staircase that gave Gamboa de Baixo residents access to the street. This association would later evolve and become the political body of local residents that advocated collectively for safety, basic sanitation, family planning, and public education. This gave rise to the prominence of women's activism within the community, establishing an identity of political activities as women's work.

The organizational capacity and legitimacy of women activists in Gamboa de Baixo has been definitive during crucial moments for the neighborhood, such as the outbreak of cholera in Salvador in 1992. During this outbreak, local activists mobilized their neighbors to demand that the municipal government provide the necessary assistance to the community in fighting the disease that killed three residents. During this time, the women organized the Association of Friends of Gegê Residents of Gamboa de Baixo (Associacao Amigos de Gegê dos Moradores da Gamboa de Baixo), named after one of the cholera victims and led by his widow (Dona Lenilda) and daughter (Lueci Ferreira). The movement from the women's association to the neighborhood association as the main reference of community organization in the struggle for social improvement is confirmed by statements by former community leader, Valquíria Boa Morte:

> I was the first person who went to the radio. By the time I got home, EMBASA [The Bahia Water and Sanitation] was already researching putting in a fountain. The death of Mr. Geraldo, the father of Lueci, reinforced the struggle, and I was mobilized at this time because I knew the family, father and mother and all the little ones. I was at home when I heard he was going to the hospital with cholera, and other residents had already gone. Another boy had died, so I

called two women, Toni and Mel, and went to the radio. After that, other women arrived: Tinda, Solange, Hilda, after Lueci. We took steps, and they brought us running water. So it was that we started the struggle to organize Gamboa, which was only a marginalized community before then.

Dona Lenilda, another leading activist, recalls:

[The other women] encouraged me to join the movement. What I wanted was a better life for my family, for my children. We had seen their father pass on and more people, you understand? So I wanted a decent life with running water, a toilet, and not to work for nothing. If we live in a place, we have to deal with it. The association was founded as an instrument of dialogue with the organized political forces.

After the 1992 cholera outbreak, the Gamboa de Baixo neighborhood continued to mobilize for general infrastructural improvement that envisioned a greater participation as citizens having rights to the city's resources. In the mid-1990s, the struggle intensified when residents learned of forced relocation of black communities of the city center to the distant periphery. Women activists focused on mobilizing their neighbors in defense of permanent land ownership and adequate housing. As one of the most vocal activists in the early neighborhood, the late Dona Iraci, stated in a 2000 interview, "when we saw [the police] evicting [the inhabitants of the Agua Suja neighborhood], that's when we became even stronger."

Dona Lenilda explained how relocation influenced her decision to become involved: "the government wanted to take all of us away from here, and we did not want to leave. We do not need to ask people for anything, right? For so many years we had been living in wooden shacks, but they were ours. The politicians and developers wanted to remove us, but we did not give up... I thought, we have to do something to strike the government. I began to work on that song. That's when I started to carry forward this anthem, and we won." They engaged in direct action protest, such as burning tires on the Contorno Avenue, stopping traffic and bringing attention to government strategies of expulsion. Through these public street protests, the community was able to garner support from civil society organizations and black movement activist groups.

In the process of confronting the threat of expulsion, the activists developed a project proposal that fit the reality of Gamboa de Baixo community residents, and envisioned a better quality of life. They teamed up with professors and students from the Faculty of Architecture at the Federal University of Bahia (UFBA). This political process of combining technical knowledge with the local experience and wisdom of residents forced urban developers to consider the construction of new houses instead of relocation away from the city center. This challenged how urban planners interact with communities during negotiations over how to develop the city, and it also changed the extent to which women participate in policy debates that impact entire black communities. As a result, the community gained participation in a national housing program that guaranteed the construction of better houses for families in the community.

Despite these gains, the late 1990s and 2000s were marked by tense discussions and debates about poor quality of the houses that were eventually constructed, and the activists' insistence that there were very apparent contradictions in statements made by public officials on several occasions over the past two decades. For example, one official stated, "This coastal land is not an area for black and poor people to live." This statement best sums up the racial dynamics of the socio-spatial order of Salvador's city-center as it undergoes rapid restructuring and renewal. These are the conditions that gave rise to black women's activism at the neighborhood level.

Conversation on Gender, Sexuality, and Activism

The history of the neighborhood struggle provides the backdrop for the conversation that took place between the authors in January 2007 on the political formation of black women in the Gamboa de Baixo grassroots movement. When we sat down to have this conversation, we had the intention of co-theorizing how black women's activism emerges and the kinds of questions around race, gender, and sexuality that have become central to how we organize within and outside our neighborhoods. We were writing an article for a Brazilian academic journal, but we also wanted to take the time to reflect on our shared understanding of how blacks, women, and working people come to grassroots politics. We tried to grapple with the question of why and how black women organize differently, if they do at all.

Ana Cristina: So, we went through this period of the cholera outbreak, and arrived at another moment that may have been even more difficult to fight than a disease like cholera. The truth is, we were fighting against government power, macho power that is in fact the power of men in Bahia who govern Brazil. The fight to make them guarantee the permanence of the community became even more complicated. Once again, we had to deal with their disrespect and contempt.

First, we, the women, were those at the front [of the movement]. We women wanted to call attention to the issues; we wanted to make noise and they [the government officials] thought that any little side talk or conversation would put us in their pockets. They thought they would co-opt us, give us a little job. These women come from the grassroots they do not come from a background of formal education that brings with it a distinguished level of knowledge. They were women who came from the very bottom, from the community—women who did not know anything and had to learn during the process. It is more difficult to co-opt these people.

Today, we have a mostly male fishermen's association, and we help them organize. So we have a majority female neighborhood association dealing with a fishermen's association that has a majority male leadership.

Keisha-Khan: What is the difference?

Ana Cristina: The difference is that the women are serious. They are honest in the majority. They really work for the collective, and they put their necks on the point of the blade to defend the community. It is as if a mother were defending her children. I think that is the difference. The women come from the grassroots.

Keisha-Khan: In a 2004 protest, residents of Gamboa armed with whistles, banners, and a megaphone ambushed the entrance to the state water company in a surprise protest, shouting "We want water!" The director asked to speak with the president of the neighborhood association. Securing her baby on her hip, Luciene shouted back at him, "We don't have a president. We only have residents!" Can you talk about the structure of the organization?

Ana Cristina: I joined the association when I was nineteen years old. Today, I am thirty-two years old, and between then and now I have seen many things. I think I have seen some of my comrades, by virtue of being in leadership, forget that community leadership is a processual thing that is passed from one person to another. To organize a community is not to organize it by yourself. It is to prepare the others to face diverse social policy demands. I cannot prepare to face them without preparing my comrades or community, because if I am not able to be there today, I need to have another person who can do the same as me or better than myself.

Comrades who have failed to take this qualitative leap in thinking have not reached the stage where they understand that today they are the leader in the front, but tomorrow they will be beside or behind someone. Leadership is not a monarchy, a king who dictates. There is a group that is organizing, preparing everyone, so that everyone knows how to talk about the same things; they know how to respond to whatever question, and they know how to prepare for battle—for a war if need be. What else are we preparing for if it isn't a war with the government, a war on tourism, a war on speculation? We can even be quite frank and say that, during the course of ten years, we have not been co-opted by politicians, and we will continue to work this way. These are strategies most privileged by the collective. We will not go anywhere without the community.

Keisha-Khan: For poor black women in Gamboa de Baixo, getting things done has meant, when necessary, collectively getting in the face of the powerful and demystifying their power and control. After having gone through a process so complicated and so beautiful at the same time—the process of organizing the Gamboa struggle—why was it difficult?

Ana Cristina: Gamboa had to create several alternatives to ensure that we remain in our houses today. We had to fight police. We had to burn tires. We had to spend months and months seeking meetings with representatives of government institutions. And all of us had to develop a dialogue around a project that we believed was suitable for our community to ensure a certain structure, a certain condition of survival. So it was not easy, but oftentimes we have had the support of men. We can count the many times when we needed to shut down the Contorno Avenue; the men would come up there, and they believed in what we talked about, and they supported it, you know? They fought alongside us and the children.

Keisha-Khan: Many activists recall when former neighborhood association president Lueci, at eight months pregnant, was forcibly removed from a meeting. Activists immediately got up from the table and fought the security guards. Sometimes the men do not step to the front, but at other times they will go forward. At key moments they go to the streets, too.

Ana Cristina: You know what I feel? It seems like, despite the fact that the experience is a little different than Gamboa, Marechal Rondon [another neighborhood in Salvador] has a nice board with a majority of men. But of course you see women there—women talking, women fighting. In Gamboa, I feel that the men put themselves at our disposal in key moments as a matter of strength, physical strength. Women deal with the issue of discussion. It seems that the men really appreciate us, and have told us so. In Gamboa, men do not feel capable enough to discuss the issues. When it has to do with a protest, the men are on our side, carrying weight, taking action for the betterment of our community.

Keisha-Khan: Why is it complicated? It is not simply that they are *all* co-opted, but there are also men who say, "my wife cannot participate."

Ana Cristina: Absolutely.

Keisha-Khan: Today, I'm sure the government thinks twice before they implement their projects in certain communities. For example, the practices of the state have changed from the time that communities started to come with their ideas, and started questioning things. Of course the black movement has had a key role, but the base has played a role, too.

Ana Cristina: In reality, the black movement, some NGOs, and some other groups have contributed a lot in this matter, but I think [the base] made things different, which really made the government rethink its interventions. Like I said in the beginning, when people begin to organize within the community they do not know anything. Because of the arbitrary projects of the government, they felt the need to defend themselves, to defend their space. So these groups, in an effort to defend themselves, are able to make change, and show that things had to be different. Projects had to be discussed within, discussed with us, and discussed not just with the women, but also with the men and the community as a whole. I think that really, for the most part, women made a difference.

Keisha-Khan: I think people in general, at least in the academic world, have not given much value to black women in this sense.

Ana Cristina: And you know something, Keisha? Even the colleges that usually visit the communities at the end of the semester normally get scared when they arrive at Gamboa. First, because they were expecting a man or woman leading. And if a woman greets them, the expect a woman

of a certain age, never a young women as is our case. They never expect
women of twenty, twenty-eight, twenty-one years old, as is our case.

Keisha-Khan: Do you think that Gamboa has changed? For example, some women have had trouble with their husbands in terms of
freedom. Do you think that this has changed?

Ana Cristina: *Porra e como!* Do I think that Gamboa has changed
in terms of the question of women's freedom? Of course, Keisha-Khan.
You see, before, women were the most repressed, oppressed. We couldn't
do anything. We couldn't talk about anything. Today, we can even agitate
with all the craziness that we do. The question of women's freedom in
Gamboa changed a lot. People are more at ease, saying what's on their
mind. If I can recall, for example, Ivana—before Ivana started participating in the meetings, going to the street protests, speaking at a meeting
for more than fifty, seventy people, speaking up and speaking out, doing
what we have to do to defend ourselves. Before then, it was Ivana-in-
the-house. I never saw Ivana, but today, who is Ivana? Single, she leaves
the house, she gets home in the early morning. Perhaps we can say, "Is
this what we consider to be freedom?" Yes, this too is freedom, because
before, she would never have done that kind of thing. Not only would
her husband not allow it, but neither would society, nor the community.
It was after this [political] process, Ivana, Rita, me, Lia, we learned that
we could do anything, that we had the right to certain things.

What taught us that? It was the struggle against eviction in Gamboa.
It was the struggle around the racial question, self-esteem, you know, as
blacks. It was the struggle around the question of being a woman, of
gender, that I can do this; that I don't have to do that. And what is gender? For instance, the question of sexuality, the discovery of sexuality: we
now have the courage to discuss sex in a meeting. Before, we wouldn't
talk. We didn't have the courage to talk about a bunch of things. The
neighborhood association and the struggle taught us a lot. It taught us
that the struggle for housing is not just to blockade the street and say
that we want houses. It taught us that the struggle for housing is to say
that we want houses, we want employment, we want education, we want
women's rights. We want to occupy spaces as women, and in order to do
this, we have to sit in a circle only as women to discuss our pain, to ask,
"How is your relationship with your husband? Is it good, bad? And your
husband who is flirtatious with me, how is he with you when he sees
you flirting with another man?" We have to discuss these various kinds

of things. We have to talk about sexual pleasure. [Laughter] You know, it was like that for me, for Rita, and for a lot of women in Gamboa, in terms of the freedom that we did not have. Just the fact that, today, any of us can speak with great facility about the question of sex, this shows how much we have liberated ourselves, how the organization of women in Gamboa gave us our right to be free.

Before, you would come down to Gamboa, you would go into the houses, and normally the men would be working. Most were at sea, of course; Gamboa is a fishing community. Some work on the streets [outside the home], the women work in the home. Today, you might be likely to see ten men in the house and fifteen women working outside the home. So women learned that one way to ensure their own freedom in relationship to men was the question of financial independence. Women are more free, they are more beautiful, women are even more warrior like, and there are more lesbians. [Laughter]

Keisha-Khan: This issue of sexuality is important. Do you think that this has changed much in Gamboa?

Ana Cristina: Yes, I do.

Keisha-Khan: We see more openly lesbian women.

Ana Cristina: This thing of freedom made more women courageous in terms of self-esteem. It was so important in our process, that women could discover all aspects of themselves. Even the issue of sexual orientation, which before we did not have. We could not say that we did or did not have lesbians, because you did not see them. You know, it was something so subtle, hidden, so that people would not feel at ease. They would be afraid. The prejudice was great, and for you to have an idea, just in the neighborhood association today, I can count three people who the community knows.

Keisha-Khan: Three lesbians and one gay man.

Ana Cristina: The people respect these men and women as community leaders. So, you see, this process of organization has made a difference.

INTERLUDE

EXIT AND TERRITORY:

A World-Systems Analysis of Non-State Spaces

Andrej Grubačić

"Is it possible, somehow to convey simultaneously both the conspicuous history which holds out our attention by its continual and
dramatic changes—and that other, submerged, history, almost silent
and always discreet, virtually unsuspected either by its observers or its
participants, which is little touched by the obstinate erosion of time?"

—Fernand Braudel

"We occupy. We occupy and we talk about territories. We situate
ourselves as a node crossed by thousands of circuits. Circuits and
accelerated currents. We are in the very mouth of the monster. We
move, we decide, we talk politics. We situate ourselves and unmask
our own bodies, our own lives, our own inhabiting of this city, this
neighborhood, this social center."

—Maria Serrano and Silvia López

As the first section of this book has shown, land grabs are ways of en-
closing the "outside" to exploit potential resources. But how do we think
about the non-state spaces that resist these land grabs? Are these experiences of self-organization "regions of refuge?"[1] Is it the "borderlands?"[2]
Or are they, perhaps, best understood as the "middle ground?"[3] I would
like to suggest a possible "braudelian" approach to the study of non-state
spaces as a systemic part of the capitalist world economy.

Fernand Braudel, in his monumental study *The Perspectives of the
World*, sends us on a search for "black holes in world-economy."[4] These

---

1   Gonzalo Aguirre Beltrán, *Regions of Refuge*, Society for Applied Anthropology
    Monograph no. 12 (Washington, D.C.: Society for Applied Anthropology, 1979).
2   Jeremy Adelman and Stephen Aron, "From Borderlands to Borders: Empires,
    Nation States, and Peoples in Between in North America," *American Historical
    Review* 103, no. 3 (June 1999): 814–841.
3   Richard White, *The Middle Ground: Indians, Empires, and Republics in the Great
    Lakes Region, 1650–1815* (New York: Cambridge University Press, 1981).
4   Fernand Braudel, *The Structures of Everyday Life: The Limits of the Possible*
    (New York: Harper & Row Publishers, 1981).

are the zones (almost) outside of the commercial exchange and contact, "black holes outside of the world time." We can find these "backward islands" in the mountains or other inaccessible places where they "share primitive destinies."[5] "There can be no doubt whatsoever," writes Braudel, "of the existence of these neutral zones,"[6] but they are a fleeting presence. Historians interested in these zones had better get ready to undertake research not unlike "underwater expeditions," where they are bound to swim up to the surface disappointed with the paucity of evidence.

Braudel's "black holes" are self-organized spaces structured outside of the realm of the interstate system, formed in response to the encroachment of the capitalist world economy into external areas. As the study of long term, large-scale social change, world-systems analysis can best recover the experience of these non-state spaces from an analysis of capitalist economy and politics. Such a research project would aim at a careful historical reconstruction of intertwined processes of land grabbing, community making, and identity shaping in both antagonistic and dependent relationships with the state-building projects of capitalist modernity.

Living without a state remains not a socio-historical anomaly but the standard human condition. In all of these cases, we encounter a social structure that thwarts both incorporation in state structures and emergence of internal state-like structures. The most ambitious attempt to understand these structures was made by James Scott in *The Art of Not Being Governed*.[7] Expanding on the work of his mentor Pierre Clastres,[8] Scott makes a forceful argument for what he calls an anarchist history. This is a history of those who "got away," history of people's "struggle against the state." According to Scott,

> An open common property frontier seems particularly vital… Just as fixed, inheritable property in land facilitates permanent class formation, a common property frontier equalizes access to subsistence resources and permits the frequent fission of villages and lineages that seems central to the maintenance of egalitarianism. The further away in terms of friction of terrain such people live from state centers and

---

5   Ibid., 40.
6   Ibid., 42.
7   James C. Scott, *The Art of Not Being Governed: An Anarchist History of Upland Southeast Asia* (New Haven: Yale University Press, 2009).
8   Pierre Clastres, *Society Against the State: Essays in Political Anthropology* (New York: Zone, 1987).

the more mobile their substance routines—foraging, pastoralism, shifting cultivation—the more likely they are to maintain the egalitarian, stateless option. Enclosure of the commons and encroachment by the state are everywhere a threat to such arrangements."[9]

With Scott, we find land grabs the gravest threat to the egalitarian project of stateless spaces.

Scott identifies a pattern of state-making and state-unmaking that produced, over time, a periphery composed as much of refugees as of peoples who had never been state subjects. It is here in such zones of refuge, or "shatter zones," "where the human shreds of state formation and rivalry accumulated willy-nilly, creating regions of bewildering ethnic and linguistic complexity."

[We can find non-state spaces] wherever the expansion of states, empires, slave-trading, and wars, as well as natural disasters, have driven large numbers of people to seek refuge in out-of-the-way places: in Amazonia, in highland Latin America…in that corridor of highland Africa safe from slave-raiding, in the Balkans and the Caucasus. The diagnostic characteristics of shatter zones are their relative geographical inaccessibility and the enormous diversity of tongues and cultures.

The proposed collective project of "alternative area studies" would assume comparative research of common diagnostic characteristics, as well as a rich repertoire of state-repelling and state-preventing strategies, or *strategies of escape*.

Breaking the State

Aside from the geographical principle of evasion are the agriculture and social organizations of escape. Shifting cultivation has been the most common agropolitical strategy against state-making and state-appropriation. Particular crops were better suited to escape as well. The "escape grain" of choice in Southeast Asia was maize, which could be grown in areas that were too high, too steep, too dry, and too infertile for hill rice. The favorite escape crop of the "New World" was cassava. In general,

9   Scott, *The Art of Not Being Governed*, 278.

some crops allow people to disperse more widely and cooperate less than others. Wider dispersal encourages a social structure more resistant to incorporation, hierarchy, and subordination.

If the agriculture of escape is a strategic choice, so is social organization. In most cases, social structure is anarchically egalitarian and designed to both evade and prevent state formation. Non-state spaces served as "cracks" in the status quo, functioning as "magnets, attracting individuals, small groups, and whole communities seeking sanctuary outside the reach of colonial power."[10] Somewhat controversially, in the spirit of arguments first offered by Clastres, Scott sees illiteracy, which he chooses to call nonliteracy or orality, as a strategic choice designed to impede appropriation, since the world of writing is, for stateless people, indelibly associated with states. People without (written) history are choosing not to have history, at least as fixed history, as this maximizes their room for cultural maneuver. Finally, prophet-led, millenarian, and Holy-man revolts in non-state spaces, together with rebellious cosmologies, are another high-stakes technique for thwarting state incorporation.

Today, however, we are moving from an encounter to enclosure—a great enclosure movement that starts from a world that is all periphery and almost no center, to the all-encompassing architecture of the modern state that encloses these non-state spaces, moving from "little nodes of power," as Scott calls them, to "the modern state, in both its colonial and its independent guises, a power that has had the resources to realize a project of rule that was a mere glint in the eye of its precolonial ancestor: namely to bring non-state spaces and people to heel."[11]

In other words, after a "stateless" era, an era of "small-scale states," and an era characterized by the "expansion of state power," we are now finally entering an era in which virtually the entire globe is "administered space," and the periphery has been enclosed. The aim of enclosure is to integrate and monetize the people in the name of progress, literacy, or social integration, and essentially to make sure that all activity was "legible, taxable, assessable, and confiscatable."[12] Not only Zomia, but other non-state regions analyzed in the book, from Africa to Latin America,

---

10 Ibid., 132.
11 Ibid., 15.
12 James C. Scott, *Domination and the Arts of Resistance* (New Haven: Yale University Press, 1990).

are now increasingly "statified" through processes incorporated in what we might call the Global Land Grab.

Another possible approach to the study of non-state spaces has been elaborated recently by Raúl Zibechi in his book *Territories in Resistance*.[13] There is a new relationship between people and spaces as a consequence of neoliberal shock therapy and the crisis of the state-form. Intensified internal migration widened the rifts in which the poor have been able to create "new forms of sociability and resistance."[14] People are moving towards spaces where capital has a limited and distant presence. Hence, new settlements have new characteristics in what Zibechi calls "dispersed space." This new space comes with a new autonomous urban economy:

> Production of livelihood in the territories signals a second radical break from the industrial past. The popular sectors have erected for the first time in an urban space a set of independently controlled forms of production. Although these remain connected to and dependent on the market, vast sectors now control their forms and rhythms of production, and are no longer dominated by the rhythms of capital and its division of labor.[15]

Zibechi explicitly relates these new urban spaces and popular survival networks to recent revolutionary events in Latin America. Dispersed spaces are a home of an underground politics:

> In the daily life of divided societies, public time dominates the scene; the only audible voices are those of the economic, political, and union elites. For this reason, the Argentine insurrection was both "unexpected" and "spontaneous" to those elites, who could not hear the underground sounds, despite the fact that for more than a decade the voices had been echoing from below anticipating the approaching event.[16]

In Bolivia, anti-state movements forged in non-state urban spaces practice a directly democratic style of politics often called "back seat driving." This style requires a different way of doing politics, which is expressed

---

13   Raúl Zibechi, *Territories in Resistance* (Oakland: AK Press, 2012).
14   Ibid., 50.
15   Ibid., 203.
16   Ibid., 213.

"in the designation of representatives to go before 'them' (*ante ellos*), in the way of controlling these representatives and relating to them, and in the way of moving in a bloc which, from behind, guides and directs the steps of those that this group has placed up front."[17]

While Zibechi's magnificent book incorporates political economic perspective, it lacks an historical one. There is nothing spontaneous or surprising about the emergence of non-state spaces. He is not entirely correct when he detects a "new relationship between people and territories." This relationship is anything but new. It is specific and original, but as a predictable response to the very same logic of exit inscribed in the *longue durée* of historical capitalism. While Zibechi might be correct in his view that new territoriality "breaks with the system of representation," it is more difficult to see why this would not hold true for historical examples presented by Scott. We should be seeing a long term, large-scale historical process of state making and state breaking, of ongoing and uneven incorporation and exilic re-appropriation.

A comparative study of state-breaking—as opposed to state-making—would make an important contribution to the field of anarchist sociology, because it presents the obverse to state formation, without which state formation cannot be understood properly. Without an adequate analysis of non-state spaces in the overall context of historical capitalism, we are left with several problems. First, the state appears to be an ahistorical subject understood not as a modern "collective misconception of capitalist societies," nor as an illustration of an "exercise in domination" that could only be grasped historically,[18] but as an entity that has existed in more or less the same way since the early agrarian states. Second, enclosure becomes conceptually divorced from the ongoing process of incorporation into the capitalist world economy. Finally, a historical comparison of mechanistic and formal non-state attributes, such as geography or agriculture, may eliminate more nuanced and dynamic comprehensions of individual local histories as part of unified historical processes of capitalist development on a world scale.

The appropriate unit of analysis is the capitalist world economy, and non-state formations should be studied as a part and parcel of larger

---

17 Ibid., 26.
18 Philip Abrams, "Notes on the Difficulty of Studying the State," *Journal of Historical Sociology* 1, No.1 (1998); Philip Corrigan and Derek Sayer, *The Great Arch: English State Formation as Cultural Revolution* (Oxford: Blackwell, 1985).

historical processes within the modern capitalist world system. This consideration of world systems seeks to illuminate how non-state spaces were mutually constitutive with the processes of capitalist world economy, and how our analysis of non-state spaces might be deepened and extended as a study of non-state formations on a world scale. What I am proposing, then, is to revisit world-systems analysis for suggestions about how we might work through, at once historically and theoretically, the relations between capitalist economy, interstate system, and non-state spaces.[19]

Towards an Anarchist World System

What are the implications of non-state spaces for the politics of the world economy? The modern state is an invention of the modern capitalist system.[20] It exists only in plural. Its distinguishing feature is participation in an interstate system, which is understood as a "political superstructure of the world economy."[21] Thus, the modern state is defined by the framework of states within which it exists. This political superstructure, in turn, is defined by its role in the capitalist economy as the expression of capitalist accumulation. Economic processes are located in a zone far larger than that of any particular political authority, and are not totally responsive to political decisions of any state. The states, together with households, ethnic/national/status groups, and classes, form the "institutional vortex that is both the product and the moral life of the capitalist world economy."[22]

Systems produce anti-systemic movements as crucial social intermediaries of global systemic change generated at the political level

---

19 As Jason Moore recently pointed out, world-systems analysis has a strong historical-geographical content, where "world-historical sociology is complemented by a world-historical geography" (Jason W. Moore, "Sugar and the Expansion of the Early Modern World-Economy: Commodity Frontiers, Ecological Transformation, and Industrialization," *Review* XXIII, No.3 (2000): 310).

20 In a recent text Wallerstein modified his positions somewhat by defining capitalism as a historical system defined as "an integrated network of economic, political and cultural processes the sum of which hold the system together" (Immanuel Wallerstein, *Unthinking Social Science: The Limits of Nineteenth-Century Paradigms* (Philadelphia: Temple University Press, 1991), 230).

21 Immanuel Wallerstein, *The Politics of the World-Economy: The States, the Movements, and the Civilizations* (New York: Cambridge University Press, 1984), 51.

22 Ibid., 36.

of the world economy.[23] According to one of the classic formulations, "The concept of anti-systemic movements is one which presumes an analytic perspective about a system. The system referred to here is the world-system of historical capitalism which, we argue, has given rise to a set of anti-systemic movements... We are in search of the system-wide structural processes that have produced certain kinds of movements, and which have simultaneously formed the constraints within which such movements have operated."[24] These movements have taken two generic forms since their arrival on the historical stage in the nineteenth century: socialist movement organized around class, and nationalist movement organized around nationality. Just like individual nation-states, anti-systemic movements are tactically and strategically constrained by the interstate system: it is impossible to transform a system that operates on a world-scale by privileging the control/administration of the nation-state.[25] No socialist control of the nation-state would alter the location of a country in the international division of labor. Nationalization of the economy and control of the nation-state contributes to the statist illusion of eliminating the inequalities of the capitalist world-system on the level of the nation-state.[26] Our task requires a significant theoretical reinvention of the world-systems perspective that calls for a different analysis of both the capitalist world economy and the process of incorporation through which the capitalist system is formed, as well as the political realm of the world economy.

Important inroads have already been made by Dale Tomich and Anibal Quijano, both of whom understand the capitalist world economy as the totality of relations forming historical capitalism. World economy is a historical economy constructed through the mediation of various interrelated and interconnected processes, always historically specific, mutually constituted, and integrated as a socio-historical whole.[27] It is an articulation of diverse relations of production,

---

23 Ibid., 105.
24 Giovanni Arrighi, Terence K. Hopkins, and Immanuel Wallerstein, *Antisystemic Movements* (New York: Verso, 1989), 1.
25 Wallerstein, *Unthinking Social Science.*
26 Ramón Grosfoguel, "From Cepalismo to Neoliberalism: A World-System Approach to Conceptual Shifts in Latin America," *Review* 19, no. 2 (1996): 131–154.
27 Derek Sayer, *The Violence of Abstraction. The Analytical Foundations of Historical Materialism* (Oxford: Basil Blackwell, 1987).

exchange and power; a "unified, structured, contradictorily evolving totality;"[28] a spatio-temporal whole defined by the interrelated nature of its processes. More than a sum of economic processes, world economy is a unified network of political power, social domination, and economic activity—a socio-historical whole that presupposes the unity of global and local, and recognizes the complex relations within as both necessary and contingent. It is "necessary because of the systemic unity imposed by the interdependence of the forms of production, exchange, and political power; and contingent because the particular character of those forms is always the product of specific, complex, uneven historical processes within the relational network."[29] Within this framework, capital is a social relation based on the commodification of the labor force, while the wage relation forms heterogeneous relations between capital and all other forms of labor. Historical capitalism is a system that links all forms of control of labor with capital as its central axis: it is world capitalism, "a new pattern of global control of labor, its resources, and products."[30]

Modernity, as Anibal Quijano maintains, is about "processes that were initiated with the emergence of America, of a new global power (the first world system), and of the integration of all the peoples of the globe in that process."[31]

> It is a global process, through which each sphere of social existence—all historically known forms of control of respective social relations—are articulated, configuring in each area only one structure with systematic relations between each component and, by the same means, its whole... In the control of labor and its resources and products, it is the capitalist enterprise; in the control of sex and its resources and products, the bourgeois family; in the control of authority and its resources and products, the nation-state; in the control of intersubjectivity, Eurocentrism... Modernity involves totality of global population and all the history of the last five hundred

---

28 Dale Tomich, *Through the Prism of Slavery: Labor, Capital, and World Economy* (Lanham, MD: Rowman and Littlefield, 2004), 29.
29 Ibid., 55.
30 Anibal Quijano, "Coloniality of Power: Eurocentrism and Latin America," in *Neplanta: Views From the South*, ed. Walter Mignolo (Durham: Duke University Press, 2000).
31 Ibid., 547.

years, all the worlds or former worlds articulated in the global model
of power, each differentiated or differentiable segment constituted
together with (as a part of) the historical redefinition or reconstitution of each segment for its incorporation to the new and common
model of global power.[32]

The nation state is a modern form articulating other historic power
relations—ie, the control over the distribution of collective authority.
Relationships that exist within capitalist modernity are not unilinear
or unidirectional: "the integration of heterogeneous, discontinuous and
conflictive elements in a common structure, in a determined field of relations, implies and indeed requires that those relations be comprised of
reciprocal, multiple and heterogeneous elements."[33] Thus, the world of
historical capitalism is a negotiated reality of a historically and structur-
ally heterogeneous whole where one or more components have a primacy, but not as determinants or bases for determinations.[34]

If the capitalist world economy is conceived, as Tomich and Quijano
suggest, as a complex and structured totality permeated by many contradictions, the role of comparative historical sociology is to theoretically
reconstruct a historical development of specific local experiences that are
produced by, and constitutive of, the overall unit of analysis. We need to
construct and reconstruct fundamental categories of analysis from historically specific constitutive elements. This method allows us to connect
local processes and histories to diverse processes of politics and economy.

Exilic Space

"Non-state space" is not the best term to capture the complexity of the
historical experience of such sites. I think it provides more clarity to
see them as instances and territories of exit, examples of what might be
termed *exilic spaces*.[35]

---

32 Ibid., 545–46.
33 Quijano, "Coloniality of Power," 7.
34 Tomich, *Through the Prism of Slavery*.
35 Exit is a concept adopted from the work of Albert Hirschman (*Exit, Voice, and
    Loyalty: Responses to Decline in Firms, Organizations, and States* (Cambridge:
    Harvard University Press, 1970). Hirschman's famous categorizations of eco-
    nomic responses to consumer dissatisfaction with a company's product include:
    loyalty (decision made despite dissatisfaction), exit (defection to an alternative),

Exilic space, a term borrowed from Obika Gray's insightful work on urban poverty and autonomy in Jamaica, seems to me the best way to describe particular spatial organization of exit.[36] Using exilic space as a broader concept gives us the possibility of connecting such disparate experiences as the Cossack territory with urban slums in postcolonial Jamaica. As I have already noted, an important limitation of Scott's approach is that he does not explicitly relate his non-state spaces to historical processes of world capitalism. Processes of exit in capitalist world economy are processes of what I suggest we call *exilic self-activity*. Spaces of exilic self-activity represent not only an escape from the state, but exit from the totality of hierarchical relations that form the capitalist world economy, of which the state is only a part. What distinguishes exilic self-activity from other instances of exit is that it assumes an alternative construction as well as a characteristic spatial organization.

Exilic self-activity takes two principal forms: territorial exit and structural (logical) exit.[37] These latter spaces are at the same time moral/symbolic and material/physical. In contrast, Cossacks, Zomians, Maroons, and the Mexican Zapatistas are all examples of a *territorialization of exit* and instances of territorially situated self-activity. In some ways, they bear structural resemblance to intentional utopian communities. Their distinctive quality, however, is that they do not require an *a priori* utopian vision of a "better" society. Exilic spaces are not always islands of desirable politics. They might imply a considerable degree of egalitarian economic and political practices, but this is not their defining characteristic.

Political activists looking for uncomplicated examples of "usable history" should look elsewhere. Exilic spaces are important, and often frustrated and incomplete, creation. They are marked by contradictory elements, including complicit involvement with state spaces or hierarchical

---

and voice (anger, demands, and open dissatisfaction). According to Hirschman, to embrace exit means deciding on an alternative strategy of resisting the opponent who could probably win any open confrontation.

36   Tomich, *Through the Prism of Slavery*.
37   Exilic social space is both psychological and physical, a "relatively sequestered" and multi-class site of contestation that serves as refuge for marginalized and morally excluded people in the Jamaican ghetto, and all those who "wish to evade the state" (Obika Gray, *Demeaned but Empowered: The Social Power of Urban Poor in Jamaica* (Kingston: University of West Indies Press, 2004), 93–119). These are the places where "the poor typically retreated…as both a social site for dissidence and venue for the repair of cultural injuries," performing the cultural labor of "self-making and self-recovery." (Ibid., 94).

processes of the world economy. We need to avoid the functionalist Scylla of seeing these spaces as irrelevant, and the romantic Charybdis of seeing them as utopian islands of prefiguration. There is a complicated relationship where power is not a zero-sum game but a shifting dialectics of compulsion and resistance between systemic pressures and exilic responses. There is a dialectical relationship of being that is demeaned within the predatory context of a capitalist world economy and empowered by the negotiated refusal and partially autonomous realities of the escape.[38] Unlike utopian communities, exilic spaces are products of a complex encounter between peoples of many ethnicities and political tastes escaping the hierarchical relationships of capital and the state. However, self-activity does not automatically imply an egalitarian form any more than the simple fact of decentralization does. Such complexity makes them even more interesting for study.

Future exiles make a decided choice to escape the harsh, hierarchical reality of emerging states and capital, leaving them for uninhabited territories (or structural cracks within the everyday life of modern world economy). It is in these new exilic spaces, through the complicated and fascinating encounter of diverse practices and identities, that they create new capital-refusing and state-repellant structures in order to attempt an autonomous existence within the larger context of a capitalist world economy. But this autonomy should not be exaggerated. Exilic spaces are autonomous, but only to a certain degree. World capitalism does not allow a complete outside. As such, exilic spaces are inhabited by an interesting paradox: they are, at the same time, inside and outside of the system; they are extra-state, but intra-systemic.[39] While they might be outside of the immediate state-space, all forms of exilic self-activity are still within the larger context of the hierarchical processes of the capitalist world economy, and, as our historical examples demonstrate, in parasitic relation to it.

---

38 Ibid., 176.

39 This is probably what Mignolo and Dussel have in mind when they talk about "exteriority:" it is not a pure outside, it manifests itself in degrees, but an outside constituted as excluded by hegemonic processes of the world system. My notion of exit complicates this notion, as this is "exteriority by design," to paraphrase Scott, where people constitute themselves as "others," in the exteriority of the system (Enrique Dussel, *Filosofía de Liberación* (México: Edicol, 1977)). This is an outside that is created against the inside (Walter Mignolo, *Local Histories/Global Designs: Essays on the Coloniality of Power, Subaltern Knowledges and Border Thinking* (Princeton: Princeton University Press, 2000)).

As Braudel reminds us, capital is never able to commodify everything—there is always an active, dialectical process of contestation/negotiation.[40] Only a history that is sensitive to the interrelation and unity of diverse processes can help us understand the paradoxical location and production of exilic spaces in our capitalist world economy. It seems to me that we can hope to understand this exilic reality only if we develop a heuristic strategy at two distinct levels: first, we need to understand and conceptualize exilic spaces as specific configurations in relation to the immediate state-spaces; second, we need to address their simultaneous embeddedness in spatiotemporal frameworks of world economy as a whole. Their consequences and possible political significances are only clear when contextualized in relation to the structural transformations of the world economy.

Indeed, they comprise a diverse pattern of exilic self-activity formed within distinct historical temporalities, and unified through multiple dimensions of world economy. Imagine a complex movement of global pressures and local responses conditioned by a variety of contexts in a contested ambience of world-systemic conflicts and contingent local outcomes. Systemic regularities produce distinctive local spaces within a unifying global framework of "world time." Seen in this way, exilic self-activity is an immanent part of the making and the remaking of the capitalist world economy and political power. Exilic spaces are always in process; they are always being made and remade, composed and decomposed. But they never go away. There is nothing spontaneous or surprising about the emergence of the Zapatistas, for instance, who are an example of what I would call *exilic re-appropriation*.

---

40 Without a wish to venture too far and too deep into many exciting theories of place, which surfaced recently with surprising vigor in geography and feminist political economy, I would only suggest that, perhaps, in a dialogue with Gibson-Graham (J.K. Gibson-Graham, *The End of Capitalism (As we Knew it): A Feminist Critique of Political Economy* (Minneapolis: University of Minnesota Press, 2006)) and other modern theorists of place, we should talk about places instead of spaces, as places are "the excluded dimension of modernity's concern with space, universality, movement, and the like" (Arturo Escobar, *Territories of Difference. Places, Movements, Life, Redes* (Durham: Duke University Press, 2008)). Place, in this perspective, implies "emplacement," or a politics of the production of subjects and places, a politics of becoming in a place (Gibson-Graham, *The End of Capitalism*). Places are never fully capitalist, but are inhabited with economic and other differences, with a potential of becoming something other, a possible site of an alternative construction.

Hidden Transcripts and Infrapolitics

In order to understand territorialization of exit from a world-historical perspective, I suggest that we should read Wallerstein and Scott together, and against each other, in a way that corrects their respective weaknesses. One possible step towards this theoretical-historical synthesis is to apply twin notions of "hidden transcript" and "infrapolitics" to our (re) examination of the politics of the world economy.

Hidden transcripts are a set of practices developed by the weak:

> Every subordinate group creates, out of its ordeal, a "hidden transcript" that represents a critique of power spoken behind the backs of the dominant. The powerful, for their part, also develop a hidden transcript representing the practices and claims of their rule that cannot be openly avowed. The comparison between the hidden transcript of the weak with the hidden transcript of the powerful, and of both hidden transcripts to the public transcript of power relations offers a substantially new way of understanding resistance to domination.[41]

Hidden transcripts are, in rare moments, spoken publicly and directly in the teeth of power: "hidden transcript was perhaps improvised on public stage but had been rehearsed at length in the hidden discourse of popular practice and culture."[42] However, for the most part, we must look for the hidden transcript from afar, in the "social sites where this resistance can germinate."[43]

Infra-politics is a related concept that refers to "an unobtrusive realm of political struggle,"[44] which includes a "wide variety of low-profile forms of resistance that dare not speak in their own name."[45] Infra-politics are essentially a strategic form of resistance that subjects must assume under

---

41 James C. Scott, *Domination and the Arts of Resistance* (New Haven: Yale University Press, 1990), xii. The bulk of my discussion here is drawn from Scott's *Domination and the Arts of Resistance*.

42 This is, of course, another way of thinking about Hirschman's voice: "what is refused in public transcript finds its full-throated expression backstage" (Scott, *Domination and the Arts of Resistance*, 38, 75.

43 Ibid., xii.

44 Ibid., 183.

45 Ibid., 38.

conditions of great peril.[46] In other words, infra-politics provide a "structural underpinning for more visible political action, not as a substitute, but as its condition."[47]

What is the hidden transcript of our capitalist world economy? What happens if we try to "emplace" politics, contextualize it in actual geographic places located in the exteriority of the system? I suggest we refer to the production of such forms of place-based politics within cracks of global capitalist system as *infra-politics of the capitalist world-economy.* That is to say that infra-politics describes the very process of breaking from systemic processes of state and capital; (self-)organization of a separate, relatively autonomous, and partially incorporated geographic space.

We can see these territories of exit as elaborations of an offstage hidden transcript, an alternative reality produced against the official public transcript of power relations within the capitalist world economy. An infra-political analysis of place-based politics urges us to be attentive to what might lie beneath the surface, or more accurately, in the interstices of the world economy. The entirety of the political should not be reduced to complete hegemonic compliance (loyalty) and anti-systemic uprisings (voice). Infra-politics of exilic spaces, as an interstitial process of production of resisting and repelling structures, exists in the vast territory (Critchley's "interstitial distance") in between the two opposites. *Pace* Scott, the process of neoliberal globalization made these spaces and regions not less relevant, but more explicitly political. They are not merely a "state effect," but, more accurately, a "system effect," system-evading spaces constitutively inseparable from the system, in a sense that they represent a "dark twin" of an "integrated network of economic, political and cultural processes the sum of which hold the system together."

Politics of place-based exit are, as already noted, usually not regarded as politically relevant. Exilic territories are, after all, spaces of refuge for bandits, criminals, outcasts, and "villains of all nations," where "the worst of the worst" hide from the law. Therefore, much of the historical experience of territorial exilic spaces had been lost. We do not know much about the Cossack frontier, and even less about pirate ships. Recovering this "waste of experience" requires what Sousa Santos calls the "sociology of absences and emergences." It is a sociological journey that takes us in to swamps, forests, and mountains. One of the goals of such

---

46 Ibid., 199.
47 Ibid., 58.

adventurous sociology would certainly be to understand how, and under what kind of conditions, "muted" politics developed within exilic spaces, become vocal, anti-systemic protests against the dominant transcript of capitalist modernity.

The modern day Zapatistas are an excellent illustration of a moment when the hidden transcript of exilic politics shoulders its way onto the public stage of capitalist world economy. It seems to me that this introduction of the anarchist sociology of state-breaking and self-organization would help avoid some of the rigid functionalism put forward by world-systems theorists, and, at the same time, give historical and political-economic framework and structure to recent anarchist (anti-state) interventions in anthropology. The Zapatistas are a part of a continuum of historical experience where the partial and reversible nature of incorporation into the capitalist world-system created possibilities for appropriation, and later, for exilic re-appropriation of insurgent territories. This logic of inquiry, of course, should apply to both forms of exilic self-activity: to territorial and to structural exit.

Conclusion: A Place of Exile

The exiled alternative is inscribed in geography. It sits in places. It is critical for the development of a more complete understanding of the politics of world economy to point out hidden transcript, exemplified by emplaced processes of exilic self-activity in *la longue durée*. The infra-political view from "in between," from a vantage point of self-constituted cracks in world-systemic geography of the Global Land Grab reveals the complicated nature of economic expansion and offers a possibility for a more nuanced understanding of the processes of the world economy. In the process of incorporation, systemic pressures produce specific forms of place-based exilic refusals that are, at the same time, simultaneously constitutive of the global system. Yet systemic processes do not simply produce or "give rise to" anti-systemic politics.[48] Rather, in a complex multi-play of structure and contingency, a relation might appear contingent on one analytical level and organized by structural forces on another.[49]

It is not just the noise of the dominant system and the voice of the resisting movements that produce dissonant notes in the world system;

---

48 Arrighi, Hopkins, and Wallerstein, *Antisystemic Movements*, 1.
49 Tomich, *Through the Prism of Slavery*, 53.

the struggle is also expressed in silences, in refusals—perhaps less vocal, but not less confrontational. Such silence and refusals exist in "far away" spaces, in exilic spaces and exilic territories. These are refusals that used to travel on ships, and live in jungles, steppes, and mountains; refusals that now live in Zapatista and Aymara regions, as well as in urban exilic spaces of neighborhoods, *asientos*, slums, Roma settlements, and, why not, occupied town squares.[50]

An infra-politics of self-organized geographic sites "where resistance can germinate" is a "structural underpinning for more visible political action," not its substitute, but its condition. Infra-political dimensions of the politics of world economy, understood as state-breaking and territorial self-organization—this fascinating "exercise in de-legitimization" and state *de*formation—rests on a relational and constitutive tension between place-based exilic energy and the world economic processes it is directed against (the ongoing expansion of capitalism, interstate system, and accumulation by dispossession). It is in this partial and reversible triumph of capitalist expansion, and in the accompanying stubborn refusal—sometimes uttered in silence and at high altitude—that one should find reasons for optimism even, or especially, today.

---

50 It is interesting to note Quijano's proposal for a "socialization of power" in the context of our discussion (Quijano, "Coloniality of Power"). Quijano, following Mariategui, proposes "socialization of power," an extension of social equality and democracy to all spaces of social existence. What is interesting to our purpose is that Quijano explicitly links the utopian promise with exilic territories like Andean indigenous communities and the new urban exilic social places where reciprocity and solidarity are the main forms of social interaction. He introduces the notions of non-state public and social-private to oppose capitalist/state-socialist notions of private and public.

PART TWO

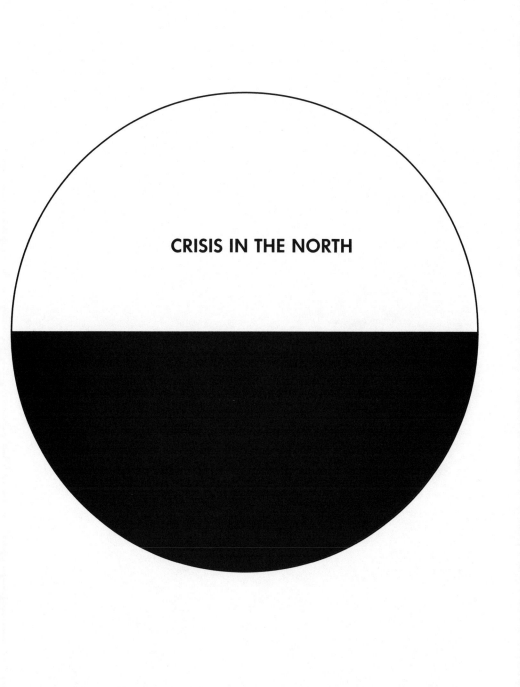

CRISIS IN THE NORTH

TAKING BACK THE COMMONS:

An Introduction

Alexander Reid Ross

Delinking from Systemic Racism

Western Europe has declared itself the final outpost of civilization since it began to write its own histories. This notion of Imperial dominion arose through the oppression of European peasants at the hands of the nobility and clergy, who enclosed commonly held land holdings under the auspices of private accumulation. The Church, Crown, and Bourse attempted to suppress and enclose collective organizations, which fought back in recursive political and spiritual struggles for the commons. By the nineteenth century, European philosophers had generally accepted the notion that the European individual, in its spiritual and political form, manifested the ultimate goals of Enlightened rule and, by extension, humanity. For example, the respected nineteenth century philosopher G.W. Hegel's *Lectures on World History* moves swiftly from East Asia to Europe in an attempted timeline of private accumulation, settling on Germany as the hierarch of individual refinement. After the Holocaust, however, philosophers of the twentieth century such as Hannah Arendt, Angela Y. Davis, Franz Fanon, Herbert Marcuse, Anibal Quijano, and others determined to radically rethink the entire notion of the individual.

Liberation and decolonization became the watchwords of Third World struggles and of the Civil Rights Movement in the US. This was not liberation from above—a sort of recolonization of Western European thought—but liberation as a careful and cautious accounting of the history of oppression and colonialism, along with the freeing of bodies, minds, and collectivities to explore the fullest capabilities of life. On this level, movements from the Kenyan "Mau Mau Uprising," more accurately referred to as the Manjeneti, to the subaltern struggles of what Katsiaficas calls "Asia's Unknown Uprisings," as well as the Liberation Theology movement of Latin America sought not only to recast the role of the individual along the lines of Marx and Engels's scientific socialism, but more indigenous, localized traditions of resistance as well.

Liberation, as a revolutionary instrument in the hands of the oppressed, actualized the redistribution of land and the forgiveness of debts.

In the US, liberation struggles hit an incendiary climax in the late 1960s–early 1970s. However, the sensational race riots that burned through most major cities have been used by liberals and conservatives alike to obscure the legacy of grassroots, radical programs that proliferated throughout the cities of the US to bring food, education, and healthcare to poor people of color. To subvert such popular representation and urban uprising, major military, economic, and political strategists of the US constructed a plan called "Spatial Deconcentration." Implemented from the late 1970s on, Spatial Deconcentration relied heavily on a planning apparatus called the Urban Institute, with its deep military connections, including former Deputy Secretary of Defense Cyrus Vance and former Secretary of Defense Robert MacNamara as trustees. The Urban Institute worked with the Urban League and other reformist civil rights groups to deploy "Mobility Programs" that shifted people of color living in inner-city Section 8 housing or other subsidized housing projects to the outer-suburbs.

The Mobility Programs coincided with Urban Renewal programs at the onset of neoliberalism, a system that further undermined manufacturing jobs in the US along with subsistence farming in the Global South. As joblessness increased, the inauguration of the drug war led to the rapid rise of the prison-industrial complex as former manufacturing hubs began to empty out. This outcome was precisely the vision of Anthony Downs, who took part in the Urban Institute's program (along with other military and political elites) and whose influential "triage" report set forth a plan by which US agencies might coordinate a program to "depopulate" urban centers. In 1980, economic justice activist Yolanda Ward revealed the scheme in detail in a short speech at a conference of economic justice advocates shortly before she was murdered, execution style, by two well-dressed white men on a Washington, DC sidewalk.[1]

In her speech, Ward explained Downs's strategy: "Community Development funds should be withheld from inner-city neighborhoods so as to allow 'a long-run strategy of emptying-out the most deteriorated areas.' A city's basic strategy, he wrote, 'would be to accelerate their abandonment…' The land having been 'banked,' it could be redeveloped

---

1   Ward was singled out among a group of friends one night in Washington, DC, ordered to lie face down on the sidewalk, and shot in the back of the head.

for the gentry. He argued that instead of being given increased services, minority neighborhoods should be infused with major demolition projects."[2] Today, with the depopulation of the major cities in the Midwest, and the wholesale removal of people of color, not only from neighborhoods of color, but from the housing market entirely, we bear witness to the apotheosis of Spatial Deconcentration. This part of *Grabbing Back* expresses the spirit of liberation in community between rural and urban spaces whose struggles are intertwined in the bloody triad identified by Walter Mignolo as Capitalism-Modernism-Racism.

The Spoils of Class War

John D. Rockefeller once said, "The way to make money is to buy when blood is running in the streets." The story of how he entered the oil business reflects this murderous impulse. In 1865, Samuel Van Syckel constructed the first oil pipeline, dominating a transportation industry that until that point had been composed of teamster carts moving oil on horse-drawn carriages. In response, the teamsters cut lines, burnt oil, and tried to drive prices out of reach. At this point, when the pressure was on, Rockefeller entered the oil business not through production, but refining and infrastructure. Rockefeller quickly bought up every stage of the production process to drive his own expenditures down and force others' prices up. Though he approached his competitors with the language of cooperation, they knew that if they did not sell out, they would be taken over. By 1877, Rockefeller owned 90 percent of the oil refineries and pipelines in the US—an empire attained through threats, sabotage, and blackmail. In one infamous example, a mechanic at an independent refinery in Buffalo, New York, confessed to sabotaging a still under the instruction of Standard Oil's subsidiary, Vacuum Oil, Co.[3] In coming decades, Standard Oil's empire would intervene often in Latin American affairs, sponsoring Paraguay in a war with Bolivia (and Royal Dutch Shell) over the Gran Chaco region. Fought amidst the dry alluvial plains and sub-tropical lowlands of Chaco, La Guerra de la Sad (the War of Thirst) would become the most deadly South American war of the twentieth century.

---

2   Http://www.abcnorio.org/about/history/spatial_d.html.
3   Matthew Josephson, *The Robber Barons: The Great American Capitalists* (New York: Harcourt, Brace and Company, 1934), found online at http://www.yamaguchy.com/library/josephson/josephson_index.html.

At the same time, JP Morgan, James Fink, and Jay Gould consolidated power over the railroads quickly stretching across the US. As the workers unionized, the robber barons fought back. In 1886, the Texas and Pacific Railway fired a Knights of Labor leader, sparking a strike that snarled traffic on the railroads. Strikers set out to sabotage the works, with dozens of workers mobbing a roadhouse and dismantling twelve locomotives. A pitched battle between workers and police saw seven strikers killed in East St. Louis, and the subsequent arson of a freight depot. The next month, May 1886, a general strike froze production in protest against the slaughter of workers in St. Louis while demanding an eight-hour workday. At a related meeting in Chicago's Haymarket Square, a bomb was thrown, leading to a police riot and media frenzy, costing, in the end, the judicial assassination of seven Anarchist leaders. The martyrdom of the Haymarket Anarchists sparked a greater movement for solidarity and the eight-hour workday, which was won soon thereafter.

Not since that era has such a colossal expansion of extractive industry been seen in the US as we are seeing today. The biggest banks have cut back on lending, bringing them an excess of deposits, which they can invest into securities for collateral on loans. The banks borrow money based on the excess deposits invested in securities, and use that leverage to buy up assets like stocks and companies on the repo market.[4] Morgan Stanley admits to being engaged "in the production, storage, transportation, marketing and trading of several commodities, including metals (base and precious), agricultural products, crude oil, oil products, natural gas, electric power, emission credits, coal, freight, liquefied natural gas and related products and indices."[5] Goldman Sachs declares its heavy investment in "the production, storage, transportation, marketing and trading of numerous commodities, including crude oil, oil products, natural gas, electric power, agricultural products, metals (base and precious), minerals (including uranium), emission credits, coal, freight, liquefied natural gas and related products and indices."[6] It would appear that the banks are leading a new scramble for infrastructure points in the US

---

4   Ellen Brown, "The Leveraged Buyout of America," *CounterPunch*, August 27, 2013 http://www.counterpunch.org/2013/08/27/the-leveraged-buyout-of-america/.

5   MorganStanley.com, Form 10-K, December 21, 2012, http://www.morganstanley .com/about/ir/shareholder/10k2012/10k2012.pdf.

6   GoldmanSachs.com, Form 10-K, December 31, 2012, http://www.goldman sachs.com/investor-relations/financials/current/10k/2012-10-K.pdf.

along with the rest of the world. Why? Perhaps because the new bank-held properties—including electric power production, oil refining, and even uranium mining—comprise highly sensitive choke points in the industrial supply line, and can be very handy in terms of financial specu-lation. In 2008, confidential data leaked by Bernie Sanders showed that major banks, along with the Koch Brothers, drove the price of oil up by speculating in just this fashion: not only investing in numerous private exchanges, but physically buying up tremendous quantities of oil, and leaving it on tankers and large containers. With ownership of airports, tollbooths, etc., banks and holding companies can play merchant elite, funneling rent and profits from every industry into their coffers.

Echoing Rockefeller's monopoly pipelines, the Koch Brothers, in cahoots with the banks TD Economics and CIBC, are making a play on the TransCanada's Keystone XL Pipeline to increase their own power-ful grip on the world's oil supply. Unfortunately, the US government is complicit. Both of the state-hired private contractors commissioned to perform the environmental-impact analysis on the Keystone XL have been economic partners with TransCanada for some years. Keystone XL cuts a swath of land grabs through the US on its 1,700 mile route from the tar sands in Alberta to Houston, but it is backed by the courts in cases raised by companies like Texas Rice Land and citizens like Julia Trigg Crawford. Meanwhile, oil and gas production is breaking records by expanding operations in tar sands and shale areas throughout the US and Canada.

The US's rail lines have taken on more than two-hundred thousand oil trains per year, to meet the infrastructure requirements for the boom in oil production—an increase twenty-times over from 2008. In 2012, Warren Buffett's coal- and oil-hauling Burlington Northern Santa Fe Railroad made $1 billion. More natural gas is being extracted from the US today than ever before in history, because the EPA has censored proof that fracking pollutes clean water systems, according to leaked re-ports. It is clear that the US is in the midst of a sweeping push towards extractive industries and private control over city planning at whatever the social cost, and the profits will go to the banks and holding com-panies, not to the people, as racialized systems of environmental and economic injustice persist in keeping the poor unsafe and hungry while the rich feast on the spoils.

Crisis in the North

Noam Chomsky sparks the discussion by calling for an analysis of the Global Land Grab amongst activists in the North Atlantic, drawing parallels and creating bonds of solidarity through an international Poor Peoples Movement. Grace Lee Boggs and friends enter into this terrain of emancipation with a historical consideration of the brilliant work of poor peoples' organizing to bring life back to the decaying city of Detroit.

Next comes Ahjamu Umi's personal accounts of gang bangers, bankers, and anti-austerity protesters in Africa, making a connection between resource extraction abroad and the housing market crash domestically. Umi shows that the racist system of global finance relies not on the crafty interventions of consciously racist planners, but on the implications of everyday institutionalization of racism that pervades society and economics within as well as outside the banking system. The system relies on individual inaction to keep the systemic racism in place; only individual empowerment and community action can intervene to halt the oppression.

Max Rameau follows Umi's intricate analysis with a discussion about strategy and tactics of land-based movements that have emerged from nearly a decade of dogged organizing through the grassroots organization, Take Back the Land. Rameau's discourse opens the space for more discussion on land reform and the involvement of US activists in reimagining social relations not only along the lines of economic conditions, but also in connection to ecology. Throughout the history of the US, the accumulation of capital has been underscored by the oppression of labor and the often-brutal extraction of raw materials.

As Cathy Kunkel, Andrew Munn, and Jenn Osha show in their article about mountaintop removal and land reform in Appalachia, the liberation of the latter has always been connected to the circumstances surrounding the former. Next, Miles Howe reports from the front lines of the volatile Indigenous resistance against the energy company South West Natural and the government of New Brunswick. scott crow follows Howe's report with more stirring examples of solidarity networks and poor peoples' organizing—this time against disaster capitalism in the wake of Hurricane Katrina.

Andrew Herod comes next with an insightful and interesting essay on the crucial resistance of dockers and longshoreman to unfettered capitalism, followed by an account of the upwelling of resistance to fossil fuel infrastructure and tar sands megaloads from the Port of Portland, Oregon to Nez Perce lands in Idaho. Recalling Zibechi's formulation discussed in Grubačić's introduction, Alex Barnard closes out the section on emancipation with an article about his experiences forming "dispersed spaces" in Occupy-Cal and the community farming projects that followed. Finally, an interview conducted by myself with Michael Hardt rounds out the chapter with a discussion on altermodern thinking and solidarity between ecological and workers' struggles.

RECONSTRUCTING THE POOR PEOPLES MOVEMENT

Noam Chomsky[1]

The New "Great Game"

The Global Land Grab refers generally to the purchase of lands in the Global South for agricultural production for rich countries. It is part of a more general effort to take over the resources of the weaker and poorer societies and use them for the benefit of systems of power and domination. For people who have followed Occupy Wall Street, the Global Land Grab is not really on the radar of their immediate concerns, but it can and should be.

In Colombia, where I have repeatedly visited the regions that are under threat, there is a constant effort to take away the lands and opportunities of peasants, indigenous populations, and Afro-Colombians for international mining corporations and agribusiness, etc. That means eliminating sustainable agriculture and biodiversity, and using the land for industry run by big corporations and ranchers. Consider also what is happening in Ecuador, where the indigenous populations are opposing the exploitation of resources. Something similar is happening in Bolivia, and everywhere there are activist indigenous populations—India, Australia, everywhere. What is happening in Latin America is no different from Saudi Arabia, among other states, buying up land in Africa.

The process goes back centuries to the enclosures of England, for example: the privatization of the commons—that is, land that is used and cared for by everyone—for mineral, agriculture, or energy resources. This turn towards raw material production is not an effective way to develop economically, because it leads to dependency. Beyond that, the extraction of fossil fuels is going to destroy the possibility of decent existence by the lives of our grandchildren, if even that far off. At this point in history, human action may destroy the prospects for the human species to survive in any decent fashion, along with plenty of other species as well.

If you look around the world, the people who believe in doing something about the crisis are the indigenous nations: the First Nations in

---

1   This piece was edited together from two interviews that took place by telephone on March 6, 2012 and March 15, 2013.

Canada, tribal societies, indigenous societies in South America. They are pressing hard for measures to reduce the crisis, mitigate it, or repel it. On the other hand, even the mild, leftist governments in Ecuador and Bolivia want to develop the resources. So a crucial conflict exists between the developmentalist programs of governments that are based in part on the indigenous populations on the one hand, and the interests of indigenous populations in preserving both their own lifestyles and preventing their destruction on the other. That kind of conflict ought to be of concern to activists in the US, because it is very similar to local headline-grabbing struggles, like the effort to stop the Keystone XL Pipeline. Shall we exploit fossil fuels—not for jobs of course, but for profit of major corporations, and to maintain a lifestyle built on wasteful use of fossil fuels? Shall we move forward, seriously endangering our survival down the road?

Hugo Chavez gave a speech in the General Assembly in 2005, which went unreported for a long time. He said, "For the year 2020 the daily demand for oil will be 120 million barrels. Such demand, even without counting future increments—would consume in twenty years what humanity has used up to now. This means that carbon dioxide will inevitably be increased, thus warming our planet even more... Now more than ever—we were saying—we need to retake ideas that were left on the road such as the proposal approved at this Assembly in 1974 regarding a New Economic International Order."[2] Media in the US did not pay attention to that position, whereas what has happened in Latin America over the last ten years is quite astonishing. Latin America has emerged from Western, mainly US, domination for the first time.

The US has almost no military bases left in South America. To mention another example, in 2013 the Open Society Foundation published a study of what they called "Globalizing Terror" about the US campaign of globalizing its torture apparatus of external rendition.[3] Over fifty

---

2   Missing from the quotation above: "...It is unpractical and unethical to sacrifice the human race by appealing in an insane manner the validity of a socioeconomic model that has a galloping destructive capacity. It would be suicidal to spread it and impose it as an infallible remedy for the evils which are caused precisely by them." The full text is available online, see President Hugo Chavez, "President Chavez's Speech to the United Nations," September 16, 2005, found at Venezuelanalysis.com/analysis/1365.

3   Amrit Singh, *Globalizing Torture: CIA Secret Detention and Extraordinary Rendition* (New York: Open Society Justice Initiative, February 2013), found at http://www.opensocietyfoundations.org/reports/globalizing-torture-cia-secret -detention-and-extraordinary-rendition.

countries participated—most of Europe and the Middle East, as well as most of the rest of the world—the one region that is notable by its absence is Latin America. Not a single Latin American country was willing to participate in Washington's globalizing torture campaign. That is pretty astonishing. Not many years ago, Latin America was in the pocket of the United States, and during that period it was also one of the world's centers of torture. Now those countries are refusing to participate in it. Those are big changes.

Strategies and Tactics in the Twenty-First Century

The Occupy movement has been comprised primarily of urban movements, so the questions of land grabs, mining in Colombia, or taking agricultural lands in Africa have remained on the periphery. As for what the Occupy movements will become, it is really early to say. There is a big transition right now. The occupy tactic has probably run its course. It was fairly successful, but through a combination of state repression and exhaustion of the tactic, it has come to the point where it's going to have to move on, and the question is where? You could ask the same question about the *indignados* of Spain. They could be part of a large-scale, global, popular movement. They all have potential, but realizing it in the face of many barriers, including state repression is a hard, long task.

If we look at the Spanish Revolution in 1936, we see some important potentialities. First of all the 1936 revolution was both urban and rural. So there was collectivization of land in the peasant areas of Aragon and others, and there was also a collectivization of industry in Barcelona where there was heavy industry. They were integrated within a functioning society with interchanges in agricultural production and industrial production. The Spanish Revolution did not have a long enough period of time to develop. It was wiped out by international force in about a year by a combination of fascists, communists, and world democracies—they disagreed on a lot more, but they agreed on crushing the revolution. Within that year, however, the revolution was certainly making moves toward collectivization—holding moves in that period of war. The most difficult question becomes, "How can that model be of use to us today?"

A kind of horizontalist approach seems to me very healthy, but not beyond the limits of cooperation. The union movement in the US provides a special example. The US has a very violent labor history, and if you go back to the early union movement, which was quite significant, organizers were highly committed to worker solidarity (obviously true of the IWW, but also with the Knights of Labor and other movements). When the CIO was organized in the 1930s, it attempted to break down the craft-based unions of the AFL and to unite the various components of the union within the industrial system. The unions also reached out elsewhere; they had become part of a general social policy. Every union is called an international, because they are supposed to be built on international solidarity. Of course, that's far from the reality.

The unions in the US failed to maintain the general social commitment that was true of, for example, the Canadian unions. This is why Canada has a national health system while the US does not. The same unions (UAW on both sides of the border) picked different approaches during the 1950s. The Canadian unions struggled for health benefits for everyone; the American unions struggled for health benefits for themselves. So the UAW in the US got a pretty good health benefit system for themselves, but didn't extend it to others. It was a compact between the unions and management, and when management decided they didn't like it anymore, they discarded it using the government as their instrument. In Canada on the other hand, the national health care system was established. It has been chipped away at, but it has to be chipped away at in less direct ways.

The Promised Land

There is not only a need, there's a desperate need for a more robust working-class movement in the US. In 2013, a study came out from the OECD, the organization of the rich societies, that measures the thirty-one richest societies by the usual measures of social justice. The US ranked twenty-seventh out of thirty-one, right next to Mexico.[4] Remember, this is the richest, most powerful country in history with enormous advantages shared by no one. The key reason for the recent impoverishment of the US is that the labor movement has taken such a battering over the years that it can barely function.

---

4   See "Strong Variations in Social Justice within the OECD: Bertelsmann Stiftung publishes Social Justice Index for 31 OECD countries," Bertelsmann Stiftung, October 27, 2011, http://www.bertelsmann-stiftung.de/cps/rde/xchg/bst_engl/hs.xsl/nachrichten_110193.htm.

If you look over the years, organized working classes, specifically, have been near the front or at the front in struggles for civil rights, economic rights, and social justice most of the time. In the early 1960s, the Civil Rights Movement was focused overwhelmingly on the voting rights and the rights of the South. As long as that was the focus, it had fairly good support in the liberal centers of the North. When you listen to the oratory on Martin Luther King Day, it typically ends with the "I Have a Dream" speech of 1963 with a lot of enthusiasm, excitement, and so on. As long as the Civil Rights Movement was condemning racist sheriffs in Alabama, Northern liberals thought it was fine. But then Martin Luther King Jr. shifted the movement towards Chicago to deal with housing as a right. He moved on to try to see if he could organize a movement of the poor—the Poor Peoples Movement. Attitudes towards him changed radically. King was bringing up class issues and class privileges, and his popularity among the privileged, including liberal elites, sharply declined. He also started to speak openly about the Vietnam War, which was also intolerable. He gave another "I Have a Dream" speech, which you don't hear much about on Martin Luther King Day. It was in 1968, the day before he was assassinated.

He was in Memphis, Tennessee to support a public workers' strike and to take steps towards organizing the Poor Peoples Movement that was supposed to march towards Washington, and he declared, "Like anybody, I would like to live a long life. Longevity has its place. But I'm not concerned about that now. I just want to do God's will. And He's allowed me to go up to the mountain. And I've looked over. And I've seen the Promised Land. I may not get there with you. But I want you to know tonight, that we, as a people, will get to the Promised Land!"[5] He could see the promised land, it would be a land of rights, not just voting rights for African Americans but fundamental rights for the poor, for housing, for decent living, and so on. He could see it, he didn't know if he could make it, but you could get there if you keep struggling.

Although he was assassinated, the march took place. It was led by his widow, Correta Scott King. It went through the South. It went up to Washington, where they set up a tent city. They were allowed to stay for a while, and then the police were sent in, in the middle of the night, to

---

5   Martin Luther King, "I've Been to the Mountaintop," speech delivered April 3, 1968, Mason Temple, Memphis, TN, found at http://www.americanrhetoric. com/speeches/mlkivebeentothemountaintop.htm).

destroy the tent city and drive everyone out of town. The Poor Peoples Movement was an effort much like Occupy, and it was beaten down. Reconstructing it ought to be a crucial part of our efforts today.

A DETROIT STORY:

Ideas Whose Time Has Come

Matthew Birkhold, Grace Lee Boggs,
Rick Feldman, and Shea Howell

Detroit: City of New Possibilities

The story of land in Detroit is the story of people reimaging productive, compassionate communities. The land, poisoned and abused by industrial capital for much of the nineteenth and twentieth centuries, holds the relics of mass production. As technologies advanced and capital became more mobile, Detroit and its people were abandoned. Yet within this devastation, people began to see the opportunity to create something new. Calling on the deepest resources of memory, spirit, and imagination, abandoned land is being reclaimed as urban gardens; old factories hold the possibilities of aquaponics, art studios, and bicycle production; neighborhoods ravaged by drugs and violence are organizing to create peace zones where people take responsibility for public safety and personal problem solving. Detroit, once the symbol of industrial mass production, holds the possibility of becoming a new kind of self-sufficient, productive, creative, and life-affirming city.

The year 1980 was a turning point in Detroit. For more than two centuries, Detroit had seen steady growth. Colonized by the French in 1701, it began as a small trading fort and gradually evolved into a manufacturing center. In the 1800s, as a port on the Great Lakes and north of the river separating the US from Canada, it became increasingly important for shipping raw materials from forests, mines, and farms; the tanning of leather, and manufacturing bricks, springs, ovens, bicycles, and carriages. At the beginning of the 1900s, it was home to the first Model T automobile. With the Model T came the mass assembly lines that would ultimately drive the industrial power of the city and the nation. By World War II, Detroit was synonymous with industrial might. Within the next decade, however, Detroit began the long, slow slide away from industrial production. Peaking in 1950 with nearly two million people, Detroit began to lose population as deep structural changes altered urban landscapes.

The sources of these interrelated changes are well known. First the end of WWII and the GI bill fostered suburban home ownership. Then, the emerging interstate highway system, the lifting of restrictive home ownership, and increased individual automobile ownership opened suburbs to white working people. At the same time, automation was advancing rapidly, replacing people with machines on the assembly line, creating a growing, permanent underclass. This underclass was increasingly young people of color. Finally, capital was becoming more mobile, leaving the industrial north to open new plants in the southern US and other countries, especially those in the developing world with unorganized labor and little or no safety and environmental protections.

On the national scale, right wing political forces dominated public consciousness. Ronald Regan was swept into the White House on a promise of restoring US military power abroad and the prestige of white men and women at home. At the same time the deindustrialization of Detroit intensified. The automobile industry had taken severe blows with the OPEC oil embargo and an escalating recession. Once a city of nearly two million people, Detroit dropped from the fourth largest city in the US to number six, with barely a million people. Over the next thirty years, this decline in population was to continue, making it the first US city to have reached a million people and then decline below that number.

Today, Detroit is 139 square miles. Its physical footprint could contain all of Manhattan, Boston, and San Francisco. Fully one-third of the land has been abandoned, much of it being reclaimed by the prairie, as wild flowers, pheasants, coyotes, raccoons, opossum, and hawks return to vast sections of open land. The recent recession and foreclosure crisis accelerated this abandonment. At the peak of the crisis, Michigan ranked fifth nationally for foreclosure rates and Detroit was the number one city for foreclosures in the nation with nearly 5 percent of all homes in some stage of foreclosure. Detroit lost 25 percent of its population in just ten years. From 2000 to 2005 Detroit lost nearly 27 percent of its manufacturing jobs.

Detroit's recent bankruptcy filing by Emergency Manager Kevyn Orr acknowledged the reality that our city, which has been abandoned by a million people and thousands of businesses, is not financially viable and must re-imagine and re-invent itself. However, the state-appointed Emergency Manager did not include in his filing the shameful story of how the legislatures of Michigan and other states, which are now controlled by conservatives like the Koch Brothers, have been strip mining cities by privatizing almost all services, attacking public workers and their unions, while at the same time providing billion dollar tax cuts for large businesses and cutting revenue sharing to the cities.

From Rebellion to Revolution

In 1980, only a few people realized this decline was part of a larger transition in human evolution, as great as the shift from hunting and gathering to agriculture, or from agriculture to industry. Most people were still looking for ways to "reindustrialize" Detroit, to entice jobs and people back into a rapidly emptying landscape.

Prior to 1980, the political work of those of us involved in the James and Grace Lee Boggs Center was shaped by the ideas and practices that flowed from the major social movements of the twentieth century. We were especially influenced by the humanizing questions of Labor, Black Power, Civil Rights, and Feminism. After the uprising in Detroit in 1967, we found it important to make a distinction between rebellion and revolution. We understood rebellion as a righteous uprising, expressing the grievances of people. Revolution, on the other hand, was an effort by people to advance our most human qualities of social responsibility, reflection, care, and compassion. In *Revolution and Evolution in the Twentieth Century*, James and Grace Lee Boggs emphasized the role of revolution in advancing our human capacities. They wrote:

> A revolution is not just for the purpose of correcting past injustices.
> A revolution involves a projection of man/woman into the future.
> It begins with projecting the notion of a more human human being, i.e., a human being that is more advanced in the specific qualities which only human beings have—creativity, consciousness, and self-consciousness, a sense of political and social responsibility...
> A revolution is a phase in the long evolutionary process of man/woman. It initiates a new plateau, a new threshold on which human beings can develop, but it is still situated on the continuous line between past and future. It is the result of both a long continuous line between past and future. It is the result both of long preparation and a profoundly new, a profoundly original beginning.[1]

---

1   James and Grace Lee Boggs, *Revolution and Evolution in the Twentieth Century* (New York: Monthly Review Press, 1974), 19.

We had already rejected what we saw as static models of revolution-ary struggle aimed at seizing the means of production and state power. We were deepening our understanding that the US had become techno-logically overdeveloped, while being humanly underdeveloped. And we were acutely aware that US capital, able to produce more and more with fewer and few people, was entering a new stage.[2]

Poletown: A Community Betrayed

As we were doing this theoretical work, General Motors announced it would build a new automobile plant in Detroit. The proposed site of the plant encompassed the old Dodge Main complex owned by Chrysler. Once one of the largest industrial plants in the world, employing over forty-five thousand people during World War II and through the mid-1960s. Dodge Main closed in 1979 with less than two-thousand work-ers. Like many old factories in Detroit, it was abandoned. No one could afford to tear it down. GM soon bought the entire 135-acre facility for $1, and used it as a corner stone for its new plant. Plans for the new plant included an additional 330 acres, most of it inhabited by people living in small, working-class homes that had evolved over the years to support Dodge Main.

Over the next year an intense struggle ensued, with the residents of what was called Poletown organizing to oppose the sacrifice of their community to a private corporation. General Motors, Mayor Coleman Young, and the Detroit City Council, operated under the authority of a new Michigan "Quick Take" law that allowed local governments to seize private property and give it to another private party for a public purpose. In this case, the "public purpose" was the promise of 6,500 jobs.

The dimensions of the Quick Take were staggering. The City agreed to clear 465 acres. This included flattening 1,500 homes, 144 business-es, sixteen churches, a school, and a hospital. About 3,500 people were forced out so that the land could be turned over to GM for its new Cadillac plant.

At first, neighbors organized resistance through letter-writing campaigns, public meetings, and demonstrations, including the bash-ing of a GM car in front of its world headquarters. Ralph Nader, fresh from his victories challenging GM safety violations, agreed to join the

---

2   Ibid.

Neighborhood Council, and sent a team of organizers helping to challenge the Quick Take Law in court.

But the forces against the residents were too great, the appeal for jobs too urgent. GM and the City were joined by the UAW, the Arch Diocese, and the local media, claiming that the destruction of the neighborhood was essential to progress and jobs. There was no alternative, they declared. Ultimately, even the occupation of the Immaculate Conception Church by neighbors, supporters, and several elderly Polish women could not stop the wrecking balls. After enduring withdrawal of city services, including police protection and garbage pick up, as well as a series of arsons set by thugs encouraged by the City, the court challenge was lost. In 1981 the Michigan Supreme Court approved the forced relocation and sale of lands, removing the last legal barrier to development.

The destruction of Poletown caused us to think more deeply about what was happening in our city. Our earlier hope that black political power would provide the impetus for new, more human forms of development was clearly mistaken. Grace Lee Boggs summed up our assessment when she said, "The whole Poletown Fiasco was a very dramatic example of destroying a community in a futile effort to bring back the past."[3]

Post-Industrial Era: New American Dream

We began to understand that Detroit, once the epitome of industrial society, was now in the forefront of the newly emerging post-industrial era. Central to that new era was the use and abuse of land.

Facing rising unemployment and continued deterioration of the community during the 1980s, we began to organize among people who were locked out of any possibility of productive jobs. Through the Michigan Committee to Organize the Unemployed, we protested forced overtime and deepened our understanding that twentieth-century America was "a society in which the trade of lives for dollars has become the essential bargain and has come to define the American Dream."[4]

The people coming to our meetings were less and less concerned

3   Jeanie Wylie, *Poletown: A Community Betrayed* (Champaign: University of Illinois Press, 1989), 109.
4   Richard Feldman and Michael Betzold, *End of the Line: Autoworkers and the American Dream* (Champaign: University of Illinois Press, 1988).

about what was happening in the plants and more and more concerned about the loss of humanity in the community. For them, the symbol of this inhumanity was the "cheese lines" where the federal government distributed surplus food once a month. The distribution took pace on one day per month at four centers around the city, each center attracting fifteen- to twenty-thousand people. People would line up the day before, even in the snow, for the food. A survival-of-the-fittest mentality ruled. At organizing meetings, people told stories of elders being knocked over, people in wheel chairs being pushed aside, and young men stealing from mothers and children to resell food on the black market. Soon it became apparent that the community was our primary focus. Reflecting our growing consciousness of the need to transform our communities, by 1985 we had renamed our group Detroiters for Dignity.

The first task Detroiters for Dignity assumed was to change the free food distribution system. We began asking the distribution centers to simply add one additional day for distribution and to divide up the recipients alphabetically. We offered to organize volunteers to help maintain peaceful relationships and to assist in the packing and distribution. All of our proposed changes were soundly rejected, first by city administrators of the programs, and then by Mayor Young who had us forcefully removed from his office. Ultimately, the City Council invited Detroiters for Dignity to testify at one of their meetings about the conditions on the cheese lines. The emotional descriptions, especially that given by Geneva Smith, led to City Council action to reform the distribution system, including setting in place a cadre of volunteers to deliver food to the elderly and people with limited mobility. This hard-fought victory positioned Detroiters for Dignity as a voice for human values in the city.

From this perspective, we became involved in two related concerns: the increasing youth violence, due to the emergence of crack cocaine, and efforts by the Young administration to bring casino gambling to the city. Detroiters for Dignity joined to support the newly emerging organization, Save our Sons and Daughters (SOSAD) in 1986. Organized by Clementine Barfield and Vera Ruckers, SOSAD was an effort to transform the grief of parents who had lost children to gun violence into a positive force for peace. Also as crack dealers began to change the character of neighborhoods, we joined with WePros (We the People Reclaim Our Streets), marching weekly to draw attention to crack houses. In one neighborhood our persistent weekly marches reduced crime 80 percent.

These neighborhood organizations joined together with faith-based groups, city council members, and community leaders to oppose Coleman Young when he announced that his next effort for creating jobs in the city would be casino gambling. Thus, we formed Detroiters Uniting.

Revolution, Transformation, Reimagining Community

It was this growing experience within community-based struggles that deepened our understanding of revolution as a transformation of ourselves as we struggled to transform and create new systems for work, for safety, for education, and for play. Mayor Young, furious at our opposition to his plans, called us a bunch of "naysayers" and challenged us by asking, "What is your alternative?" We knew that alternative forms of development needed to emerge if the community was to take charge of its own future.

Central to these alternatives was the recognition that no one else was going to solve our problems but us. In Detroiters Uniting we said, "We are convinced that we cannot depend upon one industry or one large corporation to provide us with jobs. It is now up to us—the citizens of Detroit—to put our hearts, our imaginations, our minds, and our hands together to create a vision and project concrete programs for developing the kinds of local enterprises that will provide meaningful jobs and income for all citizens."[5]

Recognizing it was up to us opened up new ways of thinking about the city. As we began to explore alternative paths for developing ways of living outside of industrial capital, we were able to see more clearly that much of what industrial capital had discarded and disrespected—young people, elders, and the land—held the potential for rebirth.

Our thinking during this period was very influenced by the work of ecofeminists, especially Maria Mies, Vandana Shiva, and Starhawk.

This theoretical work was deepened by our experiences in the community, especially the older women who still remembered community life. Most of them, having migrated to Detroit in the 1930s and 1940s, brought with them the memory of communities that had endured and survived the Jim Crow South. We were beginning to see that in post-industrial cities, building community—transforming ourselves as we transformed our institutions—was essential to revolutionary change. In 1963, James Boggs wrote,

---

5   James and Grace Lee Boggs, *Revolution and Evolution*, 10–11.

Up to now we have not depended upon ourselves to build community. But now that corporations are abandoning and destroying our
communities it is up to us to build community. That means we need
a two-pronged approach. On the one hand we must resist the efforts
of the corporations to destroy our communities by closing down our
places of work and of the urban planners who are working for the
mayor to turn Detroit into a tourist center and develop the riverfront
to lure back those folks who have abandoned the city…but at the
same time we must be building the communities necessary for the
human identity of ourselves and our children.[6]

As he said later, building community depended on our "continuing
faith in people, even when all around us we see so many of our brothers
and sisters without faith, without hope, and living such empty lives."[7]

Building Alternatives

Out of this faith, and drawing on this experience of more than a decade
of community-based organizing that aimed to raise questions of how we
value one another—how we create bonds of community and restore local
economies—we launched Detroit Summer in 1992. We had come to
understand that young people were not "problems to be solved," but held
the solutions to many of the problems we faced. By challenging them to
use their skill, imagination, vision, and heart to help rebuild the city, they
would also be able to develop themselves.[8]

Critical to Detroit Summer was the idea of urban gardening. Under
the influence of Gerald Hairston, a lifelong Detroiter, master gardener,
and community activist, we began to see that land, abandoned by capital,
was a new opportunity. It provided the space to begin to redevelop our
communities by providing for our most basic necessities. As Gerald liked
to say, "A city that feeds itself, frees itself."

Gerald had been the main support for the then-fledgling urban gardening movement that was begun by elderly women who had mostly
migrated from the South to Detroit during the 1940s and '50s. These

---

6   James Boggs, *The American Revolution: Pages from a Negro Worker's Notebook*
     (New York: Monthly Review Press, 1963), 334.
7   Ibid.
8   Ibid., 113.

women, watching neighbors leave, saw the space left behind not as vacant, abandoned property, but as open land offering new garden space. Throughout the 1980s, with the encouragement of the Detroit Farm a Lot program run by the city, and tools lent out through local libraries, small groups of women began turning vacant lots into flourishing gardens. Some of these expanded, long-standing backyard plots were started generations ago by Detroit residents reluctant to abandon their rural ways. Sometimes they were efforts to keep community memory alive, as with Lillian Clark who organized her neighbors to capture the perennials planted throughout their neighborhood to mark family occasions. Rosebushes for anniversaries; apple trees for graduations. Lilacs for the birth of child were lovely, rescued from abandonment and replanted in the memory garden with the hope that one day the plant and its story could be passed on to new families. Most often, gardens were to provide food for families and neighbors.

When Detroit Summer began, Gerald Hairston estimated there were around 130 such gardens. Over the next twenty years, the urban garden movement came to dominate the Detroit Landscape, putting Detroit in the forefront of a new global movement to reimagine cities as self-sufficient and self-sustaining. Studies currently predict that Detroit has the capacity, with the addition of hoop houses, to provide 75 percent of all the vegetables and 40 percent of all the fruits it would need to survive well.

Through these efforts, we realized that creating gardens was also recreating community, uniting neighbors across generations. In a recent article by Jose Flores, we get a picture of the solutions that are emerging out of our efforts to create community. Mr. Flores writes of his conversation with Rick Feldmen:

> At the old abandoned Packard plant just outside downtown Detroit, Feldman reflects: "It's the end of the economic American dream, which was also very destructive. On one level we have to grieve, but we also have to welcome it. Now we can move on to create another kind of American dream that is based on quality of life versus a standard of living."
>
> Out of necessity, the people of Detroit are shaping alternatives to the urban wreckage left by the collapse of the auto industry. And new possibilities are emerging across the city: Eastside residents have

transformed their neighborhood into an outdoor public art exhibit with waste materials collected from vacant lots. Just a short drive away, a group has purchased storefronts, planted fruit trees along a few city blocks, and renamed the area "Hope District." Elsewhere, another group has reclaimed two acres of unused and underutilized land in the city to grow produce that feeds community members. In short, the movement in Detroit is putting forth a model for creating solutions rooted in frontline communities and place-based relationships.[9]

Growing Freedom

According to Tyrone Thompson of Feedom Freedom Growers, urban agriculture can work to heal people from the alienating nature of wage labor. Because Feedom Freedom's work is not exploitative, workers are freed up to think about the purpose of work in different ways. In comparison to wage labor, Tyrone describes his work at Feedom Freedom as physically tiring, but adds that, "spiritually it refills you. It's rejuvenative. It has medicinal power. You grow stronger, and more diligent, the more you work out there." Working in agriculture, Tyrone says, "you can go take a nap and be sweet afterward, then go back and do your thing. You got to take vacations from your 9–5 plantation job to spend time with your family and enjoy life. Then you go back out there and do your thing out there. But here, shit, every day is a vacation. You go and do your work, you eat good, spend time with your family working, you go to sleep and wake up and you look forward to doing it."

Freed from alienating labor, human beings become aware of their capacity to create and experience the type of freedom that allows them to experience revolutions in their values and identities. In a clear example of how this kind of work facilitates changes in consciousness, Myrtle Thompson of Feedom Freedom says that working in urban agriculture taught her to completely reconstruct her understanding of time, spirituality, and nature, because she began to see that the earth is not made of dirt, but is made of soil. Farming has taught her biology, geography, and broadened her understanding of human consciousness. According to Myrtle, "All these things we've put aside by just going to the grocery store and getting some food wake up in you."

9   Jose Flores, "Detroiters Find 'Way!' Out of No Way," *Weaving the Threads* 17, no. 2 (2010).

Because she saw that she could create food that was better for her than food she could buy in a store, she eventually quit her job as a cook. There she would make something for someone and think, "you don't really want to be eating this."

Simultaneously she began to recruit youth to participate in Feedom Freedom because the process of growing and consuming locally produced food "is much better for them, physically, spiritually, mentally, environmentally, the whole nine yards." Adding, "When you know better, you should do better," and that "sometimes its hard to shake that off because we are so conditioned."

Myrtle is not alone. According to Monique Thompson, by "working in the garden, the saying, that who doesn't work doesn't eat, really came to life." This realization helped her understand that she is connected to people throughout the world. Everything that goes into getting food on the table," Monique asks, "who's doing this for me when I go to the grocery store and get it, and what do I owe them?"

Understanding Feedom Freedom's farm as something like a liberated zone, organizer Wayne Curtis declared, "This is our environment that we are able to develop and grow in… The youth that are participating in this process, when they get older maybe they won't be suffering from the same psychological idiosyncrasies that we have now."

Struggle Over Different Visions

These community-based efforts have been able to grow, because land throughout the city was not contested. The sheer magnitude of abandonment overwhelmed city administrations. Until recently. Within the last few years a new coordinated effort by business, foundations, and government has emerged to take over land and reshape the city.

In 2009, Detroit elected Dave Bing as mayor. A former basketball player with no government experience, Bing promised a mature, business-like approach to government. Exhausted and embarrassed by the sex scandals and bad boy attitude of former-Mayor Kwame Kilpatrick, Detroiters looked forward to a new era of cooperative no-nonsense government.

Shortly after his election, however, Mayor Bing announced a new initiative. In response to the loss of population and abandoned houses, he wanted to "shrink the city." In February of 2010, Mayor Bing made an almost off-hand comment on a conservative radio show that he planned to force residents from sparsely populated areas out of their homes by cutting city services to them.

He said, "There is just too much land and too many expenses for us to continue to manage the city as we have in the past. There are tough decisions that are going to have to be made. There will be winners and losers, but in the end we've got to do what's right for the city's future."

This announcement was met with a huge outcry within the city. Images of Poletown and the devastation of countless "urban renewal" projects (including the destruction of Hastings Street, the heart of the thriving African-American community in the 1930s and '40s, the leveling of China Town, and the division of the Latin-American community in Southwest Detroit) surfaced in the collective memory of the city as a powerful indictment of the Mayor's plan.

Meanwhile, the foundations, especially Kresge, Kellogg, Ford, and Skilman announced the Detroit Works Project. Clearly aligned with the Mayor, business interests, and the newly appointed state emergency manager of the schools, the Detroit Works Project, set about getting citizen consent for the plan to shrink the city.

The first meeting of Detroit Works was attended by over a thousand people, the vast majority angry and upset. Efforts by the organizers to break the meeting into small groups were rejected by those attending. After a year of these gatherings, almost everyone agreed that the Detroit Works effort had failed to garner any support. In fact, it was widely assumed that the high-paid consultant brought in to lead the team would be removed, and the project rethought.

However, by the spring of 2011 Detroit Works reinvented itself. In the hands of a well-respected local planner, Dan Pitera, Detroit Works was recast, first as a public short-term planning process, then as long-term process with the charge of producing a plan to reshape the city by August 2012.

This process appears to be little more than a public-relations stunt, for while the "engagement" continues, the mayor announced the dimensions of his shrinking effort.

On May 20, 2012, the combined *Detroit News* and *Free Press* published the mayor's latest plan to reshape the city by concentrating services in selected areas. About one quarter of the city was labeled distressed. Introducing the plan to shut off services, the article began, "The city of Detroit can no longer afford to give the same services to all areas.

Neighborhoods now are ranked according to a market type that will determine which city service an area receives. Among the factors considered are how many people live in the neighborhood, the number of bank-owned houses, and whether there are stores, schools and other amenities."

This was followed by an editorial endorsing aggressive action against residents in the "distressed neighborhoods," saying, "Now that its de facto triage process is public, it can only behoove the city to make sure residents understand as clearly as possible the likely destiny of their own neighborhoods. The campaign to cajole, entice or otherwise redeploy Detroiters to more densely populated neighborhoods is certain to meet resistance, and spawn occasional injustices. But in the long run it is the only path forward."[10]

In contrast to this mainstream media cheerleading, we wrote a response in the *Michigan Citizen*. There we said: "To anyone who has been following city development over the last few years, this was no surprise. It is exactly the plan everyone knew was coming. It clearly intends to free up land on the east side of the city, now openly talked about by developers as the next opportunity for them."[11]

This plan is completely illegitimate, and quite possibly illegal. It is nothing short of a declaration of war on neighborhoods. It did not emerge from any citizen process. It was never presented in any public meeting, and it is hard to believe that even in this weak and often misguided City Council there would a majority of members callous enough to support it.

The essence of the plan is the forced removal of people from their homes. Even the *Detroit News* had to acknowledge this in its lead paragraph about the plan. It said, "The city is trying to encourage—or push—people out of rundown neighborhoods that are largely vacant."[12] How will it "encourage or push" them? By cutting off services. The services being "stopped" are street lights, which haven't been on in many neighborhoods for years; tree trimming; removal of abandoned houses, a process that continues at a glacial pace even the best of neighborhoods; and police services, whose absence might not be noticed. The city is vague about what it intends to do with water, fire protection, garbage pick up,

---

10 "Editorial: No Improvement without movement in Detroit's stressed neighborhoods," *Detroit Free Press*, May 22, 2012.
11 Shea Howell, "Disaster plan," *The Boggs Blog*, May 27–June 2, 2012.
12 Cecil Angel, "In Detroit's distressed areas, the neighbors left, and now services disappear," *Detroit Free Press*, May 20, 2012.

and basic sanitation. If past history is any guide, these, too, are likely to be cut off. Certainly that was the strategy used in what is now widely considered one of the most shameful episodes in city development, the destruction of Poletown. Folks living in the neighborhoods targeted for clearance would do well to learn the lessons from that effort, and begin immediately to develop local safety and support organizations to resist the plan to force them out, house by house.

Behind all of this is the effort by the city to evade using eminent domain, made more difficult thanks to the residents of Poletown, who attempted to ensure that what happened to them would not happen to anyone else. After years of court battles and legislative effort, the city cannot simply declare areas cleared for development. Further, the city cannot take homes without fair compensation. In other words, it's a lot cheaper to try to drive people out than to legally take property for public purpose.

Every one who cares about the future of our city should reject this inhumane, vicious plan. How dare public officials and their appointees declare war on the poorest, most elderly among us? How dare they think a city that denies aid to elders is a city anyone thinks is worth living in? How dare foundations and corporate interests who are orchestrating this plan for their own benefit pretend they are interested in our people?

The mayor told the truth about one thing. He didn't have a plan. He had a declaration of war on the poor. All of us who care about the future of our city need to make clear that the only plans acceptable for our future begin with the recognition that every life is valuable, every home is sacred. The mayor's plan is a disaster.

Clearly, two very distinct visions of the future of Detroit are emerging. On the one hand the business-foundation-government view sees a smaller, whiter, wealthier city, with more small businesses designed to cater to the workers of large corporations and privatized city services. Their nod to urban agriculture appears to be some urbanized version of large-scale, industrial farms on the land that was once populated by the poorest among us.

The other vision is the one that has been slowly, but surely, emerging for decades as people are choosing to live, work, and play in new cooperative and life affirming ways. Rebecca Solnit, visiting Detroit shortly before these latest struggles, saw the hope and possibility of a different kind of city. She wrote:

It is here where European settlement began in the region, that we may be seeing the first signs of an unsettling of the very promises of colonial expansion, an unsettling that may bring a complex new human and natural ecology into being.

This is the most extreme and long-term hope Detroit offers us: the hope that we can reclaim what we paved over and poisoned, that nature will not punish us, that it will welcome us home—not with the landscape that was here where we arrived, perhaps but with land that is alive, lush and varied all the same....Detroit is a harsh place of poverty, deprivation and a fair amount of crime, but it also a stronghold of possibility.[13]

That "stronghold of possibility" has deep roots now throughout our community. We will not be moved.

---

13 Rebecca Solnit, "Detroit Arcadia: Exploring the Post-American Landscape," *Harpers Magazine* (July 2007): 73.

CAPITALISM, RACISM, RESISTANCE[1]

Ahjamu Umi

Banks Owe Us

On May 1, 2012 hundreds of people moved Alicia Jackson back into her house. At the time, I said that was only the first time that was going to happen, and I didn't lie. The Blazing Arrow Organization, along with other Portland-area groups such as the Portland Liberation Organizing Council, have executed several foreclosure resistances since then, involving activists moving home-owners back into their own homes, police attempting to evict them, and home-owners fighting back with the help of the community. Today, we have five houses that we are more-or-less defending in the Portland, Oregon area.

We are trying to raise the question of housing to the youth as people in this community who are growing, participating, and paying taxes. In our view, housing is a human right. Everybody should have a place to live whether they can afford it or not. We are trying to encourage people to think, "Why should somebody profit off of you having a place to live?"

To many people today, that does not make any sense. We have been programmed to believe to live somewhere means to pay somebody. We see the bankers getting rich, and we want to be rich like them. There is no reason to question the system, because it manifests the model that we want to emulate in our lives.

But Wells Fargo, Bank of America, Chase Manhattan Bank, and JPMorgan Chase are not powerful because they worked hard. The best illustration of this point comes through a historical analysis. How did the banking system in this country get started? How did the richest people in the richest country in the world get their money?

Banking got started in this country by investing in the Triangular Slave Trade. The reason historians call it Triangular Slave Trade is that Europeans went to Africa, enslaved the people, brought them to this part of the world, and sold the people for products like hemp, sugarcane, cotton, and then those products were sent to Europe. That is why there

---

1   This essay was transcribed from a guest lecture delivered on March 21, 2013 at Concordia University for Nicholas Caleb's "Introduction to Cultural Geography" (GEO-110) class.

were three angles: Africa, the United States, and Europe. The banking system—Lloyd's of London, Barclays Bank, Bank of America, Wells Fargo—invested in that process and that is how their hegemony was established.

In the last five years, almost all the banks I just mentioned have reluctantly acknowledged that they became established through the institution of slavery and the slave trade.[2] So we see many people today questioning the system considering this simple fact: "Because the banks got rich by exploiting my ancestors, I don't see why I should have to pay them anything. *They owe me* if anything. I don't want their money, because there is no price tag that can be placed on the suffering."

Gentrification in Portland

Let's discuss the Oregon Land Donation Program. It is not like Goodwill. As the growing metropolises of the East Coast grew overcrowded, opportunities for employment began to dwindle. The South lost the Civil War, and fell into economic ruin. People came out West to build a better life for themselves and the next generation. When they came out here, there was a program created called the Oregon Land Donation Program to remove the Indigenous people and give the land as legal property to white people.

The people who came to Oregon, and built these cities became eminently powerful through theft, murder, and destruction, and the same historical process remains important to economic development as we see it today. In my youth I lived in Crenshaw, South Los Angeles, and was a gang member. I have numerous friends in prison for theft and murder. I can live with that, but if there is justice in the system then the bankers ought to be in prison too. We see this sentiment echoed today: "Why should my friends go to prison and suffer as the person who tells us, 'You have got to pay the price when you do wrong,' builds an empire on the same crimes." The greatest irony is that my friends who are in jail were imitating those power-brokers, only on a very small level.

For an example of the crimes being committed on a daily basis, perhaps we can look to Mrs. Steele, an eighty-year-old woman living in

---

2   Kate Benner, "Wachovia apologizes for slavery ties," *CNN Money*, June 5, 2005, http://money.cnn.com/2005/06/02/news/fortune500/wachovia_slavery/; Makebra Anderson, "JP Morgan Chase & Co. admits link to slavery," *The Final Call*, February 9, 2005, http://www.finalcall.com/artman/publish/article_1797.shtml.

Portland. Blazing Arrow is making a demand on her bank in Seattle to return her house to her. Too often, the question asked is, "Why is this home-owner failing to pay back the loan?" We think the real question is, "Why is the bank foreclosing on Mrs. Steele in the first place?"

Why is the current crisis underway? Why are so many home-owners failing to pay the mortgages back? Mrs. Steele has a loan right now that she is supposed to pay until she is 103, and then when she is 103, she is supposed to pay a $52k balloon payment. She did not understand that payment regimen when she signed the papers, and there was no disclosure. In other words, the banker did not explain the regimen properly, and failed to have Mrs. Steele sign a document confirming that she understood the conditions of her loan.

Both Mrs. Steele and Alicia Jackson, another foreclosure resister, had 750 credit scores. If you have a credit score like that you always have options. If a banker puts a client in a more expensive loan than necessary, the banker must ask the client to sign something acknowledging the outstanding terms and conditions of the loan. But in many cases where foreclosures are concerned, the bank could not produce disclosures, because they did not go through the proper procedure. That is fraud.

That is why Blazing Arrow is moving these people back into their houses. How does this happen? The banker tells the client what she wants to hear—"The house will cost $500 a month, and that house you love is going to be yours." The client is elated, thinking that she can afford the house, as if the $100,000 lump sum payment somehow gets lost amidst the paperwork. It is, in fact, hidden in the paperwork. Then, five years later, the home-owner receives a statement that says she owes $500 this month and $100,000 next month.

Hence, the "Justice" Department in DC is suing Wells Fargo for predatory lending. There is a national lawsuit against Wells Fargo and Bank of America.[3] Multnomah County is suing the Mortgage Electronic Registration System, because there has been massive fraud happening, as in the case of Alicia Jackson and Annette Steele.[4]

---

3   US District Attorney's Office: Southern District of New York, Press Release: "Manhattan US Attorney Sues Bank of America for over $1 Billion for Multi-Year Mortgage Fraud Against Government Sponsored Entities Fannie Mae and Freddie Mac," October 24, 2012, http://www.justice.gov/usao/nys/press releases/October12/BankofAmericanSuit.php.
4   Multnomah County, "Multnomah County board votes to sue Mortgage Electronic Registration Systemis, Inc. for unpaid recording fees," November 19, 2012,

I am a recovering banker, so I do speak about this with some level of authority. I have developed loan programs for credit unions in three or four different countries. People have always had mortgages. People have always used equity from their houses to buy boats, or do whatever they want to do, but they have always paid it back. That is how the system works. What has changed in the last five or six years that people do not necessarily understand is that an entire industry is being created based on foreclosing on people. It has become a separate, profitable industry to "poach" people's houses.

Many people in the developed world blame the home-owner, saying, "You sat there and signed the paperwork, you should know what you signed." We hear that, "The reason why this is happening is that the home-owners should have been responsible like me, and not bought houses they can't afford." Everything that happens seems to be based on personal decision: if people make the right decision, good things will happen; if people make the wrong decision, bad things will happen. But can we have a discussion about the Rule of 78s financing and simple interest financing? Most home-owners—even the most privileged and condescending—do not know what is in a mortgage contract, because those inscrutable contracts are written by mortgage attorneys. The bankers don't want people to know. We just sign it, and pay the bill.

Institutionalized Racism and Banks

Many people simplify racism as something that happens when somebody does not like somebody else because of their color. That is not what racism is at all. If a person does not like another because of their color, it generally has a minimal impact compared to the much broader effects of systemic racism. To think that racism is akin to personal dislike is to suggest that people of color need some kind of social benefits from white people, rather than autonomy and self-determination. Kwame Touré said it best: "If a man wants to lynch me that's his problem, if he has the power to lynch me, that's my problem." Racism is institutionalized discrimination.

How does racism function in the US? A banker or a police officer does not necessarily say to themselves, "That person's black" or "That

---

http://web.multco.us/news/multnomah-county-board-votes-sue-mortgage -electronic-registration-systems-inc-unpaid-recording-.

person's Mexican, and I'm going to discriminate against them. I'm going to mark it off on my calendar." The financial impacts of racism are much more insidious.

For a police officer, they have to arrest people, so the question is who is going to get arrested and who is not going to get arrested? I will tell you a quick story: my ex-wife lives in Sacramento. She is a therapist. Before she did that, she was a YMCA councilor, and one of her kids was the son of Thomas Cecil, the Superior Court Judge in the State of California. When I was living there, helping the young men get out of gangs, I had to go in front of this guy four or five different times. He was always this "law and order" right-wing kind of guy: "You broke the law, you are going to prison, I don't want to hear anything about your circumstances." The Cecils asked my ex-wife to house sit while they went camping for the weekend. They gave their seventeen-year-old son a credit card, meals at the country club, a new BMW; the only rule was that he couldn't have anybody in the house. But they didn't get the RV two blocks down the road before he had people coming over and a band coming. So she called me and said, "Can you get these kids out of here?" So I went over there, did my gang banger thing, and got them all out. The Cecil child got in that BMW, and he ran straight into a light pole. He calls Judge Thomas Cecil, who comes back from the camping trip, goes down to the police station and just swoops his boy up. No booking, no questions. Just, "Where's my son? I'm taking my son."

If one of the gang members I mentored was in the same position, Judge Cecil would have said, "He broke the law, and he has got to go to jail." I can personally live with the law, but judges' sons should have to go to jail, too. But when cops arrest somebody, they arrest somebody who is less likely to have important social or political connections. They arrest some black gang bangers or some Mexican gang bangers. That's how racism works.

With the mortgage crisis, the situation is remarkably similar. If a woman of color comes into the bank, a situation of socialized behavior unfolds. People of color are inculcated from a very young age to understand that complaining will not lead to positive consequences. As one white comedian said, "I love all minorities, as long as they act white." That is the terrain that people of color navigate throughout college, and it is often upheld by parents and teachers. So when a person of color goes into a car dealership or a bank for a mortgage loan, and the banker issues a mortgage rate at a much higher-than-fair interest rate, they know we are much less likely to complain.

The banker knows that if he gives people of color higher interest rates, it will not be challenged. Since the bankers make money by adding points on the interest rate, they are truly "just doing their job." That is how the racism works. That is why we have predatory lending where we have people of color who are paying much higher interest rates. It is not a question of the banks saying, "I don't like black people so I'm going to charge them a higher interest rate." It is much more complex and sophisticated than that.

Fighting Back

There are many people across Europe and North America today who are fighting against austerity, but when I lived in Africa in the early 1990s, people were already doing that. The US uses one-fourth of the world's oil and 45 percent of the world's resources. That unequal distribution represents the greatest reason for which people throughout the world struggle. I lived in Guinea-Bissau, Guinea, some of the poorest countries in the world. People were fighting, they were striking, they were fighting back.

Guinea has 50 percent of the world's bauxite reserves. Bauxite is a mineral that they use to make aluminum. Companies like Alcoa suck the minerals and profits out of the country as if they were using a straw. The global economic system is secured to insure that host corporations are able to exploit resources cheaply, and the North Atlantic countries can afford to consume them.

As the global movement increases and expands, it is going to have a bigger impact on the more alienated North Atlantic countries. Iraq burned the oil fields during the first Gulf War so that the US would not be able to exploit the resources of a colonized country. That is similar to what people around the world are doing with regards to agriculture. From GMOs in Haiti to palm oil in Madagascar, people are rejecting (and sometimes burning) crops grown through exploitation and land grabs.

For similar reasons, an increasing number of people in the North Atlantic are having to deal with the problems of inequitable distribution of capital and land. The problem does not stop at housing—less people are able to afford the basic products that they used to accumulate through the exploitation of the Third World, let alone the housing and equity that used to comprise the American Dream.

That is why Blazing Arrow asks, "Why should we have to help somebody profit off of someone else living there?" There are many different models. Even in Portland right now there are housing co-ops, where people own a building and they pay for the upkeep of the building, they pay a certain percentage to live there. They have neither a landlord, nor a bank. People are not just going to sit on the side of the streets and die, they are going to fight back. People are going to do whatever they can to survive.

TAKING BACK THE LAND[1]

Max Rameau

Understanding the Global Land Grab

There is an allure of the US being the freest country in the world. It is something that most people think and believe—even the far Left, who think and believe it in a different kind of way. However, after a look at the best patterns and practices for housing rights in the world, it becomes obvious that none of them are found in the United States. So, both in terms of the way societies work and in terms of the way that social movements work, people in the US have to start thinking outside of the US as well as inside of the US, in order to think about what basic human rights are and how they can be applied.

For example, in South Africa, housing is a constitutional right, so as a result of a case that was brought in the summer of 2011, the South African Supreme Court ruled that foreclosure is not grounds for eviction. In the US, when we think about foreclosure and eviction, we think about who is being foreclosed on, and who is being evicted, because one leads directly to the next. In South Africa there is no direct connection between the two. We need to experience what some of these best practices are, and in the US, we actually have a lot to learn from what is happening in the Third World.

The idea of public space and particularly the idea of the commons, a space to which all people have equal rights, is disappearing very rapidly in the US. We call it public space, common space, and the commons, but it means exactly the same thing in the end: the expectation of a collective right of access to a particular area. Other places in the world are hanging on to those concepts dearly, but in the US the idea of the commons is hanging on by a thread. If you go to any major city, you will find problems of development and gentrification.

Gentrification happens when you can buy the property cheap now, fix it up, and sell it high later. Usually the process is accompanied with one of a few things, such as a big public works project. Just take Miami for example: a section of Miami downtown was, until recently, dedicated

---

1   This essay was compiled from two interviews conducted on April 4, 2012 and September 21, 2012.

to the waterfront—not necessarily a beach area, but a park where people could walk and look at the water and that gigantic water space open to public access where people used to go picnic with their children or throw the Frisbee. It was leased, not sold, to a professional sports team, and they built a basketball stadium less than one mile away from an existing basketball stadium, which the public was still paying for. They used public money in order to build a stadium, which now blocks people from access to the water.

When that stadium went up in Miami, all the property values around it went up. People knew about the stadium happening, and the first thing they thought about was not parking, but about what the property values would be like. Immediately, developers tried to buy up as much land as possible while trying to force people out. They knew that, whatever they bought it for today, they would be able to double in five years after the stadium was built. That is gentrification: buy low, fix it up, evict the people, and sell high.

The idea that a pay-to-get-in basketball stadium right on the water is public space was just completely absurd, and spoke to the extent to which the ideas of public space and community are eroding in this country. There are cities where gentrification is still happening—there are poor neighborhoods where property values are increasing—but due to generally low property values, there is also the creeping intervention of the Global Land Grab that is distinct in several ways from the classical definition of gentrification.

By 2008, housing prices in the US were coming down. It was clear that the price at which speculators bought land today would be lower in two years, whether they improved the property or not. If the meaning of gentrification is buy low, make repairs and upgrades on the property, and sell high tomorrow, then the term did not apply at that point. This did not mean that gentrification had become somehow outmoded, but that gentrification, as a cycle that leads to particular things, was temporarily on the decline.

The amount of land that banks and corporations have accumulated since then is mind-boggling, with both individual speculators and corporate speculators turning a profit. Bank of America owns literally hundreds of thousands of homes that they say they do not want, and the foreclosure crisis has not yet concluded. It is not difficult to imagine that in ten years or so, the US will have four or five landlords (Bank of America, JP Morgan Chase, Wachovia, Wells Fargo), and instead of owning their own homes, which they could fix up or do whatever they want to with, everyone else is renting from those financial institutions. The working class is pushed into a technology-driven feudalism where the majority of people cannot escape one of these landlords. So it seems like there is a long-term cycle taking place that is distinct and in some ways related to the cycles of gentrification. People are still being evicted from their homes, but in places controlled by Emergency Financial Managers for example, dispossession is happening for reasons that are other than gentrification.

Occupy Strategy

One of the brilliant and controversial things about Occupy was that there were no specific demands. It would have meant a huge mistake if we as a movement had come out at that time with demands after making such a huge splash and with those in power so nervous about it. So when I went to New York, I said, "Do not make demands. We do not know what this particular historic movement portends."

In 1954, Rosa Parks goes, and she gets on to a bus. She sits down. A white man sits behind her. The bus driver asks her to get up and move. She refuses to get up, and that starts the Montgomery Bus Boycott (MBB). What was the demand of the MBB?

One would think it would be the end of segregation, but that was not the demand of the MBB. The slogan of the MBB was, "Segregation with dignity," and the demand was not that people could sit wherever they want on the bus. Originally, blacks had to sit in the back row first and move their way forward, and whites had to sit in the front row first and move their way backwards. So the problem would seem that, if Rosa Parks sat in the middle of the bus, and there was a seat open in front of her and behind her, and a white guy walked in and he ended up sitting behind her, the white guy wasn't at fault, Rosa Parks wasn't at fault, both of them should have just sat on their sides. You can look at the pictures from that time, and see all the black people jam-packed on their side, and only one or two white people on their side. Why?

In 1954, "Segregation with Dignity" was all that people thought was possible. No one in their right mind thought that we could win the end of segregation in 1954. Ironically, if we would have gotten our demands in 1954, it's very possible that we would still be living in a segregated society today. The boycott would have won completely, they would have gotten everything they wanted, and there would still be segregation. At the time, they did not recognize the potential of that moment in history, so it is a good thing that the demand was not met. The conditions on the ground move so quickly that what at one time was moderate Left will be at another time moderate Right.

I think there are similarities to the present situation. First of all, several years ago, we would not have been able to get principle reduction for families by doing eviction defense. Such a victory would have been front-page news, a huge thing. Everyone would be thrilled with it, because at that time no one had won such a victory. Today, however, everyone is winning principle reductions. It is no longer viewed as a far-Left victory. So we need to understand what the victories are for these times, and push the envelope.

Now, we on the Left have an assessment of what the potential for this time is, and the potential for some of these actions that people are engaged in. Take Back The Land (TBTL) says, "We want control of this territory, and the way that we control this territory is not by giving it to the city. We liberate it entirely to create alternative structures." I do think that we are headed in that direction. We will have these alternative structures where people will have the real ability to control land and make decisions about what will happen in their community.

That raises all kinds of other questions, but interestingly enough, the Right is complaining that we are talking about government handouts, but when we are talking about alternative structures we are explicitly taking that discourse outside of the purview of government. We are explicitly *not* asking the government for anything. We are trying to establish that we ourselves can, and should, control this particular thing or entity, and the only thing that upsets the right and the government more than asking the government for something is telling them that we don't want anything from them.

Liberation

Liberation is not just claiming that we do not want places controlled by the banks. People have to be involved in their own process of liberation. It is the collective process of people rising up and participating that makes liberation a transformative process, not just a destination. The way people obtain a connection to public land is by fighting for it, and our real job is to create the space in which they can be involved—a political structure and framework that they can feel connected to. I cannot take back someone's house and give it to them, because they would have a different relationship to that house.

On the first action, TBTL liberated land in a small inner city section of Miami, and we called it Umoja Village. Native Americans came down to bless the land, and we took that process very seriously. Then we moved towards opening up government-owned and foreclosed homes. We have to engage in these fights not just for housing, not just for farmland, but for land, itself. When more than one person does that, all the people involved are going to feel some sort of ownership, or belonging. They are going to feel some sort of ownership of and belonging to the campaign, and that will give them a connection to the land. So, when there are attacks on that land—when there is an attempt to perform an eviction, or there is an attempt to sell that house—the people who feel tied to it are going to rise up and fight back.

Such direct action fundamentally transforms the people who are engaged in it. Umoja Village was a shantytown, but there was something about taking over that land and building our own housing units that transformed people. At the point where we were offered the land, itself, and the city said, "We'll give you the land, but you'll have to build standard housing there. You'll have to get a contract." We talked about the possibility that the residents would feel alienated from the housing if they had not used their own labor to build their house. Housing would mean less to them. It would not seem like theirs, because they had not built it with their own hands. Are we saying, "We want people to live in boxes"? No, of course we want them to live in professionally built housing—standard, up to code housing—but how do we do it in a way residents feel connected to it?

While taking this step forward, we recognize that we have some obligation here to win the battle—not just the physical battle that happens when we hold an eviction defense, blockading and preventing the police from carrying out an eviction, but the battle in the minds of people who we have to challenge the idea of common space. It is in taking this step that we think we have some areas of cross-interests with people who took part in Occupy. People in the Occupy movement reimagined, re-envisioned what space means; not only thinking about it in one location of public space, but to decentralize it and think about it in terms of the hundreds of thousands of vacant and government owned houses out there that need to be reused and put back for public use.

In a more specific sense, TBTL is actively working on building important relationships with several organizations. We have a strategic partnership with Abahlali Basemjondolo. (This is also called the shack dwellers' movement, and they are one of the biggest eviction-defense organizations in the world.) There is also the Nairobi people's settlement movement in Kenya. We are working on building strategic partnerships with organizations doing eviction defense work in Haiti, and have meetings forward with Afro-Colombian groups in Colombia. We are actively looking at how we can connect with these international organizations, and build an international movement towards gaining control of the land.

Alternative Structures

What if we liberated all kinds of land, and we had it all under community control? We would create an entirely different structure for people to participate in democracy. It would be, in a sense, creating an alternative power structure in an autonomous area with egalitarian ways of relating to one another, relating to land, and how we use it to socialize those ways.

I have had very important conversations with Gopal Dianeti about what alternative structures mean, and how they relate to his economic analysis of the means of production—who controls them and the role of the government versus that of private industry. The traditional economic view is that the workers will own and control the means of production. At some point we would own the factories, and then we would not be exploiting one another. Now, however, with the environmental crisis that is well underway, we have to recognize that, while things like worker-owned cooperatives are a prerequisite, they are no longer sufficient for solving the world's problems. For example, what if we replace the rich fat cats—for example the head of GM or the head of Ford or the head of Chrysler? If we turned all of those corporations into workers' cooperatives, and we still created these gas-guzzling cars by polluting the air?

We are not talking about a two-dimensional map where there are economic concerns on one side, race or gender concerns on another side, and the compass is pointed north-south-east-and-west. We also have an extremely complex system of environmental problems as well. The problem turns into a multi-dimensional puzzle rather than a two-dimensional map. How then do we do the things we want to do; how do we provide the things that we want to provide without destroying the planet in the process?

We have to make our movement sustainable over a long period of time by solving a broad range of problems, but first we have to agree on our objectives.

What usually happens in social movements is crystallization around an agreement on objectives—like a woman has a right to vote, the right of everyone to marry regardless of their essentialized identity, the end of legalized segregation, and so on. There are movements built around objectives that involve tremendous disputes over the methods, strategies, and tactics to achieve those objectives. Today, we have an incredible amount of unity over the tactics that we are using—eviction defense—and no unity around the objectives, which is a really bizarre arrangement. The problem with that is that we have huge eviction defenses, and then an organization works out a deal with the bank and with the city. When they announce what the victory is, or what they have come to terms with, someone is going to be unhappy, or a large percentage will be unhappy, because they never talked about what the objectives actually are.

There are many instances where people who believe that houses are a human right also believe that mortgage principle reduction for individual families is, in a way, against the idea of housing as a human right, or that homes should be handled completely in terms of a land trust. This is almost a mutually exclusive range, yet all of these folks were being packed into the same movement. We are starting to see the splits in the movement based on the fact that we are starting to talk about objectives. At the end of this mobilization of Occupy, at the end of this particular historic era, what is this movement going to become, and what is this society going to look like?

For TBTL, the ultimate objectives are elevating houses to the level of human rights and securing control of the land. If people are willing to achieve those things, and are able to engage in direct action in order to achieve them, then they certainly are able to link in to be a part of TBTL.

Education

We say all the time that TBTL is a land organization. We are in talks right now to do land takeovers for urban farming, for example. We feel that people are going to start understanding the potential of alternative structures when we have local groups that do urban farming, and take over common space like closed-down, boarded-up schools and parks, and of course rural farms and businesses as well.

Education and social spaces are becoming increasingly important. In the Bay Area there was a neighborhood school that closed down due to budget cuts. After the school closed down, a group cut off the chains, they opened up a Freedom School, and it remained open for most of the summer. Through this work, people reimagine their relationships to land and to each other and to institutions. Who actually runs this thing? The answer to that used to be, in the US, "Government runs that." The way we grapple with that question today is going to be the extent to which communities self-organize and build their own institutions.

There are a couple of forms of pedagogy that are going to make a lot of sense. First of all is the importance of a certain amount of common curriculum set to happen across borders. That does not mean the whole thing has to be common, because that would be harmful. With Movement Catalyst, the nonprofit organization that I work for, we are trying to create a curriculum on three levels: political education, which would have a mass use; leadership development, which would be more for people who are trying to move to positions of leadership; and then advanced leadership development. It is not only important that people understand the same concepts. There is something really exciting about being in a group watching a video or reading a text that can be studied with the full knowledge that there are hundreds of other groups looking at the same texts or the same video and discussing them together. That is how we are going to develop huge amounts of political unity.

The other important thing is that these types of places are open to people of color. There are communities of color that live like islands surrounded by the general normativity of "whiteness," so it is important for the ideology of people of color to sink all the way through from top to the bottom of these alternative structures. Theories of geography and economy written by European men from the 1800s and 1900s will not deal with the Land Question in the same way that Third World people of that time and, since then, have dealt with it. The theory presented in academia is often very different from the Third World, but also from poor peoples' movements in the US. It is very different from the way the Panthers would have talked about land and geography, even though the economic analysis of things like the commons, of course, are right. I certainly encourage finding pieces, terminology, direct connections to historic land rights movements, and writing things about it. Kwame Nkruma, Sekou Toure, Franz Fanon, and Amilcar Cabral all have pieces on land. There are no direct writings from Queen Nzinga, but Queen Nzinga is the queen of land liberation and defense. Space will be created for people of color if the framework comes from people of color.

Entering the consciousness of non-Native Americans in America is this sense of post-colonial analysis. Now settler people in the US are learning from examples around the world of what they have done. There are class considerations that are not just the relationship to the means of production. They are about the relation to land. Of course in peasant societies, the land is the means of production. Nonpeasant societies where the land is not the means still recognize that people cannot live without land. Occupy is bringing to the table the class question outside of the question of the factory, but it has been a long time coming.

ORGANIZING THROUGH DISASTER FOR LIBERATION AND SOLIDARITY

scott crow

"All at sea again
And now my hurricanes have brought down this ocean rain
To bathe me again
My ship's a-sail
Can you hear its tender frame
Screaming from beneath the waves"

— Echo & the Bunnymen, "Ocean Rain"

Everything Comes from Somewhere

In the telling of stories about the aftermath of Katrina, we often forget about the lands and ecosystems; the efforts to stop home evictions and the closing of public housing; the restoring of the wetlands; and how some communities created autonomy despite the red tape and bureaucracies. This essay barely scratches the surface, illustrating some ways these communities resisted and fought, and how anarchists in an organization called the Common Ground Collective worked to support these struggles against the odds that we all faced.

In the fall of 2005 the Hurricane named Katrina rolled ashore. An amazing thing happened. Thousands of people stepped in to do what governments would not or could not. Instead of waiting for permission, they acted on principles and belief with their emergency hearts to help and support communities in a time of crisis and beyond. Katrina shined light on the two worlds occurring within the confines of what people call America.

The Common Ground Collective (or Common Ground Relief) was an anarchist-inspired organization that arose in the floodwaters of New Orleans and the surrounding areas in the storm's aftermath. It was just one of many, but it was one of the handful of grassroots organizations that refused to let the government or the non-profit industrial complex control its operations by the carrot and the stick.

When it came to our collective part in the battle for New Orleans—to resist and rebuild—a genesis framework based on mutual aid quickly sprouted and developed further out of necessity and openness. We expressed collective liberation as "Solidarity Not Charity." The Common Ground Collective was very fluid, with thousands of people bringing dynamic change. Any given week could bring hundreds of volunteers into the streets under the auspices of the Common Ground umbrella. At its height, up to a hundred projects were going on simultaneously.

Land and housing have always been issues to the people of New Orleans and beyond in the greater Gulf Coast. In Louisiana's history, land was taken, people displaced and the environment destroyed between the mad rush of industry, annexation, and the business of slavery in the pursuit of profit or power.

Homes Are More Than Wood and Bricks

> "And the jobs ain't hiring, unemployment is gone
> They going to repo your car and foreclose your home
> Me I suggest you get yourself a shotgun
> So when they come to evict you can make them run
> The banks got bailed out but we still suffering…"

—Killer Mike, "Burn"

From almost the beginning, unscrupulous landlords within New Orleans were evicting people from non-flooded rental property. Large parts of the city still remained closed, and there was a lack of services (electricity, water, gas) except in the few neighborhoods that had not been affected so severely by flooding or damage.

The city government tacitly allowed them while setting ambiguous deadlines allowing people to return. These evictions were illegal: landlords simply tossed belongings to the street with minimal notification. Meanwhile developers and landlords pushed to expand what they were doing illegally. Soon people were removed from rented homes, whether or not they had been contacted. The landlords had ulterior motives. Rental and housing prices in New Orleans were skyrocketing. The contractors, governmental and non-governmental, were pouring into the city and driving up the rental prices. Landlords, developers, and real estate agents wanted to cash in on the new money. Housing rights activists used lawyers to stop outright fraud and abuse while they lobbied the city council about zoning, taxes, and other things that would effect the restructuring of whole neighborhoods. However, it was imperative to take direct action, stopping landlords from forcing people from their homes in real time.

There were some Common Ground volunteers who formed an eviction defense group as part of a larger anti-eviction coalition with Forest Park Tenants Association, Hands Off Iberville Coalition, and volunteers from People's Hurricane Relief Fund (PHRF.) We called it N.O.H.E.A.T. (New Orleans Housing Emergency Action Team) using direct action to un-evict people from their homes. When landlords removed belongings, the eviction defense team returned them to their homes and set everything back up. In a number of cases, the landlords did not check back to see if the housing had been re-occupied, and families were able to stay in their places longer; or, in the cases of unoccupied homes, the belongings were returned instead of being ruined on the streets. It was a short-term tactic, part of a strategy of giving people a chance while bringing larger housing issues to light.

Through our own eviction defense teams and N.O.H.E.A.T., we stopped a number of evictions. We also protested city and federal housing authorities, using public events, media events, and legal maneuvers to expose and stop landlords. Homes and apartments were on the cusp of being erased, house-by-house, neighborhood-by-neighborhood, from working class areas to the poorest, hardest-hit communities. People deserved to be able to come back to their homes. Eviction defense was necessary, because many of these people had almost nothing and they were being driven out by easy money. For us it was easier, because often the affluent landlords were absent from the city.

As time passed, Common Ground's efforts also included organizing legal clinics for tenants. Through our coalition efforts, we worked to ensure that landlords did not evict tenants because they were not able to return. We also focused on supporting the fourteen thousand evacuated public-housing residents in resisting the destruction of their homes with a combination of direct action and legal means.

Gentrification and Resistance

In addition to dwindling rental stock, there were homes and neighborhoods devastated by flooding. There had been a great diaspora when the federal government had finally evacuated people from the Gulf Coast.

Tens of thousands of people had been scattered all over the country without any plans or support to get them back home. During these times the local governments decided to bulldoze "flooded" and "uninhabitable" homes—even when people were unable to come back and at least look for remnants of their previous lives.

New Orleans is full of *intergenerational housing* that has been handed down informally in families without deeds, titles, and definitely not insurance. These are not bluebloods, but everyday "shotgun houses" with kids, an auntie, and maybe some cousins living there too. If they did have insurance, the insurance companies often refused to cover damages, because they valued the home less than the repairs. If the insurance company paid anything, it would have been a pittance, due to the low values of these homes pre-Katrina. These homes and neighborhoods became fodder for the land grab that ensued by governments and developers to take cheap land for new development by destroying homes, neighborhoods, and public housing. Real estate worth $10,000–15,000 before the storm became prized, as thousands went without alternatives or say in their own futures.

Common Ground in coalition with other organizations used various methods to help people keep the houses from being demolished. Volunteers used civil disobedience to physically block bulldozers, and protested at public hearings on housing issues. We had thousands of students from all over the US come in and gut thousands of houses to make them habitable for free. We also provided free materials and labor to rebuild their houses and long-term construction training. These methods provided much-needed support for individuals and neighborhoods as they worked to regain their lives.

During all of this time Common Ground volunteers contributed to, even as they fought against, gentrification along the way. The most obvious way was by taking up valuable rental stock that was available. All of the volunteer forces and contractors that descended onto the area were driving up the prices for lower-income families. A house that rented for $200 could be worth $1,000 to a contract worker, or NGO staff or volunteer. We had volunteers that were part of that mix.

We also inadvertently played into neo-liberal plans. We approached our work from a liberation practice with the intentions of small, localized neighborhood and community groups leading the way and getting outside support. The large NGOs or corporate/state partnerships stepped in, and on, community groups or projects. They funneled money to established or national groups that could work the red tape of the grant-specific funding. It was taken out of all of our hands.

Members of the People's Hurricane Relief Fund (PHRF) coalition, which encompassed about forty local grassroots organizations, called us out for contributing to problems of gentrification. Internally, we were consumed by questions around housing. If Common Ground volunteers were contributing to the rebuilding then where should they stay? Was there any way to mitigate any of this?

There was tension between different local organizations with different organizing structures, objectives, and strategies. Many of the problems had more to do with our organizing tactics and beliefs than with our presence. But it was easy for frustrated groups to target each other than to turn and face Power—at least in the short term.

Indigenous Solidarity in the Gulf Coast

When we talk about a Global Land Grab, and when we talk about territory in the US and land in general, we must always come back to the fact that this is stolen land now occupied largely by a white, settler mentality.

Most of the Katrina stories we are told and retold address what happened in New Orleans, but there are invisible, tragic, and different histories that happened to communities along the coast, itself—places where land, housing, and the surrounding ecosystems are vital to people's lives and livelihood. These are the villages and small towns of Cajun, Creole, rural black, Vietnamese, and indigenous communities along the Gulf Coast who were directly hit by the hurricane storms and flooding. Ignored or de-prioritized in the on-the-ground triage by relief agencies, governments, and the media in the aftermath, they remained out of view to most people. Some of these villages were completely wiped off the map. The extent of damage, and even location of some of these places, was largely unknown. It was invisible and tragic.

After Common Ground's inception, one of the first things that a handful of volunteers did was try to locate some these communities to lend help and support. The reports we heard about "no response," even from Red Cross, must have been exaggerated, we thought. Co-founder of Common Ground, Malik Rahim, and others knew about these communities, and we felt late in coming two to three weeks after the storm.

The heartbreaking truth was that Common Ground volunteers were the first outsiders in these areas providing medical aid, direct aid support, or in some cases search-and-rescue by boat in the bayous. No one had come. They were fending for themselves with little supplies or access.

The indigenous communities, which are largely under the broader Houma Nation banner, are actually made up of about fifty different tribes of all sizes. Some are small communities of fifteen to twenty people while others are made of hundreds or thousands. In the smaller communities, we continued to run mobile clinics and distribution centers out of large trucks in the outlying, sparsely populated rural areas for a year after the storm. In larger communities, we helped build aid distribution centers and medical centers, which their community members started running by the end of October. By that point we were just providing material aid like tools, lumber, medical supplies, and media support.

Marginalized communities have their own grassroots power, skill sets, and political analysis; sometimes they just need support—the access to money, the labor, the material support, or media—to build their infrastructures and exercise that power. Historically marginalized communities also deserve to have their autonomy, self-determination, and solidarity outside of disasters. We simply asked, "How can we provide it?" Solidarity and mutual aid together helped us build bonds and avenues for power sharing where we all had a stake in the outcomes regardless of our social capital.

Naomi Archer and other early Common Ground organizers left to form Four Directions Solidarity Network to continue this support work. Initially, Four Directions received material support and volunteers from Common Ground, but eventually became completely autonomous. It was the first project of many to spin off from Common Ground in a networked fashion.

Restoring the Wetland and Community Gardens

Due to the longstanding environmental degradation of the barrier reefs, sand bars, and the massive wetlands themselves, in the name of commerce and progress the natural protections from storms has been compromised or utterly destroyed. Common Ground with some of the coastal communities initiated and still today operates a Wetlands Restoration Project focusing on advocacy and action in actively replanting the diminishing wetlands of the Gulf Coast while working to bring attention to the valuable ecology. This grass-planting effort restores some of the lands inhabited by migrating birds, fish, and other creatures. Through tours and media, the Wetlands Restoration Project also highlights the destruction of the areas that were largely invisible to most people until Katrina and the BP oil spill. It has also provided limited jobs for community members in villages transitioning to better lives.

Food security is one of the root projects of rebuilding that we have tried to tackle. How do we provide food security that is locally grown, healthy, organic, and affordable? As part of Solidarity Not Charity we embarked on rebuilding community and individual gardens while also scaling up many more community and individual gardens in places lacking access to good food. Our liberation analysis is rooted in security and independence from outsiders, corporations, or the state. Also, it creates small-scale economic engines of business in depressed workforce areas.

Support for neighbors building community gardens and growing food in their own yards is important for the short term and for rebuilding communities for the long term.

Local Action Realizes Global Solidarity

It took hundreds of years of capital to create these inequalities, and brute force to maintain them. These disasters and governments' responses to them have only magnified the inequalities in real time. We struggled with these communities for self-determination around housing issues from the bayous to the wards of New Orleans in solidarity or mutual aid.

We came to support people living their lives with dignity in hope of creating better futures. Working in solidarity does not mean that we can or could have provided all the needed support for all the people all the time. Those of us with access to resources provided support where we could in meaningful ways for the autonomy of others and ourselves. That is solidarity.

As movements, we need to think globally, toward solidarity with Arab Spring and the *indignados*, and so on, but in order to recognize our kindred spirit and the bonds of collective liberation, we must do the work in our own localized communities, in solidarity with people who are right next door. Colonialism, gentrification, all these issues take place at every location. We do not have to look five thousand miles away to help forward the practice of collective liberation. It is happening here and now. So one of the questions that we need to ask is, "How do we build solidarity, and how do we do create collective liberation within our own communities without a crisis?" How do we do this in our day-to-day lives?

The rebuilding of collapsed infrastructure needs to happen everywhere in all of our communities, but it starts from asking first: "What can we do?" It is a question that leads to some problems that we might not have answers for today, but we should be willing to build the road by walking. Pretending that there are "three steps towards revolution" is a sham, because civil society is complex and these steps are all transitional from today. Sometimes the correct path may be rewilding areas; in other places it may be localized industry; it may be rebuilding infrastructure in a way that we have never thought about it before.

We are in a revolutionary set of times. If we can remove the cynicism and get back to hope then we *can* do these things (not the Obama-brand "hope," but real hope)—our emergency hearts will move us further than pessimism and fear. Civilization as we know it, and capitalism will fall eventually, but it's probably not happening tomorrow. So why live under such fear or expectations? And if collapse does not happen, but we still do all these things—power sharing, food security, new communities with love and caring—then we still helped make the world a better place for ourselves, animals, other communities, and the planet.

If we do nothing, or work to destroy, then we have no hope and no future. Collective liberation seeks to resist and rebel against injustice, but also to create better futures. As movements, we add to our analysis by building things. We learn by looking back at what came before us—especially strategies, tactics, or programs—while simultaneously moving forward to create our unwritten futures. These personal and political histories are what shape us, from people and events, to culture—even our relationships within larger civil society provides foundations to spring from. Common Ground Collective was just one small opening of these collective ideas that still have power to spread, because they have a root value to them. How can we create this together day-to-day beyond the obvious crisis?

OCCUPIED MOUNTAINS:

Resisting Mountaintop Removal and Corporate Land Ownership

Cathy Kunkel, Jen Osha, Andrew Munn

The coalfields of central Appalachia are geographically far from Wall Street—and culturally even farther. The urban nature of the Occupy Wall Street movement, with its inner-city occupations and massive general assemblies, does not seem to bear much relevance to what is going on in small-town, rural Appalachia. Yet in central Appalachia—as in other communities impacted by resource extraction—a similar narrative of the 1% versus the 99% has unfolded for more than a century. This resistance has taken the form of successful labor struggles and vigorous opposition to surface mining, but increasingly attention is turning to land ownership and its foundational relationship to the empowerment or disempowerment of communities in West Virginia.

The history of central Appalachia since the late 1800s has been dominated by attempts of outside interests to extract the resource wealth—coal, timber, oil, and natural gas—of the region. In her work, *Absentee Landowning and Exploitation in West Virginia, 1760–1920*, Barbara Rasmussen argues that this early history of landownership greatly affected the political and economic future of southern Appalachia. Rasmussen states, "...from the earliest colonial days, Virginia's political system was carefully structured to protect the interests of those who owned vast lands, not the independent mountain farmers who generally claimed fewer than five-hundred acres a piece."[1]

These independent mountain farmers often ended up signing away their rights to lands and/or minerals by signing a "broad-form deed." The broad-from deed was the primary legal tool used by land-holding and coal companies to dispossess mountain farmers and residents of the rights to their land and minerals. Coal River historian Rick Bradford writes, "the 'broad-form' deed when signed gave the coal or land company the

---

1   Barbara Rasmussen, *Absentee Landowning and Exploitation in West Virginia, 1760–1920* (Lexington: University Press of Kentucky, 1994). See also Paul Salstrom's *Appalachia's Path to Dependency* (Lexington: University Press of Kentucky, 1997).

right to use the surface in any way 'convenient and necessary' to excavate the minerals." Bradford continues, "it absolved the company from any liability for damages caused directly or indirectly by the mining operation on that land; and it passed on ownership of that particular tract of land 'to the parties of the second part, their heirs and assigns.'"[2]

Not only has the coal industry controlled the natural resources, they also sought economic and social control over the workforce. Workers were imported from outside the region to work in the mines. Many miners lived in coal-company-owned homes in company towns. They were often paid in scrip which could only be redeemed at company-owned stores, resulting in ever-increasing debt despite long hours and dangerous work. By the beginning of the twentieth century, miners in West Virginia had a death rate five times higher than their European counterparts.[3] Large-scale resistance against the coal industry first took the form of labor struggles, the violent "mine wars" of the 1910s and 1920s, as the United Mine Workers of America attempted to organize the southern West Virginia coalfields.

Historically and presently, cultural stereotypes of Appalachian people have masked the inherent social inequities of resource extraction in central Appalachia. Perhaps the best illustration of this injustice can be seen in the pubic portrayal of the Hatfield-McCoy feud, well known as an example of the ignorance and backwardness of mountain residents. In stark contrast to this stereotypical image, the research of historian Altina Waller linked timber and coal extraction drives from outside of the region to the ongoing feud. The McCoy side of the feud was taken up by an emerging elite capitalist class in Kentucky in the 1880s in order to prosecute Anse Hatfield and force him into selling off his valuable coal lands in southwestern West Virginia. What is more, the image projected to the rest of the nation of backwards, feuding mountaineers—when much of the violence was in fact precipitated by outside hired detectives and bounty hunters—helped justify the "modernization" and industrial exploitation of the region.[4]

---

2   Rick Bradford, "History and Social Geography: Absentee Land Ownership," http://auroralights.org/map_project/theme.php?theme=coal_river_101&article=14.

3   Jim Wood, *Raleigh County, West Virginia*, 367, from journeyupcoalriver.org.

4   Altina L. Waller, "Feud: Hatfields, McCoys, and Social Change in Appalachia, 1860–1900," (Chapel Hill: University of North Carolina Press, 1988). And WV Film History Project, "Transcript of interview with Altina Waller, June 27, 1992, for the film *West Virginia*, http://www.wvculture.org/history/wvmemory/filmtranscripts/wvwaller.html.

The absentee corporate interests' early establishment of control over the region's natural resources set the stage for the present-day situation in which the contrast between the "1%" of the coal elite and the "99%" is extreme. West Virginia consistently ranks as one of the poorest states in the nation in terms of median household income.[5] The largest coal-producing county in West Virginia, Boone County, produced twenty-seven million tons of coal in 2009, which sold for an average of $70 per ton, or $1.9 billion in a single year.[6] Yet, despite its rich resource wealth, 15.7 percent of the families in the county live in poverty, compared to 10 percent for the US as a whole. The median household income in Boone County is $39,900.[7] Meanwhile, the CEO of Alpha Natural Resources, one of the major mining corporations in the county, earned $6.7 million in 2011.[8]

Not only does the local population not benefit from their vast resource wealth, they also disproportionately bear the costs of extraction. The control of the land and resources by outside interests with no stake in the community enables the environmental and humanitarian disasters we have seen from the coal industry. Mine safety is compromised, mechanization reduces employment options, and extreme forms of extraction like mountaintop removal are practiced with little regard for surrounding communities. The impacts of coal mining on local communities include flooding, blasting damage, overweight coal trucks, and coal dust, not to mention the occupational hazards of working in the mines. Furthermore, with so much of the surface controlled by coal interests, there is little opportunity to create other economic options. Indeed, West Virginia ranks forty-sixth in the nation in terms of economic diversity.[9] Concentrated

5   Ted Boettner, Jill Kriesky, Rory McIlmoil, and Elizabeth Paulhus, "Creating an Economic Diversification Trust Fund," WV Center on Budget and Policy, January 2012.

6   US Energy Information Administration, "West Virginia: State Profile and Energy Estimates," http://www.eia.gov/state/state-energy-profiles-data.cfm?sid=WV#Prices, 2012. And West Virginia Office of Miners' Health, Safety and Training, "2009 Coal Production and Employment by County," http://www.wvminesafety.org/2009%20Annual%20Figs/CNTYSUM2009.pdf, 2010.

7   US Census Bureau, "American Community Survey (2008–2010 three-year estimates)," 2012.

8   Alpha Natural Resources, "Notice of 2011 Annual Meeting of Stockholders and Proxy Statement: To be held May 17, 2012," http://files.shareholder.com/downloads/ALNR/1873273777x0x557094/73929bc7-ad75-46a3-902b-879063f485ea/Alpha_2012_Proxy.pdf.

9   Boettner et al., "Creating an Economic Diversification Trust Fund."

absentee corporate ownership of resources has been the constant, thus far unswayable, force that removes the power of decision making from communities and extracts both the resources and the wealth from West Virginia's mountains.

Absentee Ownership of Resources

The underlying problem of absentee control of resources has long been recognized by Appalachian social movements and justice-seeking organizations. Interest in land reform reached a previous height through the work of the Appalachian Alliance in the late 1970s and early '80s. In 1977, heavy flooding caused widespread damage throughout central Appalachia, particularly the coalfields. Dissatisfied with government response to the disaster, citizen groups concerned with a range of issues, including housing, strip mining, health, welfare, workers' rights, and others, convened a meeting in Williamson, on the Kentucky-West Virginia border. The Appalachian Alliance emerged from this meeting as the body through which separate community-based organizations could share resources for disaster relief and efforts for environmental and economic justice.

Members of the Appalachian Alliance knew of, and had experienced, countless pieces of anecdotal evidence that pointed to absentee land ownership as an undergirding force in producing the persistent poverty of central Appalachia. To address this, they formed the Land Task Force. Comprised of academics and citizen activists, the Land Task Force held its first meeting in 1978 and laid out an ambitious plan to document land ownership patterns using participatory research in rural areas of eighty Appalachian counties in West Virginia, Kentucky, Virginia, Tennessee, North Carolina, and Alabama.

The study used participatory methods to gather data from eighty county courthouses for at least two purposes. The sheer scale of the project and the pre-digital format of the data necessitated an unaffordable number of people-hours. More important to the mission of the Appalachian Alliance and its members, however, was the empowerment of Appalachian people to take control over their lives and the conditions in which they lived. The training of dozens of volunteer researchers in communities across central Appalachia brought together a network of knowledgeable local people, and gave them ownership over the study and its implications.

The final study report contained policy suggestions, and the participatory process of executing the study laid the groundwork for grassroots political pressure to implement them. Foremost in the study's many political impacts was the formation of Kentuckians for the Commonwealth, which organized across the state to finally end the broad-form deed, and to start taxing unmined minerals held by corporations, in 1987.[10]

The study's findings have also had profound implications, highlighting the degree to which locals have lost control of the resources. Across the eighty Appalachian counties it surveyed, the Appalachian Alliance found that 99 percent of the people owned less than 47 percent of the land. The fraction of minerals owned by the local population was an even smaller percentage—about a quarter in West Virginia. Furthermore, the study found a high degree of concentration, with the top 25 percent of surface owners controlling 85 percent of the land, and the top 25 percent of mineral owners controlling 90 percent of the minerals.[11]

This high degree of concentrated absentee ownership has profound implications for the political economy of the region. The Appalachian Alliance highlighted the fact that absentee owners do not pay their fair share of property taxes, leading to underfunding of schools and local infrastructure. In the eighty counties studied, the top 1 percent of property owners owned 22 percent of the land but paid less than 5 percent of the property taxes.[12] As a result of this disparity, decisions regarding the use of natural resources have overwhelmingly been taken out of the hands of local communities and placed on the tables of boardrooms across the globe.

There have been some attempts over the years to address the economic inequalities endemic to resource-extraction-based economies, by retaining more of the industry's wealth within the state. Successes have been few and far between, due to the large amount of political power and connections between the industry and political elite in the state. In the 1950s, for example, West Virginia Governor William Marland proposed that the

---

10 Organizing against the broad-form deed occurred in Kentucky and not West Virginia because West Virginia law interpreted "broad-form deeds" differently than Kentucky. Under West Virginia's interpretation, the idea of strip mining would not have been within the contemplation of the parties that signed a deed in the early 1900s and therefore such deeds did not give the mineral-owner permission to strip the surface owner's land.

11 Appalachian Land Ownership Task Force, "Land Ownership Patterns and their Impact on Appalachian Communities," February 1981.

12 Ibid., 128.

state institute a severance tax on coal that could be used to support the state's schools and road system. In language that is rarely heard from West Virginia's politicians today, Marland spoke of the need for such a tax:

> Whether we like it or not, West Virginia's hills will be stripped, the bowels of the earth will be mined and the refuse strewn across our valleys and our mountains in the form of burning slate dumps. This refuse will continue to be dumped into our once clear mountain streams. We are paying a fearful price to allow the coal to be extracted from the hills of West Virginia. It is only right that we should be able to point with pride to improved roads and schools as a result of this awful toll that we are taking of the beautiful State of West Virginia.[13]

Marland's severance tax proposal lost, and Marland was never again elected to public office. A coal severance tax was not passed until 1987. During the past two legislative sessions, there has again been discussion of keeping more of the state's natural resource wealth in state by creating a permanent mineral trust fund. If the severance tax on coal and natural gas were increased, the money could be directed into a trust fund for long-term economic diversification. Mineral-rich western states, including Wyoming and New Mexico, have already done this. An additional 5 percent severance tax on coal and natural gas going into a trust fund could be generating $2.4 billion per year for the state by 2025.[14] That is money that could be invested in making higher education more affordable, providing better child health care services, and workforce development.

Resistance: Past, Present, Future

There has been a long history of resistance to the coal industry's dominance of central Appalachia. Arguably the most successful economic resisters to the coal companies were the unions, which were successful in empowering miners to regain some measure of control over their lives. Unfortunately, the A.T. Massey Coal Company was largely successful in breaking the union in the 1980s, and today there are few union mines left in the region.

---

13 Marland, William. "Message to the Fifty-First Legislature: Regular Session February 23, 1953," http://www.wvculture.org/history/government/marland01.html.

14 Ted Boettner, "Creating a West Virginia Mineral Trust Fund," presentation to the Alliance for Appalachia, August 29, 2011.

A major symptom of outside-interests' domination is the exploitation of local communities by surface mining. Thus, much of the local resistance has centered around opposing surface mining. Large-scale resistance to strip mining began in the 1950s and 1960s. Particularly in Kentucky, much of this resistance was directed against the broad-form deed, which allowed companies to strip the surface to mine coal without the consent of the surface owner. Resistance frequently involved direct action efforts to block bulldozers from destroying peoples' property. The Appalachian Group to Save the Land and People was perhaps the most famous of these early anti-strip mining groups. These resistance efforts were unsuccessful in abolishing strip mining, but did provide enough political pressure for it to be regulated through the Surface Mining Control and Reclamation Act of 1978—a highly controversial piece of legislation within the movement, which some feared would only legitimize the destruction caused by strip mining. Local organizing did score a major victory in Kentucky, however, with Kentuckians for the Commonwealth spearheading a state constitutional amendment that banned the broad-form deed in 1987.[15]

Currently, much of the grassroots resistance work against the coal industry is centered on mountaintop-removal mining. The process of mountaintop removal mining began in the 1970s, grew throughout the 1980s, and exploded through a combination of advanced mining technology, lenient regulatory interpretation of federal legislation, and the national demand for low-sulfur coal. Its share of Central Appalachian coal production has steadily grown since the '70s.[16] Mountaintop removal mining is a way of using fewer workers to extract the coal and also allows companies to reach seams that wouldn't necessarily be mine-able with conventional, underground methods. The process of mountaintop removal coal mining entails removing mountaintop rock and soil above multiple horizontal seams of coal. After the coal is removed, the rock and soil are returned and reclaimed in an effort to restore the approximate original contour of the

---

15   Organizing against the broad-form deed occurred in Kentucky and not West Virginia because West Virginia law interpreted "broad-form deeds" differently than Kentucky. Under West Virginia's interpretation, the idea of strip mining would not have been within the contemplation of the parties that signed a deed in the early 1900s and therefore such deeds did not give the mineral owner permission to strip the surface owner's land.

16   Rory McIlmoil and Evan Hansen, *The Decline of Central Appalachian Coal and the Need for Economic Diversification* (Downstream Strategies, 2009). Available online at http://www.downstreamstrategies.com/documents/reports_publication/DownstreamStrategies-DeclineOfCentralAppalachianCoal-FINAL-1-19-10.pdf.

mountain. The excess rock is used to fill adjacent mountain hollows and create valley fills. Enormous landscape change occurs as a result of clear cutting the timber, using explosives to remove the overburden, filling in headwater streams with the overburden, and leaving the area denuded and flat. As of a 2008 USGS report, surface mining is now the dominant driver of land use change in central Appalachia.[17] Over 1.2 million acres have been mined and five-hundred mountains have been leveled across Central Appalachia as of 2009.[18] The creation of valley fills has destroyed nearly two thousand miles of streams in Central Appalachia, with eight hundred miles of direct stream impact in West Virginia alone.

MTR is the cheapest way to mine coal, due to the externalization of both current and long-term environmental and social costs. The use of massive draglines allowed coal companies to reach multiple seams of coal after using dynamite to blast the tops off the mountains. Therefore, MTR can recover a higher percentage of coal, use less manpower, and meet the demands for low sulfur coal. Mountaintop removal does not occur in all coal mining states: in fact, in Appalachia it is widespread only throughout eastern Kentucky, West Virginia, and southwestern Virginia. Even though regional coal production actually peaked in 1997,[19] the destruction of the land has escalated due to mountaintop removal mining. Mountaintop removal mining's share of production has increased because it is typically a cheaper method of extracting coal, and central Appalachian coal is finding it increasingly difficult to be price-competitive with the open-pit coal mines of Wyoming's Powder River Basin.

The expansion of mountaintop removal throughout the 1980s and 1990s met with challenges across the coalfields. Organizations such as Kentuckians for the Commonwealth and Save Our Cumberland Mountains had already formed in response to the social and economic impacts of strip mining.[20] The Citizens Coal Council started in 1987 in Lexington, KY, as a coalition of community-based coalfield organizations from across

---

17   Kristi L. Saylor, "Land Cover Trends: Central Appalachians," USGS, 2008, http:// landcovertrends.usgs.gov/east/eco69Report.html. Accessed 20 February 2013.

18   Ross Geredien, "Extent of Mountaintop Mining in Appalachia 2009," *I Love Mountains*, http://www.ilovemountains.org/reclamation-fail/details.php#extent_study.

19   Ibid.

20   Stephen Fisher, ed., *Fighting Back in Appalachia: Traditions of Resistance and Change* (Philadelphia: Temple University Press, 1993).

the country. The Ohio Valley Environmental Coalition has also worked since 1987 to preserve the mountain ecosystems and culture of the Central Appalachian region, making ending mountaintop removal/valley-fill strip mining the primary issue. In 1998, a flood in White Oak, on the Clear Fork, killed two people, and in the same year, members of Coal River communities created Coal River Mountain Watch to fight for the social, economic, and environmental wellbeing of southern West Virginia against the destructive practices of MTR and the coal companies.[21] Prominent national figures such as NASA climate scientist James Hansen and Robert F. Kennedy, Jr., who called mountaintop removal the "worst environmental tragedy in American history"[22] have stepped forward to stop mountaintop removal and, in particular, to save Coal River Mountain.

Outside of Appalachia, mountaintop removal mining is most often discussed in terms of its environmental impact. Now, however, increasing attention is being given to the impact of mountaintop removal mining on public health in surrounding communities. Recent research has documented "serious environmental impacts that mitigation practices cannot successfully address" from the burial of headwater streams beneath valley fills[23] as well as a "high potential for human health impacts" from exposure to polluted streams or airborne toxins.[24]

❦

The current period of resistance, while unsuccessful at banning MTR at the federal level, has scored some local victories. Although the central message of the anti-mountaintop removal movement has been the abolition of mountaintop removal mining, local organizing work has addressed mountaintop removal in the context of broader impacts of the coal industry on community health and safety. For example, there have been successful local efforts to control dust pollution from coal-processing

21 For more information and resources about and from Coal River Mountain Watch, see *Coal River Mountain Watch*, http://www.crmw.net.

22 Robert F. Kennedy, "A president breaks hearts in Appalachia," *The Washington Post*, July 3, 2009, http://www.washingtonpost.com/wp-dyn/content/article/2009/07/02/AR2009070203022.html.

23 M. Palmer, E. Bernhardt, W. Schlesinger, K. Eshleman, E. Foufoula-Georgius, M. Hendryx, A. Lemly, G. Likens, O. Loucks, M. Power, P. White, and P. Wilcock, "Mountaintop Mining Consequences," *Science* 327, no. 5962 (2010).

24 M. Hendryx and M. Ahern, "Mortality in Appalachian Coal Mining Regions: The Value of Statistical Life Lost," *Public Health Reports* 124 (2009).

facilities, class-action lawsuits on behalf of communities whose water has been poisoned by underground coal slurry injection, the successful relocation of Marsh Fork Elementary School away from a slurry dam and coal processing plant, and attempts to better regulate overweight coal trucks.

Since the beginning of 2009, there has been a steady upwelling of direct, non-violent civil disobedience to stop mountaintop removal and raise awareness about the dangers of slurry impoundments. The first action occurred on February 3 when fourteen people were arrested and six people chained themselves to a bulldozer up on Coal River Mountain. The direct-action movement to end mountaintop removal began under the name of Climate Ground Zero, with more than 150 residents and activists arrested, and continues through the group Radical Action for Mountain People's Survival (RAMPS). The mission statement of RAMPS highlights the realization for many in Appalachia that ending MTR is about taking on the 1% who control the land and the resources:

> We are here to fight for the survival of the land and people of Appalachia, the right to a healthy and sustainable future with clean air and clean water, and the right to a livelihood that nurtures that future. To achieve these goals, we are up against much more than an unjust mining process. We are fighting decades of repression by the coal industry and its agents. We are fighting the inept, if not corrupt, regulation agencies and government. We are fighting out-of-state land companies who hold this land and therefore its people's lives as a commodity to be auctioned off. We are fighting national ignorance and indifference to the oppression of the Appalachian people.[25]

In addition to local organizing, allies around the country are supporting the work in Appalachia by making connections between the financial industry and what is going on in Appalachia. The consolidation of capital in the mining industry and the increasing mechanization of the industry have been bankrolled by Wall Street. The worst banks, in terms of financing mountaintop removal mining and coal-fired utilities, are Bank of America, JP Morgan Chase, and Citi.[26] There is a growing recognition

---

25 RAMPS, "Mission Statement," http://rampscampaign.org/about-us/.
26 Rainforest Action Network, BankTrack, and Sierra Club, "Dirty Money: Coal Finance Report Card 2012," 2012, http://ran.org/sites/default/files/ran_coal_finance_reportcard_2012_web.pdf.

that outside capital and financial interests are making decisions that affect our communities—from mining communities to those impacted by the housing crisis. The 2012 Bank of America shareholders' meeting in Charlotte, NC was dubbed "Bank vs. America" by a coalition of groups who came to make the connections between the bank's profits and its impact on communities. In addition to its role in financing mountaintop removal and coal, Bank of America is also the largest foreclosure profiteer and has been repeatedly sued for predatory lending.[27]

Thus, over the past two decades, a variety of tactics and messages have been used to build a movement against mountaintop removal, both inside and outside of coal-producing areas. Though these efforts have found success in attracting the intervention of federal authority to limit the scope of surface mining and make it less economically attractive, the thus-far intractable regime of corporate land and mineral ownership stands as a barrier to a true shift in the balance of power in West Virginia's coal-burdened regions.

The Beginnings of Land Reform

The issue of absentee and corporate land ownership is the linchpin of persistent poverty and the political disempowerment of communities in Central Appalachia, and it has foiled efforts to create a diverse local economy. The Coal River Wind Campaign was a high-profile effort undertaken by Coal River Mountain Watch in 2008. It pitted the renewable energy aspirations of communities in the Coal River Valley against Massey Energy's plan to remove over six-thousand acres of Coal River Mountain in Raleigh County, WV. It sparked and fueled a passionate state-wide dialogue on the fate of southern West Virginia's coal-bearing mountains—demolition for short-term profits or development for long-term profit. The debate, however, was over before it began.

Rowland Land Company owns more than twenty-four thousand acres on Coal River Mountain and the surrounding area. The decision about what to do with Coal River Mountain was made in 1993, when Rowland Land Company leased 8,241.5 acres of land and minerals to

---

27 Mariah Blake, "Miami and Los Angeles Sue Banking Giants Over the Sub-Prime Mortgage Debacle," *Mother Jones*, December 23, 2013, http://www.motherjones.com/mojo/2013/12/cities-sue-banking -giants-over-sub-prime-mortgage-debacle.

Marfork Coal Company, a subsidiary of Massey Energy, with the express permission to use surface mining methods to extract the coal. After twelve years of sitting on the coal, in 2005, Marfork Coal applied for a permit to begin mountaintop removal mining on Coal River Mountain. In October 2010, after five years of citizen opposition to the mining at public hearings, meetings with company and public officials, international media attention, and civil disobedience, blasting commenced on the Bee Tree Surface Mine on Coal River Mountain.

The Coal River Wind Campaign articulated a vision for prosperity in southern West Virginia that balanced the historical land-use of root digging, hunting, gardening, and animal husbandry with twenty-first century wind-energy technology. But the hopes of hundreds who stand to lose their health, heritage, and well being to mountaintop removal were not enough to break the structural barriers presented by absentee and corporate land ownership. Present realities of land ownership in the region rendered this vision and other possible community-based visions for structural economic changes unattainable. For this reason, organizers in Central Appalachia, especially in West Virginia, have taken a renewed interest in issues of land ownership and land reform.

Land reform is a way to organize a broader base of people for a positive vision of land use in their communities. As the rise of the natural gas industry unfolds and the economic and social unraveling of Central Appalachian communities continues, land ownership and reform becomes increasingly important. By transferring resources, and keeping control of these resources from coal, gas, and land companies to local people and organizations directly accountable to local people, a successful land reform strategy will gradually the energy industry from causing ecological devastation. Like the strategies of land acquisition and consolidation employed by the agents of industry more than a century ago, efforts to change the pattern of land ownership will unfold over decades.

Historically, land-reform efforts around the globe can be generalized as efforts to decentralize wealth and power from concentrated ownership by elites to distributed control by a larger portion of a society's population. It addresses and is motivated by a group's need or desire for a bigger piece of the economic pie. This is still a central aim and motivation of land reform, but twenty-first century land reform should also be understood as a strategy of preparation and adaptation for the consequences of climate change and resource-depletion-caused economic contraction and destabalization. It is a confluence of the movements for economic justice and sustainability, not out of ideological abstraction, but necessity.

Two strands of land-related work are already underway in West Virginia. The first is an effort to document present-day land and mineral ownership. As of December 2012, participants in this effort have completed a pilot project, documenting the land and mineral ownership in Boone and Doddridge counties. Upon releasing the pilot project results, the West Virginia Land Study will determine whether or not to scale it up into a state-wide study and possibly partner with organizations in other Central Appalachian states to replicate the study in their areas. Organizing for land reform, the second strand of land-related work, is in its inchoate form.

The New Land Study

The current land study is not an end in and of itself, but the kindling to reignite public dialogue on land ownership in West Virginia, and begin organizing for land reform. A segment of the group undertaking the study is also setting in motion a participatory process to define a collective vision of land reform and possible strategies to achieve it, drawing upon the strengths of established land-reform-tinged projects. This group will attempt to situate the created vision and strategies within the context of historical forces at work in the region, and the global trends that will increasingly touch every aspect of life in the decades to come, including the depletion of coal reserves in Appalachia, shifting demographics, commodification of the biosphere, climate and resource-depletion-driven destabilization of the global economy, and other trends uncovered in the land study and in the process of vision and strategy definition.

In looking to expand strategies for land reform, it is important to pay special attention to the places in which land has either remained under community control or been reclaimed by community organizations. The Clear Fork Community Land Trust in eastern Tennessee is a four-hundred-acre land trust that gives ninety-nine-year leased sub-parcels to families who wish to live on the land trust. Residents own improvements they make to the properties, and live in accordance with land trust principles of sustainable land use. The Big Laurel Land Trust is not a residential land trust, but provides an educational center in Appalachian culture, ecology, and sustainability in Mingo County. The Stanley Heirs Park is a fifty-acre park in the midst of a ten-thousand-acre mountaintop removal mine on Kayford Mountain. Retained by the Gibson family, the park provides a community gathering place for the anti-mountaintop removal movement and family gathering place for residents of Cabin Creek, many of whom have seasonal cabins on top of the mountain. Places like this hold lessons in maintaining community ownership in areas dominated by extractive industries.

Other new projects undertaken by grassroots organizations in West Virginia already overlap with land-reform efforts. The Heritage Homeplace strategy advanced by the relatively new anti-strip mining organization, Keepers of the Mountains, focuses on identifying land owners concerned about the impacts of surface mining, and working with them to become land trusts or use deed easements to protect their land in perpetuity. Protecting land presently in the hands of local people is an important starting point for a broader land-reform effort involving public lands.

The struggle for Blair Mountain, site of the 1921 labor uprising by striking miners during the West Virginia Mine Wars, has been the focus of a campaign to protect the mountain battlefield as a park. The mountain is presently the site of mountaintop removal operations by Alpha and Arch Coal.

While these campaigns address issues of ownership, many more organizations advocate for policies that limit the use of lands independent of the question of ownership. Watershed and local conservation organizations across the state advocate and create county and municipal policies to protect specific areas or limit development through zoning. The approach of most anti-mountaintop removal organizations is to ban surface mining as a legal use of land by advocating for federal legislation and enforcement of existing laws.

Land Reform and Resistance in the Midst of Resource Depletion and Climate Destabilization

But the coal industry in Central Appalachia is currently in decline—a fact that may open up new directions for resistance work and opportunities to break free of the "jobs versus environment" box. According to the Energy Information Administration, we are in the midst of 50 percent decline in Central Appalachian coal production from 2008–2014.[28] This means that there is now more of an opportunity to advocate for economic

28   Energy Information Administration, "2011 Annual Energy Outlook."

diversification, as more people are beginning to realize the need to think about a future beyond coal. This also gives more opportunity to think about longer-term efforts to reform patterns of land ownership, since the current patterns of absentee landholding are a serious barrier to local economic development. We may see more of a shift towards organizing around some of these broader issues of economic inequality and control of resources, which are not often emphasized in environmental discussions of mountaintop removal and the impacts of coal. These themes, however, do resonate with previous decades of Appalachian resistance.

As extraction picks up in the Powder River Basin, however, coal production is expected to decline from the central Appalachian basin.[29] As the industry goes dormant, the trickle of resources it does provide will dry, and the land that they control will sit unused. New uses of the land and resources in the region will need to emerge to form the basis of the post-coal economy in Appalachia. By bringing decision-making power over the use of land and resources into local communities, land reform can provide the basis of new, community-oriented economies.

While this region-specific economic trend unfolds, global forces of climate change and resource-depletion driven economic contraction and destabilization will also begin to be felt. As a resource-rich outlying area, central Appalachia will be among the first to see the withdrawal of public services, but the tendrils of extractive industry will attempt to maintain hold here for as long as there are fossil fuels in the mountains. Land reform can provide the basis for local material self-sufficiency and resiliency as the services provided by the national and global economy withdraw, and can act to box out extractive industry for as long as property law is recognized and enforced or rights of ownership can be defended by local people.

Vigorous opposition to mountaintop removal must continue to defend communities from the environmental and social impacts of coal extraction. Additionally, behind the shield of resistance to mountaintop removal, it is important to begin to sketch out and actualize strategies to begin transferring ownership of West Virginia's land and resources to communities through institutions with direct ties of accountability to them, and acre by acre, build the power of the 99%.

---

29 Coal production is expected to decline by 46 percent: from 235 million tons in 2008 to 127 million tons in 2020. Rory McIlmoil, Evan Hansen, Nathan Askins, and Meghan Betcher, "The Continuing Decline in Demand for Central Appalachian Coal: Market and Regulatory Influences," *Downstream Strategies*, May 14, 2013.

MI'KMAQ AGAINST THE GAS GRAB

Miles Howe

Beginning in the summer of 2013, a chain of important blockades and actions against natural gas exploration in what is known as the Maritime provinces of Canada brought global attention to the struggle of First Nations against ongoing colonial exploitation.

The Maritime provinces of Canada, the name we settlers commonly call Mi'kma'ki, is statistically speaking, among the poorest regions in the Dominion. We also represent among the least formally educated segments of the population, even more so when you escape from the metropolitan areas. More traditional, self-sufficient and sustainable enterprises, fishing and logging in particular, have seen themselves annihilated by large-scale, local and international players.

Maritimers, especially rural Maritimers, are now the transient grunts of the Canadian economy. They are the infantry in the Army, and the pipe fitters in the Alberta tar sands.

There is also something of feudality in the air here. Old and well-moneyed families control many aspects of life, from food to transportation to media to land. The population, to a degree, has an aspect of feudal docility to it—many are descendants of indentured Irish workers, Scots fleeing persecution and Acadians returned from exile—made all the more real by the fact that those who would protest risk protesting directly against their employer.

The mandate of the Media Co-op, the grassroots news organization with which I am strongly allied—and employed as an editor— is to report on unreported or under-reported stories, especially in relation to marginalized communities. We offer journalistic training to interested groups as well, and consider that peoples affected by issues are often in the best position to be able to truthfully relay those stories to an inquiring audience. We also operate on a sustainer-based model, so the blurred lines between editorial policy and advertorial influence are in effect circumvented. We attempt to fashion ourselves as the peoples media.

So it was that I began to report on Indigenous issues in the province of Nova Scotia. It was not a conscious effort to go out and seek Indigenous-related issues, but was more-so a vague feeling that here were some of the most glaring stories of inequality, in a region of Canada that is rife with inequality.

Colonial Era Land Grab

Mi'kmaq interactions with the British Crown, have, from the outset, been dubious and based on original falsehoods. Upon signing the Treaty of Utrecht with France in 1713, the British wrongly assumed that they had inherited French territories in the "New World," which included much of Mi'kma'ki. In fact, all that they had inherited—from the perspective of international sovereignty—was the potential for a working relationship with a peoples historically astute and well-versed at treaty making.

Strong-arm tactics by the British, fueled perhaps by delusions of landlord-ship, led almost immediately to outright war, which lasted for years. The first recorded treaty between the Wabanaki peoples (four treaty-bound tribes, including the Mi'kmaq) and the British was signed in 1725 at the then-Nova Scotia capital of Annapolis Royal. Far from being a mutually sought after agreement, as is classically presented (if and where it is presented at all), the agreement was attempted by the British lieutenant governor of Annapolis Royal on three occasions before Wabanaki representatives met with him.[1] It was the British, out manned in an unknown environment, who, in effect, sought peace with a more formidable foe.

A series of treaties were then signed between the Mi'kmaq and the British throughout the mid-1700s. Such treaties, which still did not cede territory on the part of the Mi'kmaq, were punctuated by British bad faith and genocidal tactics, such as the issuance of a scalping proclamation in 1749 and the distribution of disease-ridden blankets as "gifts." In effect, these early British attempts at pacification of a people who had been inhabiting the land since time immemorial failed. No land was ceded.

The Royal Proclamation of 1763, issued by King George III, was, at least on paper, an admittance that Aboriginal title did exist. In essence, the Royal Proclamation gave the original inhabitants title to all

---

1   For more information, see the website of Mi'kmaq historian Daniel N. Paul, http://www.danielnpaul.com, and Daniel N. Paul, *We Were Not the Savages* (Nova Scotia: Fernwood Books, 2007).

traditional lands,, and made it illegal for anyone to purchase lands from "Indians" except for the British Crown. But the Proclamation, as with the rest of the "Covenant Chain" treaties, exists only as paper truths, and was ignored as colonial expansion continued.

As British control of its American colonies began to slip, Loyalist immigration to Mi'kma'ki increased. During the last few decades of the eighteenth century, waves of unsettled colonists, still loyal to the British Crown, began to further encroach upon unceded Wabanaki territory. Despite the signing of the Royal Proclamation, settlement in traditional lands continued without consultation of the Mi'kmaq populations.

The Malicete and Mi'kmaq peoples did in fact try to evict the British colonists through a notice dated as early as 1778. The notice, presented to a congregation of British bureaucrats at Machias, states as follows:

> We desire you to go away with your men in peace and to take all those men who has been fighting and talking against America. If you don't go directly you must take care of your men, and all your English subjects on this River for if any or all of you are killed, it is not our faults, for we give you warning time enough to escape.[2]

Post-Confederation Interactions with the Crown

Mi'kmaq historian and grassroots Treaty scholar Kevin Christmas sums up the post-confederation period as comprised of Mi'kmaq reactions to what the Crown was doing to his people, starting with Diamond Jeannese in 1945:

> He framed the twenty five year plan to assimilate the Indians of Canada. As an anthropologist he was immediately given legitimacy, and the residential school plans became real. This was coupled with the centralization of all the Mi'kmaq into two reservations, the denial of ceremonies, the enforcement of day passes for ration, the implementation of the Indian Agent system, as well as the denial of access to the forests and the fishery.

---

2   For the full document, see Miles Howe, "Tit for Tat – As SWN issues injunction against anti-shalers, Treaty Scholar Patles brings out eviction notice from 1778," *Halifax Media Co-op*, October 4, 2013, http://halifax.mediacoop. ca/story/tit-tat-swn-issues-injunction-against-anti-shalers/19123.

Fishing, cutting, gathering, stewarding, protecting, nursing, caring for all the living things that require water [were unlawful]. We survived by working as migrant labor in the United States because it was unlawful to have money, and only a credit or chit system was in place and only on two days a week, and only at specific stores.

You could not be Indian, and you were prohibited in all occupations and livelihoods because you were Indian. Your children were taken away, you were forced to go away, you were tortured, abused, denied, and treated like children, and all conducted under the auspices of the catholic church.

1969 was the last year of the twenty five year plan for the assimilation of Indians into Canada. Jeannese is still celebrated as the most wonderful custodian of aboriginal culture and traditions.

Then Prime Minister Pierre Trudeau came along with The White Paper in 1969 when the job was finished. From 1969 until today, we have experienced the impacts of these measures. Only remnants of ideas, concepts, legitimacy, tradition, hope, and pleasure remained. Every policy, every effort, every promise was housed in a place of destruction. What we see before us are those that benefited from our displacement from society, not our integration or assimilation. The governments, business, and public sector all benefited from this mad man Jeanesse. All of them bought into the unholy promise to eliminate us forever by casting aside everything we are entitled to and valued, and gave it to someone else to spite us.

The twenties were similarly bleak, the thirties worse, and by the forties folks were glad for war. It began when they returned. They defeated a menace then menaced our people. These people were unstable and in charge.

The answer?

Get rid of them, the Indians and along comes Diamond Jeanesse. Every terror since 1945 has been unleashed upon our people, and all in a concerted attempt to destroy by denial and neglect, in the extreme. To get the Indian out of them... our friends have beaten back many demons and many misguided anthropologists who convince people in charge that they know what is good for us. Was any parent of a residential school child asked for their consent?[3]

---

3   This quotation derives from a personal interview with the author, December
     2013.

SWN versus the Mi'kmaq

SWN Resources Canada, a subsidiary of the Texas-based company Southwestern Energy, is a corporation with deep pockets riding the current fracking wave of shale gas development across North America, and indeed the world. Southwestern Energy is the fifth largest gas company in the United States of America, with gas plays in numerous states. Less reported by the mainstream, it is also engaged in a variety of lawsuits, especially in Pennsylvania and Arkansas. These lawsuits are directly related to the pollution and destruction of the environment, and poisoned water.

In 2010, the then-New Brunswick provincial government of Shawn Graham issued exploratory gas licenses to SWN Resource Canada. Shawn Graham, who won the Kent County political seat in 1998, is a member of one of New Brunswick's dynastic old-money families. Shawn's father, Alan Graham, is a massive landowner in Kent County, and was the Member of the Legislative Assembly (the provincial government house for New Brunswick) for Kent County from 1967 to 1998.

Alan Graham served as Minister of Natural Resources under the Frank McKenna government from 1991 to 1997. McKenna now serves on the board of the TD Bank Group, one of Canada's largest financial service institutions, as well as on the board of directors of Canadian Natural Resources, Canada's second-largest "independent" natural gas producer. Although out of direct political power, McKenna still wields enormous influence as a power player in New Brunswick, and he is a firm proponent of shale gas development as a cure-all to New Brunswick's economic woes. In early 2013, two years after a seismic testing campaign was thwarted in an adjoining county, SWN turned its sights to Kent County, the Graham seat of power. Seismic testing lines (to locate potential locations for fracking injection wells) were slated to pass directly through land owned by Alan Graham. While the royalty scheme in New Brunswick is still being developed, land owners are expected to receive direct royalties from any shale gas plays developed on their land.

The environmental dangers of hydraulic fracturing for shale gas were perhaps ill-understood in New Brunswick in 2010. Grassroots resistance to, or even knowledge of, this water-intensive and environmentally polluting technique was fairly minimal, and limited to a few key voices of former-oil-rig workers turned environmentalists, as well as a few Indigenous activists. However, SWN's 2013 plans to seismic test in Kent

County took into account the potential of Mi'kmaq resistance—especially from the nearby community of Elsipogtog First Nation, one of the largest reserves in New Brunswick. Towards neutralizing that possibility before testing even began, SWN hired former RCMP informant and admitted gang rapist Stephen Sewell, under the company name Chief to Chief Consulting Ltd. Sewell. A Mi'kmaq man from nearby Pabineau First Nation in New Brunswick, Sewell provided SWN with the optics of "Indigenous approval," and several mainstream media articles focused on his inherent Aboriginal expertise, rather than his extremely questionable, criminal and violent history.[4]

In April 2013, Sewell proposed to Elsipogtog Chief Aaron Sock and his elected band council the possibility of hiring several local young men in order to work a variety of security-related duties for SWN. Elsipogtog band council balked at the offer, but Sewell, through a deal orchestrated by the North Shore District Micmac Council Inc (a private enterprise whose board of directors is comprised of eight local New Brunswick Mi'kmaq chiefs) managed to secure funding for the positions. The positions were sub-contracted through Industrial Security Limited (ISL), an Irving-owned company (Irving being among the richest Canadian families, and undoubtedly the most central old-moneyed family in the Maritimes).

In Elsipogtog, unemployment is estimated as high as 80 percent.[5] The possibility of a decent paying job was a definite allure for certain individuals, and Sewell's sub-contracted positions were filled with at least a dozen young Elsipogtog men. Of note, one of Sewell's first hires was Gary Augustine, who was at the time the appointed "War Chief" on the reserve. This had the effect of adding further confusion to the on-reserve situation. Gary Augustine's position as Elsipogtog War Chief was quickly terminated by his brother, Keptin of the Grand Council (a facsimile of a traditional form of government), Noel Augustine.

---

4   Jorge Barrera, "Security firm protecting SWN hired company owned by ex-con who claimed undercover work for RCMP in Akwesasne," *APTN National News*, November 14, 2013, http://warriorpublications.wordpress.com/2013/11/14/security-firm-protecting-swn-hired-company-owned-by-ex-con-who-claimed-undercover-work-for-rcmp-in-akwesasne/.

5   Vincent Schilling, "Getting Jobbed: 15 Tribes with Unemployment Rates over 80 Percent," *Indian Country Today Media Network*, August, 29 2013, http://indiancountrytodaymedianetwork.com/2013/08/29/danger-zone-15-tribes-unemployment-rates-over-80-percent-151078.

With testing beginning, a power vacuum opened up in a community now in need of war-time leadership. Noel Augustine, as Keptin of the Signigtog District of the Grand Council, appointed Sun Dance leader John Levi to the position of Elsipogtog War Chief. Throughout the summer, the Mi'kmaq of Elsipogtog, under Levi, spearheaded theon-the-ground resistance to SWN's attempts to work.

Collaboration and Resistance

Throughout June and July of 2013, actions were limited mostly to highway-side protests. June 21, 2013, along Highway 126 in Kent County, presented something of a minor turning point in the summer's protests. On that day, which also happens to be Canadian "National Aboriginal Day," twelve protesters were arrested. An eight-and-a-half-month pregnant Mi'kmaq woman was arrested, and an Mi'kmaq grandmother was roughed up enough by RCMP that she was bleeding from the mouth by the time she was arrested. The community of Elsipogtog was understandably up in arms.

In response, on June 23, Tobique First Nation member Wendell Nicholas was introduced to the community at an emotional community hall meeting. When first brought before the community of Elsipogtog, Nicholas was introduced as a "UN Independant [sic] Observer." His rather vaguely defined mission at the time was related to making observations and preparing an upcoming report for a branch of the United Nations.

Claire Stewart Kannigan, working for *rabble.ca*, noticed the misprint on Nicholas's shirt ("UN Independant Observer") and started snooping.[6] When Kannigan could not find an established connection between Nicholas and the United Nations, and proceeded to out him on *rabble*, Nicholas promptly re-branded himself—with the assistance of a press conference led by Chief Aaron Sock—as the leader of a new "peacekeeping" team known as the "Elsipogtog Peacekeepers."

In the midst of a heated summer of protests, with residents tired of watching their community members being roughed up by the RCMP,

---

6   Claire Stewart-Kanigan, "Midnight confiscation of drilling equipment at New Brunswick anti-fracking protest," *rabble.ca*, June 25, 2013, http://rabble.ca/news/2013/06/midnight-confiscation-drilling-equipment-new-brunswick-anti-fracking-protest.

the press conference introducing Nicholas was awash with hand shakes, ceremony, and praise for Nicholas—even if his role was not entirely understood or defined as being more than a liaison between Elsipog-tog band council and the RCMP.[7] But Nicholas is an old hand in the game of liaising between First Nations communities and the RCMP. In fact, he wrote the modern-day manual, in the form of the Public Safety Cooperation Protocol (PSCP), which is amongst the memorandums that facilitates sharing information between Indian Act chiefs and the RCMP on Indigenous unrest across Canada.[8] When former Assembly of First Nations (AFN) Chief Phil Fontaine was outed and discredited for collaborating with the RCMP to quash Indigenous unrest in 2007,[9] his intelligence sharing with the police reflected the Nicholas-penned PSCP agreement.

As for Nicholas, he hired members of the Elsipogtog community on as "peacekeepers," and also hired people from outside of the community. Suddenly summertime anti-shale gas protests alongside of the highways in Kent County were highly monitored affairs, with people wearing bright orange "Elsipogtog Peacekeepers" t-shirts wandering around ev-erywhere, some speaking to the police, some taking notes on clipboards.

One of those protest monitors was former US National Guardsman and police officer—and Nicholas's cousin—John Deveau. At some point, possibly due to failing health or prior commitments, Nicholas stopped being the public face of the Elsipogtog Peacekeepers. Handing over the daily duties to Deveau, Nicholas retired to a behind-the-scenes role as Elsipogtog's Public Safety Advisor, where he appears to remain.

Deveau took over the directorship of the "peacekeeping" team, and is actively drawing a salary of $60,000 a year as the director of the "Wa-banaki Peacekeepers," complete with a budget for equipment, three oth-er full-time salary positions, and a salaried part-time staff that can swell to five members, as needed.

---

7   CBC News, "Elsipogtog chief appoints 'peacekeeper' in shale gas dispute," June 27, 2003, http://www.cbc.ca/news/canada/new-brunswick/elsipogtog-chief-appoints-peacekeeper-in-shale-gas-dispute-1.1365143.

8   Royal Canadian Mounted Police, "Public Safety Cooperation Protocol Between the Assembly of First Nations and Royal Canadian Mounted Police," May 18, 2004, http://www.rcmp-grc.gc.ca/ccaps-spcca/psc-csp-protoc-eng.htm.

9   Tim Groves and Martin Lukacs, "Assembly of First Nations, RCMP co-operated on response to mass protests in 2007," February 15, 2003, http://www.thestar.com/news/canada/2013/02/15/assembly_of_first_nations_rcmp_cooperated _on_response_to_mass_protests_in_2007.html.

All summer long, and into the fall, the Deveau-run, joint AFN/
RCMP crisis response team liaised with SWN, the RCMP, and Elsipogtog band council, all the while presenting itself as a neutral negotiating
body to grassroots activists on the ground.

Summoning the Warrior Society

Towards the end of July, Elsipogtog band members who had been active in the grassroots resistance for months requested the assistance of the
Mi'kmaq Warriors Society, an independently run organization that operates outside of the scope of both Indian Act and Grand Council leadership.

There was a certain tension between the Society, which does maintain its own ranking system (including "Chiefs"), and Elsipogtog War
Chief John Levi and a group of his staunch supporters. Levi, named
War Chief through the Grand Council, had no titled standing with the
Society. Levi, as a community member of Elsipogtog, was also largely
responsible and loyal to Chief Sock. The Society, for its part, although
responsive to the needs of the Elsipogtog community that had invited
them, operated with a certain degree of military regimen. The Society
was also staunchly against the Indian Act, and favored a treaty-based
solution to the immediate issues at play. Something of an inner power
struggle began to fester, especially as youth from Elsipogtog began to
seek out membership in the Society.

The summer campaign of protest against SWN came to a head on
July 28, when several key pieces of SWN's seismic-testing equipment
were seized along a dirt road. With Levi participating in the annual Sun
Dance in Elsipogtog, community members and members of the Society blockaded SWN's work crew, and three women chained and locked
themselves to a blockaded truck.

RCMP presence was formidable. Although the cover of darkness
made impossible a full accounting of the police forces on hand, estimates
range into the dozens of officers. Due to failed negotiations, which heavily featured Deveau's Peacekeeper team, the stand-off lasted for about
eight tension-filled hours.

The next day, RCMP seized the launching point for the blockade, a
"Ski-doo" shack filled with supplies and water over which flew the ubiquitous Warrior flag. The RCMP, it was relayed, were treating the shack as
a crime scene. Upon hearing that the shack had been seized, members of

the Society returned to the scene, and chased off several RCMP officers. Amidst the celebratory mood, it was learned that SWN had decided to stop seismic testing for the summer months. The company noted that they would return in mid-September to continue with their search for shale gas deposits.

Interestingly enough, during the remainder of the summer, members of the Society began to make key inroads into inter-cultural allegiances. The surrounding non-Indigenous population was, to a degree, allied with the anti-shale gas movement during the summer months, but was not necessarily activated into on-the-ground roles, per say.

On paper, over two-dozen interest groups in New Brunswick had called for a moratorium on the process of hydraulic fracturing. But time and again, the absence of on-the-ground capacity, especially as it pertained to the greater non-Indigenous community, was one of the key hindrances to the possibility of direct action. In effect, it was the Indigenous community members, specifically from Elsipogtog, that were paying the price—in terms of arrests—while the non-Indigenous supported from the sidelines.

The Blockade within a Blockade

It was the Society, with the allure of a quasi-military force at least open to the potential of increased degrees of action against SWN, that began to attract like-minded individuals from the Kent County environs. The Society spent the remainder of August and September forging allegiances, especially with the Acadian population in nearby "settler" communities.

Eight weeks later, in late September, SWN's sub-contracted All-Terrain Vehicles were spotted on Highway 11 near Kouchibouguac National Park, New Brunswick. As well, numerous pieces of seismic-testing equipment, including five "thumper" trucks, were located in an Irving-owned, fenced-in compound at the junction of Highways 134 and 11, near the town of Rexton, New Brunswick.

The focal point of the re-energized protest movement became the main entrance to the compound. Aside from two dirt tracks, there was only one gravel road into the compound. With five thumpers inside the compound, along with numerous boxes of currently unidentified equipment, it was a trove of equipment, which, if contained, would present a stumbling block to SWN's intentions to perform seismic testing.

By September 29, RCMP forces closed off automobile access to the Irving-owned compound, from both north and south exits to Highway 134 off the Highway 11, as well as Highway 134, itself, in both directions—ostensibly for the protection of those protesting. In response, on September 30, members of the Society, assisted by community members, felled several pine trees and lit fires along the highway. With police presence heavy along both extremities of the encampment, the anti-shale gas fight in Kent County had taken on a new and risky dimension.

As the blockade-within-a-blockade continued, a more pointed philosophical schism began to develop between those actively participating in the encampment.

On the one hand were those aligned with Elsipogtog First Nation Chief Aaron Sock. For the most part, this paradigm was comprised mostly of members of the Elsipogtog community. Sock, from a public perspective, had come down firmly against SWN's presence in his traditional territories. On October 1, for example, buoyed on by the support of hundreds, Sock read from a Band Council Resolution stating that his community was prepared to reclaim all unoccupied Crown Lands in Signigtog District, which comprises most of present day provincial New Brunswick. Councilor Robert Levi from Elsipogtog then announced that the Elsipogtog band chief and council would be issuing SWN Resources Canada an eviction notice to have all their equipment removed from the currently blockaded compound by midnight, October 1. Jim Pictou, representing the Mi'qmaw Warriors Society, noted that the Society would personally escort them out of the province of New Brunswick. Chief Candice Paul of St. Mary's First Nation then offered the support of members of her community in assisting the Warriors in their escort. It was a heady announcement, to be sure, and was coupled with Sock's determination that there would be "no more negotiations with anybody."

But by midnight, Sock and his council were nowhere to be found. The RCMP went on high alert in preparation for some as-yet unknown action. The Society, ostensibly the security force on the side of the protesters, had not been informed of any Elsipogtog council-led action. This was the beginning of deep-seated misunderstandings.

On the other side of the philosophical divide were members of the Society and their supporters, who appeared fixed on a Treaty-based resolution to the blockade, and to the larger issues of illegal colonization of traditional territories. This philosophy, which would necessarily render all Indian Act chiefs into little more than representatives of the colonial, federal government, is often referred to as "extremist," as having it come to fruition would require deep transitions in the current, established system of colonially-imposed Indigenous governance in Canada.

Towards these ends, negotiations—if they could be termed negotiations—between the RCMP and the Treaty-based Society were peppered with lists of demands that had hung like so many elephants in the room since colonial times. On October 9, treaty scholar Suzanne Patles presented a list of demands, which included:
- Produce all Bills of Sales, Sold, Ceded, Granted and Extinguished.
- Lands for New Brunswick.
- Produce documents proving Cabot's Doctrine of Discovery.
- Produce consents for Loyalists to land in Nova Scotia/New Brunswick.
- Produce records of Townships created and consents by Chiefs to allow this.
- Produce agreements or consents by all New Brunswick Chiefs who agreed to Confederation of 1867.
- Produce all documents creating border divisions, that divide the Wabanaki confederacy.
- Produce the Orders from the Lords of Trade to the Governor of the Colonies.[10]

Patles herself was doubtful that the provincial government would respond to these demands, lest it acknowledge itself as an illegal, corporate entity without the deed to be doing the things it had done since first contact.

The rift between those backing Chief Sock's approach and those committed to the Society's treaty-based stance was solidified in a series of meetings between Sock and New Brunswick Premier David Alward. Despite consulting amongst themselves at the encampment on Highway 134 for several days prior to the series of meetings, participants from numerous local interest groups, which included representatives from the Society, were ultimately not invited (or invited to only one, quickly arranged meeting in Moncton with the premier).

To make matters worse, a series of hand-written notes between Sock and the premier surfaced from one of these meetings. Although taken

---

10   Miles Howe, "Selling the farm without the deed," *Halifax Media Co-op*, October 9, 2013, http://halifax.mediacoop.ca/story/selling-farm-without-deed/19187.

in point form, the contents of the notes suggested that Sock was enter-taining the idea of removing the blockade and accepting incentives of various forms for his cash-strapped community, in exchange for SWN's exploration program to continue. It was also revealed that John Deveau, of the Elsipogtog Peacekeepers, was also on provincial payroll as an ap-pointed advisor to Sock.

The Society, which found itself represented at the one-off meeting by non-Society members from Elsipogtog, interpreted this as a serious slap in the face. Communication with Sock and his representatives, who remained on site, disintegrated to the point that the encampment was essentially divided into a Warriors Society section and a non-Society section. At one point, food and supplies were even delivered to the two alternate encampments, depending on where one's allegiances lay.

RCMP Raid, Fallout

On October 17, the RCMP raided the entire encampment with an un-til-then unprecedented force. Literally hundreds of Tactical Unit mem-bers from the provinces of Nova Scotia, Prince Edward Island, Quebec, and New Brunswick descended upon the encampment in the pre-dawn hours. The Tactical Units were supported by several units of Emergency Response Teams, or ERTs, armed with less-lethal firearms as well as assault rifles. Also present were K-9 units with short-leashed dogs.

The original raid on the encampment resulted in about fifteen ar-rests, as the RCMP focused primarily on disabling members of the Warriors Society and liberating SWN's equipment. As members of the surrounding community were made aware, through social media, that an RCMP raid was underway, dozens of people, mostly from Elsipogtog, attempted to break through what was now an established line of RCMP Tactical Units. More less-lethal rounds were fired, residents were beaten and pepper sprayed, and in all about forty people were arrested.

While most of those arrested, myself included, in the initial raid upon the Warrior encampment were released within twenty-four hours, four members of the Society were to bear the brunt of the charges laid from October 17. As it turns out, the RCMP, working in conjunction with Irving's ISL security force, had managed to finesse a narrative in which members of the Society had been "escalating tensions" at the en-campment since at least October 15. Three of the four members of the

Society who remain incarcerated have charges laid upon them related to threats, assault, and unlawful confinement related to October 15 and 16.

For the anti-shale gas movement in Kent County, the obvious setback was the incarceration and momentary blow dealt to the Society, as well as the RCMP-assisted liberation of SWN's seismic-testing equipment. But from the ashes of the encampment, and the polarizing—and eventually crippling—philosophical differences of approach between those aligned with the Indian Act and Chief Sock and those aligned with a treaty solution, sprang an arguably stronger anti-shale gas movement.

As SWN figured to promptly begin seismic testing along stretches of Highway 11 in Kent County, a new encampment sprang up. Images of the brutal raid had flashed across the country, and assistance from Indigenous supporters from various nations, as well as from non-Indigenous supporters from around the world, rained down upon Kent County. In this renewed anti-shale gas fervor, emanating now from many corners of Canada, the differences in approach and philosophy suddenly became secondary behind the primacy of stopping the Texas-based company however possible.

Stifled again by the daytime slowdowns and nighttime raids on equipment, SWN attempted to impose a new legally binding injunction against the anti-shale gas activists in order to finish their seismic-testing program and move on to the next stage: fracking. While a judge granted the injunction, issuing the RCMP the right to arbitrarily arrest people within a 250 meter front-and-back and twenty meter side-to-side parameter of SWN equipment, protesters responded by lighting tire fires along the highway for three successive days.

For reasons that are not yet apparent, on Friday, December 6, SWN issued a press release stating that they had completed their seismic testing in New Brunswick, and would return in 2015. The press release thanked New Brunswickers for their "continued support." Missing from the press release was the fact that in Kent County, the company had only obtained about 50 percent of their planned data. As far as the remainder of their licensed areas in New Brunswick, an area that covers millions of acres, it remains unclear whether they are currently testing, or have plans to test.

The fallout from the 2013 anti-shale gas actions in Kent County continues to unfold. Four members of the Society remain incarcerated, related to the raid of October 17 and supposed activities on the 15th and 16th. The threat to water related to SWN's shale gas exploration program has led to new allegiances both between Indigenous communities, as well as in the broader context of non-Indigenous allies—especially in the "threat zone" of Kent County. Still, there is serious trauma and a breakdown of relations between the RCMP and, especially, members of the Elsipogtog First Nation.

This is certainly not the first "modern day" clash between armed forces representing Crown and corporate interests and the Mi'kmaq people. The resistance at Elsipogtog, and especially the raid of October 17, does mark a serious example of Crown-imposed violence upon the Mi'kmaq. It is difficult to contextualize it in the notion of a breach of trust, as it is unclear from an outsider's perspective whether trust did indeed exist prior to this moment. The fallout remains to be understood in the months to come.

PORTS AS PLACES OF STICKINESS IN A WORLD OF GLOBAL FLOWS

Andrew Herod

Ports, airports, and land-based border crossings are key control points of the global economy through which goods and people must pass as they move between different, absolute spaces—say, from the spaces of international waters to the spaces of domestic sovereign territory or from the spaces of one nation-state to those of another.

Bearing this in mind, it is noteworthy that in recent years the image of the shrinking globe has become a popular one to represent processes of globalization. As travel times diminish and as people on different sides of the planet carry on conversations in real time via Skype or email, the importance of geography and location allegedly diminished. Significantly, central to this discourse is the depiction of globalization as a process whereby other spatial scales of social life are eclipsed—globalization, then, is presented as the "delocalization"[1] and/or "denationalization"[2] of economic and political life. The only scale that counts, we are told, is the global.

It is arguably management guru Kenichi Ohmae who has been most associated with the idea of the inevitability of a growing placelessness and borderlessness in the face of global capital flows. For twenty-three years a senior partner in McKinsey & Company, the international consulting firm, Ohmae has argued that the boundaries that have served as the circumscribers of various absolute spaces—most particularly the nation-state but other spaces too (e.g., the jurisdictional boundaries of cities and regions)—are becoming increasingly porous to capital flows and thus of less and less significance in how the global economy functions. Within the kinds of neoliberal writing exemplified by Ohmae and others, it has become quite fashionable to suggest that globalization is birthing a borderless world, a world of "superconductive"[3] and "friction-free"[4]

1   Paul Virilio, *Open Sky* (New York: Verso, 1997); J. Gray, *False Dawn: The Delusions of Global Capitalism* (New York: New Press, 1998).

2   Saskia Sassen, "Globalization or denationalization?," *Review of International Political Economy* 10, no. 1 (2003):1-22.

3   Lowell Bryan and Diana Farrell, *Market Unbound: Unleashing Global Capitalism* (Hoboken: Wiley, 1996).

4   Bill Gates, with Nathan Myhrvold and Peter Rinearson, *The Road Ahead* (New York: Viking, 1995).

capitalism in which capital—whether in its money or its commodity form—is increasingly able to flow across the planet's surface without hindrance.[5] The future, we are told, will be one in which there are single global markets, in which "all goods for sale in the world will be available for you to examine, compare, and, often, customize," and in which the "information highway will be able to sort consumers according to much finer individual distinctions"[6] so as to bring to them tailored products from across the world more quickly than ever before.

In contrast to such proclamations about the death of space and nation-states wrought by global capital, one group of workers—dockers—can serve as important actors in this globalization drama, facilitating the smooth flows of goods at some moments but disrupting it at others. The power of place is, then, a location from which to intervene in a world of global flows.

Dockers as Agents of Stickiness in the Global Economy

Despite the rhetoric that "national borders are far less constrictive than they once were," there are in fact numerous points of potential "stickiness" in this supposed world of free-flowing capital.[7] Ports are one such point, and the workers who toil within them can play significant roles in either fostering capital flows or in impeding them. Indeed, there is a significant irony in the way in which the global economy is unfolding in that, in some ways, dockers can play a much more disruptive role in the planetary movement of goods than they perhaps could in the past because of the growing use by manufacturers and retailers of "just-in-time" (JIT) methods of fabrication and inventory control as we move towards a world dominated by what Agger has called "fast capitalism."[8]

Arguably most advanced in the automobile assembly industry, JIT developed as a system of inventory management in Japan. Its basic

---

5   This idea of frictionless interaction is not new. Over a century ago Clapp suggested that a port's function is to bring countries "into contact and to enable them, with the least possible friction and loss of energy, to effect" exchange between them. E.J. Clapp, *The Port of Hamburg* (New Haven: Yale University Press, 1911).

6   Gates et al., *The Road Ahead*, 158, 171.

7   Kenichi Ohmae, *The Next Global Stage: Challenges and Opportunities in Our Borderless World* (Upper Saddle River, NJ: Wharton School Publishing, 2005), 20.

8   Kenichi Ohmae, "Managing in a Borderless World," *Harvard Business Review* (May 1989): 2–9.

elements were developed at Toyota in the 1950s. By the 1980s JIT had begun to be adopted by many US manufacturers. It is not confined to manufacturing, though. Many supermarkets get produce delivered just in time to put it on the shelf, thanks to more sophisticated ways of controlling their stock levels that have resulted from the use of the ubiquitous bar code, as do some fast food restaurants.[9] Growing numbers of service sector firms have also been adopting it. It is even being used in healthcare delivery.[10]

In its most basic form, JIT is a system in which parts for manufacturers and stock for retailers are delivered to a factory or store just before they are needed. For instance, in the case of automobile assemblers, components may arrive at an assembly plant only hours or minutes before they are bolted on to a vehicle moving down the production line. At the heart of any JIT system lies the *kanban* ("card" or "signboard" in Japanese), which refers to the way in which the rate of use of components controls the rate at which they are produced and sent to the shop floor. This provides manufacturers several advantages. First, it reduces the amount of a firm's capital tied up in components. In previous models of manufacturing and inventory control—sometimes referred to as the "just-in-case" model—large warehouses would typically be constructed to store huge quantities of components so that they would be on hand when needed. Not only did this require companies to purchase large amounts of land on which such warehouses could sit and to have the staff to operate them, together with complex inventory controls to be able to find components when needed, but it also meant that they might have millions of dollars in inventory sitting idly by for several months before it would be used. Reducing the amount of capital tied up in inventory increases efficiency and improves quality control because it allows defects in components to be discovered sooner. The system also places great pressures upon workers (leading to the term "management-by-stress") because everyone must now work at the same speed so that bottlenecks do not build up. Hence, whereas in the past some groups of workers might be able to "bank time" so as to build in some small relaxation

---

9   Interestingly, in the late 1940s production engineers for Toyota observed that supermarkets stock only what they expect to sell in a given period of time and customers take usually just what they need for the foreseeable future. They then sought to apply this logic to automobile manufacturing.

10   Carola Mamberto, "What factory managers can teach hospital wards." *Wall Street Journal*, June 25, 2007, B3.

interval as they waited for their confederates to catch up with them, now such abilities are seen by management as evidence that too many workers are employed in a particular part of the assembly line and that some should be reassigned. At the same time, non-problem departments are assumed to be oversupplied with labor and so this also provides an incentive for worker reallocation—the emergence of problems is deemed to be evidence of the system having reached its optimum level of labor and resource allocation. Unlike in earlier forms of production where an assembly line could only be used to produce a single product and producing a different one required closing the line and an expensive retooling, JIT also allows for a variety of models to be produced on the same line simultaneously.

JIT, then, has a lot to offer management. The greatest savings come in the reduced costs of inventory stocking and control and from greater flexibility within the labor process. However, there is one significant drawback: firms are very vulnerable to supply chain disruptions. For instance, in 1998 a strike at just two components supplying plants in Flint, Michigan, brought General Motors's North American operations to a grinding halt in only a few days—at its height, 193,517 GM workers were laid off at twenty-seven of the company's twenty-nine North American assembly plants, and some 117 components plants owned by GM subsidiaries had either to close or to cut back on production.[11] Although, then, JIT is placing shop-floor workers in an increasingly unpleasant work environment, it does also put some workers—those who find themselves at particular control points in the flow of components and other goods—in a powerful position. Dockers sit right at the heart of one of these types of nodes—ports.

Dockers' ability to halt the flows of goods that are emblematic of the globalization that has been reshaping the planet's economy—and thus to serve as agents of stickiness in what is presented as the fluid space of global flows—has been evidenced in numerous disputes. Perhaps one of the most significant has involved collaborative efforts between South African and Australian dockers, both in opposition to apartheid

---

11 Some remained open because they were supplying parts to other assemblers, like GM's joint-venture partner Toyota. Andrew Herod, "Implications of Just-in-Time production for union strategy: Lessons from the 1998 General Motors-United Auto Workers dispute," *Annals of the Association of American Geographers* 90, no. 3 (2000): 521–547. [Publisher's erratum for figures published in *Annals of the Association of American Geographers* 91, no. 1 (2001): 200–202.]

and more recently in an effort to stop union-busting efforts in Australia. Australia's Waterside Workers' Federation (WWF) frequently boycotted ships coming from apartheid South Africa, engaging in forty-eight-hour unloading bans in which union representatives would inspect arriving ships and, should the cabins of black crew members be found wanting, refusing to offload cargo until they had been refurbished.[12] Equally, members of the Seamen's Union of Australia (SUA) played a key role in the anti-apartheid struggle through imposing an oil embargo against the regime in Pretoria, a campaign coordinated with the Danish and British seafarer unions.[13]

Remembering the support that Australian dockers had given them in their own struggles, South African dockers refused on several occasions during the 1990s to unload Australian ships in protest at the attempts by the Australian federal government and several state governments to introduce anti-union legislation. They also organized union marches in Durban to oppose the new laws and supported the April 1998 strike initiated by the Maritime Union of Australia (MUA) against the anti-union stevedoring Patrick Corporation to force the rehiring of some two-thousand dockers whom the company had fired.[14] Significantly, this strike—which was arguably the most significant Australian industrial dispute of the 1990s—affected myriad Australian imports and exports, particularly those in the auto, wool, cotton, wine, beef, and fish-farming industries. Hence, Toyota Australia, the country's largest car manufacturer, was only able to avert closing its Melbourne production line when a shipload of spare parts was brought into a unionized dock at the last minute.

Some $19.5 million worth of Kia vehicles and parts being imported from South Korea were also held up on the Melbourne docks, which led company officials to fear that the dispute would bring problems for its planned launch of two new models. Non-industrial sectors also felt the pinch, with many concerned that the $2.3 billion wool export industry would be threatened if the dispute spread to P&O, Patrick Stevedores's chief rival, given that wool was Australia's third-largest export behind coal and gold. The wine industry, too, worried that wineries would have

---

12   Rob Lambert, "Free trade and the new labour internationalism," in *Free Trade and Transnational Labour (Rethinking Globalizations)*, ed. Andreas Bieler, Bruno Ciccaglione, John Hilary, and Ingemar Lindberg (New York: Routledge, 2014).

13   Diane Kirby, Voices from the *Ships: Australia's Seafarers and Their Union* (Sydney: University of New South Wales Press, 2009).

14   The SUA merged with the WWF in 1993 to form the MUA.

to shut down, a development that one industry spokesperson described as potentially "catastrophic" for the country's $487 million export industry because wineries would be unable to fill orders for the upcoming high-summer consumption season in Europe.[15]

As a way to put pressure on Patrick Stevedores and the Australian federal and state governments, the London-based International Transport Federation encouraged its affiliates in some 120 countries to campaign against the firm. In response, the US International Longshore and Warehouse Union staged protests in San Francisco whilst the Dutch FNV Bondgenoten likewise engaged in solidarity actions against ships handled by Patrick. Japanese, New Guinean, Indian, and other dockers also boycotted Patrick ships.[16] Perhaps paradoxically, given its centrality to capital's globalization, the dockers' use of the space-crossing technology of the Internet to get out to a global audience news of the dispute and to encourage supporters across the planet to take action to support the fired workers would play an important role in their ultimate victory.[17]

As a result of the close linkages that had been developed between the MUA and the South African Transport & Allied Workers Union (SATAWU), in November 1999 the two unions came together at the 5th Congress of the Southern Initiative on Globalization and Trade Union Rights (SIGTUR) in Johannesburg to sign a declaration of intent to form a global union between themselves.[18] Their main objective was to deepen connections between one another so that they could more readily respond to issues that might arise during periods of crisis. Significantly, this led the MUA to launch an initiative to similarly

---

15 Peter James Spielmann, "Australia dock strike hurts economy." Associated Press, April 19, 1998, www.apnewsarchive.com/1998/Australia -Dock-Strike-Hurts-Economy/id-40676a4ed364ea5a9a41bd8f9a9ccfa0; last accessed April 4, 2013.

16 Tom Bramble, *War on the Waterfront* (Brisbane: Brisbane Defend Our Unions Committee, 1998).

17 E. Lee, "Towards global networked unions," in *Labour and Globalisation: Results and Prospects*, ed. Ronaldo Munck (Liverpool: Liverpool University Press, 2004), 71–82.

18 SIGTUR began life as an Indian Ocean network, linking Australian unions with the newly emergent South African unions. Its goal was to develop connections between Global South unions. It has since incorporated other unions, including the Korean Confederation of Trade Unions, the Philippine's Kilusang Mayo Uno, Brazil's Central Única dos Trabalhadores, India's Center of Indian Trade Unions, and the All-India Trade Union Congress, together with unions in Malaysia, China, Indonesia, Thailand, Sri Lanka, and Pakistan.

prepare port workers and their unions across the globe through forming the Mining and Maritime Global Network.[19] More recently both the MUA and SATAWU have been involved in supporting the campaign for boycotts, divestment, and sanctions against Israel. In January 2009 the MUA's Western Australia branch called for a boycott of all Israeli vessels and all vessels bearing goods arriving from, or going to, Israel. In response, SATAWU dockers turned around an Israeli Zim cargo ship in Port Durban. The MUA has also adopted a campaign to stop the transportation of Caterpillar earthmoving and mining equipment through the port of Freemantle as a protest against the company supplying the Israeli government with bulldozers that are used to demolish the homes of Palestinians in the West Bank.

A number of labor disputes in the US have likewise illustrated dockers' ability to make ports sticky nodes within the contemporary world economy. One of the most significant took place in 2002 when the contract between the International Longshore and Warehouse Union (ILWU), representing some 10,500 dockworkers at twenty-nine Pacific Coast ports, and the Pacific Maritime Association (PMA), representing the shipping lines, expired on July 1. Efforts to negotiate a new one dragged on, largely because of disagreement over the PMA's demand to introduce new labor-saving technology (specifically, the automatic scanning of containers that would eliminate about six-hundred clerk positions), its demand for cutbacks in health care, and its unwillingness to provide for increases in pensions. Once the contract expired the union and PMA agreed to operate the ports using day-to-day contract extensions as they continued to seek a new agreement. However, although the union consented to some concessions on the matter of the new computer technology, PMA negotiators refused to guarantee that any jobs created by the new technology would be reserved for ILWU members. After several weeks of fruitless negotiations and the PMA's claim that ILWU members were engaged in a slowdown of work at strategic choke point ports, on September 27 the Association locked out the union.

The lockout lasted for eleven days before President Bush invoked his powers under the federal Taft-Hartley Act to declare a national emergency and force the PMA to allow dockers back to work until the Christmas season had passed. Such was the fear of what the dispute might do to the US economy that, according to union representatives, the Bush

---

19 Lambert, "Free trade and the new labour internationalism."

administration also threatened to remove the ILWU from under the jurisdiction of the National Labor Relations Act and place it instead under the jurisdiction of the Railway Labor Act (a move that would give the president greater powers to stop walkouts and a long-time PMA goal), to break up the union's coast-wide bargaining unit on "anti-trust" grounds (such that the union could only bargain on a port-by-port basis, which would prevent dockers in one port from striking in support of dockers in another), and to have military personnel run the ports.[20] There were even allegations that Homeland Security Director Tom Ridge and Defense Secretary Donald Rumsfeld had called ILWU President James Spinosa to suggest that any disruption of the country's economy would be viewed as a threat to national security because it threatened the "war on terrorism."

As it turned out, such fears were perhaps well founded. At the time the West Coast trade was worth about $300 billion a year and the 183 million tons of cargo imported and exported each year constituted some 42 percent of all US waterborne trade. Given that almost 70 percent of Alaska's consumer goods were being shipped through the Port of Tacoma, the port's closure soon caused food and other shortages in that state. Although a week after the lockout began Totem Ocean Trailer Express allowed ILWU Local 23 members to load its Alaska-bound ships, an action quickly followed by CSX Lines, the remaining West Coast ports remained at a standstill. Millions of dollars' worth of perishable cargo spoiled and had to be either destroyed or left to rot. Many retailers missed vital pre-Christmas deliveries, which made it difficult for them to build up inventories for the upcoming holiday shopping season. Toyota claimed to have lost $80 million in sales because of delayed shipments of vehicles and the parts vital to its JIT operations. As a result of lack of parts, the company reduced overtime at both its Kentucky and Indiana plants, as did Nissan at its assembly plant in Smyrna, Tennessee. The NUMMI plant in Fremont, California, a joint venture of General Motors and Toyota making the Chevrolet Prizm, Toyota Corolla, and Toyota Tacoma pickup trucks, had to shutter because of a lack of parts. Retailers were also impacted. The Gap laid off workers in several of its California stores because it was unable to restock shelves, an act that

---

20 Forcing the ILWU back to the old system of port-by-port bargaining would mean that actions in one port would violate the Taft-Hartley Act's prohibition of secondary boycotts.

highlights the significance of Asian factories for its operations. Many other retailers, including American Eagle Outfitters and Hobby-Town, a 150-store chain in Nebraska that relied upon the Christmas market for about 20 percent of its annual sales, were likewise negatively affected. Exporters, too, were impacted—with about half of US meat exports being shipped through West Coast ports to Asia, meat packers began to reduce slaughtering operations, which led to a drop in cattle prices for farmers as demand fell. Exports of US wheat to Japan, Taiwan, China, and the Philippines were also hurt, leading to price rises for consumers in these countries. Meanwhile, backlogged shipping companies raised container costs and charged ports dramatically inflated congestion fees.

Although the closure of the ports lasted only ten days, by the time it ended, industry analysts calculated, the lockout's overall cost to the US economy had been between \$2 billion and \$15 billion, depending upon what was considered to have been impacted.[21] Furthermore, given the importance of JIT for many businesses it is estimated that for every day the ports remained closed most firms' supply chains were backed up by one week, though for some it took six months before their supply chains fully recovered. Such was the power of the union to cripple the ports' operation that when the ILWU and PMA finally came to an agreement on a new contract in late November, the president of ILWU Local 23 at the Port of Tacoma was able to boast that it was "the richest contract we've ever negotiated."[22]

If the 2002 conflict dramatically showed dockers' power to bring supply chains to a halt, that power was again on display in late November 2012 when five-hundred members of the ILWU's relatively small Local 63A-OCU (Office Clerical Unit) struck at the ports of Los Angeles and Long Beach, California. The dispute's cause was the clerical workers' fear that the Harbor Employers' Association planned to outsource their jobs to Costa Rica and other parts of the United States (an allegation denied

---

21   Most estimates put the figure at about \$1 billion a day, nearly 4 percent of the nation's output (Brad Plumer, "Could a port strike really cripple the US economy?," *The Washington Post*, December 27). Hall explores the difficulties in getting an exact accounting of the strike's cost (Peter V. Hall, "'We'd Have to Sink the Ships': Impact Studies and the 2002 West Coast Port Lockout," *Economic Development Quarterly* 18, no. 4 (2004): 354–367).

22   Al Gibbs, "Longshore proposal called 'Win-win' deal; Negotiations: Workers' pay will increase \$3 an hour over 6 years if plan ratified in voting that begins Jan. 6," *News Tribune* (Tacoma, WA), December 27, 2002, D1.

by the HEA). The eight-day dispute was backed by some ten thousand ILWU members who refused to cross the clerical workers' picket lines. Whilst facilities for handling break-bulk cargo like raw steel and tanker traffic remained unaffected, the dispute effectively shut down ten of the two ports' combined fourteen container terminals. It was estimated to have cost the economy about $1 billion a day and to have impacted the jobs of approximately 1.2 million Southern Californians and 3.6 million workers nationally who are directly or indirectly involved in moving freight to and from the ports. Although the dispute did not greatly affect retailers preparing for Christmas, as many had received their stock several weeks earlier, towards its end it did begin to disrupt several US manufacturers' supply chains, as ships filled with parts were stuck in the ports or forced to moor offshore.

Significantly, less than a month later another group of dockers, this time East and Gulf Coast dockers represented by the International Longshoremen's Association (ILA), also threatened to flex their muscles to show their capacity to be agents of stickiness in the global economy.[23] Cautioning that they were going to strike in ports from Massachusetts to Texas should their demands concerning container royalty payments not be met, this would be the first coast-wide strike since 1977, when a two-month walkout paralyzed the flow of billions of dollars of imports and exports.[24] The affected ports handle some 110 million tons of cargo a year, about 40 percent of all container cargo traffic in the US. A strike's impact in the New York region alone was estimated by the Port Authority of New York and New Jersey—responsible for overseeing the movement of $208 billion in cargo in 2011, the most of any East or

---

23 The union's contract had actually expired on September 30, and there had been fears in August that a strike would happen, leading some to worry that it would cost over $200 billion in the run-up to the Thanksgiving and Christmas sales season. In the end an October strike was averted by a mutual agreement to extend the then-current contract.

24 Container royalty payments are a legacy of the union's success during the 1960s in negotiating a Guaranteed Annual Income (GAI) for dockers who were to be laid off because of job losses caused by the introduction of containerization (Andrew Herod, "Labor's spatial praxis and the geography of contract bargaining in the US east coast longshore industry, 1953–89," *Political Geography* 16, no. 2 (1997): 145–169.). The GAI was phased out in the 1990s and the royalties are now used to supplement dockers' wages and to fund an ILA health care fund. In 2012, the royalties amounted to $4.85 on each ton of containerized cargo handled by ILA members.

Gulf Coast port—to be about $136 million a week in personal income and $110 million in economic output.[25] Meanwhile, the ocean carriers planned to charge a $1,000 congestion fee per container for every day the ships were held up offshore, which they saw as a way to make up for some of their own loses (carriers only make money when they actually transport goods). This would have affected retailers, who would either have to absorb the costs or pass them on to customers. Moreover, many shippers worried that goods ordered from the Far East in the run-up to the Lunar New Year celebrations in early February could be caught in supply chain choke points. Thus, retailers like Wal-Mart, Target, and Best Buy feared that a strike would delay their spring and summer shipments, given that the port of New York/New Jersey alone handles approximately 10 percent of US imports coming from China.[26]

Fears about a strike's impact were so great that the National Retail Federation sent a letter to President Obama calling upon him to intervene in much the same way that President Bush had done in 2002. Although in the end a strike was avoided when the two parties came to agreement (after several extensions) on a new contract in February 2013, the palpable dread on the part of many retailers and manufacturers that a settlement would not be reached and that waterfronts would be deserted for possibly weeks speaks to dockers' power to halt the flow of goods in a supposedly borderless global economy. This was particularly so because stockpiling parts and goods has become less of an option for manufacturers, retailers and others due to the just-in-time nature of modern business.

Controlling Space, Defending Lives

Dockers' ability to hold up shipments through ports—or air cargo handlers' ability to hold up shipments through airports—challenges

---

25 The ILA indicated that not all cargo would be affected and that dockers would still handle US mail, military cargo, perishable goods (fresh—though not frozen—fruits and vegetables), and non-containerized goods and cars (Harold J. Daggett, "Strike Preparations" memo from Harold Daggett, ILA International President to ILA members, dated December 19, 2012. Available at www.ilaunion.org/pdf/StrikePreparations.pdf; last accessed April 5, 2012). S. Greenhouse, "Dockworkers Strike Threatens to Close East Coast Ports," *New York Times*, December 26, 2012.

26 Lori Ann LaRocco, "'Container cliff': East Coast Faces 'Devastating' Port Strike." *CNBC News*, online at www.cnbc.com/id/100332472; last accessed April 5, 2013.

the neoliberal point of view that we are moving headlong into a world wherein political borders no longer matter, a world of frictionless flows of goods and capital. Instead, there are and always will be places of stickiness within the global economy that, ironically, are central to contemporary globalization. Such sticky places provide, perhaps, opportunities for workers to challenge neoliberalism.

There are, however, other geographical considerations that come from contemplating dockers' activities. For one, images of borderlessness rely upon a particular representation of the nation-state: that of a territorialized "power container whose administrative purview corresponds exactly to its territorial delimitation."[27] Through their actions, then, dockers can hinder movement into and out of this container, thereby reinforcing the integrity of the national space-economy.[28] They can be agents of capital's circulation or of its paralysis.

Such a territorial view is not the only way that the nation-state can be viewed. Latour has argued that the world's complexity cannot be captured by "notions of levels, layers, territories, [and] spheres." Instead, we must think of states as "fibrous, thread-like, wiry, stringy, ropy, [and] capillary." Likewise, Appadurai has suggested that there is an ongoing emergence of "postnational cartographies" wherein social actors are "evolving non-state forms of macropolitical organization: interest groups, social movements, and actually existing transnational loyalties." In like fashion Scholte has called for the need to develop a "new, non-territorialist cartography of social life."[29] However, such debates over how to view the nation-state raise two issues.

First, the nature of borders within a globalizing world must be rethought, for nation-states can clearly be considered in both Euclidean and non-Euclidean ways. We need a both/and approach instead of an either/

---

27 Anthony Giddens, *The Nation-State and Violence: Volume Two of a Contemporary Critique of Historical Materialism* (Berkeley: University of California Press, 1987), 172.

28 Interestingly, such actions are often quite gendered. Susan P. Mains has shown how US Border Patrol agents have frequently portrayed their actions in keeping out of the country "illegal" immigrants in masculinist terms of protecting the (female) body of the US nation-state. Susan P. Mains, "Maintaining national identity at the border," in *Geographies of Power: Placing Scale*, ed. Andrew Herod and Melissa W. Wright (Oxford: Wiley-Blackwell, 2002), 192–214.

29 Jan Aart Scholte, "Beyond the buzzword: Towards a critical theory of globalisation," in *Globalization: Theory and Practice*, ed. Eleonore Kofman and Gillian Youngs (London: Pinter, 1996), 43–57.

or approach to theorizing the geographical nature of the nation-state. As Schlottmann has argued, to understand globalization and the role played in it by various agents of stickiness in spatial entities like borders, one must understand how they "are not only produced but also continuously performed in acts of communication,"[30] and how a language of borders or non-borders is made to perform, regardless of whether borders are actually becoming more porous circumscribers of national territory. Consequently, Schlottmann insists, "instead of only searching for new and 'more adequate' spatial representations, the everyday use of the 'old' ones should also remain a subject of thorough sociogeographic inquiry."[31]

The question of borders' performance and representation leads to the second issue: namely that of the politics of geographical representation and spatial praxis. The ability of dockers to hold up flows at borders means that the "borderless world" to which we are supposedly heading is what Lefebvre calls a "representation of space" designed to discipline how we think about the world (in much the same way that a map imposes a particular worldview upon us).[32] Representations of space are part of a triad developed by Lefebvre to understand how the geography of capitalism is made.[33]

Lefebvre suggests that *spatial practice* is that social activity which "secretes" a society's space; *representations of space* are the formalized depictions of space presented by urban planners, scientists, architects, engineers, artists, and others *via* systems of verbal and non-verbal signs and images—maps, models, plans, paintings, etc.;[34] and *spaces of representation* are the physical places wherein everyday life is lived and wherein symbolic meanings are enacted in spatial form and are drawn from the built environment, as through murals, advertising billboards and architecture.

---

30 Antje Schlottmann, "Closed spaces: Can't live with them, can't live without them," *Environment and Planning D: Society and Space* 26, no. 5 (2008): 826.

31 Ibid., 823.

32 Henri Lefebvre, *The Production of Space* (Oxford: Wiley-Blackwell, 1992).

33 The following two paragraphs draw heavily upon Andrew Herod, "Social engineering through spatial engineering: Company towns and the geographical imagination," in *Company Towns in the Americas: Landscape, Power, and Working-Class Communities*, ed. O.J. Dinius and A. Vergara (Athens: University of Georgia Press, 2010), 21–24.

34 Lefebvre, *The Production of Space*, 38. This means that historical transformations in ideology can be detected through examining how the laying out of particular spaces changes over time (e.g., US cities' grid patterns in the early nineteenth century reflected new ideas about rational thinking).

These three elements correspond with what he called "perceived space" (*l'espace perçu*), "conceived space" (*l'espace conçu*), and "lived space" (*l'espace vécu*), with all spaces exhibiting simultaneously these three elements.[35] However, although these three types of space constitute a unity, they do not necessarily constitute a coherence, for each is deeply contradictory.

The ability to control certain places so as to enable or disrupt movement from one space to another can be a central element in political struggle, with the result that having an understanding of how particular spaces and places connect to one another is crucial for workers' chances of success. In other words, resistance to neoliberalism, and capitalism in general, is a deeply geographical affair. Not only can dockers and other workers involved in the logistics chains that allow globalization to unfold engage in actions at particular nodes within the emergent world of flows, thereby gumming up the works for global capital, but they are only able to do so if they have support from the communities within which they are embedded. This involves not only understanding how places that might be on opposite sides of the planet are linked and what this means for articulating struggles spatially but also, *per* Lefebvre, considering how particular spatial images and representations are presented to them—and how they might present their own—and with what import. Thus, if workers actually internalize the representation of global capitalism's spaces as becoming increasingly borderless, then they are far less likely to believe that they can challenge this process. Capitalists certainly understand the value of thinking geographically, as evidenced by the time and effort they expend in figuring out new configurations of their logistics chains. If they are to be successful in their struggles, workers need to do so too.

---

35 Lefebvre, *The Production of Space*, 40.

RESISTANCE TO ALBERTA TAR SANDS MEGALOADS IN IDAHO & BEYOND

Helen Yost, Wild Idaho Rising Tide, and
Alexander Reid Ross, Portland Rising Tide

This story of ongoing courage relates the struggle of generations of people throughout the Northwest to regain authority over their lives, consciences, and lands, as they stand before the ubiquitous, industrial machines of death and devastation. The heroic deeds of seemingly isolated struggles have ignited a regional movement, instigated the grassroots power of people across the continent, and have elucidated and united concerns about extreme energy extraction that tramples our faith in our traditions, institutions, and the natural world.

The Machine in the Garden

In May 2010, US Highway 12 traversing north central Idaho basked in the warmth of the emerging spring sunshine, radiant within hundreds of thousands of acres of verdantly pristine, mountainous, public wild lands, under fresh, azure skies with bright clouds starting their western ascent of the Northern Rockies, and interlaced with clear, emerald rivers frothing bilious rapids risked by river kayakers and rafters. Not much happens in this vast region, in terms of noteworthy national news or even progressive innovations that reactionary Idaho lawmakers notice in Boise, hundreds of miles to the south. The 1990s brought the timber wars, pitting the forest products industry and loggers against low-impact recreationists, environmentalists, and Cove Mallard Campaign forest road blockaders. Mid-1990's re-introduction of wolves in central Idaho launched ongoing judicial, administrative, and even legislative skirmishes. Otherwise, life remains resplendently peaceful in the Clearwater River valley and on the high, rolling Palouse Prairie.

But rumors began circulating during the fall of 2009 that huge transports would soon invade the "Big Wild"—the largest contiguous complex of roadless and wilderness areas and wild and scenic rivers in the lower-48 states. That summer, the Idaho Transportation Department (ITD), with meager funds and some of the most dilapidated road and bridge infrastructure in the Northwest, inexplicably widened much

of Highway 12, paved and added curbs to eleven gravel turnouts, and
trimmed roadside trees. ExxonMobil subsidiary Imperial Oil stealthily
spent $3.4 million improving another nine turnouts and moving private
utility lines.[1] This sinuous ribbon of highway winds east from Lewiston,
the lowest point in Idaho at about seven-hundred feet, 175 miles southeast then northeast to mile-high Lolo Pass on the Montana border and
Bitterroot crest, the wettest place in Idaho. On the way, it crosses the
reservation and traditional homelands of the Nez Perce tribe, through
federal easements in the Middle Fork Clearwater and Lochsa River wild
and scenic river corridors—among the first in the nation honored with
this protective designation in 1968.[2] It also skirts the rugged 1.3-mil-
lion-acre Selway Bitterroot Wilderness and surrounding roadless areas,
and traces the perilous journey and parallel route of the 1803–1806
Lewis and Clark Expedition along the Nez Perce National Historic
Trail to the buffalo grounds in the wide, western, intermountain valleys
and endless, eastern, high plains of Montana.[3]

Officially acknowledging and preserving the outstanding and in-
trinsic archeological, cultural, historic, natural, recreational, and scenic
qualities of Highway 12 in June 2002, the US Department of Transportation named Highway 12 between Lewiston and Montana the
Northwest Passage Scenic Byway. In 2005, the agency imparted one of
only thirty-one of the nation's most prestigious national scenic byway
designations: All-American Road, administered by the Federal Highway
Administration. Scant industrial development has transpired since 1962,
when Highway 12 first linked the steep labyrinth of rivers and mountains in Idaho to Montana.[4] Its federal designations and the untram-
meled nature of the place have fostered a vibrant local tourism industry

---

1   Elaine Williams, "Agency: New Turnouts Not Related to Oversized Loads,"
     The Lewiston Tribune, June 27, 2011, http://lmtribune.com/northwest/article
     _0b5857ea-65b4-5b64-a46c-0698a9fdf596.html.
2   US Department of Agriculture Forest Service, Clearwater National Forest,
     "Highway 12: A Long and Winding Road," http://www.fs.usda.gov/Internet/
     FSE_DOCUMENTS/stelprdb5401618.pdf.
3   Borg Hendrickson and Linwood Laughy, "Top 20 Reasons U.S. 12 is Special,"
     The Rural People of Highway 12 Fighting Goliath, http://www.fightinggoliath.
     org/Pages/specialaboutHwy.12.html.
4   Thomas Campbell and Ladd Hamilton, "Thousands Witness L-C
     Highway Dedication," *Lewiston Tribune*, August 20, 1962: http://news.
     google.com/newspapers?id=KL5eAAAAIBAJ&sjid=JzEMAAAAIBAJ&p-
     g=4003%2C3235536.

that has flourished even while the national economy has floundered. In the mild, moist river bottoms watered by the encompassing steep, drier mountains covered with ponderosa pine and larch, ecologically significant "coastal disjunct" plants like ferns, dogwood, and alder flourish among the western red cedar and douglas fir of the interior rainforest. These original old-growth forests of the Northwest spread from the former Idaho/Washington seacoast to the nascent Cascade slopes and new Pacific shores. Not many travelers frivolously venture the five-hour drive between Lewiston and Missoula, Montana on this remote road. So why did ITD invest so much re-construction expense on a sparsely populated, lightly traveled highway?

North central Idaho citizens first learned in May 2010 that their state government and Congressional delegates had been scheming big business dreams behind their collective back. As early as January 2009, Governor C. L. "Butch" Otter and the Idaho Transportation Department supported Port of Lewiston recruitment of oil industry shipments.[5] While Imperial Oil insisted that it would only move 207 massive tar sands modules, and Idaho and Montana officials refused to acknowledge a future "high and wide corridor" through some of the Northern Rockies' most beautiful back roads. In fall 2010, the Natural Resources Defense Council[6] translated the media reports, press releases, and contract between Imperial Oil and a South Korean megaload manufacturer, Sunjin Geotec, and revealed prospects for a decade-long, $1.5 billion business relationship extending to 2020, which could produce up to one-thousand two-hundred prefabricated modules.[7]

In October 2010, thirty-four pieces of at least 207 cheaply constructed, Korean-built modules of an Alberta tar sands processing plant arrived by barge at the port, 465 river miles inland from the Pacific Ocean. One of the wealthiest corporations in the world, ExxonMobil, and its Canadian subsidiary Imperial Oil, originally intended to haul

---

5   Elaine Williams, "Big Loads: Otter Pledged Support in '09," *The Lewiston Tribune*, August 14, 2010, http://www.portoflewiston.com/wordpress/big-loads-otter-pledged-support-in-09/.

6   The NRDC was also instrumental in procuring over eighteen-thousand comments about an August 2010 plan to bury power lines under national forest land along Lolo Creek in Montana.

7   Steve Bunk, "Environmental Group Claims Expansion of Big-Rig Deal After Translating Korean Reports," *New West*, October 15, 2010, http://newwest.net/topic/article/environmental_group_claims_expansion_of_big_rig_deal_after_translating_kore/C618/L618/.

these "megaloads" through the Clearwater and Lochsa River valleys, up the 216-mile stretch of Highway 12 between Lewiston and Missoula, to the Kearl Oil Sands Project in northeastern Alberta. Unlike the usual eighty-thousand-pound, 8.5-foot-wide, eighty-foot-long semi-tractor trailers, megaloads weigh up to 1.6 million pounds, tower thirty feet tall, and crowd the winding, two-lane road with their twenty-nine-foot widths and four-hundred-foot-plus lengths.

Rural Resistance Rallies

But Big Oil and its corporate interest in Highway 12 and other narrow, rural roadways in Idaho and Montana naively stumbled into an ambush in this rugged country. Between May 2010, when the ConocoPhillips megaloads disembarked, and January 2014, when tribal and climate activists and regional allies staged three nightly megaload blockades in Idaho, and Montana, citizens have challenged, delayed, cost, and ultimately impeded tar sands facilities' transportation and construction plans. Primarily rural residents have imposed a district court case in each state and, in Idaho, a Supreme Court defense, two administrative contested case hearings against state transportation departments, and ongoing federal-level litigation against the US Forest Service and National Highway Administration. At over eighty direct actions, communities in four northwestern states have practiced simple acts of non-violent, civil disobedience to draw Americans' attention to ongoing crimes against nature and humanity perpetrated by fossil fuel tyrants.

Our allies in the Clearwater Valley, led by Borg Hendrickson and Linwood Laughy of Fighting Goliath, have valiantly, although precariously, protected the narrow, curving wild and scenic river corridor along Highway 12 in Idaho from Big Oil's rampages.[8] Over summer 2010, the Nez Perce tribe and a coalition of organizations issued public statements of opposition and gathered petition signatures from incredulous citizens. Borg and Lin sent carefully researched alerts to ITD, Governor Otter, the media, and the public, detailing the blatant incongruences between Idaho transportation law and the oil companies' plans. Imperial Oil and ITD officials hastily scheduled two strategic divide-and-conquer "informational open-houses" in late-June 2010 in Lewiston and Kooskia, and added a third in later megaload-trampled Moscow. At all but the Lewiston

---

8   Borg Hendrickson and Linwood Laughy, "Top 20 Reasons U.S. 12 is Special."

session, hundreds of outspoken, concerned citizens turned the industry dog-and-pony show into an uproarious public forum.[9] ITD formally solicited public comments only as an afterthought during a summer month when many residents vacation.[10] The Idaho governor and ITD seemed oblivious to disapproving emails and letters pouring into the agency from across the region and state as well as the 1,700 signatures, doubled by year-end, of a petition to deny megaload permits on Highway 12.[11/12]

For some regional activists and students in Moscow, Idaho, personal promises to confront Big Oil's brutal ravages came due in 2010. Still grieving the second largest marine oil spill in US history, resulting from the Exxon Valdez reef collision in wild Prince William Sound, Alaska, on Good Friday morning in 1989, we could not bear to let the ravenous ExxonMobil desecrate another beloved wilderness haunt. Through canvassing and tabling outreach work during that summer and fall, members of the north central Idaho conservation community described with renewed fervency to thousands of residents and visitors the incredible plans of one of the biggest corporations on Earth. Along with an amazing, organically arising alliance of citizens, groups, academics, and activists from the full political spectrum—a collaborative feat in itself in the reddest of the red states, Idaho—we could not work hard enough to stop this callous onslaught.

Throughout the summer, ITD-hired contractors hurriedly resurfaced the thirty-eight-year-old Arrow Bridge over the Clearwater River about fifteen miles east of Lewiston, bolting steel plates over an eighteen-inch crack in one of the middle girders of the longest (1,248-foot) bridge in the crosshairs of Big Oil's extra-heavy loads. In August 2010, the Boise environmental law firm, Advocates for the West, initiated a progression of three lawsuits that stalled passage for five months of the

9   George Prentice, "Taking the Scenic Route," *Boise Weekly*, July 7, 2010, http://www.boiseweekly.com/boise/taking-the-scenic-route/Content?oid=1673712.

10 Idaho Transportation Department, "Kearl Module Transportation Project Responses to Public Comments," January 2011, http://itd.idaho.gov/projects/d2/us12/Final_Idaho_Comment%20_Response%20Jan%2025.pdf.

11 Kim Briggeman, "Opponents Rush to Put Brakes on Imperial Oil Plan to Send Big Rigs through State," *Missoulian*, April 27, 2010, http://missoulian.com/news/state-and-regional/opponents-rush-to-put-brakes-on-imperial-oil-plan-to/article_4cb8ce66-5283-11df-95e7-001cc4c03286.html.

12 Coalition of authors, "Petition to Deny Permits for Transport of Massively Oversized Equipment on U.S. Highway 12," June 2010, http://www.petitiononline.com/k12sfw/petition.html.

four ConocoPhillips transports, the first fossil-fuel megaloads up High-way 12. Representing three river canyon residents and private proper-ty/tourism business owners *pro bono*—Borg Hendrickson, Linwood Laughy, and Peter Grubb—Advocates attorneys requested a temporary restraining order through the Idaho County court on August 17, which Judge John Bradbury granted. In Lewiston's second district court on August 24, 2010, they argued, and the judge agreed, that the state failed to address public concerns and violated its own rules in approving meg-aload permits. The plaintiffs asserted that ITD officials narrowly focused their review of ConocoPhillips applications on potential highway and bridge damages, but did not adequately ensure public safety and conve-nience and traffic clearance every ten minutes at too few turnouts. In his final ruling, Judge Bradbury further criticized ITD's failure to address the inevitable accident or breakdown, admitted by the megaload hauler Emmert International, which could make Highway 12 impassable for days or weeks.[13] Handing megaload opponents packing the courtroom a significant legal victory and disrupting transport preparation and plans, Judge Bradbury revoked and remanded ITD's issuance of four Cono-coPhillips megaload permits to travel Highway 12.[14]

But the sweeping sixteen-page order arising from the intense two-hour hearing did not stand long. Attorneys representing ConocoPhillips filed an appeal to the Idaho Supreme Court within days, challenging the decision that ITD ignored its own regulations.[15] The corporation and state government disputed whether Judge Bradbury had inappro-priately obstructed transportation department discretion and authority to interpret pertinent state rules and whether he had ignored or con-sidered improper evidence in the administrative record. Disingenuously pleading the financial hardship of $9 million in losses from its estimated 2010 revenues of $194 billion, ConocoPhillips requested an expedited hearing in the Idaho Supreme Court, ahead of Idahoans who normally wait most of a year to air their grievances there.[16] On August 30, before

---

13 Nick Gier, "Idaho's Highway 12 and ExxonMobil's Megaloads," late June, 2010, http://www.home.roadrunner.com/~nickgier/Hiway12.pdf.

14 Advocates for the West, "Lochsa Heavy Haul Route," *Advocates for the West*, August 12, 2010, https://www.advocateswest.org/case/lochsa-heavy-haul-route/.

15 Betsy Z. Russell, "Conoco: Highway 12 Residents' Claims 'Speculative'," *The Spokesman-Review*, August 27, 2010, http://www.spokesman.com/blogs/boise/2010/aug/26/conoco-hwy-12-residents-claims-speculative/.

16 George Prentice, "Conoco Pleads 'Financial Hardship'," Idaho Supreme Court

one week passed, the state's highest court granted a fast-tracked October 1 hearing of oral arguments by ConocoPhillips joined by the Idaho Transportation Department and Clearwater Valley entrepreneurs in the Supreme Court chambers in Boise.[17]

While the region awaited the high court's decision, which usually takes about six months, the ConocoPhillips half coke drums that would have moved during the week of August 16 remained parked at the Port of Lewiston. Only days after the Supreme Court hearing, an oil tanker truck crashed on Highway 12, spilling over seven-thousand five-hundred gallons of diesel, which seeped from the ditch, under the road, and into the wild Lochsa River. It compounded similar, nearby accidents in 2002, 2003, and 2005, which together released almost thirteen-thousand gallons of fuel and cost millions of dollars in clean-up.[18] Without a high court resolution or transit permits from either state transportation departments, Imperial Oil/ExxonMobil barged the first eight shipments of thirty-four massive modules into the suddenly gated and secured Port of Lewiston on October 14, 2010. A hundred conservationists and activists from Idaho and Montana peacefully rallied on the high-traffic Memorial Bridge over the Clearwater River in Lewiston on Saturday, two days later.[19] Wielding protest signs and banners for hours and expressing their opposition to blatant political pressure pushing Alberta tar sands equipment up Highway 12, some coalition members met with *New York Times* reporters and photographers, while others explored the coastal disjunct valleys along Highway 12.[20] As winter approached and the Port of Lew-

Grants Hearing," *Boise Weekly*, September 1, 2010, http://www.boiseweekly.com/boise/conoco-pleads-financial-hardship-idaho-supreme-court-grants-hearing/Content?oid=1755899.

17 Elaine Williams, "Idaho High Court to Hear Mega-loads Case," *The Lewiston Tribune*, posted in DownstreamToday.com, September 1, 2010, http://www.downstreamtoday.com/News/ArticlePrint.aspx?aid=23902.

18 Eric Barker, "Truck Spills Diesel near Lochsa River," *The Lewiston Tribune*, September 30, 2010, http://apps.itd.idaho.gov/Apps/MediaManagerMVC/NewsClipping.aspx/Preview/51414.

19 Tracci Dial, "Protesters rally on Memorial Bridge against US 12 shipments," KLEWTV, October 19, 2010; also see Matti Sand, "More News on the Fight to Protect Highway 12," *FightingGoliath*, October 21, 2010, http://sayingnotogoliath.blogspot.com/2010/10/more-news-on-fight-to-protect-highway.html.

20 Tom Zeller, Jr., "Oil Sands Effort Turns on a Fight Over a Road," *New York Times*, October 21, 2010, http://www.nytimes.com/2010/10/22/business/energy-environment/22road.html?_r=1&.

iston and other regional residents welcomed the perceived economic prosperity brought by the controversial oil and tar sands rigs, Imperial Oil hustled to deliver more of its climate-wrecking freight up the Snake River, before the locks on three dams closed for repair between December 10, 2010 and March 26, 2011.[21]

On November 1, 2010, the Idaho Supreme Court reversed our allies' district court victory, with a three to two decision and analysis stating concerns over the procedures and jurisdiction of the lawsuit, rather than making any judgments about the merits of the proposed transports.[22] The justices remanded the lawsuit to a lower level of dispute resolution, where the plaintiffs had not yet exhausted administrative remedies against ITD and ConocoPhillips before permit issuance and filing in district court.[23] Advocates for the West swiftly requested intervenor status for several plaintiffs and petitioned for separate contested case hearings addressing impending ITD permits for ConocoPhillips and Imperial Oil megaloads on Highway 12. Replete with publicly available evidence and witness testimony, citizens sought to fully disclose the secret, shady deals that ITD had evidently struck with Big Oil. However, retaliatory Idaho lawmakers passed legislation during the next 2011 session that erects economic prohibitions by requiring potential litigants to post bonds equal to 5 percent of the value of disputed shipments, payable to ITD when they lose lawsuits.[24]

Intensive legal wrangling over the administrative intricacies of determining oversize load configurations, highway and bridge capacities, public police escorts, and timing and spacing of traffic clearance characterized two contested case hearings and numerous associated motions

---

21   Alex Sakariassen, "From Economic Optimism to Outright Opposition, Big Oil's Proposed 'Heavy Haul' Has Divided Cities and Towns along the Route," *Missoula Independent*, January 20, 2011, http://missoulanews.bigskypress.com/missoula/crossroads/Content?oid=1371483&showFullText=true.

22   Steve Bunk, "Latest Ruling on Big Rigs and Highway 12 Not About Merits of the Case," *New West*, November 2, 2010, http://newwest.net/topic/article/latest_ruling_on_big_rigs_and_highway_12_not_about_merits_of_the_case/C618/L618/.

23   Laird Lucas, Advocates for the West, "Highway 12 Plaintiffs Seek Hearings on Conoco and Exxon Shipments," November 4, 2010, http://www.idahorivers.org/images/news/Release.Hwy12.Hearings.pdf.

24   Shawn Vestal, "Megaload Law Would Put Heavy Load on Citizens," *The Spokesman-Review*, March 23, 2011, http://www.spokesman.com/stories/2011/mar/23/megaload-law-would-put-heavy-load-on-citizens/.

and appeals between November 2010 and September 2011.[25] Despite the Supreme Court decision questioning the appropriateness of individuals calling for a contested case, Boise attorney Merlyn Clark, chosen by ITD and accepted by megaload opponents as the hearing officer, concluded that the intervenors (highway residents, small business owners, Nez Perce activists along the scenic Highway 12 river corridor, and the Moscow conservation group Friends of the Clearwater) have a "direct and substantial interest" in the proposed ConocoPhillips shipment plan. He ruled that such stakeholders must be allowed to intervene in ITD permit issuance, which cannot transpire until completion of a formal contested case hearing. Clark presided over the packed, December 8 and 9 public hearing held at the Grove Hotel in downtown Boise, which revealed numerous problems with the ITD permit process.[26] This instance of refreshingly rare, rural Idahoans' ongoing resistance to our development-crazed state government generated substantial media interest and citizen participation from beyond the region, including huge ConocoPhillips workers clad in company T-shirts and bussed in from the Billings refinery. In his fifty-seven-page, December 28 recommendation that ITD issue four megaload permits to ConocoPhillips module hauler Emmert, Clark upheld the safety and minimum inconvenience of the loads and dismissed the evidence provided by the thirteen contested case intervenors that the shipments would damage scenic values, tourism, and businesses along mountainous Highway 12.[27]

Infrastructure Grabs Begin

Watching the more conventional groups and wild lands loyalists maneuver their way through the litigative and legislative maze, activists in the University of Idaho college town of Moscow knew that it was just a matter of time before all legal relief was exhausted and people would be abandoned by their bureaucrats to direct-action remedies. Because

---

25 Advocates for the West, "Lochsa Heavy Haul Route," August 12, 2012, https://www.advocateswest.org/case/lochsa-heavy-haul-route/.

26 Betsy Z. Russell, "Full House for Megaloads Hearing" and other blog articles, *The Spokesman-Review*, December 8, 2010, https://www.advocateswest.org/wp-content/uploads/2010/08/Eye_on_Boise1.pdf.

27 Associated Press, "Hearing Officer: Let the Big Rigs Roll," *Missoulian*, December 29, 2010, http://missoulian.com/news/state-and-regional/hearing-officer-let-the-big-rigs-roll/article_4decb2b0-12eb-11e0-8feb-001cc4c03286.html.

many Moscow community members had initially responded to news
of the impending megaloads with threats of personally "getting in the
road" to defend their wild places and rural homes, we felt that a direct-action workshop—a condensed version of the "International Tar
Sands Resistance Summit" hosted by Northern Rockies Rising Tide
(NRRT) outside Missoula in November 2010[28/29]—was necessary to
rekindle and impart non-violent civil disobedience skills among Moscow's primarily middle-aged contingent of anti-megaload protesters.
So in mid-January 2011, several activists from Portland Rising Tide
and NRRT led two day-long training sessions: one in Kamiah to stir
direct action with Nez Perce tribal members and one in Moscow for
mostly older conservation community members and a half dozen university students. Both meetings occurred over the Martin Luther King,
Jr. holiday weekend and unofficially marked the inception of a Rising
Tide chapter in Moscow after trainers encouraged us to start a group
over a final dinner.

Idaho Transportation Department director Brian Ness ultimately
granted overlegal load permits for the unwelcome ConocoPhillips behemoths in early 2011, after the administrative appeals of established
green groups predictably and consistently failed. Cross-state coalitions
held press conferences[30] and spurred rallies in Boise and Lewiston, Idaho, during the epic weeks surrounding the first megaload's struggle up
Highway 12, starting on February 1, 2011, and ending six months later
in Billings, due to the arduous nature of the rural route and weather.[31/32]
No lack of self-sabotaging snafus and vehement citizen vigilance has
littered the interlopers' paths at every turn. Within days of its inaugural
launch, the first ConocoPhillips shipment violated its fifteen-minute
traffic clearance mandate with a fifty-nine-minute delay, when the transport trailer scraped a rock outcropping on a sharp Highway 12 curve

28 Northern Rockies Rising Tide & Indigenous Environmental Network,
    "International Tar Sands Resistance Summit November 19–22, Missoula,
    Montana," October 27, 2010, http://tarsandsresistance.wordpress.com/.
29 Murphy Woodhouse, "Voices from the International Tar Sands Resistance Summit,"
    November 27, 2010, http://www.youtube.com/watch?v=Fyw0HMTIDvs.
30 Marsha Que Serina Productions, "Mega Load Comments 1-31-11," February
    2, 2011, http://www.youtube.com/watch?v=MgvaKhQPo10.
31 Moscow Cares, "Speech at the Anti-Megaload Rally—January 29, 2011,"
    January 29, 2011, http://www.youtube.com/watch?v=KznasPjr0Hc.
32 Gary Grimm, "Highway 12 Megaload Protesters Rally at Idaho Capitol on
    2/2/2011," February 5, 2011, http://www.youtube.com/watch?v=pbyV5CttO8Y.

between Greer and Kamiah.[33] From the 2009 onset of corporate promises of increased commerce, jobs, and economic "progress," most state and local officials have complicitly assented to oil companies' use of northern Idaho's winding rural roads as industrial corridors to the 232-square-mile complex of Canadian tar sands mines considered "the most destructive project on Earth."[34] The moral outrage of impacted Idaho citizens has swelled over the years, as spirited protesting and monitoring have confronted almost every passage of these transports hauled by garish, overbearing convoys of contracted transport, pilot, and support vehicle drivers and flaggers and industry paid state, county, and city police.

During WIRT's formative months, we protested and monitored five Highway 12 megaload movements along the historic and scenic Highway 12 byway through the Nez Perce Reservation and the Nez Perce-Clearwater National Forest. We also expanded active involvement and support, in solidarity with rural residents and tourism business owners, conservation organizations, and the Nez Perce tribe. In early March, Friends of the Clearwater sponsored the Mardi-Gras-style fund raiser, Megaload of Music, to promote awareness and donations for the community anti-megaload campaign. Providing opportunities to infuse fun and music into this good fight, the unique musical celebration featured a traditional Mardi Gras parade led by the Moscow Volunteer Peace Band, the foundation of many WIRT actions, and entertainment by local alternative-rock and country-music performers.

As tribal activists organized to counter these initial Big Oil invasions, they invited and hosted renowned indigenous trainers and leaders and spiritual demonstrations on their reservation. At a Nez Perce action camp held at the Clearwater River Casino in Lewiston in mid-February 2011, Marty Cobenais of the Indigenous Environmental Network in Minnesota led discussions with the regional network about furthering the progress and possibilities of our anti-tar-sands efforts. In the final days of February, internationally renowned Anishinaabe conservationist, writer, and twice Green Party nominee for US vice president with presidential candidate Ralph Nader, Winona LaDuke of the White

---

33 KREM TV, "Megaloads Hit Mega Snag, Again," February 4, 2011, http://www.krem.com/news/local/new-plan-required-after-megaload-causes-long-delay-115300374.html.

34 Environmental Defence, "Canada's Toxic Tar Sands, The Most Destructive Project on Earth," February 2008, http://environmentaldefence.ca/reports/canadas-toxic-tar-sands-most-destructive-project-earth.

Earth reservation in northern Minnesota visited with north central Idaho tribal and climate activists. At the public meeting at a Lapwai church, she talked about regional campaigns against the Highway 12 megaloads and oil companies' exploitation of Alberta tar sands and indigenous communities.[35]

Inspired by LaDuke's no-holds-barred calls for environmental justice, Nez Perce tribal activists created and organized two events welcoming local, regional, and national tribal and non-tribal community members. In support of ending the destruction of the lands and health of Canadian First Nations people who live downstream of Alberta tar sands mines, participants in the March 19 Preserving Mother Earth Solidarity Run/Walk ambled together from the Port of Lewiston to the Clearwater River Casino and shared a small rally and refreshments. Runners continued on past Green Creek to Kamiah throughout the day. On the following afternoon, March 20, people gathered at Riverfront Park in Kamiah, to join a peaceful protest, called March to the Heart of the Monster, against the megaload "heavy haul."[36] After walking across the Kamiah Bridge to the sacred site of the birthplace of the Nimiipuu (Nez Perce) people as told by Coyote, the Heart of the Monster, concerned community members respectfully prayed about and discussed the megaloads and their impacts on Native people, treaty resources, environmental safety, and Mother Earth.

Because Idaho citizens had effectively blocked tar sands traffic on Highway 12 throughout 2010, Imperial Oil began to ship an estimated seventy-five shorter transports from the Port of Vancouver, Washington, in December 2010. At the Port of Lewiston in January 2011, the oil company also hired out-of-state workers who eventually poured $17 million into the local economy and commenced reducing the thirty-foot-tall modules to fourteen- and fifteen-foot heights. Imperial Oil corporate executives had previously certified to ITD and testified in various court cases that these transports were "irreducible in size" and thus could only travel on less developed rural roads lacking overpasses. After alluding for months to an alternative route for their tar sands-bound split-megaloads, while the court cases of our Idaho and Montana comrades temporarily

---

35   Winona LaDuke and Renee Holt, "Tar Sands Heavy Haul: Into the Heart of Darkness," *Honor the Earth & Ta'c Titooqan* (Nez Perce tribal newspaper), March 2011, http://www.honorearth.org/news/tar-sands-heavy-haul-heart-darkness.

36   All Against The Haul, "March to the Heart of the Monster," March 16, 2011: https://www.facebook.com/events/198018676885135/.

shut them out of their stated preferred route, Highway 12, industry representatives confirmed in late March 2011 that they intended to utilize US Highway 95, from the Port of Lewiston, north through Moscow, to Interstates 90 and 15 in Idaho and Montana, for their Kearl Module Transportation Project.

We were somewhat surprised when the oil giant announced in late-March 2011 that it would be shoving its 413,000-pound loads through the quaintly beautiful, tree-lined streets of college-town Moscow. We hastily met with our sympathetically megaload-opposing mayor to voice our concerns for the predictable infrastructure damages, First Nations genocide, and climate change impacts of this tar sands transportation and development project. Soon thereafter, we interviewed with Rising Tide North America principals, who inducted our rag-tag band of fifty conservation and peace activists as Wild Idaho Rising Tide (WIRT) on the birthday of Latino labor organizer Cesar Chavez, March 31.

In spite of rigorous citizen exposition of agency errors during a two-week contested case hearing presided over by officer Duff McKee in Boise in late-April and early-May 2011, Idaho Transportation Department director Brian Ness nonetheless granted permits in early-September 2011 for Imperial Oil shipments of tar sands processing equipment on Highway 12. Although the company never applied for these 114 permits, it did send one full-size "test validation module" through this public wild lands route in April 2011, after contractors denuded trees of their roadside limbs to thirty-foot heights throughout the wild and scenic corridor on Easter Sunday. In mute testament to effective litigation and corporate folly, the megaload remained stranded just inside the border awaiting Montana permits, protected from local scorn by ongoing private security, until it was dismantled and carried off as scrap metal to a recycling center in June 2012. During fall 2011, other corporate robber barons like Weyerhaeuser contracted Nickel Brothers to haul a couple dozen similar two-lane-blocking megaloads along the remote route to Alberta that Idahoans have struggled to close to such gargantuan machinery. In the winter of 2012–13, six other transports with similar dimensions belonging to other companies successfully reached tar sands operations and Canada on this arduous course.

As ConocoPhillips's and ExxonMobil's massive megaload convoys began to roll through Idaho and into Montana, they created a ghastly "tar sands tentacle" all the way to Canada. While resistance to thousands of proposed equipment hauls mounted throughout the Northwest during autumn 2010, iconic Montana authors Rick Bass and David James Duncan set aside other writing projects to hastily co-author and publish a tome on the topic: *The Heart of the Monster*.[37] This vitally important book illustrates the global impacts of this regional issue and considers ongoing measures to combat the "heavy hauls."

Also over the Bitterroot divide on February 7, 2011, the Montana Department of Transportation issued a "Finding of No Significant Impact" regarding its environmental analysis of the ExxonMobil shipments. A week later, on Valentine's Day, corporate sweetheart ITD issued permits for the Kearl Oil Sands megaloads, but only allowed the test validation module to move before the completion of contested case hearings brought by citizens against the state of Idaho. Surrounding passage of the first ConocoPhillips megaload, All Against the Haul and allies instigated a hundred-person protest soon after the initial half coke drum landed near Lolo Hot Springs, Montana.[38] Northern Rockies Rising Tide accomplished the first blockade of Northwest/Northern Rockies tar sands megaloads on March 10 in Missoula, when courageous, climate-concerned Ann Maechtlen, Carol Marsh, and a third protester sat down several times in front of the transport in Reserve Street but nonetheless escaped arrest.[39]

Meanwhile, supported by the public outreach of our All Against the Haul colleagues and the bold demonstrations of No Shipments Missoula and fellow Northern Rockies Rising Tide activists in Montana, Missoula County commissioners and three conservation organizations belatedly (from an Idaho frontline perspective) filed a request for a preliminary injunction of the ExxonMobil loads on April 7, only days before the test validation module departed the port for the Montana border. In response to their April 13 plea for a temporary restraining order, Montana District Judge Ray Dayton ruled, on April 18, that movement of the test

37 Rick Bass and David James Duncan, "Those of Heart and Will: The Story Behind the New Rick Bass and David James Duncan Collaboration," *NW Book Lovers*, December 22, 2010, http://nwbooklovers.org/2010/12/22/by-rick-bass-and-david-james-duncan/.

38 Allyson Weller, KLEW TV, "Montana Protesters Greet Megaload," February 15, 2011, http://www.klewtv.com/news/local/116203874.html.

39 Northern Rockies Rising Tide, "NRRT and Supporters Protest and Temporarily Block Conoco Shipments," March 10, 2011: http://northernrockiesrisingtide.wordpress.com/2011/03/10/nrrt-and-supporters-protest-and-temporarily-block-conoco-shipments/.

module could proceed but certain permits for road improvements could not. Calling upon the more stringent environmental statutes of Montana, the plaintiffs argued in their lawsuit that the Montana Department of Transportation had not thoroughly analyzed the impacts of expansion or construction of turnouts to clear traffic around the mammoth Imperial Oil loads. In July 2011, they secured a preliminary injunction against Imperial Oil use of rural, two-lane Montana roads such as Highway 200 through the Blackfoot "*A River Runs Through It*" valley and the magnificent eastern Rocky Mountain Front along Highways 287 and 89. But in mid-October 2011, at the request of parent company ExxonMobil, Judge Dayton modified this injunction to open an abbreviated portion of the original route—Highways 12 and 93 from the Idaho state line to Missoula—to "heavy haul" transports.

When our Missoula allies obtained the preliminary injunction against megaload movements on Highway 12 and other Montana roads in mid-July 2011, Moscow became the ground zero sacrifice zone for the tar-sands invasion. In light of the excellent work of Advocates for the West and Fighting Goliath in challenging ITD megaload permits, despite the solid merits of their cases, our legally inexperienced, direct-action group tried unsuccessfully to persuade more than a dozen lawyers to bring forward a similar contested case hearing against Highway 95/Interstate 90 megaloads. Undaunted, northern Idaho citizens extensively aired our concerns for shipment infringements on public safety, convenience, and access on our highways and city streets as well as cumulative damages to our tax-sponsored road and bridge infrastructure.

Moscow Gets in the Road with the Megaloads

We have engaged our state legislature and city government in myriad ways, even demonstrating with a roped replica of the size of a typical megaload and speaking as a majority of megaload opposition at a well-attended, city-hosted, mid-May 2011 public meeting before state agency and industry officials. Within a week after all but one of the sixty-six testifiers on the dilemma spoke out against use of our streets by Big Oil, the most conservative member of our City Council brashly advanced and secured passage of a position statement welcoming the megaload onslaught for its inferred economic (but actually detrimental) benefits. Representative of the impending First Nations genocide wrought by tar sands transports, on the same day as the council's statement, a saturated canyon slope above megaload-compacted Highway 12 released a huge boulder, which some observers believe shipment vibrations loosened. Rolling down to the road, it killed two young Nez Perce men riding east on Highway 12.

WIRT's demonstration on the June 18, 2011 International Day of Action Against the Tar Sands effectively spread our message through the regional media about the inappropriate and destructive nature of US-compelled tar sands development. Our protest denouncing Imperial Oil trimming of Moscow trees to accommodate Highway 95 split-megaload passage also garnered some public attention, both visually and conceptually. Nonetheless, from July 15, 2011 through March 6, 2012, a barrage of convoys of flagger and support vehicles and excessive state police patrol cars escorted seventy-five processing plant modules on hydraulic trailers conveyed by huge push and pull semi-trucks up two-lane Highway 95 several nights per week.

From the start, timing of tar sands shipments have been purposely erratic, due to corporate attempts to avoid our demonstrations and subsequent adverse publicity. For instance, when Earth First! and Northern Rockies Rising Tide staged the annual Round River Rendezvous in early July 2011, near the stranded test validation module at Lolo Hot Springs, Montana, no megaloads rolled through anticipated direct action encounters on any roads for the entire week. In their absence, Rendezvous participants occupied the Montana governor's office in the Helena capitol building, demanding Governor Schweitzer's denouncement of tar sands pipelines and megaloads.

Since the occupation of Schweitzer's office (and subsequent, raucous dance party on his meeting table), dozens of participants in our continuing demonstrations have gathered with protest signs, chanted anti-tar sands/megaload slogans, and waved banners in solidarity with impacted First Nations residents and other tar-sands- and associated-pipeline resisters. Inaugural WIRT actions in the spring and summer of 2011 included exercising our crosswalk rights to traverse our city streets with protest signs in front of the transports. Several late-night protests during the summer months brought only five to ten people to the sidewalks. But on the night of August 25, 2011, a boisterous crowd of about 150 protesters and onlookers filled Washington Street outside Moscow City Hall to protest ExxonMobil's launch of its first accurately-named "split-megaload," an approximately two-hundred-foot-long, four-hundred-thousand-pound, two-lane-wide monstrosity. Six men between the ages of twenty-five and sixty-five refused to disperse from either sitting or standing in a crosswalk, directly in the path of one of the larger Imperial Oil megaloads for nearly half an hour. Idaho state police (ISP) and Moscow police officers under their orders arrested these brave souls, held them overnight, released them with bond, and eventually fined them $240 dollars each.

On the following night, ISP patrols traveling with the same transport convoy targeted and approached a vehicle, parked roadside, that carrying four women, who were anonymously monitoring the megaload along Highway 95 near Coeur d'Alene, and gathering evidence for a belated but still-desired administrative hearing about ExxonMobil permits. The officers jailed two women, including a visiting activist, for refusing to provide documented or verbal identification (and thus resisting and obstructing an officer) after the troopers noted unbuckled back seat belts in the stationary vehicle. One of the monitors persisted in a lengthy legal battle that extended to a full jury trial in December 2012, which highlighted civil liberties violations but nonetheless granted no ultimate justice. This instance underscored the ongoing, intensive presence and policies of state, county, and city police, as they not only escorted and guarded these oil company payloads, but sought and received reimbursement for their corporate security services from the megaload hauler Mammoet.

Our October 6 Bikes not Bitumen! critical mass ride surrounding a convoy was somewhat scuttled by damp drizzle but resulted in the arrest of two twenty-something male activists, also charged with resistance and obstruction, the standard police threat for entering the roadway during megaload transit. Police unlawfully detained these cyclists after they briefly rode around a traffic-redirection sign temporarily placed in the street-side dirt path/sidewalk to accommodate the transports. All four unplanned arrests have generated even more consternation and caution among prospective demonstrators, but have advantageously inspired a potentially difficult Idaho civil liberties counter suit.

When some of the last five of the massive parts of an Alberta tar sands processing plant rumbled through the small, quiet, college town of Moscow at about 11PM on Sunday, March 4, 2012, four protesters linked arms and sat down in the middle of Washington Street to stop three of these megaloads weighing 200,000–415,000 pounds and measuring 150–200-feet long. Police arrested two men for resisting and obstructing officers, and dragged two women to the sidewalk as another forty protesters voiced their opposition to expanding tar sands mining operations. Again on Tuesday, March 6, when the final two shipments crossed this twenty-two-thousand-person city, demonstrators pounded drums, chanted slogans, played music, and engaged in street theater. A female protester tossed a cardboard protest sign at the rear of the last megaload, and air-kicked the transports and their police escorts out of town, resulting in since-modified and dropped misdemeanor charges for throwing an object at a moving highway vehicle and attempted battery of a peace officer. All three accused protesters pleaded not guilty based on the necessity of their actions induced by their moral obligation to directly confront the causes of climate change that are currently killing millions of people, plants, and animals around the globe.

The Highway 12 Rubicon

In February 2012, a Montana judge modified a temporary court injunction into a permanent stay, effectively barring Imperial Oil traffic on Highway 12 until the Montana Department of Transportation could produce a more thorough review of potential project impacts. As residents raged in the streets of Moscow during well over fifty protests, ExxonMobil shifted its transportation plans in October 2011 to the Port of Pasco and Highway 395 in eastern Washington. Spokane attorneys assisted by Gonzaga law students worked diligently throughout the winter, searching for legal recourse to megaload use of not only regional highways but of Spokane and Spokane Valley streets. By April 2012, Occupy Tri-Cities began scouting the Port of Pasco to alert regional activists to megaload departures, and WIRT members monitored the shipments on Highway 395. Occupy Spokane and allied comrades mobilized to protest every Imperial Oil passage on Spokane's Third Avenue in May and June 2012. Even while Moscow City Police questionably sought the same amount of funds for new riot gear that they had received for reimbursement of overtime hours spent guarding ExxonMobil, WIRT further expanded outreach, education, and activation of regional citizens concerned about megaloads in June 2012. Specifically, WIRT brought screenings and discussions of the tar sands documentary *Tipping Point: The Age of the Oil Sands* on a road show to eastern Washington and northern Idaho cities on the emerging industrial corridor.

After establishing the WIRT Activists House in Moscow in July, we journeyed via a hybrid vehicle carpool to Fort McMurray, Alberta, in early August, to partake in the Tar Sands Healing Walk led by First Nations elders and activists around some of the older tar sands mining facilities and miles-wide wastewater tailings ponds. Upon our return, we protested the US Secretary of Transportation's visit of the Port of Lewiston, which had received federal funding to double its dock capacity, likely in anticipation of increasing arrivals of tar sands and Bakken shale oil extraction equipment for transport up Highways 12 and 95. Port expansion, Snake River dam maintenance, and associated dredging could continue to attract such cargo, jeopardize native fish and aquatic lives and habitats, and imperil levee-protected Lewiston residents and businesses existing below the water levels of the Snake and Clearwater rivers at their doorsteps. Despite low protester and monitor turnouts, as well as requests by litigating anti-megaload partner organizations to not protest on Highway 12, all of WIRT's vigilance attained further historical significance when, in October 2012, we stood up to the first megaload—an evaporator hauled by Omega Morgan—to ever reach Alberta tar sands operations via Highway 12. In March 2013, we learned that allied regional resistance to tar sands infrastructure transportation had cost the Kearl Oil Sands project its CEO and about two billion addition Canadian dollars to finish facilities construction and initiate production.[40]

In an early February 2013 ruling in response to an Idaho Rivers United lawsuit, US District Judge B. Lynn Winmill of Boise reaffirmed Forest Service (USFS) power to stop megaload shipments traversing Highway 12 in the Nez Perce-Clearwater National Forest and the Lochsa/Middle Fork of the Clearwater Wild and Scenic River corridors. In his letter to the Idaho Transportation Department, Forest Supervisor Rick Brazell suggested stringent criteria for approval: megaloads should not stop traffic, the roadway and vegetation cannot be physically modified, and the megaload cannot take more than twelve hours to cross forest/river lands.

Like the ConocoPhillips and ExxonMobil/Imperial Oil modules that did not have highway travel permits, on July 22, 2013, Omega Morgan megaloads arrived at the Port of Wilma, against the desires of the

---

40 Bloomberg, "Imperial Boosts Kearl Oil-Sands Costs to $12.9 Billion," February 1, 2013, http://www.bloomberg.com/news/2013-02-01/imperial-profit-increases-as-refining-earnings-dboule.html.

Forest Service, the Nez Perce tribe, vigilant Idaho citizens, conservationists, and activists who love the Big Wild and oppose tar sands mining.
Rick Brazell presciently remarked that, without seeking or receiving
USFS approval, Mammoet was "setting us up for a showdown," and locals prepared for escalating direct action.

"I don't look at this as a symbolic issue," explained Silas Whitman,
chairman of the Nez Perce tribe. "Otherwise, we'd just issue a press statement, put up a few signs, and just let it go. No. We've run out of time
and initiatives. So that leaves us with disobedience, civil disobedience."

So it was that, on the balmy evening of August 5, 150 opponents
with the Nez Perce, WIRT, Idle No More, and allies met the megaload on Highway 12, as it attempted to roll into Nez Perce ancestral
lands. Police responded to the courage of megaloads opponents by driving a cruiser through the soft blockade of people standing in the road.
Threatening people with pepper spray, physically pushing activists, and
separating parents from children was not enough to disperse the brave
protest, which lasted longer than any prior megaload blockade. By the
end, nineteen blockaders had been arrested, including Whitman himself,
and that was only the beginning. The next evening, fifty opponents stood
against the megaload, and were met by an equal number of police and a
fleet of police vehicles. Blockaders met the megaload on the highway by
the Clearwater River Wild and Scenic Corridor, but were pushed to the
side of the road. Some pushed back, heaving boulders and large rocks
into the street, postponing the megaload's journey again.

Protests continued on Highway 12, with police and the megaload
becoming increasingly aggressive. Although the megaload was able to
make it through Idaho and Montana with its tail between its legs, the
following month a federal judge ruled in favor of the Nez Perce, placing
a temporary injunction on further megaloads traveling through Highway 12. The historic victory was clearly cause for celebration, so WIRT
and allies threw a fundraising concert for Nez Perce arrestees, attracting
a journalist with *The New York Times*, who then wrote a story about the
movement against the megaloads.

A Cross-Regional Network Rising

With Highway 12 shut down to the corporate dreams of an industrial corridor, megaload hauler Omega Morgan began scouting for new

veins to open. In November, activists with Portland Rising Tide (PRT) learned of a new megaload sitting in the harbor at the Port of Umatilla in Oregon. Without any public process, comment period, or even notification, the megaload was set to travel over the ceded lands of the Confederated Tribes of the Umatilla and the Confederated Tribes of the Warm Springs, and through the North Fork John Day Wild and Scenic River. The presence of the megaload awoke a strong sense of urgency among many in the Pacific Northwest to push back against big corporations looking for new industrial corridors for the tar sands.

PRT met with members of the Umatilla and Warm Springs tribes, and agreed to converge at the port to express opposition together. On the chilly evening of December 1, 2013, a group of fifty people joined together to oppose the megaload, and two activists locked down to the 901,000-pound, 376-foot-long, twenty-two-foot-wide megaload for two hours, before being removed by police. Because of the inspiring actions of those two individuals, the megaload was delayed for the first night, setting the pace for a difficult ride through Oregon.

The next night, a Umatilla tribal elder was arrested for sitting down in front of the megaload. One day later, Seattle Rising Tide (SRT) occupied Omega Morgan's office in Fife, Washington. On December 12, PRT occupied Omega Morgan's headquarters in Hillsboro, Oregon, after disrupting a meeting with songs and chants. While PRT activists negotiated with a dozen police officers in Omega Morgan's lobby, SRT held a solidarity action in the Bellevue, Washington office of Resources Conservation Company International, a General Electric subsidiary that manufactured the equipment being shipped.

In spite of the public outcry, Omega Morgan continued to carry the megaload through the rugged terrain of eastern Oregon—critically, the North Fork John Day Wild and Scenic River, home to bald eagles, black bears, elk, threatened bull trout, and other anadromous fish. The escalating, cross-regional actions against the megaload, then, culminated in a December 16 blockade on Highway 26 outside of the town of John Day in rural eastern Oregon. Launched by the new regional network, including Portland and Seattle Rising Tide and Cascadia Forest Defenders, the direct action was the expression of a budding constellation of activists known for dramatic tree sits, long-lasting forest occupations, intense port shutdowns, and concerted grassroots organizing. Taking place on a frosty winter night, the blockade began at 7:30PM, when activists placed a car with deflated tires in the path of the megaload. With the passenger seat removed and a hole cut into the floor, a space was created inside of the car for one individual to sit in the passenger area and lock themselves to another individual who had crawled underneath. With the megaload idling in the distance, police descended on the car, smashing the windows out and cutting it apart with the "jaws of life" to remove the activists.

One hour later, a second blockade emerged down the road, consisting of a six-foot deflated trailer parked in the middle of the highway. One individual was locked to a barrel of cement on the trailer, and another was locked to the axle underneath. Police lifted and pulled the trailer, and some reported that pain compliance was used to remove the activists. In total, sixteen activists were arrested that night—most of whom had not participated in any blockading, had followed police orders, and were standing on the side of the road. As the megaloads crossed into Idaho and Montana after long delays due to inclement weather, they were met with growing protests from 350 Idaho, Blue Skies Campaign, Indian Peoples Action, Northern Rockies Rising Tide, Occupy Boise, Spokane Rising Tide, WIRT, and allies.

On the evenings of January 22 and 24, 2014, fifty protesters stood in solidarity with the Nez Perce, Shoshone-Bannock, Umatilla, and Warm Springs tribes and the First Nations in what is now called Alberta, Canada, who are most affected by tar sands mining expansion. The protests consisted of a round dance in the road in front of the megaload, but when police disallowed the ceremonial engagement, three grandmothers stood their ground. One of the blockaders, seventy-one-year-old Carol Marsh, was at the first Northern Rockies Rising Tide sit-down blockade of megaloads in March 2011, and she returned on the night of January 24 to take action once again. In the meantime, megaloads through Oregon have been stalled by the threat of two new lawsuits regarding Oregon Department of Transportation regulations and ecological protections of Wild and Scenic Areas.

After a total of thirteen arrests and citations and four years of resistance in Idaho and Montana, as well as nineteen arrests in Oregon, the movement against the megaloads continues to grow. It joins in the cross-continental struggle against the encroachment of risky, expensive, and destructive fossil-fuel infrastructure, transporting resources from expanding points of extraction to expanding points of production—all of which relies on the dispossession of land-based communities to feed the industrial nightmare of climate change.

Why We Resist Tar Sands Infrastructure

Myriad, offensive social and environmental injustices have already resulted and will continue to result from these transportation projects that hasten the Alberta tar sands development, which climate scientist James Hansen has warned would ensure "game over for the climate."[41] Alberta tar sands processing plants release substantial carbon dioxide, greenhouse gases, heavy metals, and even the dirty tar mixture called bitumen that they treat. Energy- and water-intensive mining and upgrading processes spew toxic emissions and wastewater stews that fill vast lagoons. This extensive pollution not only poisons downwind and downstream water, air, and soil; plant and wildlife communities; and First Nations villages, it contributes to the single greatest point source of global climate chaos in North America. For billions of people around the planet, climate-change-driven warming and destabilized weather are threatening the health and lifeways of human populations with intensifying storms, flooding, drought, desertification, famine, and rising sea levels.[42] The conservative International Energy Agency reported that, unless we shift our infrastructure demands from fossil fuels to low-carbon alternatives within the next five years, "the results are likely to be disastrous."[43]

In northern Idaho, megaloads have imperiled the safety and schedules of travelers, delayed and blocked traffic with their sixteen- to twenty-four-foot, two-lane widths and lengthy convoys, impeded public and private emergency services, caused personal injury and property damage through numerous collisions with vehicles, power lines, cliffs, and tree branches, degraded highways with washboard ruts in lane centers, and pummeled saturated road beds, crumbling shoulders, and outdated

---

41   James Hansen, "Silence Is Deadly, I'm Speaking Out Against the Canada-US Tar Sands Pipeline," *Energy Bulletin*, June 4, 2011, http://energybulletin. net/stories/2011-06-04/silence-deadly-i%E2%80%99m-speaking-out-against-canada-us-tar-sands-pipeline.

42   United Nations Environment Programme, "Potential Impact of Sea-Level Rise on Bangladesh, 2000," http://maps.grida.no/go/graphic/ potential-impact-of-sea-level-rise-on-bangladesh.

43   Fiona Harvey, "World Headed for Irreversible Climate Change in Five Years, IEA Warns," *The Guardian*, November 9, 2011: http://www.guardian.co.uk/ environment/2011/nov/09/fossil-fuel-infrastructure-climate-change.

bridges.[44] Citizens concerned about the lax state oversight and myriad impacts of these overlegal loads, who have monitored, documented, and protested dangerous convoy practices and conditions, have additionally faced unwarranted targeting, surveillance, intimidation, harassment, and arrest by state troopers and county and city police sworn to serve public safety, but who instead protect corporate interests that challenge Idahoans' civil liberties and risk the health and wellbeing of people, places, and the planet.[45] To date, police have arrested twelve WIRT activists in connection with this campaign.

Idaho residents monitoring, protesting, and blocking tar sands megaloads are not radicals but concerned citizens compelled by our consciences to take a courageous and persistent stand for a livable world. We understand that our government is broken, that Americans need to abandon use of oil, coal, and natural gas, and that humans and all other life forms may not be capable of adapting their physiologies, as the US Chamber of Commerce insists, to a rapidly warming climate hotter than humans have ever experienced. The true radicals are US Congressional members, who mock widely accepted scientific evidence of climate change, and the fossil-fuel industries, who alter the chemistry of the Earth's atmosphere and who hire public relations firms to confound energy issues.

Idaho, Montana, Oregon, and Washington activists seek only to preserve the global homes that we know and love for the benefit of everyone, but particularly for the youngest and most vulnerable people. We are standing on our convictions in solidarity with other communities in the path of this industrial juggernaut, near dozens of tar sands pipeline and transportation routes and refineries. Over the last four years, we have come to understand that resistance to Big Oil is not futile but essential and mandatory for people of good will to bequeath a livable planet to all of its present and future inhabitants. Every resistance movement that has ever changed the world began with just a few people expressing their dissatisfaction and defiance, empowering their fellow citizens, and deepening their resolve to effect long overdue changes. But we are only

---

44 Wild Idaho Rising Tide, "Megaload Facts," http://wildidahorisingtide.org/megaload-facts/.

45 Wild Idaho Rising Tide, "Media Release: More Charges Brought Against Tar Sands 'Megaload' Protesters in Moscow, Idaho," March 10, 2012, http://wildidahorisingtide.org/2012/03/10/media-release-more-charges-brought-against-tar-sands-megaload-protesters-in-moscow-idaho/.

among the first wave of a rising tide of resistance that tar sands profiteers can expect across our nation.

When vehicle-dependent Americans—who consume 97 percent of Alberta tar sands products—import the majority of their foreign oil from Canada but export a surplus, steam cleaning oily sand to obtain the purported best and most secure new source of petroleum, it appears not only unnecessary but expensive and excessive. Further tar-sands development in Canada and the American West would prolong the US oil addiction admitted by George W. Bush, exacerbate global warming, and forestall transitions to safe, clean, infinitely sustainable energy sources. Political leadership independent of unaccountable multinational corporations, which channel millions of dollars reaped from tar sands production to American and Canadian administrative and legislative officials, must effectively resolve the biggest challenge that humanity has ever faced.

Although President Obama on his campaign trail heralded "the moment when the rise of the oceans begins to slow and our planet begins to heal," Americans continue to reel from the insidious, deadly effects of fossil-fuel extraction, as victims of the shameful aftermaths of the Exxon Valdez and BP Deepwater Horizon spills, water contamination from coal mining and hydraulic fracturing, and extensive tar-sands-related devastation. We cannot rely on state and national politicians, dirty energy executives, or industry workers to honor and protect people's most basic rights and interests. As life around the world struggles with the consequences of our collective delay in taking responsible actions to reverse climate change, we can only hope that investors and finance managers realize that smart money will abandon tar sands projects soon, before emerging grassroots initiatives reduce the value of their fiscal commitments to outmoded energy sources.

Catalyzed by projected atmospheric carbon concentrations of more than 450 parts per million, feedback mechanisms could overshadow efforts to reasonably shape energy policy, as chaotic weather rapidly transforms our landscapes and infrastructure. A more stable economic future already thrives through the development of abundant domestic sources of wind, solar, geothermal, and other non-depletable energy. Responsible energy providers can safely harvest these ample resources in perpetuity and offer enough power and mobility and better long-term security to meet energy needs. Our international energy crisis and widespread ignorance of the clear scientific consensus on climate change may indeed represent the eleventh hour for humanity; our shared response could also signal its finest hour.

DEMANDING THE LAND AT A PUBLIC UNIVERSITY:

Space, Place, and Occupation at the University of California, Berkeley

Alex Barnard

Revisiting a Radical Legacy

On November 15, 2011, thousands gathered at the University of California, Berkeley, for what was then the largest General Assembly held by the Occupy movement in the United States.[1] The assembly came at the end of a daylong student strike that saw ordinary classes canceled and replaced with over twenty "teach-outs" taught by both students and faculty. Some covered more traditional academic topics, ranging from "democratizing public education" to "the California state budget crisis," while students also had a chance to take part in "skill-shares" that spanned Capoeira to "silk screening." Towards the end of the day, the students erected an encampment, replete with artwork, a library, and even a piano. As one demonstrator explained it, the goal of Occupy Cal was to "build on these steps a truly free university,"[2] one which fully lived up to the lofty ideals of universal public higher education embraced by the California state legislature in the 1960s. As with other Occupy encampments around the country, the day's activities were an exercise in what anthropologist David Graeber calls "prefigurative politics"[3]—an attempt not just to advocate for a democratic, open university, but to actually try to enact it in the present.

The site of Occupy Cal's General Assembly, Sproul Plaza, contained historical significance as the focal point of student protests in 1964. Those actions over the right to free political expression on campus

---

1   Dupuy, Tina. "Occupy Cal Makes Occupy History at Berkeley" *The Atlantic Monthly* (November 16, 2011). Available at: http://www.theatlantic.com/politics/archive/2011/11/occupy-cal-makes-occupy-history-at-berkeley/248555/#.

2   Victoria Pardini and Aaida Samad, "Occupy Cal General Assembly Votes to Re-establish Encampment," *The Nation*, November 16, 2011, http://www.thenation.com/blog/164636/occupy-cal-general-assembly-votes-re-establish-encampment.

3   David Graeber, *Possibilities: Essays on Hierarchy, Rebellion, and Desire* (Oakland: AK Press, 2007).

marked one of the first moments of wide visibility for what eventually became the anti-war, women's liberation, and free speech movements that defined the decade. The open university of November 15 was a powerful attempt to both commemorate and reclaim this legacy, especially when one speaker re-iterated the words of student-activist Mario Savio, which he delivered at the same place forty-seven years before:

> There's a time when the operation of the machine becomes so odious—makes you so sick at heart—that you can't take part. You can't even passively take part. And you've got to put your bodies upon the gears and upon the wheels, upon the levers, upon all the apparatus, and you've got to make it stop. And you've got to indicate to the people who run it, to the people who own it, that unless you're free, the machine will be prevented from working at all![4]

Many of those in attendance, young and old, mouthed the words along with the speaker, acknowledging the sense of history hanging over the plaza. When another participant asked for all those who had been present during the first demonstrations at Berkeley in the 1960s to stand up, scores of people rose, to cheers and applause. It was a moment where the memories and stories embedded in the physical environment came back to shape actions in the present.

Yet while the events of November 15 seemed to reaffirm the popular linkage between Berkeley and radicalism, that connection has in fact become increasingly tenuous. Occupy Cal was, in the end, far surpassed by the more militant and diverse Occupy Oakland. Occupy Berkeley, its non-student counterpart, was "barely a blip on the radar."[5] This was no mere fluke. Instead, it reflects the steady transformation through privatization of the University of California system, the university's consistent use of force to restrain student protest, and the steady gentrification of Berkeley writ-large. In short, both a memory of past radicalism and a reality of present-day repression and de-mobilization have imprinted themselves on Berkeley's campus and become indelible parts of political action there.

---

4   Mario Savio, "On the operation of the machine," December 2, 1964, *YouTube*, Uploaded August 9, 2010, https://www.youtube.com/watch?v=PhFvZRT7Ds0.
5   Zaine Muhammad, "Occupy Berkeley: Why So Quiet?" *New America Media*, October 29, 2011, http://newamericamedia.org/2011/10/occupy-berkeley -why-so-quiet.php.

The long arc of protest leading up to and beyond the events of November 15, 2011 highlights two theoretical points about the role of space and place in contemporary mobilizations. First, although the problems of the university that led to the protests were impacted by such broad global forces as neo-liberalism, globalization, and the economic downturn, they took their most concrete and contentious form in struggles over the meaning and uses of the physical space of the university itself. As the tents on Sproul Plaza so aptly demonstrated, even in an era of transnational activist networks, global capital flows, and "e-movements" mobilized on the internet, the most dramatic moments in Occupy Cal occurred surrounding the control of the spaces activists need to survive, grow the movement, and envision alternative political possibilities.

Second, the historical and geographic context of Berkeley played a crucial role in shaping the movement's manifestation and trajectory. Although Occupy presented itself as offering resistance to such huge and impersonal forces as global capitalism and corporate political domination, we cannot fully analyze the various Occupations that arose around the world in the fall of 2011 without careful attention to the narratives and histories tied to the specific places where the movement manifested itself. Movements depend on space, in the abstract, to survive; they gain strength, however, through their connection to particular places of significance. Throughout Berkeley's history, a narrow selection of seemingly trivial places—like Sproul Plaza—have become imbued with significance that shapes the struggles taking place within them. Looking at the transformations in those spaces helps to understand why Occupy Cal was both a continuation and representation of Berkeley's (perhaps receding) radical legacy.

Space and Place in Social Movements

Despite the "spatial turn" that swept through social sciences in the 1990s, the role of space and place continues to receive short shrift in the study of social movements.[6] Of course, the classic objects of social movement analysis acquire clear spatial dimensions: peasant movements demanding control of land, labor movements seeking ownership of their factories made space the central object of their claims, and so on. Yet as the sociological gaze shifts towards so-called "New Social Movements," the

---

6   For a review, see Deborah Martin and Byron Miller, "Space and Contentious Politics," *Mobilization* 8, no. 2 (2003): 143–156.

role of space has become more ambiguous. Movements for gay rights, women's liberation, or ecological sustainability typically seem far more focused on identity and lifestyle than more traditional claims for territory or space.[7] Yet they are frequently grounded in place-based realities—for instance, Stonewall in '69, or the Castro in the days of Harvey Milk; the office or the home as sites of women's struggles ("the personal is political"); or free states in ecologically sensitive areas.

The precipitous shift away from appreciating space in social movements had a practical—not just an academic—effect on the movements that defined the decade leading up to Occupy. The counter-summits organized by the Global Justice movement, starting at the World Trade Organization meeting in Seattle, 1999, seemed like the exemplar of a new form of social protest that knew no borders, and was bound to no place.[8] It seemed as if, irrespective of where the leadership of international financial institutions or major global institutions chose to meet, the deterritorialized, nomadic networks of activists that made up the Global Justice Movement would be there to counter them. Activists, from this perspective, had transcended the particularities of specific locales and constraints of distances, moving into "spaces of flows"[9] that allowed them to follow global capital wherever it went. While this might seem like post-modernist rhetoric, these shifts rest on real and tangible technological advances. The growth of the Internet as both a tool for mobilization and a site of mobilization, itself, has led to speculation that "movements" will soon be able to exist without activists ever having to meet face-to-face.[10] The future of social movements, some argue, is one in which the confines of space and place are bound to disappear entirely.

Of course, most social movement scholars acknowledge that meaningful, contentious political action still has to take place *somewhere*, whether in the streets outside of an international financial institution summit or inside a city council meeting.[11] Indeed, one recent line of

---

7   Alberto Melucci, *Challenging Codes* (Cambridge: Cambridge University Press, 1996).

8   Sidney G. Tarrow, *The New Transnational Activism* (New York: Cambridge University Press, 2005).

9   Manuel Castells, *The Castells Reader on Cities and Social Theory*, ed. Ida Susser (Hoboken: Wiley-Blackwell, 2002); Alberto Melucci, *Nomads of the Present* (London: Hutchinson Radius, 1989).

10   Jennifer Earl and Katrina Kimport, *Digitally Enabled Social Change: Activism in the Internet Age* (Cambridge: The MIT Press, 2011).

11   See, e.g., Charles Tilly, "Spaces of Contention," *Mobilization* 5, no. 2 (2000):

research has highlighted the importance of "free spaces"—locations in which activists can gather to debate tactics, educate one another, and generate a shared sense of identity and solidarity without being harassed or policed by the authorities.[12] In these treatments, however, "space" often is used as little more than a proxy for network ties between groups of people, and are often completely divorced from any analysis of the physical characteristics that make one space different from another.

Our analysis of "space" in the abstract, then, must be coupled with one of "place"—the unique spaces within which various material objects are arrayed and to which human actors ascribe various meanings.[13] As Gieryn explains, places are constructed along two different dimensions: they are both physically carved out and "interpreted, narrated, perceived, felt, understood, and imaged."[14] These dual processes make places into "storehouse[s] of culture and history"[15] that have, by their very nature, a political character. As a consequence, the socially-constructed meanings and physical forms embedded within a given place, in turn, come back to shape the forms of actions taking place within them. The history of a given place, sociologist Harvey Molotch argues, tends to repeat itself—an intuitive insight that has nonetheless received limited attention in the study of social movements.[16]

Scattered throughout the literature of sociology, however, are examples of how this kind of spatial and place-based analysis can be used to explain the dynamics of protest. The 1989 student uprising and violent state response in Tiananmen Square, China, is one such case. The historical significance of the square was eminently spatial: the square had long served as a physical transition point between the "inner" realm of the rulers and the "outer" zone of the ruled.[17] As a result, it was virtually guar-

---

135–159.

12 Francesca Polletta, "'Free Spaces' in Collective Action," *Theory and Society* 28, no. 1 (1999): 1–38.

13 Thomas F. Gieryn, "A Space for Place in Sociology," *Annual Review of Sociology* 26 (2000): 463–496.

14 Ibid., 465.

15 Dolores Hayden, *The Power of Place: Urban Landscapes as Public History* (Cambridge, MA: MIT Press, 1997), 9.

16 Harvey Molotch, William Freudenburg, and Krista E. Paulsen, "History Repeats Itself, But How? City Character, Urban Tradition, and the Accomplishment of Place," *American Sociological Review* 65, no. 6 (December 1, 2000): 791–823.

17 Linda Hershkovitz, "Tiananmen Square and the Politics of Place," *Political Geography* 12, no. 5 (1993): 395–420.

anteed that any pro-democracy protest, seeking greater access to the state, would occur in that particular place, where the exclusion of the masses was at its most visible. The crucial moment of the protest, argues Hershkovitz, came when protesters erected a "Goddess of Democracy" statue, challenging the state's control over the iconography of the square. Indeed, the violent ending of the occupation, in part, exposed the realization on the part of the state that "the power of the students' message depended in large part on their continued physical occupation of the square."[18]

As this case reminds us, because all social movements must exist within space, they also mobilize in concrete places. It follows, then, that *all* social movements—even the seemingly placeless "New Social Movements" of students or global justice activists—are shaped by the physical and symbolic particularities of place. While space provides a necessary physical infrastructure for protest, places are also infused with narratives and histories that provide a template for action taking place within them.

Twenty-Six Feet of Pavement: Public Space and the '60s Legacy

Long-running conflict over the space necessary for political action is an often-forgotten undercurrent of activism in Berkeley. The emergence of the New Left in the 1960s, of course, represented the culmination of a host of demographic and cultural shifts, as well as the extension of the tactics and ideologies of the black civil rights movement to new issues.[19] The initial spark that turned Berkeley from a sleepy, conservative suburb of San Francisco into a bastion of radicalism, however, was something much simpler: a twenty-six-foot section of sidewalk at the entrance to campus, just outside Sproul Plaza.[20]

Historically, political action on campus was confined by administrative fiat to this tiny strip of pavement. In the fall of 1964, the university closed even this space, just as dozens of Berkeley students returned from a summer spent campaigning for civil rights with a desire to bring their activism back home. Without a place for outreach, of course, the closure amounted to a de facto ban on *all* political activity on campus. Over the next three months, disagreement over this piece of pavement—and

---

18   Ibid., 414.
19   Doug McAdam, *Freedom Summer* (Oxford: Oxford University Press, 1988): 162–163.
20   Joseph P. Lyford, *The Berkeley Archipelago* (Chicago: Regnery Gateway, 1982).

the different attitudes towards the appropriate role of activism and free speech on the campus it quickly came to symbolize—escalated. At one point, a student was arrested for handing out literature, and three thousand students surrounded the police car carrying him for thirty-two hours. Shortly thereafter, 783 students were arrested for a sit-in at an administrative building off of Sproul Plaza. It was during this conflict that Mario Savio delivered his famous speech, attacking the university administration for treating students as little more than "raw materials" to be ground up by a corporate-educational machine. This struggle on UC Berkeley's campus became known as the "Free Speech Movement," and provided some of the inspiration for subsequent student mobilizations around the country.[21]

As *the idea* of Berkeley became a public symbol of leftist politics, though, the reality of Berkeley *the place* remained far more complicated. Even though the Free Speech Movement wrung from the administration a guarantee that speech on campus would only be restricted in "time, place, and manner," students still felt that the spaces they had available for political action were too limited. In 1969, students and community members seized an abandoned parking lot near campus that was owned by the university, and declared it "People's Park." On May 15, three-hundred police cleared out the park and dispersed a demonstration outside, killing a student who was watching from a nearby building. The next day, park advocates were distributing a handbill declaring that the growing conflict over the relatively inauspicious handful of acres they had claimed was, in fact, a proxy for "struggles over who would control the institutions and property of the United States."[22] Two weeks later, a march of thirty thousand retook the park, while a banner flown by a plane overhead declared, "Let 1,000 parks bloom."

As geographer Don Mitchell demonstrates, the initial fight over Sproul Plaza, the ongoing conflict over People's Park, and—I would argue—the broader trajectory of activism leading up to Occupy in Berkeley were rooted in two competing visions of the meaning of public space.[23] For the activists who founded the park and the leaders of the Free Speech Movement, public space is "politicized at its very core; and it tolerates

---

21 McAdam, *Freedom Summer.*
22 Lyford, *The Berkeley Archipelago,* 46.
23 Don Mitchell, "The End of Public Space? People's Park, Definitions of the Public, and Democracy," *Annals of the Association of American Geographers* 85, no. 1 (1995): 108–133.

the risks of disorder… as central to its functioning."[24] This was only one of the dimensions of public space that made it so important to activists. The motto of the park—"everyone gets a blister"—reflects the aspiration of its founders to forge solidarity between diverse groups through collective investment of time and labor in a single, physical place.

Mitchell points out that the actions and policies of the university, on the other hand, have continuously impoverished the meaning of "public space" and weakened its significance. In its attempts to maintain control over campus and the park, the university has insisted that political action must be carefully circumscribed. The university does selectively appropriate and commemorate its radical history: for example, the Berkeley website celebrates a "tradition of engagement"[25] and, upon the death of Ronald Reagan, noted with an element of tongue-in-cheek pride that, as governor, Reagan "launched [his] political career using the Berkeley campus as a target."[26] The campus library even hosts a "Free Speech Movement" Café decorated with a sanitized set of photographs and plaque celebrating Mario Savio—albeit without referencing his harsher denouncements of the university administration.

The history inscribed onto campus and inculcated among the student body, then, is a selective one. The movements of the sixties are remembered as being opposed to things taking place *off* campus, like the Vietnam War. Often missing is any acknowledgment that the Free Speech Movement and its progeny were also focused on more local issues: the control of campus space and the undemocratic conduct of the university administration. While the Berkeley campus still buzzes with political activity—one administrator told me there are over fifty registered protests a year—spaces for more transgressive political action are constrained and under constant threat. As of 2012, the university and local business leaders were pushing a plan to "beautify" People's Park, which would more heavily regulate the space and push out its permanent residents.[27]

---

24 Ibid., 115.

25 "Activism: A Tradition of Engagement," *University of California, Berkeley*, n.d., http://berkeley.edu/about/hist/activism.shtml.

26 Jeffrey Kahn, "Ronald Reagan Launched Political Career Using the Berkeley Campus as a Target," *Berkeley News Center*, June 8, 2004, http://berkeley.edu/news/media/releases/2004/06/08_reagan.shtml.

27 Roland Peterson, "UC Must Transform People's Park's Legacy," *The Daily Californian*, February 3, 2012, http://www.dailycal.org/2012/02/03/uc-must-transform-peoples-parks-legacy/.

There are, then, two competing ideologies of public space deeply imprinted on the physical place of Berkeley itself. In one view, public space is open, inherently disorderly, and a launching pad for transformative political action. For the university, on the other hand, public space is only open to those willing to adhere to a narrow set of rules and prescriptions that prevent protest from getting out of hand. These ideologies, and the various strategies that both activists and administrators have historically employed to enact them, provide a crucial backdrop for the battles over public education that intensified in 2009 and led to Occupy Cal.

"Demand Nothing, Occupy Everything": Privatization Comes to Berkeley

Just a few months after the protests in Zuccotti Park started, Occupy Wall Street was already surrounded by innumerable myths as to its origins. Popular narratives tend to present social movements as "immaculate conceptions" that emerge organically in response to new grievances or problems.[28] Social movements themselves often describe mobilization as happening "like a fever" that suddenly grips previously apathetic people and compels them to take action.[29] Stories about social movements often deliberately ignore and hide the patient organizing within pre-existing networks of activists that invariably go into collective action, as well as the long, place-based histories that underpin any movement. The origin stories told by the Occupy movement about itself are multifarious. Ask an occupier for her or his inspirations, and the answers might include the Arab Spring, the Chilean Student Movement, the Zapatistas, or the Spanish *indignados*. In this way, the Global Justice movement has not simply disappeared, as is stated by some activists, but has evolved to include more localized sites of globally important action.

One historical moment that may receive less than its due share of attention in the historical trajectory leading to the protests of fall 2011 is the occupation of Wheeler Hall at UC Berkeley on November 20, 2009.[30] That day, over forty students seized a building on campus and

---

28 Verta Taylor, "Social Movement Continuity: The Women's Movement in Abeyance," *American Sociological Review* 54, no. 5 (1989): 761–775.

29 Francesca Polletta, *It Was Like a Fever: Storytelling in Protest and Politics* (Chicago: University Of Chicago Press, 2006).

30 "After the Fall: Communiques from Occupied California," *Issuu.com*, 2009, http://issuu.com/afterthefall/docs/communiques.

held it for nearly a day. On first glance, the occupation was a reflexive response to the announcement, the day prior, that student fees would be increased by 32 percent. Yet closer analysis shows that the Wheeler occupation marked a new moment of contestation within the longer battle over the meaning and uses of the university's nominally "public" space. It also showed both the persisting grain of truth to Berkeley's radical reputation as well as the growing barriers to activism there.

As campus police reminded the Wheeler occupiers, by forcibly evicting and arresting them for trespassing, that the land of UC Berkeley does not belong to the broader public. It is property of the University of California Regents. Constituted to ensure the university was kept "entirely independent of all political or sectarian influence,"[31] the regents today exercise more control over the university system than almost any other university governing board. Thus, although the ten campuses of the University of California system were built with public tax dollars, the "public trust" created for the universities by the California Constitution of 1879 keeps public control of the university to a minimum.[32]

The regents—most of whom are appointed by the governor to twelve-year terms—are a who's-who of California's 1%: investment bankers, corporate board members, and political insiders.[33] Regent Richard Blum, the husband of US Senator Dianne Feinstein, chairs a private investment firm with nearly $700 million in shares of private, for-profit higher education companies—holdings that raise serious doubts about his commitment to preserving a public, not-for-profit university system.[34] In 2004, years before the financial crisis, which has been so often invoked to justify cuts to education, the regents committed to gradually replacing state-provided funds with student fees. Unlike state money, which is "restricted" insofar as a portion of it must be spent on instruction, student fees can be used for any purpose, and, most importantly, be

31 Article IX, California State Constitution (1879) http://content.cdlib.org /view?docId=hb409nb2hr;NAAN=13030&doc.view=frames&chunk. id=div00001&toc.depth=1&toc.id=div00001&brand=calisphere.

32 Gina Patnaik, "Breaking Trust: The Past and Future of the University of California," *Zunguzungu*, December 8, 2011, http://zunguzungu.wordpress.com/2011/12/08/ breaking-trust-the-past-and-future-of-the-university-of-california/.

33 Aaron Bady, "The Regency," *Zunguzungu*, December 1, 2011, http://zunguzu-ngu.wordpress.com/2011/12/01/the-regency/.

34 Michael Hiltzik, "Is UC Regent's Vision for Higher Education Clouded by His Investments?," *Los Angeles Times*, July 14, 2010, http://articles.latimes. com/2010/jul/14/business/la-fi-hiltzik-column-20100714.

used as collateral for borrowing money.[35] The fungible uses of student tuition vis-à-vis state funding has also led the UC system to allocate an increasing number of places to out-of-state students, who pay substantially more to attend.[36] An increase in affluent, out-of-state students leads to fewer spots for lower income and minority students from California (compounded by the elimination of affirmative action in 1996), jeopardizing the university system's historic claim to be an engine of upward mobility.

The perverse consequences of the University of California's shift from an institution for public education into an engine for private profit are visible in the gradual re-shaping of the campuses themselves. Even as class sizes have skyrocketed, library hours been slashed, and entire departments threatened with elimination, the University of California has continued to invest billions in construction projects that funnel student fees and public bond money to private firms.[37] At the time of writing, the University of California system had $8.9 billion in ongoing capital projects—far more than the $2.65 billion in state money that has been lost in successive rounds of budget cuts since 2008.[38] Interest on construction bonds totaled $1.1 billion a year, even as some newly constructed buildings lay vacant for lack of operating funds to staff and maintain them.[39]

For all the talk of the growth of online education, brick-and-mortar campuses are not disappearing. Instead, the physical space of the university is becoming an important engine for profit and accumulation. More in-depth investigations have revealed the deep imbrication of the UC system with some of the financial mechanisms implicated in the 2008 economic downturn.[40] While public universities like the UCs were

35   Nathan Brown, "Five Theses on Privatization and the UC Struggle," *Reclaim UC*, November 17, 2011, http://reclaimuc.blogspot.com/2011/11/five-theses-on-privatization-and-uc.html.
36   Kevin Yamamura, "Capitol Alert: UC Sets Records for Applicants, Admits, non-Californians," *The Sacramento Bee*, April 17, 2012, http://blogs.sacbee.com/capitolalertlatest/2012/04/uc-sets-records-for-applicants-admits-non-californians.html.
37   Peter Byrne, "The Regents Club," *Sacramento News & Review*, October 7, 2010, http://www.newsreview.com/sacramento/regents-club/content?oid=1854684.
38   Jon Marcus, "Despite Massive Budget Cuts, There's a Building Boom in U.S. Higher Education," *Washington Monthly*, March 30, 2012, ttp://www.washingtonmonthly.com/college_guide/blog/despite_massive_budget_cuts_th.php?page=all.
39   Ibid.
40   Charlie Eaton et al., "Swapping Our Future," http://publicsociology.berkeley.edu/publications/swapping/swapping.pdf.

originally envisioned as spaces partially detached from the overall logic of the market economy, within which free inquiry and the development of citizenship could flourish, the private sector, right-leaning state governments, and university administrators have now identified the land of the university as a form of revenue-generating capital.

Given the obvious contradiction between the use of university space for profit and for public education, it is unsurprising that the Wheeler occupiers targeted the Office of Capital Projects and Real Estate Services—the nerve center of UC Berkeley's debt-financed building boom. The occupation was more than just a symbolic act intended to pressure the regents into reversing the tuition hike handed down the day prior, though. The Wheeler occupants' message of "Occupy Everything, Demand Nothing" also articulated a new strategy for combating privatization. The protesters didn't want to grab the attention of policy-makers, articulate a list of reforms for the university system, and then leave. Instead, the goal of the occupation was to make a "material intervention into the space and time of capitalism,"[41] a tangible and physical rupture of the day-to-day operation of the neo-liberal university that forced an immediate response.

The Wheeler Occupation thus presaged by two years the defining political logic of the Occupy movement. The protesters recognized that the privatization of the University of California system was not an inevitable outgrowth of globalization or economic downturn, but the result of deliberate choices made to reconfigure the university, including its physical space, for the benefit of private capital. The erosion of their university as a *public* university was being directed by real people working in real places. It is at these sites—concrete, identifiable physical places—that privatization is coordinated and controlled, and meaningful challenges are made. The Wheeler occupiers, to borrow Mario Savio's words, sought to "throw themselves upon the gears" and prevent "the machine" from operating.

As they recognized, though, doing this meant seizing control of space. What space, exactly, depends on the local form that "the machine" takes. While in Berkeley, a material intervention into capitalism meant occupying an administrative building, two years later the same strategy meant disrupting foreclosure auctions in New York or blockading the port in Oakland. As in the 1960s, Berkeley may not have been the direct progenitor of the movements that came afterward, but it was a forerunner in articulating how space writ large and, in particular, certain key

41   Marcus, "Despite Massive Budget Cuts," 6.

places, could be a central object of contention. Moreover, the Wheeler occupation reinforced, for both activists and the administration, a recurring pattern of conflict over space that would shape events two years later.

Fall, 2011: Repression Repeats Itself

For activists within the public-education movement at Berkeley, the fall of 2011 brought new threats to the university and, with it, opportunities to re-mobilize and recapture some of the momentum that had dissipated after 2009. Early in the new semester, the regents announced that, in November, they would consider an 81 percent hike in tuition. The result would be that the cost of a nominally "public" education, which had been just above $5,000 a decade prior, would rise to over $22,000 a year.[42] During planning meetings in September and October, activists realized that the growing visibility of the Occupy movement offered a chance to broaden the movement's message. In the language of social movements analysis, the Occupy movement provided a "master frame"[43] that diagnosed a social ill—a growing divide of wealth and political power between the 99% and 1%—and proposed a strategy—occupations of public space—to address it. The power of the occupy frame, though, stemmed from the way it could be mapped onto more local concerns and circumstances. In Berkeley, the Occupy discourse provided a way to link increasing fees, which seemed like an individual trouble for students, to a broader critique of the commoditization of previously non-market government services and the expansion of student debt.

On November 9, after a relatively sedate rally and march (which were permitted by the university administration), the newly-constituted Occupy Cal General Assembly voted to establish an encampment on Sproul Plaza. Although perhaps not as dramatic or disruptive as a building occupation or strike, the "Open University" which was to be established at the encampment nonetheless was intended as a drastic break with the university's regular business. By inviting all members of surrounding communities to participate in free classes and skill-shares, the encampment

---

42 Bob Samuels, "Changing Universities: UC Might Increase Tuition 81 percent Over the Next Four Years," *Changing Universities*, September 12, 2011, http://changinguniversities.blogspot.com/2011/09/uc-might-increase-tuition-81-over-next.html.

43 Robert Benford and David Snow, "Framing Processes and Social Movements: An Overview and Assessment," *Annual Review of Sociology* 26 (2000): 611–639.

on Sproul Plaza was intended to dramatize the university's failure to meet its obligations under California's "Master Plan" of 1960, which promised "universal access" to higher education.[44] Furthermore, the encampment would integrate education with ongoing political action on campus, a fact that made another conflict between the two competing notions of public space circulating within Berkeley almost inevitable.

Within minutes of the first tents being erected, campus police appeared and ordered their removal. When protesters refused to comply, the handful of officers disappeared, and returned shortly thereafter with several dozen riot police. Many of the officers were from the Alameda County Sheriff's Department, and as a later police review revealed, were on campus staging for a violent intervention *before* the encampment was even set up.[45] After delivering an order to disperse, the police attacked the protesters surrounding the encampment, jabbing them in the ribs with batons, grabbing some by their hair, and arresting a small number of students and one faculty member. The police review noted that the police made no plans for a mass arrest and the time-consuming processing of arrestees that would entail. Instead, their goal was to remove the tents and disperse the protesters as quickly and easily as possible.[46] The disproportionality was striking: a tiny patch of grass by the corner of Sproul Hall—a site typically used only by sunbathing students—had become a battleground. Control of this particular place was, in effect, symbolic of who, ultimately, wielded power within the university.

Although the police action in Berkeley on November 9 was not the most violent moment in the repression of the Occupy movement, it stands out in other ways. Encampments in other cities were allowed to stand for weeks or even months before they were dismantled. In "radical" Berkeley, the police intervened after only a few minutes—even though the university's regulation against overnight camping had not yet even been broken.[47] Why did the administration order the police to remove

---

44   University of California Office of the President, "Master Plan" (1960), http://www.ucop.edu/acadinit/mastplan/.

45   University of California Police Department, "Operational Review of the Events of Police Actions, Sproul Hall Protests, November 9th, 2011" http://administration.berkeley.edu/prb/PoliceReview.htm.

46   Ibid., 26.

47   Eve Weissman, "Addendum to the Police Review Board's Report on November 9," *Reclaim UC*, June 6, 2012, http://reclaimuc.blogspot.com/2012/06/addendum-to-police-review-boards-report.html.

the encampment in broad daylight, rather than at night when there would be fewer onlookers to document abuse and a clearer legal basis for the intervention?[48] The answer rests, I would argue, in the narratives and histories inscribed in the physical place of the protest and the recurring patterns of conflict over space at Berkeley.

As Francesca Polletta argues, the stories that actors tell themselves in conflict situations often "take on the status of common sense." As a consequence, an awareness of history can lead actors to "rule out tactical options," which, from a detached and objective perspective, might seem more logical and effective.[49] In this case, when the university administration looked at the encampment on Sproul, they didn't see a handful of tents: they saw an extension of the forty-two-year occupation of People's Park or a new iteration of the Wheeler Hall protests. University Chancellor Robert Birgeneau indicated as much the next day when, in an email to the campus community, he explained that the university's insistence on "no encampments"—a dictum that had been backed up by police force—was "born out of past experiences that grew beyond our control and ability to manage safely."[50] Additional emails released in response to requests for public records showed administrators commenting that, among the crowds on November 9, were protesters who had caused trouble for the university in the past.[51] The university permitted a march, but clearly had realized the danger in allowing students to create an ongoing, and more effective, protest through the autonomous control of space. After all, in forty-three years, the university had never managed to evict the occupation of People's Park.

Shortly after the initial violence, a representative of the administration returned to the area of the plaza where the protesters were still

---

48 As a report into police action against Occupy at UC Davis noted, the encampment prohibitions in the UC system apply only to overnight lodging. Conor Friedersdorf, "Reports Reveal Two New Scandals in the Pepper-Spraying at UC Davis," *The Atlantic*, April 19, 2012, http://www.theatlantic.com/politics/archive/2012/04/reports-reveal-two-new-scandals-in-the-pepper-spraying-at-uc-davis/256058/.

49 Polletta, *It Was Like a Fever*, 170.

50 Robert Birgeneau, "Campus Administrators Send Out Message Responding to Occupy Cal Demonstrations," *The Daily Californian*, November 10, 2011, http://www.dailycal.org/2011/11/10/campus-administrators-send-out-message-responding-to-occupy-cal-demonstrations/.

51 Jordan Bach-Lombardo, "UC Berkeley Administration's Occupy Cal Emails Released," *The Daily Californian*, March 3, 2012, http://www.dailycal.org/2012/03/28/occupy-emails/.

gathered. The representative presented to the General Assembly an offer: protesters would be allowed to gather on Sproul Plaza twenty-four hours a day for a week, so long as they did not have any tents, sleeping bags, or kitchen equipment. The university's offer was, of course, meaningless: a *symbolic* space for protest means little if activists cannot provide for their *physical* needs. It is hard to imagine the Tahrir Square occupation in Egypt succeeding over time without the infrastructure of tents, kitchens, and toilets that allowed activists to sleep, eat, and care for one another. In this respect, the offer was one more attempt to superficially maintain the university's "tradition of engagement" without allowing the inconveniences and material disruptions of space that meaningful political action almost always entails. The protesters nearly unanimously rejected the administration's offer, and set up another encampment. In the second raid, the police arrested thirty-two students and community members.

The University leadership's post-hoc justifications for the police's violence once again hinged on the administration's narrow conception of the appropriate users and uses of public space. The police review claimed that police action was necessary to prevent a contingent from the encampment in Oakland—Berkeley's much poorer and racially diverse neighbor to the south—from moving to the Occupy Cal location.[52] In analogous language, administrators at UC Davis attempted to explicate the now-infamous pepper-spraying of seated student-demonstrators based on a fear of "unaffiliated" non-students invading university property.[53] These rationalizations, however, elided the obvious question: Under what grounds can police keep California residents off the grounds of a public university? Notes UC Davis English Professor Elizabeth Freeman: "This is a public, land-grant university, whose mandate is to be open and accessible and to serve the people. All California residents, indeed all residents of the US, are 'affiliates' of the UC system."[54] As she points out, it is difficult to see what exactly is "public" about a space that is only open to those paying, through student fees, to use it.

The administrative crackdown also reiterated a message first

---

52 UCPD, "Operational Review," 17.
53 Larry Gordon, "Pepper Spray Report Sharply Criticizes UC Davis Leaders, Police," *Los Angeles Times*, April 12, 2012, http://articles.latimes.com/2012/apr/12/local/la-me-0412-uc-davis-20120412.
54 Elizabeth Freeman, "Gender, Sexuality, and the Kroll/Reynoso Report," *UC Faculty Supporting Students*, April 12, 2012, http://ucfacultysupportingstudents.org/2012/04/12/481/.

delivered when Sproul Plaza was closed to outreach and leafleting in 1964: transgressive political action has no place on campus and should be taken elsewhere. While some upper administrators expressed sympathy for the public education movement, they repeatedly urged protesters to take their case to the state legislature in Sacramento. The point was hit home when thirteen leaders of the public-education movement received criminal charges for their participation in the November 9 action. At the behest of the university, the courts gave them "stay-away" orders, which banned them from university property. The only exception was to come to campus to engage in "lawful business," which was narrowly defined as attending class or teaching. As a group of those charged pointed out, strictly excluded from this conception of "lawful business" was any kind of political action that might challenge "business as usual."[55]

In short, the events of November 2011 brought to a head the long-standing question of to whom the "public" university belonged and the ends to which "public" space ought to be put. The more-subtle, long-running exclusion, created by tuition increases and the withdrawal of affirmative action, became viscerally evident in the use of physical violence to keep certain kinds of politicized bodies and particular forms of disruptive political action from becoming spatially rooted on campus. Throughout the fall, the university administration's message was clear: if students wish to engage in political action, they must do so elsewhere. The physical space of the university is designated for capital investment, the production of future workers, and only a modicum of relatively meaningless political action. While Occupy might have taken it to a new level of visibility, the conflict in Berkeley followed a well-worn trajectory, with both sides acting in ways consistent with their historical roles, albeit one in which the forces of reaction had gained the upper-hand.

Occupy Gets "Back to the Land"

On November 17, two days after the university strike flooded Sproul Plaza with protesters, the university police returned, this time in the middle of the night. They rousted the thirty-five occupiers who had set up a new encampment, sending the students home and arresting

---

55 "On the November 9 Stay-Away Orders: The University and Its 'Lawful Business'," *Berkeleynov9*, March 21, 2012, http://berkeleynov9.wordpress.com/2012/03/21/on-the-november-9-stay-away-orders-the-university-and-its-lawful-business/.

two who refused to leave. Shortly afterward, a backhoe and bulldozer appeared, destroying the small library and artwork that had served as the seeds of the free and democratic university that Occupy Cal had imagined. Occupy Cal continued to meet and plan actions, including a successful building occupation that reversed cuts to library hours. But like so many other Occupy groups, it struggled to maintain its visibility and involve new groups without a physical space for discussion, outreach, and community building. Debates and disagreements that were manageable in face-to-face meetings became destructive and divisive when conducted online. If nothing else, the difficulties encountered by the Occupy movement in its post-encampment phase should remind us that the digital commons is, as of yet, no substitute for true public space and direct action.

Yet the saga of the Occupy movement at Berkeley was not quite over, especially once injected with a jolt of energy from activists previously focused on Occupy Oakland. On April 22, 2012—Earth Day—activists cut the locks and entered the Gill Tract, fifteen acres of UC property in the small town of Albany, which is adjacent to Berkeley. Unlike other occupations, this one was planned in secret and had a clear and singular objective: to establish an urban farm on some of the last remaining high-quality soil in the East Bay. When I arrived a few hours later, the farmers were already in the process of planting some fifteen-thousand seedlings they had brought with them, as well as establishing a children's patch and permaculture garden. In a sense, the farm was an exemplar of the prefigurative logic behind Occupy, which sought to create new, democratically organized institutions and spaces right in the heart of existing society. As one journalist observed, while the action carried a message about the importance of urban farming and food sovereignty, "this message is secondary to the action. The farm is not only and not really a message—because it is a farm."[56]

Of course, the seventy rows of crops that occupiers were able to plant would, even under the best of circumstances, produce only around one-hundred pounds of vegetables per week.[57] Despite its limited scope, however, "Occupy the Farm" pushed the conflicts over the university space to new extremes and laid even barer the contradictions created by

---

56   Susie Cagle, "Occupy the Farm Dug In, Dug Up," *Truthout*, May 17, 2012, http://truth-out.org/news/item/9202-occupy-the-farm-dug-in-dug-up.

57   Ibid.

the privatization of a nominally public university. When Occupy activists explained that they wanted the farm to serve as a center for education in urban agriculture, they invoked the University's original mission, which an 1868 legislative act had declared to be providing "objective practical education in agriculture and landscape gardening."[58] As with other aspects of the university's public mission, this one had been subject to a gradual abdication. In 1988, the University of California signed a $25-million partnership with Novartis, the world's largest agribusiness company, which gave the corporation partial control over publications and exclusive licensing rights for innovations coming from the University's Department of Plant and Microbial Biology.[59] Although the agricultural research conducted on the Gill Tract itself was still publicly funded, a 2004 plan slated the remaining land for development into a commercial and residential area.[60]

After months, during which time a series of Occupy projects and encampments had been destroyed after only a few days or weeks, the optimism behind the action—a farm, after all, would take years to fully mature—was exceptional. One farmer explained to me confidently that "Berkeley is still a hippie place; they're not just going to come in here with riot police and uproot everything. It would look terrible." The Occupy the Farm activists made concerted, and by some measures, successful efforts to reach out to and partner with members of the Albany community who had been working to preserve the Gill Tract for over a decade. The "Ladybug Patch"—a children's garden transplanted from the Occupy Oakland encampment's children village—further suggested that this was an occupation with broad appeal, avoiding the perceived nihilism and extremism of other occupy actions.

In light of the university's history of violent actions to maintain control of space, though, the optimism behind Occupy the Farm proved, unsurprisingly, to be unfounded. For three weeks, the university gradually cracked down on the farm, blocking entrances, shutting off the

---

58 "Landscape Heritage Plan," *University of California, Berkeley*, 2004, http://www.cp.berkeley.edu/lhp/significance/history.html.

59 Eric Holt Gimenez, "Occupy the Farm: Democracy for Land Grant Universities?," *Huffington Post*, May 8, 2012, http://www.huffingtonpost.com/eric-holt-gimenez/occupy-the-farm-democracy_1_b_1494968.html.

60 Facilities Services, "Final Master Plan" (University of California, Berkeley, June 15, 2004), http://www.indybay.org/uploads/2012/04/24/masterplan_061804.pdf.

water, and delivering daily dispersal orders. Farmers and community members responded by staying focused on their stated mission, passing a steady stream of jugs and buckets of water over fences for hours a day as police watched and taped their actions. Even when it became clear a raid was imminent, an occupier told me that "the plan is just to keep farming until we're in handcuffs." At last, on May 12, a force of one hundred officers from eight separate UC campus police forces barricaded the tract, and arrested nine people. When asked why some officers were armed with shotguns, a UC spokesman explained, "You're dealing with people whose emotions are running high, and there's lots of farm equipment around. Every piece is a potential weapon. We had to be prepared in case someone picked up a hoe and attacked a police officer."[61]

Hyperbolic fears of violence by farmers aside,[62] the university's actions and justifications were eminently predictable. A press release circulated immediately after the raid explained that police action was necessary to "secure our fundamental property rights" and "protect a core value that is an indivisible part of who we are: academic freedom."[63] While presented separately, these two reasons could be read in tandem with one another. In the era of neo-liberalism, "private" property is a prerequisite for research, even at a supposedly "public" university. Noted one blogger: "The University's ultimatum to those farming on the Gill Tract implies that academic inquiry, in order to be free, should occur entirely within the bounds of the university, and that it should be carried out using university property, undisturbed by any thing or person not bound contractually to the UC Regents."[64] Simultaneously, both the physical and spatial boundaries of campus and the symbolic boundaries of the university community were becoming steadily more impenetrable and constrained.

---

61   Cagle, "Occupy the Farm Dug In, Dug Up."
62   In truth, when the raid came, the farmers did exactly what they said they would: they kept farming. One youtube clip showed a mask farmer running, with water cans, up and down rows of crops while being chased by police.
63   Public Affairs, "UC Issues a New Statement About the Gill Tract," *University of California, Berkeley*, May 14, 2012, http://newscenter.berkeley.edu/2012/05/14/gill-tract/.
64   "Occupy the Farm and the Conditions of Academic Freedom," *Reclaim UC*, May 6, 2012, http://reclaimuc.blogspot.com/2012/05/occupy-farm-and-conditions-of-academic.html.

Conclusion

Berkeley may not, in the end, be the beacon of leftism that it is so frequently presented as. Indeed, part of the aim of this chapter has been to show the close and inseparable intertwining of radicalism and repression throughout Berkeley's activist history. Although Berkeley was once at the vanguard of social protest, activists and community members have often paid a high and hidden price for their leadership. Paradoxically, Berkeley's historical significance may come as much from its position as a catalyst and testing-ground for New Right reactionary conservatism as its role in advancing social justice. By the spring of 2012, it was clear which of these competing forces was winning. Rising housing prices and the changing composition of the student body, one person explained to me, meant that the city was "gentrifying itself into irrelevance," and many longtime activists were wondering whether the Berkeley community could continue to mount meaningful resistance to privatization.[65]

Whatever happens to Berkeley itself, a sociological analysis of Berkeley's activist history yields some broader insights about the role of space and place in social-movement analysis. The recent iterations of the Berkeley student movement have used all the tools of online organizing and social media to plan actions and spread that agenda. Nonetheless, it was only when political action became rooted in physical space that the university administration and other authorities perceived it as threatening enough to merit a violent response. The spectacularly disproportionate responses to the Wheeler occupation, the university encampments, and the Gill Tract farm all show that, even in an era of transnational and globalized protests, movements still draw their greatest strength and potential from having a space of their own.

Of course, the movements in Berkeley have not just sought "space" in the general, abstract sense, but particular, and often unique, "places." These places, I have argued, can become intertwined with particular issues, narratives, and histories, which shape the actions taking place within them. For more than fifty years, Berkeley activists and administrators have made only limited improvisations upon ideologies and roles passed

---

65 For a more thorough discussion of changes in Berkeley city politics, see Zelda Bronstein, "Progressive Incoherence in 'Radical' Berkeley," *Dissent Magazine*, August 1, 2013, http://www.dissentmagazine.org/online_articles/progressive-incoherence-in-radical-berkeley.

down to them from previous conflicts. Just as it is no coincidence that Occupy Oakland directed its ire at the police, and Occupy Wall Street was focused on finance, the actions taken by both sides of Occupy Cal are best interpreted through the lens of past conflicts over public space and the meaning of public education.

ADVANCING THE ALTERMODERN

An Interview with Michael Hardt on the Land Question[1]

Alexander Reid Ross: I want to start out the interview by asking about some of the concepts of altermodernity, and I wanted to do that by asking you to define modernity as you and Antonio Negri conceive of it.

Michael Hardt: We think of modernity as a power relationship or a relationship of domination, and that's really a contentious definition. It's not ours alone, but it's contentious with respect to how modernity has generally been conceived. Modernity has been conceived in the dominant European narrative as the process of enlightenment, democracy, and the coming of all good things. But in fact, historically, European modernity has been, both within Europe and between Europe and the rest of the world, a relationship of domination, colonization, and racialized hierarchies. If one thinks about modernity in that way, there is a logic to anti-modernity that also refuses much that is claimed by an "Enlightenment" view of modernity, and which, basing itself on anticolonialism and antiracism, tries to find an alternative to modernity.

ARR: What is the idea of altermodern that you establish in your text [*Commonwealth*]?

MH: Toni [Negri] and I are dissatisfied with the oppositional logic of an antimodern position, both for its refusal, or negations, of all things that are included in that narrative, but also for this affirmation of all things that are other than that. In some sense, what we're trying to think of with the altermodern is an alternative form of modernity, in some ways an affirmation of Enlightenment, but an alternative, different enlightenment. One can recognize the ways that domination are inherent to some of the basic concepts and pillars of modernity, but still seek a notion of reason and of an enlightenment that is not stuck with the falsely claimed accomplishments of European civilization.

ARR: David Harvey is one theorist who critically discusses your work;

---

1   This transcript was edited and compiled based on two interviews conducted in 2012 and 2013.

do you feel like your ideas on territory and his ideas on the geography of the urban have important intersections?

MH: One of the really important and central things about Harvey's urban geographies is about the notion of production. So it's not just that the city exists, and we live in it. The city exists, because we live in it; it's a product of our living interactions. That leads to the foundation of the right to the city, which in some ways has a long tradition, and not always a glorious one. The right to something is established by having produced it.

I think the sphere of production is one place where the Urban Studies geography intersects with the notion of territory and territoriality. Territory is always being produced by its inhabitation, by those who inhabit it. Territoriality connotes the qualities and characteristics that mark a given territory. So in thinking about the intersection of those two—the metropolis as a site of production, and our power to control it—is part of that production process.

ARR: What about the critique of philosophical approaches—going back to Spinoza?

MH: Philosophically, I find Spinoza quite useful in the same way that I find Marx quite useful, but I don't think that you can't get to understandings or where we need to be going through other routes. On one hand, if someone said, "We don't need to read Spinoza," I would say, "Well, fine, do it your way." On the other hand, I would not accept someone saying, "It is bad to read Spinoza, because we will mistake what's going on."

ARR: Arnae Ness, one of the original thinkers of Deep Ecology and the radical ecology movement, really broke through with his lectures about Spinoza. He looks at Spinoza's *Ethics* and what he sees, far from a Marxian organization of factories and urban areas, is a sort of utopian green-villages network characterized by horizontal communication. It's interesting that you and Negri seem to have found a way of recuperating these red and green trends in a liberating way.

MH: I like that way of thinking about it. There's one thing that gives me discomfort about this discussion of the Metropolis—by my work with Toni, in David Harvey's work, and others. Especially when saying that the Metropolis is the site for revolutionary activity, there seems to be a discounting of nonmetropolitan spaces, or the non-urban, which reinforces a distinction between urban and rural that perpetuates inaccuracy. One should not dismiss the rural and the opportunities there. The distinction between town and country, urban and rural, has been transformed in way that goes well beyond those kinds of assumptions. I think that you have also some discomfort with the dismissal of the rural, am I wrong?

ARR: You're absolutely right. The issues for me underwriting the urban focus have to do with the oppressive international legacy of capitalist development against the alternative models ideated by the Nonaligned Movement, along with the self-determination and autonomy of Indigenous peoples, the plight of farmworkers and miners, and so forth. The territorial expansion of the urban is also the crisis of the rural, because the rural must transform to suit the growth of the con-urban centralization of power. Furthermore, the geographic spread of the working class, in general, is a problem of transportation and social isolation—in Texas, where I am from, some rural folks commute all day, going from ranch to farm to building site, driving their pick-ups ten hours out of every day. So, the rural and urban crisis is also a crisis of "spaces of flows," a problem of distance and speed, but they should be distinguished to avoid a favoring of the urban, even as a site of resistance, over making empathetic connections with rural people and finding out what they need.

We have to challenge the implication that the rural does not hold a critical position of resistance to the sites of industrial exploitation that are almost like outposts of urban localities. Like if you see a mountaintop removal site, it might as well be…

MH: It might as well be a factory.

ARR: Yes! I have a dystopian nightmare that in the future such rural sites of extraction will look like a dump site in Houston, Texas, surrounded by a sea of conurban sprawl—the same thing is true with the tar sands, which in spite of their rural location is the seed of a growing complex of refineries, pipelines, and export terminals that may transform the Northwest into the Houston-model of economic growth.

MH: I think there is another way of saying the same point about the blurring of the distinction between urban and rural. I think, in terms of potential for organization and social communication, there's also a distinction being blurred. One of the most infamous condemnations of the rural in Marx is in the *18ᵗʰ Brumaire* when he's talking about the French peasantry, and trying to explain why they're reactionary, why they're supporting the dictator. What he says is: they can't represent themselves, they have to be represented. They don't communicate, they can't act as a class, so they can't act politically. They're dispersed through the French countryside.

I want to think about what he means by, "They don't communicate." He doesn't mean they don't read newspapers, and they don't know what's going on in the capital or with politicians. It's not just about information. What they don't have is that possibility of being together that creates projects of collective subjectivity, whereas urban factory workers are organized around the same machine, and can communicate in that corporeal way.

Today, the countryside, or the rural, is certainly not incommunicative. It is not only that they have plenty of information—there are certainly more opportunities for being together and acting collectively than Marx was identifying with the urban. In the late-twentieth century tradition of peasant insurrection throughout the Global South, we see rural political action through a kind of communication and being together that is equal to any urban possibilities. So whereas I agree with you in terms of a blurring of urban and rural, as well as urban waste and industry, there is also, on the other side, a potential for action in the rural and in the urban. I question the Metropolis and the City, in that it lacks some of those characteristics that take place outside of the city.

ARR: I think you may be positing the potential for a kind of transformation of the rural in contemporary political economy. Is there radical possibility in this transformation?

MH: Well let me begin with the relationship between identity and revolution. That's really our charge, what we're trying to think through. The revolutionary strain of workers' movements are really about the abolition of the category of worker and in some cases the abolition of work. But similarly, the revolutionary strains of feminist theory are really about the abolition of gender, and similarly with race theories. But that *doesn't* mean that we can quickly or immediately go to the end of such identity categories.

In all of these movements, what one learns is that they proceed as identity struggles—like workers' movements, even those revolutionary workers, struggling for the abolition of work or workers as a category, proceed as workers—so their identity-struggle is not, in itself, in contradiction with revolutionary struggles. In fact, they are necessary toward the basis of such revolutionary struggle. So it's a dual relationship that we're talking about.

There has been a difficult history that we're dealing with, where, especially in the US at least since the 1980s, there has been a commonplace conception that identity politics have done away with revolutionary struggles. We're trying to argue against that. That's not true.

ARR: So then we would have to think through what kind of urban or rural subject is being constructed or communicated before we can understand how that revolution can occur. In this sense, would one be using identity to destroy Identity, property to destroy Property, and the state to destroy the State?

MH: Let me provide one example that might help. Think about the progressive governments of Latin America over the last ten years: Bolivia, Argentina, Brazil, Ecuador, and Venezuela. In all of these examples, we have antineoliberal social movements (I would even say all of them insist on the commons) on whose backs progressive governments were elected. Hence, Chavez claimed that his power derived from the 1989 IMF riots in Caracas; Evo Morales's government came to power thanks to the social movements about water and gas in Bolivia in 2000 and 2003; and similarly with Lula and Kirchner. But in all of these cases we have very powerful conflicts between those social movements and the progressive governments in power. The recent conflicts between the Morales government and indigenous peoples in Bolivia seem like a paradigmatic example of that.

There are two alternatives that come to mind: each of which is insufficient. The first is to think that the construction of power and the acceptance of state power have led inevitably to the betrayal of the movement, and the other is to think that state power is the true representative and thus a vehicle toward the furthering of social movements. What

I see is something more complex. We've entered a stage of continuous antagonism between social movements and the so-called progressive governments. The governments can at times aid in continuing the social movements, but only because the social movements remain active and antagonistic. I see it not as a betrayal or a representation, but as a phase of antagonistic engagement. So we started off with you asking is the state necessary for the abolition of the State? Does my example say yes or no?

ARR: I don't know. It's crucial, because, in the Pacific Northwest, activists are organizing the same alliances of indigenous peoples, small farmers, and neighborhood associations against coal shipments. Elsewhere, it's natural gas or some other land-based exploitation. How can these social movements intervene, so that the state does not have the opportunity to obstruct social mobility in the name of economic development?

MH: That's a great question. I would say that the potential difference is that Kirchnerismo, Evoismo, or Chavismo are only progressive and productive insofar as they open the space for the movement, even to antagonistic struggles against the states themselves. I don't think that the actions, on their own, of these states are progressive. They are progressive insofar as they are pushed by the movements to do these things. One could think that Toni and I would have been or would still be against all these formations—against Chavez in particular, but also Evo and Lula, the Kirchners, etc. In some ways, however, the purity of that stance doesn't seem right to me. Maybe I'm being too pragmatic but I think that in certain phases the terms of struggle that we are faced with involve engaging with state power rather than refusing all engagement, because I think the ultimate goal is its abolition.

ARR: You discuss biopower with Negri as a mode of power that goes beyond conventional politics and incorporates different aspects of community engagement. Some of your thoughts about biopower and resistance make me wonder about the possibilities of reclaiming power or taking power in a permanent way from within. Can you elaborate on the tensions here?

MH: One would want to say, "Creating an outside on the inside." That's key for me to recognize the ways in which we can, while being embedded in, and in some ways being products of this system or systems, still find ways to attack and transform them. For me it goes along with being somewhat complicit and compromised within all the forms of power that we're trying to break away from.

What I think is useful and necessary and is happening all the time is the creation of new practices. Already the schema of working groups and general assemblies has real critiques, but also enormous potential in experimenting with these new practices. That's what seems to me to be really significant—new ways of creating political decisions, which were already not in the same form in Tahrir Square, Syntagma Square in Greece, Zuccotti Park. I think they were all experimenting with these democratic practices. What's more interesting to me than narratives are recurring practices.

What is clear is the attempt to create political organizations that are democratic without centralized leadership or points of dictation but rather finding ways to decide collectively. These were struggles that were born in the Argentina uprising or the assembly structure. Partly what you are recognizing here is not a theoretical legacy, but a reflection on a practical, organizational, political legacy that has been in formation over the last thirty years. The current movement has been not only powerful, but has realized what was already nascent and aspirational already some time ago.

ARR: You mentioned that Occupy may have fulfilled some aspirational model cast back in the history of social movements, which is an enormous achievement. With climate change, droughts, food shortages, speculation, how can such revolutionary practice sustainably remain hedged in ideal democratic organizing?

MH: It seems to me that climate change poses enormous challenges for democratic organizing. Many of the groups involved in climate change have trouble imagining a means of addressing the problem. That poses a huge conundrum for me. There are a variety of currents that fall into this, but the extreme version advocates a global authority or sovereignty that needs to mandate a transformation of social practices to save the planet.

Even to a less extreme version, it seems for many people involved that only state actors can make a real difference. The idea of organizing democratically seems an illusion—it seems from this perspective impossible, in a self-management way, that enough can be done to save the planet. I just recognize the pressures, difficulty, incompatibility, between friends who are activists that focus on climate change and friends that focus on autonomy and worker self-management. Some people don't know the truth, and some people can't act on the truth.

I've found one of the wonderful things about Occupy, and a whole series of encampments starting in 2011 was the ability of activists of all generations working together. There was a strong labor component, a strong ecological component, and others. There was this feeling of being together in the context of this small encampment that was very promising. Maybe I'm creating problems myself by thinking too conceptually, and activists speaking in a more grounded and practical way have less difficulty.

ARR: So the question is "opening up space" in such a democratic sense as Occupy attempted (I'm thinking especially about rural space), and whether it's possible to hold that territoriality in more than the isolated manifestations that Marx saw.

MH: Right. We've been really good at organizing a square or a park, and it's not really clear how to move that into transforming a society and its relations to the land-base. It's partly a scalar question, but it's not just a question of scale.

ARR: The last question that I wanted to ask has to remain open-ended. Having opened *Multitude* with the idea that the invasions of Iraq and Afghanistan marked a Civil War in Empire, I wonder if you will agree that the new "regionalist" approach to global politics with the BRICS countries taking the lead in some cases marks the outcome of that Civil War—a global, poly-centric Empire set up in the manner that you foresaw with Negri in 1999? And if so, where do the global uprisings since Arab Spring fit into the context of what you might call "The Global Land Grab"?

MH: I hesitated to call Tunisia and Egypt revolutions, because the removal of the dictators, although extremely important, is only the first step in what would be the revolutionary process. I do think of them much more as revolts or insurrections that may proceed towards revolutionary possibilities when alternative social relations are invented. The cycle of struggles that began in 2011 is opening new possibilities, in North Africa as well as Spain, the US, Turkey, Brazil, and elsewhere. But progress won't be linear—there will be movements forward and backward. And really we are only at the beginning.

EPILOGUE

Alexander Reid Ross

Modern radical movements have grown out of many practical problems, and perhaps most formative among these has been land. Our relation to land and to each other defines our existence on earth. As authors in this collection have pointed out, the struggle for community self-determination and security against invasion from corporations and the state is also a struggle for life, itself. When we fight for our land together, we are not only defining but also justifying our existence by defending it from ruin. The ties between land and community manifest historic bonds of radical movements against capitalism. Out of the urban/rural (as well as anti-colonial) relationships engendered by anarchist practice in the nineteenth and early-twentieth centuries, new ideas began to form to generate the potentials for radical social organization throughout the world.[1] Early manifestations of these ideas were applied by the Spanish anarchists of the Confederación Nacional del Trabajo (CNT) who advocated *autogestion*—workers self-management. The CNT found that self-managed agrarian collectives could potentially produce more food for society at more affordable, efficient rates while yielding higher relative wages for workers. During the first year of Spanish *autogestion*, several regions liberated unused, privately held lands for the usage of collective farming. It remains important to point out the problems faced by rural autogestion immediately: struggles within rural communities that raged between counterrevolutionary land-owners, their sympathizers, communists who privileged the urban proletariat, and the encroaching pressures of fascist forces.[2]

Algeria would prove another early-testing ground in the Global South for *autogestion*. As Algerians reclaimed privately held lands for popular use in the early 1960s, the administration of Ben Bella moved to formalize and regulate, rather than halt, the rapid liberation of Algeria. While progressive in its early stages of direct land reclamation, the administration attempted to reign in direct action and control autogestion.

---

1   One fascinating history of this changing time period can be found in David Berry, *A History of the French Anarchist Movement: 1917 to 1945* (Oakland: AK Press, 2009).

2   See Michael Seidman, "Agrarian Collectives during the Spanish Revolution and Civil War," *European History Quarterly* 30, no. 2 (2000): 209–235.

After Ben Bella was replaced by a military coup in 1964, Algeria solid-ified into a bureaucratic state controlled through centralized and coer-cive military command, leading to much consternation amongst radicals around the world. The difficult ethical line of solidarity with the praxis of liberation, which involves an ethical disavowal of coercion, was identified by an author writing for *Lanterne Noir*, who identified autogestion as radical in the context of "a complete destruction of the state, the end of division between manual and intellectual work, the suppression of classes and the achievement of equality among everyone, and the end of wage-labor and private property." However, as long as it "accommodates itself to the state, technology produced by capitalism, capitalist or tech-no-bureacuratic market relations, and technical and social division of labor," autogestion "is only a means for capitalism to survive."[3]

The Ejército Zapatista de Liberación Nacional (EZLN) significant-ly provides an example of the ideals of self-management over and against the desire for state power and inclusion in the state. The enthusiasm for the EZLN stems from a tradition of *autogestion* that emerged from the militancy of peasant-led anarchist movements during the Mexican Rev-olution. Under the slogan Tierra y Libertad, the Mexican journalists and revolutionary leaders, Enrique and Ricardo Flores Magón promoted and organized autonomous land expropriations from landowners in Mexico's northern regions, while Emiliano Zapata helped to organize thousands of peasants against their exploitative landlords in the south. The revo-lutionary Mexican constitution set into place economic protections to maintain self-sustaining agrarian land holdings (ejidos), but neoliber-alism slowly chipped away at the ejidos system until it was effectively liquidated by the North American Free Trade Agreement (NAFTA). On January 1, 1994, the day that NAFTA went into effect, the EZLN announced the liberation of indigenous lands of southern Mexico from the rule of the state. The Zapatistas have since assembled "good gover-nance councils" in these autonomous zones to promote health, educa-tion, sustainable agriculture, and defense of the rainforest.[4]

The principle of autogestion remains critical for collectives around the world, as autonomous direct action remains the crux of land-based

---

3   Found in David Porter, *Eyes to the South: French Anarchists and Algeria* (Oak-land: AK Press, 2011), 158–159.
4   See Subcommandante Insurgente Marcos, *The Speed of Dreams* (San Francisco: City Lights, 2007).

movements. Guillermo Delgado-P.'s elucidation of ancient, traditional Indigenous methods of agriculture indicates possibilities of future organizing, as opposed to US-backed attempts, such as the Paraguayan coup exposed by Benjamin Dangl, to stop radical land occupations. Keisha-Khan Perry and Silvia Federici have shown the critical role played by women around the world in halting the accumulation of capital that is literally starving the world. Vandana Shiva goes on to show the importance of India's rural mobilizations against big infrastructure and industrial extraction, which can be viewed alongside attempts in North America to halt the expansion of the tar sands infrastructure and the Chinese anti-pollution movement. These groups are all united in attempts to gain popular sovereignty over the machinery that displaces people from their homelands and threatens to wipe humanity off the face of the Earth through climate change.

As the activists investigating the possibility for land reform in Appalachia indicate, there is indeed much to talk about regarding the subject in the US—but we must not be fooled into an instrumental logic of technical, abstract formalization. If we break out a map of the country, we will find a vast majority of land holdings in the hands of the 1% in every state, while the majority of people in the US remain confined to relatively small houses or apartments in a rentier economy. As agribusiness decimates much of the country (especially the South, the Midwest, and the Central Valley of California) with monocrops, pesticides, and industrial fertilizers, humans live in increasingly polluted environments eating poisoned food. As I write this, California is undergoing a record-breaking drought, placing in peril one-third of the US's produce, and coastal Oregon forest is in flames during what is supposed to be the rainy season. In a situation of total irony, the bumper crop of grain from the Midwest (following the drought of 2013) is delayed on the rails by the endless line of oil trains emerging from the Bakken oil fields. Clearly the situation is changing rapidly, and while there is need for a revolutionary movement, we will not be able to adapt to conditions on the ground through a centrally managed power structure.

As *Grabbing Back* hopefully reminds us, as in the case with the Boggs Center in Detroit, communities can and are actively banding together to increase the food security and livability of their urban environs. Ahjamu Umi has shown how capitalism is irreconcilable with economic and social justice, and Max Rameau of Take Back the Land shows that what is possible on the scale of urban communities has brave potential for larger areas and even bioregions. In this context, vast areas of forestland, fresh water, and expansive desert habitats, prairies and mountains can be defended throughout, empty buildings can be reclaimed for social purposes, and participatory democracy can be enfranchised through networks of neighborhood and rural assemblies. With Andrej Grubačić, we might envision regional societies "based on voluntary co-operation and mutual aid, direct democracy of neighborhood assemblies and city federations, free associations that 'extend themselves and cover every branch of human activity,' with a self-managed economy with participatory planning, structured within the regional frame of a state-dissolving federation."[5]

This is a long process of development, but it is gaining speed and momentum as the government continues to fail to protect the people from debt and *de facto* segregation. Hence, the process of liberation and land defense for the environmental movement, as scott crow explains, is tied to the self-determination of Indigenous peoples and people of color. As Noam Chomsky suggests, the movement in defense of the land has everything to do with building a new poor peoples' movement. While scholars and intellectuals marveled at the brilliance of Occupy in bringing class into the US consciousness, the connection to land, public space, and dreams of a better world were always palpable. These connections have deep roots in US society—to the communal movement of the late 1960s, for instance, which many considered a possible precursor to autogestion in the US, and which may have prefigured some elements of the modern-day organic farming and permaculture movements.[6]

There may not be much time left to act, but there are countless ways to get involved. As we move forward, we must never forget that the world is still being created. The future is ours to imagine and bring to life.

---

5   Andrej Grubačić, *Don't Mourn, Balkanize!* (Oakland: PM Press, 2010), 267.
6   For a good exploration of the potential of the communal movement, see Ian Boal, Janferie Stone, Michael Watts, and Cal Winslow, eds., *West of Eden: Communes and Utopia in Northern California* (Oakland: PM Press, 2010).

CONTRIBUTOR BIOS (in order of appearance)

Javier Sethness Castro is author of *Imperiled Life: Revolution against Climate Catastrophe* (AK Press) and *For a Free Nature: Critical Theory, Social Ecology, and Post-Developmentalism* (LAP Lambert). His essays and articles have appeared in *Truthout, Climate and Capitalism,* Dissident Voice, *MRZine, Countercurrents,* and *Perspectives on Anarchist Theory.* He is currently writing a political and intellectual biography of Herbert Marcuse.

Dr. Vandana Shiva is a philosopher, environmental activist and eco feminist. She is the founder/director of Navdanya Research Foundation for Science, Technology, and Ecology. She is author of numerous books including, *Soil Not Oil: Environmental Justice in an Age of Climate Crisis; Stolen Harvest: The Hijacking of the Global Food Supply; Earth Democracy: Justice, Sustainability, and Peace;* and *Staying Alive: Women, Ecology, and Development.* Shiva has also served as an adviser to governments in India and abroad, as well as NGOs, including the International Forum on Globalization, the Women's Environment and Development Organization, and the Third World Network. She has received numerous awards, including the 1993 Right Livelihood Award (Alternative Nobel Prize) and the 2010 Sydney Peace Prize.

Ward Anseeuw works with CIRAD (Centre de Coopération Internationale de Recherche Agronomique pour le Développement) and the University of Pretoria (ward.anseeuw@up.ac.za).

Mike Taylor works with the ILC (International Land Coalition) (m.taylor@landcoalition.org).

Graham Peebles is an artist, writer, and director of The Create Trust, a UK-registered charity he founded in 2006. He has run education projects and teacher training programs in Palestine, India, and Ethiopia. A long-time student of the Ageless Wisdom Teachings and eastern philosophy, he is currently writing a series of essays on education.

Yangtzee River Delta EF! is a loose configuration of monkeywrenchers and allies.

Silvia Federici is a feminist activist, writer, and a teacher. In 1972 she was one of the co-founders of the International Feminist Collective, the organization that launched the international campaign for Wages For Housework (WFH). In the 1990s, after a period of teaching and research in Nigeria, she was active in the anti-globalization movement and the US anti-death penalty movement. She is one of the co-founders of the Committee for Academic Freedom in Africa, an organization dedicated to generating support for the struggles of students and teachers in Africa against the structural adjustment of African economies and educational systems. From 1987 to 2005 she taught international studies, women studies, and political philosophy courses at Hofstra University in Hempstead, NY. All through these years she has written books and essays on philosophy and feminist theory, women's history, education and culture, and more recently the worldwide struggle against capitalist globalization and for a feminist reconstruction of the commons.

Guillermo Delgado-P. is an Andean anthropologist. He teaches Latin American Anthropology and is Field Studies Director in the Anthropology Department at the University of California, Santa Cruz. He is co-author of "Indigenous Anthropologies beyond Barbados," in *A Companion to Latin American Anthropology*, ed. Deborah Poole (Malden: Blackwell, 2008), co-editor of *Indigeneity: Collected Essays* (Santa Cruz: New Pacific Press, 2012); and his most recent article is in *Los Giros Culturales en la Marea Rosa de América Latina* (Houston: LACASA Editora, 2012).

Benjamin Dangl is the author of *Dancing with Dynamite: Social Movements and States in Latin America* (AK Press), from which this article includes excerpts, and *The Price of Fire: Resource Wars and Social Movements in Bolivia* (AK Press). He is the editor of *TowardFreedom.com*, a progressive on world events and *UpsideDownWorld.org*, a website covering activism and politics in Latin America. Email: Bendangl@gmail.com

Keisha-Khan Y. Perry is an Assistant Professor of Africana Studies at Brown University in Providence, Rhode Island. She is the author of *Black Women Against the Land Grab* (University of Minnesota).

Ana Cristina da Silva Caminha is an independent scholar and long-time activist in Salvador, Brazil's vibrant land and housing rights movement.

Andrej Grubačić is Associate Professor and Department Chair of the Anthropology and Social Change program at the California Institute of Integral Studies. He is an outspoken protagonist for "new anarchism," co-author with Staughton Lynd of *Wobblies and Zapatistas* (PM Press) and editor/author of *Don't Mourn, Balkanize!* (PM Press).

Noam Chomsky is among the most influential political commentators in the world, and often described as "the father of modern linguistics." He is a professor emeritus at the Massachusetts Institute of Technology.

Grace Lee Boggs is a philosopher-activist committed to visionary organizing and the Next American Revolution whose more than sixty years of political involvement encompass the major US social movements of this century. She has written her autobiography, *Living For Change* (University of Minnesota Press), and in 2011, *The Next American Revolution: Sustainable Activism for the Twenty-First Century* (University of California Press).

Richard Feldman worked on the assembly line for twenty years and, for ten years, was an elected union representative at the Ford Michigan Truck Plant. He is currently a staff member of the International United Auto Workers, and is guided by his commitment to a two-sided revolution based upon the need to transform our thinking while we create local sustainable economies and communities.

Shea Howell has been a Detroit activist for more than three decades. She works with youth and artists for community-based development. She lectures on issues of social difference and peace, and writes a weekly column for the *Michigan*

Citizen. Her most recent work is on political ideology and community transformation. She is a co-founder of Detroit Summer and of the Boggs Center to Nurture Community Leadership. She is a professor of Communication at Oakland University.

Ahjamu Umi is a housing justice activist, working-class organizer, and Pan-African organizer. He has worked with the All-African Revolutionary Peoples Party across several decades, and has organized extensively in the US, Africa, the Caribbean, and Europe. He has worked with villagers, peasants, trade union workers, gang members, the elderly, women, students, and virtually every segment of society for positive social change. He is also a novelist who is currently working on the sequel to his first book, *Find the Flower that Blossoms* (America Star Books).

Max Rameau is a Haitian-born activist and co-founder of Take Back the Land, whose book, by that same name (published in its second edition by AK Press in 2012), explores the linkages between Marxism, Pan-Africanism, and economic justice.

scott crow is an Austin-based anarchist community organizer, writer, and trainer who began working on anti-apartheid, international political prisoner, and animal rights issues in the mid 1980s. He is the co-founder and co-organizer of several social justice groups and education projects throughout Texas and the South including Common Ground Collective (with Malik Rahim), Radical Encuentro Camp, UPROAR (United People Resisting Oppression and Racism), Dirty South Earth First!, and North Texas Coalition for a Just Peace. He has trained and organized for Greenpeace, Ruckus Society, Rainforest Action Network, ACORN, Forest Ethics, and Ralph Nader, and many smaller grassroots groups. He is the author of *Black Flags and Windmills: Hope, Anarchy, and the Common Ground Collective* (PM Press) and co-producer of the dvd, *The Angola 3: Black Panthers and the Last Slave Plantation* (PM Press).

Miles Howe is an editor with the *Halifax Media Co-op.* He would like to clarify that he is not a First Nations person. He was also not born in Mi'kma'ki, the traditional territory of the Mi'kmaq peoples that stretches across the Canadian provinces of Newfoundland, Prince Edward Island, Nova Scotia, into New Brunswick to the St. John River, north into the Gaspe Peninsula in Quebec, and south into Maine.

Andrew Herod is a distinguished research professor of geography at the University of Georgia, focusing on labor, political economy social theory, and qualitative methods.

Alex V. Bernard is an animal rights and global justice activist. He is currently a PhD student at University of California, Berkeley.

Michael Hardt is a professor of literature and Italian studies and chair of literature at Duke University in North Carolina. He has written several books including (with Antonio Negri) *Empire* (Harvard University Press), *Multitude* (Penguin) and, most recently, *Commonwealth* and *Declaration.*

INDEX

ABOUT THE EDITOR

Alexander Reid Ross is a writer and journalist from Houston, Texas. He is a co-founding moderator of the *Earth First! Newswire*, and has been published in *Climate & Capitalism, Counterpunch, Perspectives on Anarchist Theory, Science and Society, The Ecologist, The Singapore Review of Books*, and the edited collection *Life During Wartime* (AK Press 2013). He currently resides in Portland, Oregon, where he works for the Mt. Hood grassroots biodiversity group, *Bark*, and translates Bakunin in his spare time.

Support **AK Press!**

AK Press is one of the world's largest and most productive anarchist publishing houses. We're entirely worker-run & democratically managed. We operate without a corporate structure—no boss, no managers, no bullshit. We publish close to twenty books every year, and distribute thousands of other titles published by other like-minded independent presses and projects from around the globe.

The Friends of AK program is a way that you can directly contribute to the continued existence of AK Press, and ensure that we're able to keep publishing great books just like this one! Friends pay $25 a month directly into our publishing account ($30 for Canada, $35 for international), and receive a copy of every book AK Press publishes for the duration of their membership! Friends also receive a discount on anything they order from our website or buy at a table: 50% on AK titles, and 20% on everything else. We've also added a new Friends of AK ebook program: $15 a month gets you an electronic copy of every book we publish for the duration of your membership. Combine it with a print subscription, too!

There's great stuff in the works—so sign up now to become a Friend of AK Press, and let the presses roll!

Won't you be our friend? Email friendsofak@akpress.org for more info, or visit the Friends of AK Press website: www.akpress.org/programs/friendsofak